INNOVATE TO DOMINATE

INNOVATE TO DOMINATE

The Rise of the Chinese
Techno-Security State

Tai Ming Cheung

CORNELL UNIVERSITY PRESS   ITHACA AND LONDON

First published 2022 by Cornell University Press

Library of Congress Cataloging-in-Publication Data

Names: Cheung, Tai Ming, author.
Title: Innovate to dominate: the rise of the Chinese techno-security state / Tai Ming Cheung.
Description: Ithaca [New York]: Cornell University Press, 2022. | Includes bibliographical references and index. |
Identifiers: LCCN 2021054740 (print) | LCCN 2021054741 (ebook) | ISBN 9781501764349 (hardcover) | ISBN 9781501764356 (pdf) | ISBN 9781501764363 (epub)
Subjects: LCSH: Technology and state—China. | Technological innovations—Government policy—China. | National security—Technological innovations—China. | National security—Economic aspects—China. | Economic development—China. | Industrial policy—China. | China—Economic policy. | China—Politics and government—2002–
Classification: LCC T173.5.C5 C47 2022 (print) | LCC T173.5.C5 (ebook) | DDC 338.951—dc23/eng/20220201
LC record available at https://lccn.loc.gov/2021054740
LC ebook record available at https://lccn.loc.gov/2021054741

Contents

Preface and Acknowledgments

Innovate to Dominate is the second installment of an examination of the titanic struggle that the People's Republic of China has waged in the pursuit of wealth, might, and innovation since its founding in 1949. *Fortifying China* was the first account that delved into the political economy of China's defense technological and industrial development between the 1950s and the late 2000s spanning the reigns of Mao Zedong, Deng Xiaoping, Jiang Zemin, and Hu Jintao.[1] This book covers the rule of Xi Jinping, or more specifically his first decade at the helm, and goes beyond the defense technological and industrial realm to examine the broader innovation-security-development landscape.

The foundations of this book rest on a large-scale multiyear research and educational project funded by the US Department of Defense beginning in 2009 to identify and study the long-term security challenges awaiting the United States and the international community. The Minerva Research Initiative was the brainchild of the secretary of defense at the time, Robert Gates, and ably led by Tom Mahnken, whom I have had the privilege of collaborating with ever since on a wide range of projects. Over the course of the 2010s, I was able to lead a multitude of workshops, training courses, and research trips examining Chinese approaches to innovation and technological development very broadly defined. This resulted in the publication of numerous studies and the nurturing of a small but growing number of students and analysts to focus on the intersection between technology, economics, national security, and China, who are in great demand these days. This book is a distillation of many of the insights gained from this endeavor.

Innovate to Dominate has also benefited from the support of the Smith Richardson Foundation, which provided financial support but even more importantly insistent prodding to ensure that the book actually got written. Allan Song has been an able program manager in helping to steer this "just one more year" project to a successful conclusion.

Many ideas, arguments, and portions of this book have benefited from feedback that I have had from colleagues, students, and participants at numerous workshops and presentations. I wish to thank Eric Hagt, Stephan Haggard, Andrew Kennedy, James Lee, and James Cross for useful comments. I have also benefited more broadly from the intellectual interactions of University of California San Diego colleagues Barry Naughton, Peter Cowhey, and Susan Shirk.

I have had able research assistance from a staple of talented students, many of whom shall remain nameless given the sensitivity of the topic, but those who can be mentioned are Ian Brown, Patrick Hulme, and Ethan Olson.

Special thanks go to those who have played a direct role in providing editorial, administrative, and logistical support for the book project. Colleagues at the University of California's Institute on Global Conflict and Cooperation who have been especially helpful include Marie Thiveos, Lindsay Morgan, and Lynne Bush. Zethyn McKinley had the herculean editorial task of turning a butchery of the English language into a readable academic tome while Elizabeth Bond worked wonders on the graphics and artwork. I also had the honor of being among the final batch of authors that the legendary Roger Haydon at Cornell University Press worked with initially before he retired (I suspect I may have hastened his decision with my lump of coal). The baton was smoothly passed on to Michael McGandy, who also masterfully managed the project to a successful conclusion.

My final and most deep-felt gratitude goes to my family. My wife, Ai, had to endure years of distraction and incomprehensible mumblings about the intricacies of technological innovation and puzzling about the workings of the Chinese system at all times of the day and night. I also had the fortune to spend a good amount of time writing and rewriting in the peaceful English Chilterns enjoying the company and cooking of my mother, Woo Sok Yin, and sister, Wendy, and the occasional visits of Tai Wai, Fiona, and Kirstin. And a final scratch goes to Hana, my faithful canine sidekick who never doubted that I would get the book done as long as there were daily walks and I diligently attended to my duty as a generous treat dispenser.

Abbreviations

AECC	Aero Engine Corporation of China
AI	artificial intelligence
AMS	Academy of Military Sciences
AS	asset securitization
AVIC	Aviation Industry Corporation of China
BIS	Bureau of Industry and Security
BRI	Belt and Road Initiative
CAE	Chinese Academies of Engineering
CAS	Chinese Academy of Sciences
CASC	China Aerospace Science and Technology Corporation
CASIC	China Aerospace Science and Industry Corporation
CCDI	Central Commission of Disciplinary Inspection
CCP	Chinese Communist Party
CDSTIC	China Defense Science and Technology Information Center
CETC	China Electronics Technology Group Corporation
CFIUS	Committee on Foreign Investment in the United States
CMC	Central Military Commission
CMCFDC	Central Military-Civil Fusion Development Commission
CMI	civil-military integration
CNC	computer numerical control
CNNC	China National Nuclear Corporation
CNSC	Central National Security Commission
COSTIND	Commission for Science, Technology, and Industry for National Defense
CSC	Central Special Committee
CSGC	China South Industries Group Corporation
CSIC	China Shipbuilding Industry Corporation
CSSC	China State Shipbuilding Corporation
CSTC	CMC Science and Technology Commission
DARPA	Defense Advanced Research Projects Agency
DJI	Dajiang Innovations Science and Technology Co., Ltd.
DMLP	Defense Science and Technology Medium- and Long-Term Development Plan
DoD	Department of Defense

ECC	equipment contractor certificates
EDD	Equipment Development Department
FELG	Financial and Economic Leading Group
GAD	General Armament Department
GDP	gross domestic product
GGF	government guidance fund
HNSC	Holistic National Security Concept
IAD	information analysis and dissemination
IC	integrated circuit
IDAR	introduce, digest, assimilate, and reinnovate
IDDS	Innovation-Driven Development Strategy
INSS	integrated national strategic system
IP	intellectual property
MCC	military-civil combination
MCF	military-civil fusion
MCIPD	Military-Civil Integration Promotion Department
MHPSTIP	Military High-Level Personnel in Science and Technology Innovation Project
MIIT	Ministry of Industry and Information Technology
MITI	Ministry of International Trade and Industry
MLP	Medium- and Long-Term Science and Technology Development Plan
MOST	Ministry of Science and Technology
MPS	Ministry of Public Security
MSD	main strategic direction
MSG	Military Strategic Guidelines
MSS	Ministry of State Security
NDRC	National Development and Reform Commission
NDSTDSC	National Defense Science and Technology Development Strategy Committee
NDU	National Defense University
NKRDP	National Key Research and Development Program
NORINCO	North Industries Group Corporation
NPC	National People's Congress
NSL	National Security Law
NSS	national security state
NSSO	National Security Strategy Outline
NUDT	National University of Defense Technology
ONI	(US) Office of Naval Intelligence
PAP	People's Armed Police

PLA	People's Liberation Army
PRC	People's Republic of China
R&D	research and development
RMB	renminbi
S&E	science and engineering
S&T	science and technology
SAMI	selective authoritarian mobilization and innovation
SASTIND	State Administration for Science, Technology, and Industry for National Defense
SEI	Strategic Emerging Industries
SOE	state-owned enterprise
TTP	Thousand Talents Program
UAV	unmanned aerial vehicles
WEAIN	Weapons and Equipment Acquisition Information Network
WECP	Weapons and Equipment Construction Plans
WEDS	Weapons and Equipment Development Strategy
WERPL	weapons and equipment research and production licenses

List of US$-RMB Exchange Rates

This list provides the average annual exchange rate between the US dollar and the Renminbi between 2012 and the first half of 2021.

1 US$ = RMB
2012: 6.31
2013: 6.15
2017: 6.76
2018: 6.63
2019: 6.91
2020: 6.90
2014: 6.16
2015: 6.28
2016: 6.65
2021: 6.50

INTRODUCTION

Thinking about China as a Techno-Security State

Long-term strategic and economic rivalry between great powers is the defining paradigm of the international security order in the opening half of the twenty-first century. As the chief protagonists, the United States and China are contending for global supremacy across the critical domains of national power: economic, technological, military, and geostrategic. In this cauldron of intensifying competition, both Beijing and Washington recognize that the nexus between economic development, national security, technology, and innovation is a pivotal peacetime battleground. At the 19th National Congress of the Chinese Communist Party in October 2017, paramount leader Xi Jinping (习近平) spoke of building China into a strong power that would take center stage globally over the next few decades by becoming a world-class military and innovation power.[1] Two months later, the Trump administration issued a national security strategy that stressed the essential role of the "national security innovation base" in maintaining American security and prosperity.[2]

Although Chinese and US leaders use different labels, they are referring to the same phenomenon: the techno-security state. The notion of such a state is centered on the thick web of complex relationships between the state, national security, innovation, and development. A small handful of studies have peered into the state-technology-innovation-security-development nexus, especially concerning the United States, but this topic has generally attracted limited academic attention.[3] This book explores how the state is able to effectively coordinate the national security, technological innovation, and economic systems so that they can work closely together to enhance national power, especially in the strategic and military domains. Is this best achieved through state-led, top-down approaches, or market-driven, bottom-up approaches—or a mix of both? The answer will vary and depends on critical factors such as regime type (statist or anti-statist), security environment (peaceful or threatening), and the nature of coordination mechanisms employed (direct or indirect regulatory controls).

Innovate to Dominate examines the nature, evolution, and dynamics of the making of the Chinese techno-security state, especially under the rule of Xi Jinping. His grand design for establishing a techno-security great power able to challenge the United States for global leadership by the middle of the twenty-first century is anchored in two key areas. First, because Xi attributes China's inability to leverage its massive size into global strength to a chronic lack of original innovation, he has made the development of a homegrown world-class science, technology, and innovation system an urgent task. Second, Xi prioritizes the erection of a formidable national security state (NSS) as a means to defend the country's expanding external interests and safeguard internal stability. Even as China assumes an increasingly influential presence on the world stage, policymakers in Beijing see the country's national security as under serious threat—internally from political rot and social instability and externally from maritime sovereignty disputes to intensifying US-China strategic competition.

The general argument of this book—that a very different Chinese state that is far more powerful, more authoritarian, and more ambitious is emerging under Xi compared to past regimes—is not novel. Other scholars have plowed this field more broadly and produced excellent studies. Elizabeth Economy calls what Xi is doing a "Third Revolution" that is leading to the rise of a centralized state under his tight control.[4] Stein Ringen examines the governance system that Xi has put in place, which he argues is significantly more dictatorial and repressive in nature but notably has not translated into a stronger party-state.[5] The overarching theme of these studies is that there is far more change than continuity in the evolution of the Chinese state under Xi's rule. The main contribution of this book is to provide a focused, nuanced, and detailed exploration of this transformational change in the security-innovation-development nexus, which is one of the principal areas where China's impact on the world will be most profoundly felt.

What Is the Techno-Security State?

This book puts forward the concept of the techno-security state to make sense of China's comprehensive strategic rise in the first half of the twenty-first century. The techno-security state is an innovation-centered, security-maximizing regime that prioritizes the building of technological, security, and defense capabilities to meet expansive national security requirements based on heightened threat perceptions and the powerful influence of domestic security coalitions. This definition of the techno-security state brings together several different approaches in the study of the state that include the developmental state, NSS, defense industrial state, and innovation/entrepreneurial state. A detailed review of these schools of thought will take place in chapter 6 and will provide the intellectual scaffolding for the analytical framework that will be built to compare the US and Chinese techno-security states and the escalating strategic competition between them.

What are the underlying motivations, structural imperatives, and internal and external factors that shape the choices that states make in their techno-security building? Five considerations are especially relevant. First is the issue of statism versus anti-statism. In statist regimes, there is tight and direct top-down control by the state, which actively and pervasively intervenes and micromanages across virtually all areas related to techno-security issues. Statist regimes are structurally prone to authoritarian rule. In anti-statist regimes, the state adopts an indirect hands-off posture and allows the market and bottom-up forces to assume a leading role in technology and economic development. There is a healthy level of checks and balances in anti-statist regimes that places limitations on the power of central authorities. In reality, states often have both statist and anti-statist attributes and there is a constant struggle to find the right balance.

Techno-security states may differ based on whether they are offensive or defensive in their security postures and orientations. Techno-security states can be defined along a spectrum, with one end being defensively oriented states and the other being offensively minded (e.g., Germany or Japan in the 1930s). A pivotal factor at play here is how states perceive threats to their national security. Ideal-type defensive techno-security states typically view their security environments as benign and engage in restrained positive-sum balancing behavior in which the main goal is to maintain the status quo and not to maximize power. Defensive states build their security through internal resource mobilization rather than outward expansion and alliance building, and they focus mainly on domestic security and border defense, with only limited and temporary efforts at power projection. Ideal-type offensive techno-security states are more threat-oriented, revisionist, and pursue zero-sum behavior that is coercive. They rely on preemptive or punitive use of military force beyond their immediate borders, are highly repressive internally, and seek to mobilize their domestic economies and societies to support external policies. In the real world, states do not fall neatly within these two categories and often combine both defensive and offensive attributes.

A third consideration concerns the institutional design and structural arrangements of the techno-security state—namely, the degree to which the national security, innovation, and economic systems are integrated or compartmentalized. Techno-security states seek to forge deep-seated institutional alignments and connections between national security, technological innovation, and economic development to ensure there is close coordination and interdependence between these domains. This is carried out through a diverse array of structural instruments and mechanisms. The existence of a strong domestic defense and dual-use civil-military strategic innovation and industrial base is usually a highly visible landmark of an integrated ecosystem. Another is the willingness to devote a considerable proportion of state resources for strategic and national security priorities on a long-term, sustained basis.

Fourth is the goal of seeking or preserving technological self-sufficiency. Techno-security states emphasize the importance of self-reliance in the development of strategic, defense, and national security–related technological and industrial capabilities, although they are pragmatic about how and when to achieve such a goal. For catch-up countries, achieving self-sufficiency is a long-term aspiration and they accept the need to depend on imports in the meantime to ensure their national security. For advanced states, maintaining self-reliance and keeping abreast of the global technological frontier is an ongoing challenge.

A fifth and final point is that the world is in the midst of global technological upheavals—often described as revolutions—in both the military and commercial realms. The relationships between national security, technological innovation, and economic development are consequently likely to be very different going forward. The boundaries that once clearly distinguished military and civilian, national and international, and private and public are becoming increasingly blurred. This has far-reaching implications for the control and diffusion of technologies, knowledge, and national competitiveness and provides profound opportunities and challenges.

A sizable number of states past and present would fit the definition and characteristics of a techno-security state. A prime historical example is Great Britain during its golden imperial era in the nineteenth century when it was the world's most technologically advanced and dominant military power. Nazi Germany in the 1930s and 1940s would also fit the bill of a techno-security state, although very much an extreme fascist authoritarian model. In the twenty-first century, Israel, North Korea, Russia, the United States, and China would be members of this techno-security club.

In applying these points to contemporary China and the United States, China under Xi is a stridently statist regime and is in the process of shifting from a defensive to an offensive posture. The United States, by contrast, is strongly anti-statist and has a mixture of defensive and offensive attributes. Until the beginning of the twenty-first century, the US and Chinese techno-security states had limited interaction or concern for each other, but this has drastically changed and the security competition between them has become increasingly entangled since the 2010s.

The Chinese Techno-Security State from Mao Zedong to Xi Jinping

The techno-security state concept offers a coherent and integrated analytical framework to make sense of China's pursuit of economic development, military modernization, technological innovation, and national security and to assess the global implications. Although Xi represents a far-reaching and discontinuous break from China's past, many of the ideas and approaches that he is using are drawn from previous regimes, so an examination of the historical foundations is necessary from Mao Zedong (毛泽东) in the 1950s and 1960s to Hu Jintao (胡锦涛) in the 2000s (see table 1.1).

The Techno-Security State under Mao Zedong: Version 1.0

The strategic thinking and organizational design behind the twenty-first-century Chinese techno-security state owes heavily to the historical legacy of the original version that was established in the 1950s under Mao and was a core pillar of the Chinese state for the next several decades. The Maoist model was based on top-down central planning and thrived because of the acute threats China faced to its national security during this period.

The Maoist techno-security state had several key features. First was the over-riding importance of national security considerations in state priorities because of a severe external threat environment. Ensuring regime survival in the face of acute threats was the foremost concern of China's communist leadership throughout Mao's rule, so it is not surprising that national security priorities were of dominant focus. During the 1950s and 1960s, China engaged in a series of military conflicts and tense showdowns with the United States and its Asian allies around its territorial periphery. This began with the Korean War between 1950 and 1953 and continued with military crises in the Taiwan Strait in 1954–1955 and 1958, and Indochina during the 1960s.[6] The country's security environment became even more complicated beginning in the 1960s as the Soviet

TABLE I.1 Timeline of key events in the making of the Chinese techno-security state, 1949–present

DATE	EVENT
Late 1950s–late 1970s	"Two Bombs, One Satellite" development strategy for building of strategic weapons capabilities
March 1986	863 High-Technology Research and Development Plan established
May 1999	US bombing of Chinese embassy in Belgrade: China responds with launch of 995 New High-Technology Project and development of strategic deterrence capabilities
2006	Launch of 2006–2020 Medium- and Long-Term Science and Technology Development Plan. A defense S&T version is also implemented
October 2007	Hu Jintao introduces military-civil fusion for the first time in keynote speech at the 17th Party Congress
November 2012	Xi Jinping is appointed CCP general secretary and CMC chairman at the 18th Party Congress
August 2013	Xi Jinping chairs Politburo study session on military innovation
September 2013	Xi Jinping chairs Politburo study session on global trends in S&T
September 2013	China Shipbuilding Industry Corp. completes first asset securitization deal by a Chinese defense industrial corporation
November 2013	18th Party Congress 3rd Plenum previews major reforms in military, defense industry, and national security systems central in formation of the techno-security state
2014	Revision of China's Military Strategic Guidelines
January 2014	Central National Security Commission is established and holds first meeting in April 2014
June 2014	Xi Jinping makes first keynote speech on S&T at CAS-CAE conference
November 2014	US Defense Secretary Chuck Hagel publicly announces Third Offset Strategy
2014–2016	Reorganization of national S&T management and funding system into five comprehensive programs
March 2015	Military-civil fusion elevated to a national-level development strategy
May 2015	State Council issues Made in China 2025 plan
October 2015	Fifth Plenum approves establishment of Science, Technology, and Innovation 2030 Major Projects plan
January 2016	Major reorganization of PLA high command that includes creation of CMC Science and Technology Commission and CMC Equipment Development Department
March 2016	13th Five-Year Plan is launched and is followed by plans for science, technology, and innovation, military construction and development, and defense science, technology, and industry
May 2016	Xi Jinping makes keynote speech at CAS-CAE conference that officially launches the Innovation-Driven Development Strategy
July 2016	Party Central Committee, State Council, and CMC issues Opinions on the Integrated Development of Economic Construction and Defense Construction

DATE	EVENT
December 2016	State Council and CMC issues Economic Construction and Defense Construction Integrated Development 13th Five-Year Plan
January 2017	Establishment of the Central Military-Civil Fusion Development Commission
September 2017	CMC issues 13th Five-Year Military-Civil Fusion Science and Technology Plan
October 2017	Xi Jinping calls for formation of an integrated national strategic system in keynote speech at the 19th Party Congress
December 2017	Xi Jinping puts forward idea of "high quality" and "unimpeded" development that signals rise of thinking on economic securitization at annual Economic Work Conference
December 2017	US President Donald Trump issues US national security strategy that defines great power competition as the principal organizing framework for US national security policy with China as the principal competitor
March 2018	Military-civil fusion development strategy outline issued by the Central Military-Civil Fusion Development Commission
May 2018	US government imposes sanctions on ZTE Corp., which is likened to a "Sputnik" wake-up moment in highlighting China's vulnerability to dependence on foreign sources
April 2020	Xi Jinping introduces Dual Circulation Strategy at Central Financial and Economic Commission Meeting
March 2021	14th Five-Year Plan and 2035 Vision is launched at the annual meeting of the National People's Congress

Union emerged as a serious security threat through large-scale troop deployments along the Sino-Soviet border and the targeting of a sizable portion of its nuclear arsenal against China. This confrontation continued until the 1980s and China found itself in a near-perpetual state of militarization.

A second attribute was the pursuit of technological self-sufficiency in the development of strategic weapons. In the early years of communist rule, priority was placed on absorbing enormous amounts of military, economic, and technological assistance from the Soviet Union. However, when Beijing failed to obtain nuclear weapons technology from Moscow in the mid- to late 1950s, the Chinese government launched a massive effort to indigenously develop its own nuclear and long-range ballistic missile capabilities. This techno-nationalist enterprise became known as the Two Bombs, One Satellite or *Liangdan Yixing* (两弹一星) initiative and was an important source of ideological inspiration and mobilization for the development of not only the defense industry but also strategic sectors of the economy deemed critical to national security.[7]

A third characteristic was the dominant role of the defense industrial base in the national economy. The defense industrial base cast a long shadow over the

Chinese economy between the 1950s and 1980s. A large majority of the most advanced industrial sectors were either directly or indirectly associated with the defense industry, and the country's key technological goals and achievements were inextricably tied to its activities.[8] When the central government issued a twelve-year national science and technology plan in 1956 to guide long-term research and development (R&D), the top twelve tasks listed were drawn from a parallel classified defense science and technology (S&T) development plan. This included the development of nuclear energy, electronics, semiconductors, rocket technology, computer technology, and automation technology.[9] There were, however, two distinct components of the defense industrial base: a conventional weapons apparatus covering the development and production of ordnance, aerospace, naval, and defense electronics-related equipment, and a strategic weapons base working on nuclear weapons, strategic missiles, and space capabilities such as satellites.[10]

A fourth feature was the top-down and central planning nature of the Maoist techno-security state, which reflected its authoritarian nature. Politically, the Communist Party maintained tight control of decision making and policy implementation, especially on techno-security matters. This was carried out through special coordination bodies at the highest levels of the political-military leadership command, such as the Central Special Committee, which oversaw the strategic weapons programs. Economic planning and management were carried out under a central planning regime in which party-state agencies maintained tight administrative control, and there was close adherence to official orders and five-year plans. A key characteristic of this top-down approach was a strong emphasis on large-scale and highly complex science and engineering projects. Nuclear weapons, missile, space, and nuclear submarine projects required a massive and sustained mobilization effort by the state to provide the necessary technological, financial, human, and engineering resources.

A fifth attribute was the strong presence of national security coalitions at the top echelons of the political system. The military, defense industrial apparatus, and the scientists and engineers leading the R&D of strategic weapons capabilities enjoyed high-level access to top leaders. Senior military commanders with close ties to the techno-security state were appointed to top positions across party and state institutions such as the Politburo Standing Committee and government agencies. They included the likes of Marshal Nie Rongzhen, who was director of the Commission of Science and Technology for National Defense and concurrently a vice-premier; General Luo Ruiqing, chief of the People's Liberation Army (PLA) general staff and director of the National Defense Industry Office; and Marshal He Long, director of the National Defense Industry Commission and also a vice-premier.

The Maoist techno-security state is viewed by subsequent generations of Chinese leaders, from Deng Xiaoping (邓小平) to Xi, to have been extremely successful in large part because of its track record in the development of strategic weapons capabilities. As a result, key aspects of this model have been incorporated into the post-Maoist Chinese national and defense science, technology, and innovation systems. Principal features that have been retained are the political and organizational norms and routines of the Two Bombs, One Satellite approach.

The Developmental State from Deng Xiaoping to Hu Jintao

When Deng took over the reins of power in 1977, he moved expeditiously to transform the external and domestic circumstances under which the techno-security state had thrived under Mao. He sought to end China's international isolation and concentrate on economic development rather than preparing for war, which became known as the Reform and Open Door policy. Deng sought to turn the techno-security state into a developmental state.

Economic development, though, could only take place with a peaceful strategic environment. China had been on a near-permanent war footing since the outbreak of the Korean War, first confronting the United States and subsequently facing off against the Soviet Union. With Sino-Soviet relations still strained at the end of the 1970s, Chinese military chiefs insisted that the country still faced the danger of an "early war, a major war, and a nuclear war."[11] Deng regarded this Cold War thinking as outdated and a major obstacle to reform plans.

After a disastrous border war with Vietnam in 1979, Deng used the opportunity to order the PLA to begin a comprehensive review of the country's military situation with the intention of downgrading the threat posture and reducing the defense burden.[12] This review took several years to complete and it was not until 1984 that the military high command officially declared that China no longer faced the danger of major war.[13] This paved the way for major cuts in the size of the military and defense industrial establishments as well as in defense budgets.

Downgrading the threat environment also led to a significant curtailing of the political influence of the military and defense industrial coalitions. Military representation in key political bodies such as the Politburo Standing Committee and Communist Party Central Committee was reduced, and the military's role as a kingmaker in the political process dwindled. The defense industrial base struggled to cope with shrinking military outlays, which led to a sharp and sustained downturn in orders from the PLA. The once powerful military-industrial ministries saw their privileged status disappear, and they were reorganized into quasi-corporate entities. As military orders slowed to a trickle, defense enterprises had to convert to civilian output, which required them to learn to compete in the open marketplace. The techno-security state found itself in survival mode.

There were rearguard efforts to preserve important capabilities of the techno-security state. In the mid-1980s, a quartet of senior scientists from the strategic weapons apparatus persuaded Deng to support S&T development in strategic areas such as space that were deemed crucial to the country's national security and economic competitiveness. In the post-1978 reform era, funding for national security–related topics had been drastically cut and the scientists were worried that the country's strategic R&D capabilities were in danger of being lost. Deng approved the proposal, which led to the creation of the High-Technology Research and Development Plan (国家高技术研究发展计划, *Guojia Gaojishu Yanjiu Fazhan Jihua*), better known as the 863 Program, to commemorate the date of its establishment in March 1986. Funding for the 863 Program was modest in its first decade but grew substantially from the late 1990s and became one of China's most important strategic S&T R&D programs in the twenty-first century.

When Jiang Zemin (江泽民) took over from Deng at the beginning of the 1990s, China was facing a far more tense and uncertain geostrategic environment. Beijing's ties with the West were in a deep freeze after its violent crackdown on protesters in June 1989, and the sustainability of the Chinese political system—in the wake of the collapse of the Soviet Union and numerous other communist regimes in Eastern Europe and elsewhere—was uncertain.

China also confronted a series of major security challenges throughout the 1990s. This began with the First Gulf War in 1990–1991 between the US-led coalition against Iraq, which made clear to Chinese military chiefs that the PLA was chronically outdated and ill-prepared to fight a high-technology war. This was followed by rising tensions in the Taiwan Strait from the early 1990s as Beijing feared the island was seeking independence. The PLA was called into action to deter Taiwan through demonstrations of force, but it lacked access to the advanced weapons that would serve as a credible deterrent. The Deng era had left the domestic defense industrial base seriously weakened and technologically obsolete, unable to meet the PLA's pressing requirements.

Another major crisis in 1999 only added to the deepening need to revive the techno-security state. This was when the Chinese embassy in Belgrade was destroyed by a US military strike in May 1999 as part of a North Atlantic Treaty Organization bombing campaign against the Milosevic regime. The United States said that the attack was accidental, but the Chinese authorities disputed the US explanations. In response, Jiang called on the PLA and the defense industry to embark on the development of strategic deterrence capabilities to protect the Chinese homeland.[14]

In these more turbulent strategic circumstances, the Chinese authorities devoted more attention and resources to national security matters, although the overarching strategic focus remained on economic development. Defense budgets were steadily increased and leadership engagement with the national security establishment, especially the defense industrial base, intensified. Jiang paid frequent visits to defense R&D facilities and military S&T units and personally identified himself with key defense-related high-technology projects.

A key priority for Jiang, as he sought to build China's strategic military technology capabilities, was to resurrect important features of the Maoist techno-security state that had become moribund under Deng. Shortly after the Belgrade embassy attack, for example, Jiang called for the revival of Two Bombs, One Satellite as a role model and source of inspiration to help guide the embarkation of a new great leap forward in S&T. At a conference in 1999 to laud the Two Bombs, One Satellite "spirit," Jiang said that the core elements that defined this ideology could be summed up in a twenty-four-character statement: Warmly love your country (热爱祖国, *Reai zuguo*); Give selflessly (无私奉献, *Wusi fengxian*); Renewal through self-reliance (自力更生, *Zili gengsheng*); Hard and arduous struggle (艰苦奋斗, *Jianku fendou*); Vigorously promote coordination and cooperation (大力协同, *Dali xietong*); and Courageously climb up (勇于登攀, *Yongyu dengpan*).[15] The key principles, in other words, were nationalism, indigenization, diffusion, and catching up.

The Two Bombs, One Satellite approach has provided the underlying principles of political, organizational, and management design for a number of the key strategic technology development projects since the beginning of the twenty-first century, such as the *Shenzhou* (神舟) manned space flight program and the *Chang'e* (嫦娥) lunar project. The success of the various *Shenzhou* flights has been attributed to a number of key features of China's techno-nationalist strategy of which the most prominent are (1) effective mobilization of resources and capabilities, which is "one of the advantages of the socialist system," (2) being self-reliant and focusing on indigenous innovation that allows critical breakthroughs to take place, and (3) close guidance and support from the central party authorities. At the operational level, important factors identified as contributing to the program's success included strong work ethic and high motivation, willingness to take risks, and careful attention to management discipline and quality control.[16]

When Jiang passed the leadership baton to Hu in the early 2000s, the revival of the techno-security state began to gain momentum. Although economic development remained the country's foremost priority, the relationship between security, innovation, and development became more balanced. This evolution continued for the duration of Hu's leadership. Hu also paid considerable attention to the security-innovation relationship. Speaking at a meeting to celebrate the success of the *Chang'e* lunar probe in December 2007, Hu declared that "science and technology, especially strategic high-technology, has become the focus of the race for comprehensive national strength. Enhancement of indigenous innovation is the core of the national development strategy and the key to building up comprehensive national strength. It is necessary to rely on indigenous innovation for real core and key technologies in the crucial areas concerning the lifeline of the national economy and national security."[17]

Hu's remarks offer insights into the evolving Chinese thinking on the relationship between innovation and national security. First, Chinese decision makers use a grand strategic framework to view the interaction between technology and security, although the Chinese term is "comprehensive national strength" (综合国力, *zonghe guoli*). Broadly defined, grand strategy is the overarching vision of how a state coordinates and utilizes its economic, military, diplomatic, technological, and other capabilities to achieve national goals.[18] Second, in referring to the development of this comprehensive national strength, Hu described the process as "a race" and that it was crucial to rely on indigenous innovation capabilities. This suggests a zero-sum realist perspective that fits into the techno-security state mindset. Third, Hu noted that it was a necessary requirement for China to develop "real core and key technologies" by itself that are crucial for economic competitiveness and national security, which meant that it could not be reliant on external sources. These strong nationalist sentiments and security concerns coupled with a central role for the state are the essential ingredients of the techno-security state.

By the early 2010s, many of the key attributes and conditions for the emergence of a new techno-security state were in place. This included strong leadership support for technological innovation, deepening concerns over the country's external security environment, the embrace of techno-nationalist and top-down policies, and intensifying lobbying from the military and defense industrial sector. Although economic development remained the overarching priority, the security-innovation-development nexus had become more balanced.

The Techno-Security Party-State 2.0 under Xi Jinping

China under Xi is a security-maximizing state that is building its power and prestige on an increasingly capable and expansive economic and technological foundation. Xi has significantly elevated the importance of national security concerns and technological innovation in the country's overall agenda since taking charge in 2012. He has invested considerable time, effort, and political capital to establish an expansive techno-security state based on his strategic and ideological vision and under his close personal control through direct command of key institutions.

This building of a techno-security state, or what Xi calls an integrated strategic system, was pursued through four major lines of effort during the first decade of Xi's rule (see figure I.1):

- An innovation-driven development strategy that represents a new
  comprehensive model of national economic development that is closely
  coordinated with military and security goals.
- A national security strategy that integrates the domestic and external
  security arenas and emphasizes the development of internal security and
  information control capabilities across a wide array of domains under
  the watchful eye of the party-state.
- A military-civil fusion (MCF) strategy that seeks to integrate the
  compartmentalized civilian and defense portions of the Chinese
  economy into a seamless, cohesive dual-use system better able to cater to
  the needs of the military and national security apparatuses.
- A comprehensive military strengthening strategy designed to turn
  the PLA into a top-tier global military power by the mid-2030s and
  challenge competitors such as the United States for overall dominance
  by mid-century.

The central argument of this book—that Xi has engineered a decisive shift in
China's strategic posture and attendant grand strategies from development to
security—may be contested by those who see more continuity than change in China's approach to security. Taylor Fravel, for example, says only minor adjustments

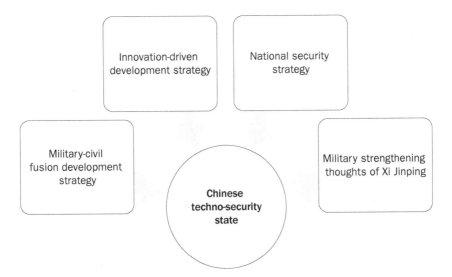

FIGURE I.1. The key components of the Chinese techno-security state

have so far been made to China's military strategy since Xi came to power, pointing in particular to limited revisions in 2014.[19] Although MCF, original innovation, and military strengthening are not new and can be traced back to prior regimes, Xi has significantly revamped these initiatives and added new policies so that the overall nature of China's approach to innovation, national security, and development under his leadership represents a far-reaching and discontinuous break from his immediate predecessors.

Organization of the Book

Each of these four components of the Chinese techno-security state will be addressed in subsequent chapters beginning with an examination of the evolution of Chinese strategic thinking on the relationship between development, innovation, and national security in the twenty-first century in chapter 1. Special attention is given to the making and implementation of the Innovation-Driven Development Strategy (IDDS; 国家创新驱动发展战略, *Guojia Chuangxin Qudong Fazhan Zhanlue*), which is Xi's grand strategy for transforming China into a global innovation power along with his approach toward military-driven innovation that goes hand in hand with the IDDS.

Chapter 2 addresses the rise of the NSS under Xi, in particular the political logic, origins, drivers, characteristics, and strategic thinking behind this transformational undertaking. Key questions examined include why Xi made a hard turn toward national security when he took power, how differently national security is viewed and managed under Xi compared to prior regimes, and what means are available to forge a powerful and effective NSS.

Chapter 3 is about the pursuit of MCF and the central role it plays in the building of the Chinese techno-security state. A key question is, what is the development vision and implementation strategy for MCF? Further, how does MCF integrate the civilian and military systems, especially in weapons and equipment research, development, and production? How is MCF being funded, and what is the best way to evaluate progress in MCF implementation?

Chapter 4 looks at Xi's military development guidance, known as military strengthening, and its relationship with the techno-security state. Key issues explored include the ties between the country's military strategy and the development of its weapons and equipment capabilities, the PLA's ability to foster military technological innovation and armament development, the efforts of the defense industrial base to reform and modernize its capabilities, a review of key defense technology and weapons development programs, and last, a generational analysis of the quality of the PLA's frontline arsenal over the past three decades.

The focus shifts in chapter 5 from the strategies and planning for techno-security development to actual implementation through a high-level techno-security-development model that leverages the core strengths of the country's political, economic, social, defense, and technological systems. This is the Selective Authoritarian Mobilization and Innovation (SAMI) model, or what is more commonly known in China as the Two Bombs, One Satellite approach. The SAMI model illustrates the relationship between innovation and industrialization in the making of China's strategic technological capabilities. The analysis of the SAMI model charts its evolution through several distinct stages beginning in the mid-1950s through to the Xi era.

Chapter 6 widens the analytical aperture beyond China to the nature of the techno-security state from a general conceptual and comparative perspective. Different schools of thought from the economic-centric and bello-centric traditions are relevant in thinking about the nature of the techno-security state and its relationship to development, innovation, security, and power. The developmental state model is identified as being especially useful in providing insights into the catch-up approach pursued by China. Other models of analysis examined include the NSS, the entrepreneurial/innovation state, and the great power state. Particular attention is paid to insights from the experience of the US techno-security state, which has grappled extensively with the security-innovation-development nexus and has been able to find effective and durable institutional arrangements enabling collaboration and coordination across the civilian and national security divide. The chapter applies these conceptual and comparative perspectives to develop an analytical framework to assess the state of and prospects for the Chinese techno-security state, especially in the growing competition with its US counterpart.

The concluding chapter considers the prospects and global implications of an increasingly potent and assertive Chinese techno-security state. Several topics are addressed, beginning with the question of how large and sustainable the Chinese techno-security state is, especially from an economic and financial perspective. How large a footprint does the techno-security base have relative to the size of the overall country and how affordable is this burden? Another important question to be addressed is how institutionalized or personalistic is the Chinese techno-security state? How much of its long-term fortunes rest on Xi? The chapter then compares the US-China techno-security rivalry in the twenty-first century with the US-Soviet Cold War and US-Japan geo-economic competition in the late twentieth century. Although on the surface there are similar themes between the US-Soviet and US-China standoffs, they are very different in nature. A standout reason is that the nature of the Chinese techno-security state is significantly different from the Soviet Union and represents a far more potent and comprehensive challenge to the United States. The chapter offers a detailed comparison of the US and Chinese techno-security states and the prospects for their long-term techno-security competition and finishes with an examination of the development path ahead for the Chinese techno-security state over the course of the 2020s and into the first half of the 2030s as laid out by the 14th Five-Year Plan and 2035 Vision. The prominence given to economic securitization priorities suggests the broadening of the Chinese techno-security state into the mainstream economic base.

INNOVATION-CENTERED DEVELOPMENT

When Xi Jinping assumed the mantle of Communist Party general secretary and Central Military Commission chairman in late 2012, he took command of an increasingly powerful and prosperous country. But at the same time, China was facing mounting headwinds that threatened to blow its rise off course. The economy's impressive growth was beginning to flag and reach the limits of its post-1978 development model. The national security apparatus was formidable but afflicted with critical flaws ranging from entrenched corruption to severe bureaucratic fragmentation. The science and technology (S&T) system was making impressive progress in catching up but showed few signs of creating truly original world-shattering innovation. A succinct appraisal was that China was big but not yet strong.

As a party cadre who had spent most of his career in provincial politics, Xi had limited exposure to national affairs, especially concerning innovation and national security. But as Hu Jintao's heir apparent between 2007 and 2012, Xi had plenty of time to carefully study, prepare his policy agenda, and forge his strategic vision. This chapter examines the evolution in thinking of Xi and his advisers on the relationship between development, innovation, and national security in the making of the twenty-first-century Chinese techno-security state.

Two broad themes are addressed in this chapter. First is the making and implementation of the Innovation-Driven Development Strategy (IDDS), which is Xi's grand strategy for transforming China into a global innovation power. The IDDS is the conceptual framework for an expansive staple of initiatives and plans that have been promulgated and implemented, such as the Made in China 2025

(MIC 2025; 中国制造 2025, *Zhongguo Zhizao 2025*) strategy and the 13th Five-Year Science and Technology Innovation Plan (十三五国家科技创新规划, *Shisan Wu Guojia Keji Chuangxin Guihua*) from 2016 to 2020. Second is an examination of the approach under Xi of military-driven innovation, which complements what the IDDS outlines in the civilian arena.

The Making of Xi Jinping's Thinking on Innovation-Driven Development

When Xi arrived in Beijing in 2007 as the heir apparent to Hu, there was little in his background to suggest that he would go on to become one of the most powerful leaders in the history of the Chinese Communist Party (CCP), even rivaling Mao Zedong. Xi had not served in the central corridors of power since working as an assistant to Defense Minister Geng Biao (耿飚) between 1979 and 1982. But what Xi lacked in his work record was more than compensated for by his insider credentials. Xi's father was Xu Zhongxun (习仲勋), one of the founding fathers of the CCP, which opened the gilded doors for the younger Xi to the exclusive personal networks of the governing elite.[1]

Xi used this access to cultivate a trusted inner circle of political confidants and policy advisers who would play a critical role in his consolidation of power upon taking office in 2012 and help shape and implement a strategic and ideological vision of China that differs significantly from Xi's immediate predecessors, especially in the realms of development, national security, and technology and innovation. Key figures who have played important roles on issues related to the techno-security state include the following:

- Wang Qishan (王岐山), head of the party's Central Commission for Discipline Inspection and a Politburo Standing Committee member during Xi's first term. Wang was responsible for overseeing the anti-corruption crackdown that became one of the most visible and hard-hitting instruments of the national security state.[2]
- General Zhang Youxia (张又侠), director of the People's Liberation Army (PLA) General Armament Department (GAD; 总装备部, *Zong Zhuangbei Bu*) and its successor, the Central Military Commission (CMC) Equipment Development Department (EDD; 军委装备发展部, *Junwei Zhuangbei Fazhan Bu*) during Xi's first term. Zhang was promoted to a vice-chairman of the CMC in Xi's second term. Zhang and Xi have had a long friendship starting from when they both grew up in the leader-

ship compounds in Beijing in the 1950s and 1960s. Zhang's role as the PLA's top armament and acquisition chief would have provided him a central seat in the making of the defense components of the techno-security state.[3]

- General Liu Yuan (刘源), the political commissar of the PLA General Logistics Department during Xi's first term, was a key military adviser on issues such as the anti-corruption crackdown that took down large numbers of senior officers.[4]

- Li Zhanshu (栗战书), head of the CCP General Office during Xi's first term and National People's Congress (NPC) chairman and Politburo Standing Committee member in Xi's second term, and was also appointed as the first director of the general office of the Central National Security Commission (CNSC; 中央国家安全委员会, *Zhongyang Guojia Anquan Weiyuanhui*) in 2014.[5]

- Liu He (刘鹤), director of the general office of the Party Financial and Economic Leading Group (FELG; 财政经济领导小组,*Caizheng Jingji Lingdao Xiaozu*) during Xi's first term and then promoted to vice-premier responsible for economic affairs in Xi's second term. Liu and Xi have been friends since childhood when they both lived in Beijing. Liu is an economic researcher and policy planner specializing in industrial policy, state-owned enterprises, macroeconomic planning, and the information economy and is likely to have played a pivotal role in shaping Xi's thinking on issues such as the IDDS and economic securitization.[6]

Other important advisers affiliated with the techno-security state include Zhong Shaojun (钟绍军), a close aide to Xi who became the director of the CMC General Office and Xi's personal office in 2017, and Cai Qi (蔡奇) who was the deputy director of the CNSC between 2014 and 2016.

At his inauguration at the 18th Chinese Communist Party National Congress in November 2012, Xi was given the stage for the first time to publicly lay out his views and ideas as to how he would govern and make China strong. Party protocol dictated, though, that the outgoing party chief would give the keynote speech detailing his successor's policy agenda. Consequently, Hu delivered Xi's vision, which included innovation and national security and their relationship to the country's overall goal of development.

A short section in the speech was devoted to science, technology, and innovation, which called for the establishment of a new IDDS.[7] The passage pointed out that "science and technology innovation provides strategic support for raising the productive forces and boosting comprehensive national strength and must be placed at the core of the overall development of the country." Key goals of the IDDS were as follows:

- China must focus on indigenous innovation and elevate the capability to conduct original innovation, integrated innovation, and reinnovation through importation, digestion, and absorption.
- China should attach importance to systematic innovation, deepen reform in technological structures, push for close integration of S&T and economic development, and speed up construction of a national innovation system.
- The Chinese government will build a market-oriented system for technological innovation with enterprises playing the lead role and combining with industry, academia, and research institutes.
- China will improve its knowledge innovation system and strengthen basic research and development (R&D) in frontier technologies.
- China will seek to occupy a strategic vantage point in S&T development by pursuing major national technology projects, make breakthroughs in major technology bottlenecks, and speed up research, development, and the application of new technologies.

This brief outline was little more than a bookmark until Xi could devote more time to fully articulate his grand vision. This occurred gradually as Xi had his hands full consolidating his power during his first months in control by, for example, presiding over the implementation of a wide-ranging anti-corruption campaign against the ruling civilian and military elites.

The rollout of the IDDS concept took a major step forward in September 2013 when Xi held a Politburo study session to "acutely grasp" global trends in science, technology, and innovation development and to "conscientiously" implement the IDDS.[8] This event was used by Xi to provide top-level leadership guidance as to what a national-level innovation development strategy should mean. Xi reiterated that it was necessary for science, technology, and innovation to be accorded a "core position in the state's development" and that this was a "major strategic choice made by the Communist Party Central Committee after comprehensively analyzing both the international and domestic trends." By contrast, previous leaderships had designated innovation as a very important, but not core, priority.

One of the central findings of this analysis was that the world was undergoing a far-reaching S&T revolution along with a fundamental transformation in industrial manufacturing. These global developments were occurring at the same time as the Chinese economy was facing the need for a major overhaul to its highly successful but increasingly flagging post-1978 economic development model. Xi noted that these external and internal trends presented a "historical convergence" that offered "a rare major opportunity for us to implement the innovation-driven development strategy." He emphasized that this "opportunity is transient. If we grasp it, it is our opportunity. If we fail to grasp it, it is our challenge."[9]

Despite Xi's strong advocacy for the IDDS concept, the initial lengthy absence of a detailed policy agenda and concrete implementation measures after its unveiling led to uncertainty about its actual significance and durability. Mu Rongping (穆荣平), a prominent academic adviser on innovation policy to the Chinese government, noted that the IDDS followed several earlier efforts to establish S&T-related national strategies in the 1990s and 2000s.[10] They included the Strategy for National Sustainable Development in 1992, the Strategy for National Reinvigoration through Science, Technology, and Education in 1995, and the Strategy for National Reinvigoration through Talents in 2004. Mu noted, however, that the policy environment for the implementation of the IDDS concept was different than in the past, especially because the triad of science, technology, and innovation "has become an increasingly important issue in policy-making procedures and must be accounted for in national development strategies."

A major reason why the Xi administration was initially cautious in pushing ahead with the IDDS concept was its highly ambitious and complex nature. Xi said that the implementation of the IDDS is "a systems engineering project, which involves all aspects of work and requires us to do many things." Xi hinted that there might be considerable bureaucratic opposition to the IDDS when he said that the most "urgent" step in preparing for the implementation of the IDDS concept was to "further emancipate the mind." In addition, Xi pointed out that other measures required for the successful adoption of the IDDS were an acceleration in the pace of reform of the S&T management system and the removal of "all obstacles restraining the concept."[11]

At the September 2013 Politburo study session, Xi provided guidance on five tasks that needed to be addressed before the IDDS could be launched. The first was to work out the relationship between the state and the market. Xi pointed out that the market should be responsible for "allocating innovation resources and ensuring that enterprises will truly become the main entities of technological innovation," while the state "should strengthen support and coordination, define the overall technological orientation and line, take advantage of the fulcrums of the state's major scientific and technological projects and major construction projects, and concentrate on occupying the commanding heights." A second key task was to promote the development of original homegrown innovation capacity. Xi stressed that it was "very important to enhance indigenous innovation ability by a great margin and strive to master key and core technologies."[12] A key means to achieve this goal was to improve incentive mechanisms and the policy environment.

A third related mission requirement was to revamp the human talent management system, especially to cultivate, train, educate, and promote domestic personnel and attract highly qualified individuals from overseas. A fourth task was to improve the governance and policy environment, which included enhancing intellectual property protection, creating a more tax-friendly framework to promote innovation, and increasing the supporting role that the capital markets can play for S&T-oriented companies. Last, Xi stated that it was important to deepen international S&T cooperation despite the need for more indigenous innovation. These five themes would become key pillars of the IDDS concept when it was eventually promulgated into an official national development strategy in 2016. There were some notable omissions in this early version of the IDDS concept. The most important was the lack of mention of military-civil fusion (MCF), which was only added a few years later.

The next important milestone in the formulation of the IDDS concept occurred in June 2014 when Xi gave a keynote speech to leading scientists, engineers, and academicians belonging to the Chinese Academy of Sciences (CAS) and the Chinese Academies of Engineering (CAE). This speech built on Xi's guidance at the September 2013 Politburo session but was directed to the scientific and engineering communities and intended to provide a more detailed action plan for the drafting of the IDDS that was under way in the planning bureaucracy.[13]

Xi noted that the "great rejuvenation of the Chinese nation" was closer at hand than at any time in China's contemporary history, and to achieve this goal, it was necessary to "unwaveringly implement the strategies of rejuvenating the country through science and education and innovation-driven development." This would allow China to "become a powerful science and technology power," because "science and technology constitutes the basis of a country's strength and prosperity." He added that "science and technology power determines changes in the balance of world political and economic power," and so "the importance of strategic innovation competition grows greater in the competition for comprehensive national strength."

One of the key themes in Xi's June 2014 speech was the compelling urgency of transforming China from an imitator into an original innovator. He noted that the existing foundations for domestic indigenous innovation were weak, which meant that China "is controlled by others in critical fields." The country needed to break out of this situation, guarantee its own national security, and avoid becoming "the technological vassal of other countries." To achieve this goal, Xi said that China's national innovation system needed to be significantly built up and had to remain actively engaged in international S&T exchanges and cooperation.

Xi devoted considerable attention in his speech to reforming the science, technology, and innovation system and offered specific guidance as to how this should happen. This required having a clear road map and timetable for key tasks; reforming the national S&T innovation strategy and the systems and mechanisms for resource allocations; improving the relationship between research, education, and production; and overcoming obstacles to the conversion and popularization of R&D into commercial output.

Xi called attention to a number of specific development issues and characteristics. One was the critical importance of mastering strategic and core technologies. He pointed out that "the Central Committee has fixed a long-term strategy for the science and technology of our country geared to 2030 and decided to implement a number of important S&T engineering projects." Xi said it was necessary to master key and core technologies in order to capture "the strategic science and technology commanding heights that have a bearing on the future and the overall situation." This 2030 timeline was subsequently extended to 2035.

Another priority that Xi highlighted was the need for better unified planning and coordination. He said that "we must work hard to overcome problems of fragmentation, including dispersion and stove-piping, and overlapping and redundancy, among the various fields of study, departments, and aspects of science and technology innovative activities." Bureaucratic fragmentation is a particularly salient problem for the Chinese S&T system, whose organizational setup and institutional culture remains closely tied to its historical roots as a central planning apparatus.[14]

Paradoxically, Xi praised the mobilizational advantage of the S&T system's socialist legacy that allowed China to "concentrate our efforts on doing big things. This is an important magic weapon for us to achieve our goals. In the past, we made important science and technology breakthroughs by depending on this magic weapon," which was a reference to the country's Two Bombs, One Satellite legacy. For Xi, the state must play a direct interventionist role in leading technological innovation, although in select areas only. "We must give better play to the role of the government in unifying and coordinating, exerting ourselves to conduct coordinated innovation and concentrating our forces to accomplishing great things. We must grasp the big, the cutting edge, and the basic, thus forming a powerful combined force that will spur indigenous innovation," Xi told the assembled scientists and engineers. This selective authoritarian mobilization model offers a key explanation as to why China has had a strong track record in a number of strategic technology development programs.

It is noteworthy that the IDDS drafting process was led by the National Development and Reform Commission (NDRC; 国家发展和改革委员会, *Guojia Fazhanhe Gaige Weiyuanhui*) and the FELG because these two entities are heavyweight players in economic policymaking and have significantly more bureaucratic clout and political influence than ministerial-level organs such as the Ministry of Science and Technology (MOST; 科技部, *Keiji Bu*), which had previously been in charge of science, technology, and innovation initiatives under the Hu administration (see table 1.1). A new State Leading Group for Science and Technology System Reform and Innovation System Construction (国家科技体制改革和创新体系建设领导小组, *Guojia Keji Tizhi Gaigehe Chuangxin Tixi Jianshe Lingdao Xiaozu*) provided coordination between state and party institutions. In addition, there was extensive consultation with local authorities, enterprises, universities, and research institutions.[15]

Xi was also involved in policy deliberations at the working level. For example, he chaired a FELG session in August 2014 examining the implementation of the IDDS.[16] He urged the participants, who represented the country's principal economic and financial agencies, to step up their formulation of the IDDS and supporting policies and plans, especially focusing on the implementation of major strategic technological and engineering projects as well as reform initiatives. This direct high-level pressure from Xi ensured that work on the IDDS concept and associated implementation plans proceeded at a rapid pace and did not run afoul of bureaucratic infighting. In March 2015, the Party Central Committee and the State Council issued "opinions" on accelerating the pace of implementation of the IDDS and reforms of the S&T system.[17] These opinions were intended to elicit feedback before the drafting was finalized and submitted for approval.

TABLE 1.1 Key party and state agencies involved in the formulation and decision making of the Innovation-Driven Development Strategy

INSTITUTION	HEAD	ROLE
National Development and Reform Commission	Xu Shaoshi	Policy research and drafting
Financial and Economic Leading Group	Xi Jinping	Decision making, coordination, and drafting
Ministry of Science and Technology	Wan Gang	Policy research and drafting
State Leading Group for Science and Technology System Reform and Innovation System Construction	Liu Yunshan	Coordination
State Council Leading Group for Science, Technology, and Education	Li Keqiang	Coordination
Central Leading Group for Comprehensively Deepening Reforms	Xi Jinping	Oversight and decision-making approval

Other senior leaders that played prominent roles in the formulation of the IDDS include Premier Li Keqiang (李克强), Politburo Standing Committee members Liu Yunshan (刘云山) and Zhang Gaoli (张高丽),[18] Vice-Premier Liu Yandong (刘延东), MOST minister Wan Gang (万钢), and Liu He, who served as director of the FELG general office and also as a NDRC vice-chairman during Xi's first term in power.[19]

The Adoption of the IDDS

The finalized version of the IDDS was approved by the Chinese authorities in the spring of 2016 and an outline (纲要) was issued by the Party Central Committee and State Council in May 2016.[20] The outline was described by Wan Gang as a top-level design and systemic plan that established the goals, directions, and priorities for China's innovation-driven development over the next three decades. Wan said the IDDS built on the 2006–2020 Medium- and Long-Term Science and Technology Development Plan (MLP; 中长期科学和技术发展规划纲要, *Zhongchangqi Kexuehe Jishu Fazhan Guihua Gangyao*) and the midterm evaluation of major S&T projects carried out under this plan.

Barry Naughton, a leading expert of the Chinese economy at the University of California, San Diego, argues that the IDDS should be considered primarily as a highly sophisticated and expansive industrial policy as it "explicitly targets a range of specific sectors and steps up the resource commitment to those sectors."[21] This is a basic feature of industrial policies and not of innovation policies, which generally do not target specific industries. Consequently, Naughton argues that the IDDS is mislabeled and should more accurately be called a technological upgrading development strategy.

The IDDS outline defines three stages for achieving China's overall modernization by the middle of the twenty-first century. The first step is for China to become an "innovative country" by 2020. This means establishing a robust innovation-friendly governance regime with improved intellectual property protection, better incentives, and a comprehensive set of policies and regulations. The outline calls for annual R&D expenditure to reach 2.5 percent of gross domestic product (GDP) by 2020, which it came close to actually achieving.

The second stage is for China to "move to the forefront of innovative countries" by 2030 (subsequently revised to 2035). This requires the country to join the top tier of advanced industrial and innovation economies, with China becoming a global leader in select areas. Annual R&D expenditures should reach 2.8 percent of GDP by 2030. The third and final stage is to become a "strong global innovation power by 2050," which would allow China to realize "its dream of national renewal." This implicitly means that China will challenge and begin to overtake the United States as the global science, technology, and innovation leader. The outline also states that China's defense S&T quality should be at world-class levels by this time.

Jakob Edler and Jan Fagerberg identify three flavors of innovation policies: (1) mission-oriented operational policies that address specific challenges of political agendas, (2) innovation-oriented policies that are more narrowly focused and concentrate on the R&D stages of the innovation process and leave exploitation and diffusion to the market, and (3) system-oriented policies that tackle system-level issues, especially related to national innovation systems.[22] Key tasks contained within the IDDS outline can be divided into these three categories with increased emphasis placed on innovation-oriented policies that have previously been secondary in priority to mission-oriented policies.

Mission-Oriented Tasks

The IDDS identifies ten broad areas in which the strategic task is to accelerate industrialization (工业化, *Gongyehua*), informatization (信息化, *Xinxihua*), digitalization (数字化, *Shuzihua*), and intelligentization (智能化, *Zhinenghua*, which refers to autonomy, artificial intelligence, and self-learning by machines) in order to promote industrial upgrades and emerging industrial clusters:

- Information network technology, which includes artificial intelligence (AI), virtual reality, microelectronics, optoelectronics, broadband mobile internet, cloud computing, internet of things, big data, high-performance computing, network security technology, especially with regard to integrated circuits and industrial controls, and the protection of national network security.
- High-end smart and green manufacturing technology and key common technologies such as basic materials, basic components, basic processes, and basic software that would be important in the development of large-sized aircraft, aircraft engines, nuclear power, high-speed rail, marine engineering equipment, and ultra-high-voltage power transmission.
- Marine and space technology, especially the development of synchronized 3D marine observation systems, space entry and exploitation systems, satellite-based remote sensing, and marine engineering equipment.
- Health technology, especially addressing the challenge of tackling major diseases and an aging population. The goal is to develop capabilities in

life sciences, Chinese traditional and Western medicine, bioengineering, biotechnology, major disease control and prevention, development of an advanced drugs pipeline, big data research in genomics and health care, and improved diagnostic technology. The COVID-19 pandemic has made this domain of even greater priority.

- Agricultural technology that emphasizes the importance of environmental sustainability, product safety, efficiency, and self-reliance. The nurturing of an independent seed industry is defined as the core priority along with developing standardized large-scale crop and animal production, improving food supply security, and developing high-end agricultural equipment.

- Energy technology that is safe, clean, and highly efficient, of which top areas of focus include clean coal, development of technology for deep-sea and deep-earth resource extraction, shale oil, nuclear energy, solar energy, new-energy vehicles, and smart grids.

- Environmental technology addressing severe air pollution, water resource utilization systems, waste management, and more efficient recycling and resource use.

- Modern service-related technologies such as e-commerce, logistics, internet banking, online education, and industrial design and engineering software.

- A catch-all domain of disruptive technologies that might lead to far-reaching industrial transformation and the rise of new industrial sectors, such as mobile internet technology, quantum information technology, aerospace technology, addictive manufacturing equipment, intelligent robots, and nanotechnology.

Another mission-oriented task that has received considerable attention in the IDDS is the execution of large-scale big science and big engineering projects that are directly related to national security and long-term development. The need to nurture teams of high-level talent that can carry out this proliferation of tasks is another highlighted priority.

Innovation-Oriented Tasks

The overarching priority in this category of tasks is to strengthen the country's pivot to original innovation and to enhance sources of high-end innovation supply:

- Strengthening of basic cutting-edge and high-end S&T research that is directed at meeting strategic needs. Of particular emphasis is the development of original innovation capabilities, scientific discovery capabilities, industrial transformation, and national security innovation.

- Supporting blue sky basic research, especially work that focuses on breakthrough research, transformative research, and the coordinated development of academic curriculums, interdisciplinary work, and the fostering of emerging scientific disciplines.
- Building new infrastructure and collaborative platforms that support high-end innovation and especially big science projects, such as national laboratories, large-scale shared experimental facilities, big data resources, supercomputing centers, and cloud computing mechanisms.

System-Oriented Tasks

The IDDS put forward a number of goals to significantly improve the country's national innovation system, especially as it transitions from catching up to becoming a front-runner:

- Optimizing the compartmentalized and often overlapping regional innovation systems so that provinces and other subnational players can perform complementary roles and focus on their core areas of competence rather than competing for the same areas of innovation capabilities. The outline recommends that coastal eastern regions focus on original and integrated innovation while interior provinces in central China pursue leapfrog-style development in emerging industries.
- Deepening MCF by forging an integrated dual-use civil-military innovation and economic system. This will require significant work to bridge a wide and deep gap between the civilian and defense sectors.
- Incubating the growth of world-class innovation-oriented enterprises, universities, and research institutions that are at the global frontiers in the development of critical industries.
- Reforming the innovation governance system with key tasks that include the establishment of a high-level national innovation policy-making consultation mechanism and the promotion of intellectual property protection, standards, and quality controls.
- Increasing financial investment through multiple channels, especially private and public sector funding mechanisms such as venture capital and government guidance investment.
- Stepping up China's leadership role in defining the norms and governance frameworks for the global innovation order.

The IDDS was officially unveiled during a keynote speech by Xi to more than four thousand attendees at the National Science, Technology, and Innovation Conference, the CAS and CAE Academicians Conference, and the 9th National Congress of the Chinese Association for Science and Technology in May 2016.[23] He compared the new development strategy to the MLP and previous long-term S&T plans and pointed out that the promulgation of the IDDS meant that science, technology, and innovation now occupies "a core position" in the country's national priorities and its main focus would be on transforming China into a "strong S&T country."

In unveiling the IDDS, Xi reiterated the pressing need for China to become an original cutting-edge innovator and said that China should take a more prominent role in defining global governance norms and assume leadership of select international S&T programs. He also praised the superiority of the Chinese socialist system to successfully pursue "big science" undertakings.

Xi also mentioned new policy initiatives. One that stood out was the decision to build large-scale national laboratories comparable to foreign counterparts such as the Lawrence Livermore and Los Alamos National Laboratories in the United States. Xi explained that "the necessity of organizing a number of national laboratories in important innovation areas . . . is a move with strategic significance in the S&T innovation of our country. . . . National laboratories should become strategic science and technology forces for tackling difficult issues and leading development."

Another important new effort that Xi touched on was a decision by the Party Central Committee at its Fifth Plenum in October 2015 to launch a long-term initiative on mastering core technologies.[24] The Science, Technology, and Innovation 2030 Major Projects (STI 2030; 科技创新 2030 重大项目, *Keji Chuangxin 2030 Zhongda Xiangmu*) plan initially covered fifteen science and engineering megaprojects, although this was subsequently increased to sixteen projects. They include aircraft engines and combustion turbines, technologies for deep-sea exploration and deep-sea stations, quantum communications and quantum computing, neuroscience and brain-related research, cybersecurity, deep-space exploration and in-orbit spacecraft, clean and efficient use of coal, smart power grids, space-earth integrated information network, intelligent manufacturing and robotics, and key new materials research and applications. Xi stressed that it was "necessary to speed up implementation centering on the needs of important national strategies, focus efforts on mastering key and core technologies, and capture science and technology strategic commanding heights that have a bearing on the future and the overall situation."

The Significance of the IDDS

The IDDS represents the Xi administration's bold grand strategy of realizing China's long-term ambition of becoming a world power by the middle of this century, if not sooner. The strategy is state directed but market funded, globally engaged but framed by techno-nationalist motivations. It seeks a seamless integration of the civilian and military domains, and employs a selective authoritarian mobilization approach targeted at core and emerging critical technologies.

The Xi administration has set the implementation of the IDDS against a Hobbesian backdrop of a life-or-death struggle for the economic and strategic renaissance of China. Its leaders see the world as engaged in an intensive zero-sum technological revolution for national and military competitiveness that requires China to urgently get its innovation house in order so it can effectively compete for the global commanding heights. This assessment was made well before the sharp deterioration in US-China relations in the mid- to late 2010s, which has only reinforced the Chinese leadership's belief that it has made the correct policy choices.

The IDDS, both in substance and the circumstances surrounding its formulation, offers telling insights into its policy significance and relevance to the making of the techno-security state. First, from an institutional perspective, the IDDS as a guiding strategy is far more authoritative than past S&T long-term plans and strategies such as the MLP. Although the MLP was issued by the State Council, it is institutionally identified as belonging to MOST. By contrast, the IDDS was drafted by the NDRC and FELG, the country's two highest-level party and state organs for economic planning, respectively, and issued jointly by the Party Central Committee and State Council. This ranks the IDDS among the country's highest-level strategic guidances.

A second related point is that the IDDS umbrella represents a whole-of-nation effort in the pursuit of technological innovation. This allows the authorities access to enormous institutional capabilities and material resources that can be applied to critical objectives. This selective authoritarian mobilization model is what Xi calls the superiority of the socialist system and has been successfully used on a number of pivotal S&T projects in the past.

Third is the issue of high-level leadership support, which is critical for states seeking to pursue more advanced forms of innovation. The IDDS is personally intertwined with Xi, who first put forward the concept and was intimately involved in its formulation, approval, and rollout. In a political setting where power rests more in the person of Xi and less in institutions,[25] the IDDS is likely to benefit from its tight association with Xi in at least two ways. First, Xi's strong commitment to the IDDS sends a clear signal to the administrative bureaucracy to vigorously implement the strategy and associated policies and plans or suffer the consequences. Second, the lifting of term limits in 2018 on Xi's tenure in power means that the IDDS can expect to enjoy an extended shelf life, which is important because of its long-term focus. By contrast, the MLP's chief benefactor was Wen Jiabao (温家宝), who as premier in a collective leadership wielded far less power and authority than Xi. This may help to explain the MLP's mixed implementation record.

A fourth point is that the IDDS framework demonstrates the breathtaking ambition and risk-taking appetite of the Xi administration in its goal of transforming China from a catch-up imitator into a world-class original innovator by the beginning of the 2030s. This will require a fundamental overhaul of how the Chinese national innovation system has traditionally been organized, incentivized, and governed. The Chinese term for this catch-up absorption approach is "reinnovation" (再创新, zaichuangxin). The IDDS calls for advancing from reinnovation, then passing through the intermediate stage of integrated innovation (集成创新, jicheng chuangxin), and finally moving to original innovation (原始创新, yuanshi chuangxin), which covers scientific discovery, technological invention, and most importantly, achieving breakthrough innovation in high-end technological fields. This grand pivot from imitation to original innovation is the centerpiece of the IDDS umbrella and will occur during the 2020s.

A fifth aspect of the IDDS framework is its emphasis on international S&T cooperation, which is influenced by techno-nationalist impulses and seeks to ensure that China has an influential say in the making of the global innovation order. Xi has said that it is essential for China to "plan and promote scientific and technological innovation with a global vision, comprehensively strengthen international scientific and technological innovation cooperation, actively integrate into the global network of scientific and technological innovation, enhance the level of opening up the state's science and technology programs to the outside world, actively participate in and lead international scientific projects, and encourage Chinese scientists to initiate and organize international scientific and technological cooperation projects."[26] One example of how China is developing its global innovation reach is through the Belt and Road Initiative, which Xi says should be used to build S&T innovation alliances, bases, and common platforms. Moreover, Xi says that it is important to enhance China's influence and rule-making ability in global science and technology governance. This includes standards setting, norm making, and the building of international regimes and institutions, such as in cybersecurity and 5G.

A sixth issue concerns the changing role of the state and its relationship with the market. The state remains of central importance in the IDDS umbrella, but its functions and responsibilities are being redrawn so it is better organized to handle a more complex and advanced innovation ecosystem. The IDDS talks about building a modern innovation governance system, which would replace the existing rigid top-down, monolithic, bureaucrat-driven, and administratively micromanaged model with a more pluralistic, decentralized, streamlined, expert-informed, enterprise-focused, and indirect governance approach that has a clearer division of labor between the state and market. In this reconfiguration of the state's guiding hand, some functions and responsibilities are being enhanced while others are being curtailed or eliminated. Areas being strengthened include strategic planning, policy formulation, supervision and evaluation, the implementation of major and strategic tasks, and supporting fundamental research.[27]

A key area where the state is stepping up its direct involvement is in the development of core and strategic technologies that China seeks to dominate. The 13th Five-Year Science and Technology Innovation Plan points out that China "will select strategic, forward-thinking, major scientific issues that can have a strong driving effect in improving sustained innovation capabilities" and that will help to "seize the commanding heights in global scientific development."[28] Many of them are included in STI 2030, which will be examined in detail in chapter 5.

In seeking to tame the pervasive reach of the state, one effort being made is to introduce more professional scientific expertise into the policy formulation and resource allocation process that would attempt to loosen the formidable grip of the bureaucratic elite. The IDDS calls for the establishment of a system of high-level S&T think tanks and consultative mechanisms that will allow academicians and other experts expanded access to policymakers to ensure more informed decision making. This reform is also being implemented in relation to how research grants are selected.

Another important arena in the adjustment of state-market ties in promoting S&T innovation is in resource allocations for promising critical and emerging technologies, especially early-stage investment and management support. In the past, state and private investment in S&T activities took place along parallel but separate tracks,[29] but the IDDS framework espouses the development of "innovation-driven institutional arrangements that organically integrate the leading role of the government with the deciding role of the market."[30] The 13th Five-Year Science and Technology Innovation Plan, for example, points out that the authorities "will fully exercise the role of national investment guidance funds for emerging industrial business start-ups as well as national development funds for small- and medium-sized enterprises in stimulating social capital to support the development of high-tech industries."

Government guidance funds are a useful example of how the "state leads" versus "market directs" concept works. Government-affiliated entities help to establish investment consortia that tap corporate investors for funds. These government guidance funds may contribute a modest share, but their principal role is to provide leadership, policy privileges, and management guidance that steer the funds into areas of state priority. The extent to which companies will be allowed to "decide" the fate of their portfolios will depend on factors such as the strategic importance of the investments in technological ventures to the national interest. Chapter 3 will examine the role of government guidance funds in financing MCF development.

The role of enterprises is also another hotly contested issue in the state-market innovation dynamic. Although the IDDS emphasizes the importance of an enterprise-focused S&T innovation system, whether market competition will be allowed to determine the fate of companies or the state intervenes to pick winners is a matter for debate. The IDDS and affiliated plans make clear that the central authorities will play an active role in picking national champions. The 13th Five-Year Science and Technology Innovation Plan points out that "we will bolster the construction of innovative enterprises and cultivate a number of internationally influential, innovative leading enterprises. . . . We will fully exercise the encouraging and guiding role of the state."

Nonetheless, the IDDS does put forward a significantly expanded and upgraded role for the market and nonstate actors across a wide range of functions, from policy consultation to providing research, financial, and talent support. The central authorities in particular are keen to promote bottom-up approaches to S&T innovation through initiatives such as mass innovation and mass entrepreneurship, especially by providing improved access to financial resources for start-ups and small and medium firms.

These reforms, if successfully carried out, will make the Chinese selective authoritarian mobilization model even more focused and effective. This will allow the state to better leverage and access market resources, especially investment funds and private enterprises. A more integrated and balanced state-market relationship is crucial to the goal of transforming China from a catch-up imitator into a truly world-class cutting-edge innovation leader.

The Relationship between Innovation-Driven Development and the Techno-Security State

The principal task of the IDDS and its constellation of associated plans and strategies is to support China's overall development, of which integral elements are national security and defense. The relationship between the IDDS and the techno-security state revolves around several strands:

- Linkages between the IDDS and counterpart national security and defense-related strategies
- Integration between the civilian and national security domains, especially the defense S&T and military apparatuses
- Building of strategic and core technological capabilities
- Development of domestically oriented national security capabilities, especially public security and surveillance technologies

When the MLP was formulated in the early 2000s, there were parallel civilian and defense versions. Drafting of the civilian plan was led by MOST, while the Commission for Science, Technology, and Industry for National Defense (COSTIND; 国防科技工业委员会, *Guofang Keji Gongye Weiyuanhui*) was in charge of the defense S&T plan (for more details, see chapter 4). The civilian MLP omitted any mention of defense-related matters but was slightly more candid on dual-use matters. For example, the civilian MLP had a list of sixteen large-scale so-called megaprojects but excluded any mention of three of them because they were classified.

In contrast to the MLP, there is only a single civilian version of the IDDS. This is because it is a national-level guidance that also incorporates national security and defense issues. This is set out in the introduction to the IDDS outline, which emphasizes that science, technology, and innovation are critical to building up the country's comprehensive national strength and must be placed at the heart of national development.

Defense S&T matters are only briefly touched upon in the IDDS, but they are referred to throughout the outline. In the discussion on building a national innovation system, for example, there is mention of the need to "build a defense innovation platform for defense science and technology integration." When the outline states that China will contend for global innovation leadership by 2050, it also notes that "defense technology will have reached global leadership levels" by this time. Xi has sought to explicitly link the IDDS with the PLA's efforts to embrace innovation. At a meeting with PLA delegates at the annual National People's Congress in March 2016, Xi called on the PLA "to fully implement the innovation-driven development strategy, place combat capacity at the center of all their work, and step up theoretical and technological innovation."[31]

There is considerably more detailed discussion of MCF in the IDDS. Four issues are highlighted: (1) improve military-civil macro-coordination mechanisms, which include organizational structures, planning, and resource sharing; (2) forge a more integrated military-civil acquisition process, which includes research, development, demonstration, engineering, and production, especially for major tasks; (3) promote the building of a basic MCF foundation, especially in basic research, the shared use of common basic raw materials and components, the establishment of joint military-civilian standards, and better information sharing; and (4) improve civilian-to-military (spin-on) and military-to-civilian (spin-off) transfers and open up access to the defense market for private enterprises. MCF matters are laid out in more detail in a special 13th Military-Civil Fusion Science and Technology Plan issued in 2017, which is covered in more detail in chapter 3.

The indigenous development of strategic and core technologies is one of the foremost priorities of the IDDS and its associated plans and consequently receives plenty of attention. Strategic and core technologies refer to capabilities that are crucial for national security and long-term national competitiveness. The IDDS puts forward a two-step development approach with the first near-to-medium stage reaching to 2020 and the second long-term stage extending to 2030, although this has since been extended to 2035. In the first step, the focus is on accelerating the implementation of megaprojects that have already been under way in plans such as the MLP. This includes core electronic devices such as supercomputer central processing units, high-end universal chips, basic software products such as operating systems, very-large-scale integrated circuit manufacturing equipment and turnkey techniques, new-generation broadband wireless mobile communication networks like 5G mobile communications capabilities, high-grade numerical control machinery and basic manufacturing equipment, large-scale advanced nuclear power plants with pressurized water reactors and high-temperature gas-cooled reactors, large-sized passenger aircraft, specifically the C919 airliner, high-resolution earth observation systems to allow the establishment of a comprehensive ground, atmospheric, and marine observation network, and manned spaceflight and lunar exploration projects like the Tiangong-2 space laboratory. This first stage also covers the period of the 13th Five-Year Science and Technology Innovation Plan.

In the 2020–2035 phase, a new batch of major S&T projects will be pursued that "embody China's strategic intentions . . . in striving to take the lead on breakthroughs in important directions." Many of them are included in STI 2030.

Another area of national security focus in the IDDS and its panoply of plans (see figure 1.1) is the development of technologies for public security and social governance applications. Although the IDDS outline does not address domestic security issues in any detail, some of the supporting plans do pay attention. The 13th Five-Year Science and Technology Innovation Plan, for example, talks about the need to develop "reliable and highly efficient public security and social governance technologies." This means public security-related capabilities for

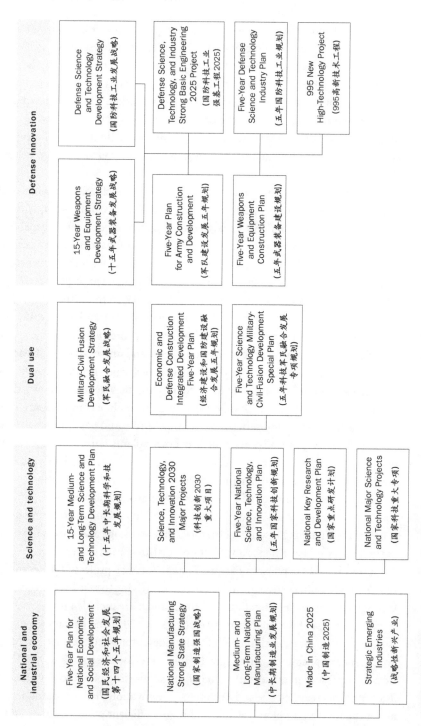

FIGURE 1.1. Chinese strategies and plans for national, dual-use, and defense science, technology, and innovation

early warning, emergency response, and surveillance, especially the "monitoring of social organizations, migrant populations, impoverished populations, and special groups of people."

Xi Jinping's Approach to Military-Driven Innovation

Xi's grand goal of transforming the PLA and the defense S&T apparatus from being big to being strong rests on a three-pronged strategy of reform, innovation, and modernization. Reform refers to undertaking a concerted roots-and-branch restructuring of the existing defense establishment to improve its readiness and ability to fight and win future wars as well as to ensure its political reliability to the Communist Party. Innovation concerns the development of new, especially novel, ways and means of strengthening China's military power and influence through hard (material, technological, and industrial) and soft (normative, strategy and tactics, and processes) factors. Modernization is the result of the implementation of the reforms and innovation on the development of defense capabilities.

Although these three components of Xi's military strengthening strategy are being pursued on parallel but separate tracks, there is considerable overlapping and coordination of their activities. Moreover, even though these endeavors are occurring concurrently, there are different time frames set for them. Xi declared at the 19th Party Congress that the bulk of structural reforms will be accomplished by the beginning of the 2020s, while overall defense modernization will be "basically completed" by 2035.[32] Achieving the goal of becoming a world-class defense innovation power on a par with the United States is envisioned for the middle of this century in time for the hundredth anniversary of the founding of the People's Republic.

Reform and modernization have been at the top of the defense establishment's policy agenda going back to the 1970s, but innovation has only come to the fore since the beginning of the twenty-first century. Both Jiang Zemin and Hu Jintao emphasized the importance of innovation, especially related to R&D, during their tenures. Xi, though, has elevated innovation to a core priority and broadened its application to far more military areas than his predecessors.

Xi's push for the defense establishment to be more innovative has been far from easy, however. Innovation in the defense domain, Xi has explained, "is more demanding and difficult than innovation in other arenas" because of the deeply conservative, insular, and change-resistant military culture and mindset. He pointed out that it is "incumbent upon us to liberate our minds and perceptions" and shift from (1) thinking of fighting mechanized wars to preparing to fight informatized wars, (2) safeguarding traditional external security to focusing on comprehensive security, and (3) conducting campaigns by a single service to conducting joint campaigns involving multiple service arms.[33]

This transformation is being carried out through a wide-ranging overhaul of the organizational structure, workings, and institutional culture of the military and defense S&T systems. Xi calls this approach a systems engineering project that "requires overall planning and a coordinated advance" on many fronts.[34] In viewing innovation from a systems perspective, Xi subscribes to the concept of a bounded innovation system consisting of a complex arrangement of actors interacting with each other through defined norms and routines. He has in particular targeted five hard and soft areas for his comprehensive military innovation drive: theory-driven innovation, organization-driven innovation, creativity-driven innovation, technology-driven innovation, and civil-military innovation.[35]

Xi first made clear how important innovation was in his military priorities at a Politburo study session in August 2013 that was devoted to examining military innovation and international military developments. Xi said at the meeting that a new global military revolution was developing "at a speed so fast, in a scope so wide, at a level so deep, and with an impact so great that it has rarely been witnessed since the end of World War II." Xi believed that "faced with such grim challenges and rare opportunities because of this new military revolution, we can narrow the gap as soon as possible and realize the new leap forward only by advancing with the times and vigorously promoting military innovation."[36]

Theory-Driven Innovation

At the Politburo session, Xi called for the development of a new innovation-driven military theory that would provide the comprehensive strategic guidance to steer the PLA's long-term modernization and development, which he defined as "military strengthening." Xi explained that

> to fulfill the goal of military strengthening is a great and arduous cause, which cannot be done without the guidance of advanced military theory. The innovation of military theory must be closely linked with this goal of military strengthening, must closely keep pace with trends in global military development, must be closely related to the changing needs of national security, must deeply study the characteristics and laws of taking the military-strengthening path with Chinese characteristics, so that it effectively turns the goal of military strengthening into a concrete road map and schedule so as to provide reliable theoretical support for the building of a big and powerful military.[37]

A central component of Chinese military theory is the country's military strategy, which represents a set of policy decisions that define the military framework for operational planning and actions. China's military strategy is known as the Military Strategic Guidelines (MSG; 军事战略方针, *Junshi Zhanlüe Fangzhen*) that "prescribe concepts, assess threats, and set priorities for planning, force posture, and modernization."[38] The PLA conducted a revision of its MSG in 2014–2015 in which the new focus is on fighting and winning "informatized local wars" with a particular emphasis on "maritime military struggle."[39] There were other notable revisions that incorporated key elements of Xi's thinking on military and national security innovation, according to one Chinese military scholar:[40]

- Taking advantage of a window of historic opportunity to shift from being big to being strong: China's growing prosperity allows the PLA to emphasize quality over quantity, which means the top priority of modernization should be on a smaller force but with much greater firepower.
- China's more complex threat environment: The MSG views China's security environment as extremely complex with challenges coming from multiple geographic and technological directions that require "across the board" planning to ensure overall strategic stability.
- A comprehensive national security perspective: The revised MSG has broadened its traditional narrow military focus to include a "holistic national security outlook," which views the country's security more expansively and includes political, economic, and social dimensions of national security.
- A more flexible and offensively oriented "active defense" strategy: The revised MSG advocates a more proactive forward-based military posture in a number of ways. One approach is to combine strategic defense with campaign and tactical-level offensives. Another way is to switch from strategic defense to strategic counteroffensive in a "timely manner." Strategic defense in the revised MSG means the "establishment of a strategic posture of resisting aggression and safeguarding national security and development interests, and serving political, diplomatic, and legal initiatives."[41]

The updating of the MSG was incorporated in the crafting of Xi's overarching military guidance issued by the Communist Party and titled "Military Strengthening in the New Era" (新时期的强军, *Xinshiqide Qiangjun*). This constitutes the military component of Xi's guiding political ideology that was enshrined in the Constitution of the Communist Party at the 19th Party Congress as "Xi Jinping's Thoughts on Socialism with Chinese Characteristics in the New

Era." The military strengthening guidance "determines the direction and priorities of military theory innovation," which in turn defines the approach for "military building and directly affects the rapid enhancement of the military's combat power," explained Lieutenant General Sun Sijing (孙思敬), the political commissar of the Academy of Military Sciences, the PLA's premier think tank on military affairs.[42] This was reiterated by CMC executive vice-chairman General Xu Qiliang (许其亮), who pointed out that Xi's military strengthening guidance has provided a "golden key" for the PLA as to "why to strengthen the military, what to do to strengthen the military, and how to strengthen the military under the new historical conditions."[43] The military strengthening guidance provided the road map that allowed the PLA to forge "a new system, a new structure, a new pattern, and a new look," Xi proclaimed at a ceremony to celebrate the ninetieth anniversary of the PLA's founding in August 2017.[44] A detailed examination of the military strengthening initiative is conducted in chapter 4.

With the military strengthening guidance providing top-level direction, there has been extensive formulation and revision of new and existing development strategies and strategic guidances covering military doctrine, and defense S&T since the mid-2010s. They include the long-term Weapons and Equipment Development Strategy and a national security outline for the national security apparatus. A number of medium-term defense implementation plans and programs have also been drafted, such as the Defense Science and Technology Industry Strong Basic Engineering Project 2025 (国防科技工业强基工程 2025, *Guofang Keji Gongye Qiangji Gongcheng 2025*), which is the counterpart to the civilian Made in China 2025 and the 13th Five-Year Defense Science and Technology Innovation Plan.

Organization-Driven Innovation

Turning next to organization-driven innovation, this domain has also been a pressing priority for Xi and has gone hand in hand with structural reform of the high command and other parts of the military and defense S&T systems.[45] Of particular relevance to the Chinese techno-security state has been the revamping, beginning in 2016, of the military's armament management system that is responsible for overseeing scientific research, development, and acquisition issues—especially in two areas:[46]

- The GAD was reorganized into the EDD and given responsibility for the unified management (集中统管, *jizhong tongguan*) of the military armament system.[47] One of the now-defunct GAD's chief roles was to oversee the armament development of the ground forces. The GAD units responsible for this have been transferred to a newly created PLA Army command.

- The GAD Science and Technology Committee was elevated to a commission-level rank reporting directly to the CMC and renamed the CMC Science and Technology Commission (CSTC; 军委科技委员会, *Junwei Keji Weiyuanhui*).

The promotion of the CSTC from the GAD to the CMC demonstrates that the Chinese military authorities, and especially Xi, are increasingly serious about engaging in higher-end innovation pursuits. The establishment of a high-level coordinating mechanism through the CSTC will provide operational leadership and guidance.

The ability of the EDD to carry out its mandate of providing centralized management of the armament system has a greater chance of success than the GAD, which was hamstrung by its institutional bias toward the ground forces. The nature of the relationship between the EDD and the armament departments belonging to the service arms will be critical in determining how much jointness versus compartmentalization will be present in the PLA's armaments development. The authority and influence of the EDD initially benefited from the appointment of GAD director General Zhang Youxia as its head. Zhang has close ties with Xi through princeling-related links and was subsequently promoted to be a CMC vice-chairman in October 2017.[48] Zhang was replaced as EDD director by Lieutenant General Li Shangfu (李尚福), who spent much of his career working in the space launch system before serving as a GAD deputy director and then as a Strategic Support Force deputy director.[49]

In parallel, the state defense industrial bureaucracy formulated new strategies and plans for a less ambitious but still significant adjustment to the defense industry and to chart its medium- and long-term transformation. One of these key plans was the 13th Defense Science and Technology Five-Year Plan.[50]

Creativity-Driven Innovation

A third innovation domain that Xi has paid considerable attention to is creativity-driven innovation. Xi has spoken of the need for more creative thinking and more open-minded and highly qualified personnel to establish a forward-thinking and innovative military institutional culture. He has argued that human agency is the most critical factor in innovation.[51] "There is a pressing need," Xi said at a meeting with NPC military delegates in 2016, to develop a critical mass of "high-end talented people to push for our army's reform and innovation."

However, Xi recognizes the enormous challenges that need to be tackled to train and educate adequate numbers of high-quality talent. He has pointed out that China in general "lacks world-class science and technology masters, and our leading and cutting-edge human talent is lacking. The cultivation of engineering and technical personnel has become disconnected from the practice of production and innovation." To address these issues, Xi said that "we must reform the mechanisms for human talent cultivation, importation, and utilization," explaining that this must be a long-term effort and should be prioritized over shorter term demands. "We must avoid hastily seeking immediate success," Xi warned. Another normative barrier that Xi highlighted was the risk-adverse nature of the S&T system, which meant that innovation was not highly valued. "We must actively create a positive atmosphere that encourages daring and courageous innovation and that is also accepting of innovation. We must value success but must also be tolerant of failure."

When Xi took office, the defense establishment was already pursuing a series of initiatives to promote creativity-driven innovation. Much of this effort was directed toward talent development of the officer corps, including armament and S&T personnel. The marque undertaking was the Military Talent Development 2020 Plan (2020 年前军队人才发展规划, 2020 Nianqian Jundui Rencai Fazhan Guihua) that was issued by the CMC in 2011 and provided unified strategic guidance for human capacity building across the entire armed forces.[52] Subordinate military commands put together their own talent development initiatives. The army command in 2018 established a five-year Army Science and Technology Innovation Talents Priority Support Program Implementation Plan to build one hundred innovation teams to work on military theory and technology innovation issues, cultivate one thousand promising and high-caliber S&T personnel, and support another ten thousand troops working in technical professions such as equipment maintenance.[53]

In the armament and S&T arena, the GAD in 2012 issued its version of the Talent Development 2020 Plan, and a special Military High-Level Personnel in Science and Technology Innovation Project (MHPSTIP; 军队高层次科技创新人才工程, Jundui Gaocengci Keji Chuanxing Gongcheng) was also established in 2009 in which two hundred promising scientists and other military technical personnel would be selected every two years for advanced training, including the opportunity to be mentored by academicians and leading experts.[54] The GAD also established its own version in 2010.[55] A review of the MHPSTIP program after its first two years pointed to impressive progress. This included the establishment of ninety-six "high standard" S&T innovation teams that made up the research staff of many state-level key laboratories.[56] Some of the personnel selected for this program were involved in the Shenzhou manned space program and the development of the Tianhe high-performance computer project. More than one hundred academicians from CAS and CAE were said to have participated in this program as mentors. Another examination of the MHPSTIP in 2016 showed that its impact was growing. The program had recruited more than 550 leading experts, academic faculty, and academicians, and participants were involved in many of the country's most important defense S&T projects, including those belonging to the 863, 973, 048 (indigenous aircraft carrier), and 995 projects.[57]

The GAD (now EDD) Military Talent Development 2020 Plan was aimed at cultivating specialized professionals required for the management of an increasingly large-scale and complex armaments acquisition and maintenance system.[58] The plan had ten main goals, which included cultivating highly qualified command-level officers able to conduct joint operations, fostering high-level technological experts, training better qualified military representative system personnel, and enlarging the limited noncommissioned officer pool of equipment specialists. One of the biggest human resource challenges that the PLA armaments system faces is a huge gap between its work responsibilities and the capacity of its workforce to manage these missions and tasks. The GAD in the early 2010s, for example, had only around eight thousand qualified acquisition personnel to manage its rapidly expanding equipment procurement system.[59] When compared to the size of the US defense acquisition workforce, which has around 135,000 personnel, the Chinese system is chronically undermanned.[60]

Xi has added new initiatives to promote creativity-driven innovation, especially aimed at the high end of the innovation spectrum in the pursuit of cutting-edge and breakthrough R&D. Perhaps the most consequential of these initiatives was a far-reaching overhaul of the military academic system in 2017 centered on the three institutions at its pinnacle: the Academy of Military Sciences (AMS), National Defense University (NDU), and National University of Defense Technology (NUDT). At a ceremony unveiling the changes, Xi said, "Our military academies, scientific research institutions, and training institutions are the backbone forces for pushing forward the rejuvenation of the armed forces through science and technology."[61] These three institutions had previously functioned on parallel but separate channels with limited interaction between them and the topics they focused on. AMS was primarily engaged in policy and theoretical research, NDU was responsible for advanced training of senior officers, and NUDT specialized in S&T training and research. A central aim of these reforms is to bring about greater convergence in their areas of responsibility, especially linkages between military strategy and technology. In reference to AMS, Xi said that it was necessary to "closely integrate military theory and military science and technology." As for NUDT, Xi said the revamped institution is "a high ground for training high-quality and new-type military talented personnel and for indigenous innovation in defense science and technology."

The CMC Political Work Department (军委政治工作部, *Junwei Zhengzhi Gongzuo Bu*) and its extensive network of party organizations is primarily responsible for the management of the key components of the creativity-driven innovation portfolio, especially on matters related to human talent development. However, this task of nurturing a more permissive environment for intellectual inquiry and debate appears to run counter to the Political Work Department's overarching mission of ensuring strict political reliability of military personnel to the Communist Party. Xi, though, has rejected arguments that the PLA's professional responsibilities and political obligations are at cross-purposes. He insists that the corrosive influence of domestic and foreign trends such as corruption means that "political work should only be strengthened, not weakened."[62] This has resulted in a significant tightening-up of ideological discipline during Xi's tenure. As part of this crackdown, Xi has directed that only politically reliable personnel should be recruited and promoted who "will not be swayed by negative ideological trends" and that there should be "innovative development of political work." Xi pointed out at the PLA's landmark 2014 Gutian political work conference that "innovation is the soul of a military's development and progress, and is also the inexhaustible driving power for strengthening and improving political work." As to what political work innovation means, Xi has said that it "must be oriented to the development of the times."[63] With political reliability the defining requirement in Xi's creativity-driven innovation framework, it is unclear whether the PLA will be able to meaningfully forge a more innovation-friendly institutional culture under these severe constraints.

Civil-Military Innovation

The PLA's relationship with the Communist Party also figures prominently in civil-military innovation, which is the fourth key domain in Xi's efforts to turn the PLA into an innovation-minded institution. Xi has sought to reconfigure the nature of civil-military interactions in both the political and economic domains through a combination of reforms and innovation. In the political realm, civil-military relations have undergone far-reaching realignment. When Xi first came to office, he had serious concerns about the PLA's obedience to the Communist Party as well as the trustworthiness and professional competence of the military leadership. There were several occasions during Hu's rule as CMC chairman when the PLA appeared to be operating independently with little oversight from the civilian leadership, especially on matters related to foreign and security policy. Xi moved quickly to address this emerging gap in party-army relations under the guise of a sweeping and prolonged anti-corruption drive into the top military ranks. More than one hundred generals and many lower-ranking officers were arrested and imprisoned, including some of the PLA's most senior commanders, such as former CMC vice-chairmen General Guo Boxiong (郭伯雄) and General Xu Caihou (徐才厚).

The political commissar system was identified as one of the hotbeds of corruption and an extensive purge of its ranks took place from the top down. This meant that the political monitoring and control system that had been the bedrock of the Communist Party's grip on the PLA had been seriously compromised. In response, Xi overhauled the long-standing commander-commissar parallel rule system in 2016 by adding a robust disciplinary governance mechanism so that it could more effectively monitor the political work system. This disciplinary governance apparatus includes a more high-level and powerful CMC Discipline Inspection Commission (军委纪检委员会, *Junwei Jijian Weiyuanhui*), a political-legal affairs committee to oversee the work of the military judicial system, and the elevation of the CMC Audit Office.[64]

The economic component of civil-military innovation is MCF, which Xi elevated to be a national priority in 2015 and defined as a development strategy. The Chinese authorities have been promoting the convergence of the civilian and defense components of the national economy since the beginning of the twenty-first century but with little tangible success because of limited high-level leadership attention, unclear strategy, ineffective implementation, and poor coordination between civilian, defense regulatory, and military agencies. Chinese authorities see this integration as essential in the country's drive for original innovation and defense modernization.

Technology-Driven Innovation

The fifth and most important and visible component of Xi's military-driven innovation campaign is technology-driven innovation. Xi has given a set of ambitious instructions aimed at turning China into a world-class defense technological leader within the next two decades. First, there should be an all-out effort to shift as quickly as possible from reliance on foreign sources to homegrown original innovation. Ever since its founding, the People's Republic has been overwhelmingly dependent on foreign sources for its defense technological needs. When this access was cut, as happened in 1960 with the rupture in Sino-Soviet relations and again in 1989 with the severing of military ties with Western countries, China was left isolated and unable to keep pace with global technological trends. Through concerted efforts since the late 1990s, the Chinese defense industry has been able to narrow the technological gap and steadily increase the quality and level of domestic content in its weapons production. A considerable amount of this "local" technology has been obtained and "reinnovated" from foreign sources through legal and illicit means. But at the same time, China's defense and dual-use S&T system is demonstrating that it can indigenously develop high-quality products that—from appearances at least—are getting close to advanced global levels.

Second, Xi has stated the importance of accelerating the implementation of major projects.[65] This point was included in his authoritative 19th Party Congress work report. Although Xi did not offer any details of these major projects, maritime, cyber, and space have been highlighted during his tenure. Specific major defense projects that have been fast-tracked through research, development, and acquisition include the J-20 fighter, the country's first stealth-like combat aircraft that entered operational service in 2018, and the navy's first indigenously built aircraft carrier. The development pipeline for major weapons and dual-use projects is impressive, including a significantly larger and more advanced locally built aircraft carrier, a new generation of nuclear ballistic missile and attack submarines, ballistic missile defense, satellite navigation systems, and next-generation exascale high-performance computers.

Third, urgent priority will be directed to the development of a select number of core and emerging defense and strategic technologies that would allow China to advance to the global frontier ahead of other competitors. Many of the strategic technologies are dual use in nature and are listed in key national plans such as STI 2030, Made in China 2025, Five-Year Science and Technology Innovation Plans, and the MLP. They include aircraft engines, deep-sea technologies, quantum communications and computer technology, cybersecurity, semiconductors, deep-space exploration, and space-earth integrated information systems. Defense-specific technologies that Chinese defense research institutions are already working on include directed energy weapons, hypersonic missiles and glide vehicles, autonomous systems such as drones and robots, and AI-related capabilities.

A fourth requirement by Xi was to build a more robust, systematic, forward-looking, and integrated planning process combined with increased investment in early-stage research that would allow Chinese defense planners and scientists to "see things before they happen, know things before they occur."[66] At a CMC reform conference in November 2015, Xi said that "we must select the right points for breakthroughs, make planning ahead of time, and strengthen major technological research with forward-looking, pioneering, and exploratory features."[67] A number of organizational mechanisms have been created to enhance long-range defense S&T research and planning. They include the CSTC, CMC Military Scientific Steering Committee (军委军事科学研究指导委员会, *Junwei Junshi Kexue Yanjiu Zhidao Weiyuanhui*), whose existence was revealed in 2017, and the Defense Industry Development Strategy Committee (国防科技工业发展战略委员会, *Guofang Keji Gongye Fazhan Zhanlue Weiyuanhui*), which was established by the State Administration for Science, Technology, and Industry for National Defense (SASTIND; 国家国防科技工业局, *Guojia Guofang Keji Gongye Ju*) in June 2015.[68] Moreover, the PLA and defense S&T system have been forging closer linkages with the civilian research community to bolster basic research. The National Natural Science Foundation of China, for example, signed a strategic agreement with the CSTC in August 2016 to expand civil-military basic science cooperation.[69]

Xi stressed that the "PLA must pay greater attention to the development of strategic cutting-edge technologies, seize the initiative through autonomous innovation, make good offensive moves, and do well in seizing initiative in combat. It is necessary to correctly choose follow-up and breakthrough strategies, choose major directions of offensive and breakthrough points accurately, arrange setups in advance, draw up plans in advance, and step up forming unique advantages in some major areas. There is a need to step up and do a good job on transformation and utilization of innovative and breakthrough results and turn innovative results into tangible combat strength."[70]

Assessing Xi Jinping's Military Innovation-Driven Development Campaign

This examination of Xi's military-driven innovation campaign offers insights into the evolving nature of Chinese military power and the long-term evolution of the Chinese techno-security state. Xi is using innovation as an instrumentalist tool to fundamentally remake the Chinese defense establishment in his own image, that is, as a strong, self-reliant, globally competitive, professionally capable but politically obedient, and military-led but civilian-controlled institution that is under his absolute personal authority. Innovation is a politically expedient cover to overcome deeply entrenched bureaucratic interests, long-standing but outdated practices, and fragmented power structures that have been resistant to incremental reform efforts by previous leaders. Xi is employing shock-and-awe tactics to engage in disruptive change that is defined as innovation.

Xi has thrown his full political authority along with a considerable amount of time behind this military innovation campaign. In addition to his role as CMC chairman, Xi leads several entities at the center of the formulation and implementation of key military reform and innovation initiatives. One of the most important is the CMC Leading Group for the Deepening of Reforms in Defense and the Armed Forces (军委深化国防和军队改革领导小组, *Junwei Shenhua Guofang He Jundui Gaige Lingdao Xiaozu*) that was established in 2014 to draw up and execute the far-reaching reform of the military high command, service arms, theater commands, and other key elements of the defense apparatus that began in 2016.[71] Xi also is the head of the Central Military Civil Fusion Development Commission, which is responsible for guiding MCF, and the chair of the 995 Leading Group, which coordinates major weapons development projects. Xi's direct and committed engagement in the innovation and reform drive is critical to addressing intensive bureaucratic and political resistance.

For Xi to be effective in realizing his military innovation vision, he requires a capable leadership team and associated institutional mechanisms that can accurately translate and robustly implement his agenda. However, in the first few years of his rule, Xi had a group of senior military commanders and civilian leaders who were reliable administrators but had little experience or background dealing with technology or innovation-related issues. They included GAD director General Zhang Youxia, State Council vice-premier Zhang Gaoli, SASTIND director Xu Dazhe (许达哲), and CMC vice-chairman General Xu Qiliang, who is responsible for defense modernization matters. General Zhang is a career ground forces officer who served almost exclusively in operational command roles at the divisional, group army, and military region levels before being appointed as GAD director in 2012. However, Zhang graduated from NUDT and has had preliminary training on S&T matters.[72] Zhang Gaoli was a career party cadre who spent much of his career at the provincial level before being promoted to the central leadership at the 18th Party Congress in 2012 and given an economics portfolio as vice-premier that included overseeing defense industrial matters that he had little experience dealing with. Xu Dazhe was the most knowledgeable on defense innovation issues within the leadership team because of his training as an aerospace technical designer and his extensive career working in the aerospace industry that was capped with becoming the head of the China Aerospace Science and Industry Corporation (CASIC) in the late 2000s. However, Xu served less than three years as SASTIND director between 2014 and 2016, so his impact was limited. General Xu Qiliang also had some exposure to technology and modernization issues as the commander of the PLA Air Force in the late 2000s to early 2010s. However, his career background was as a pilot and operational commander with little dedicated involvement in S&T or acquisition matters.

Since the mid-2010s, the leadership team responsible for military innovation and defense S&T issues has become more technically qualified, especially with the inclusion of Lieutenant General Liu Guozhi (刘国治), director of the CSTC, into Xi's inner circle. Liu spent much of his career engaged in advanced defense and high-technology R&D.[73] Besides Liu, other officers with technology backgrounds have assumed senior slots in the military innovation leadership team, such as aerospace expert General Li Shangfu, who became EDD director in 2017.

Xi views innovation from a top-down systems perspective, which means that there are numerous moving parts, a complex structural layout, and close linkages among the different components. This is why he describes his innovation campaign as a systems engineering project. Only by pursuing a comprehensive, coordinated, and systematic approach that addresses both hard and soft factors will the Chinese defense establishment successfully adopt innovation, especially advanced innovation. This requires sustained top-level attention over a prolonged period.

Although Xi takes a comprehensive approach to the sources of military innovation, his overriding laser-focused imperative is for China and its defense establishment to become a high-end, self-reliant innovation power. This can be termed as the cult of gold-plated innovation, which is the prevailing model for defense S&T development in the United States and other military pacesetters, in which the pursuit of next-generation technological capabilities trumps all other considerations including affordability, suitability to end-user needs, and development schedules. However, there is growing debate in the United States and elsewhere about the sustainability of this approach amid calls for less expensive and faster alternatives. This is especially ironic for the Chinese defense acquisition system because it has become proficient in the "good enough" model of defense S&T development, which is quicker, cheaper, and can be produced in greater volume. This approach has allowed China to significantly narrow the innovation gap with its competitors. A key long-term question is whether the cult of gold-plated innovation will push China to abandon its "good enough" model or whether Xi and the Chinese leadership can find a workable balance between these tracks.

What are the prospects for success from Xi's innovation makeover? There are at least two areas to consider. The first is whether Xi's wide-ranging efforts will lead to a significant shift in the insular, conservative, status quo–minded, and deferential institutional culture prevalent in the military and defense S&T systems to a more inquisitive, open, and challenging mindset. The tight ideological climate that has accompanied Xi's rule has seriously hampered efforts to instigate normative changes. Xi has insisted that the country's scientific, academic, and research workforce must be both creative and absolutely loyal to the Communist Party.[74] This is a throwback to the Maoist requirement of being red and expert. There may be some improvements in specific subareas such as the R&D system where much of the reforms and initiatives are targeted, but it will take far more time and effort to fundamentally alter the existing military institutional culture.

Will this defense innovation campaign enable the military and defense S&T systems to reach the goals of becoming a first-tier military innovation power by

2035 and contend for global leadership by 2050? The initial phases of planning, defining, and preparing the reform and innovation initiatives followed by the early stages of full-scale implementation have made robust progress so far. If this momentum continues and the leadership remains supportive, engaged, and willing to continue to invest significant political and financial capital, the odds appear favorable that China will meet or come close to meeting these objectives. The increasingly adversarial competition with the United States provides added incentive and momentum to this endeavor.

THE NATIONAL SECURITY STATE

Xi Jinping was expected to continue the highly successful path of pursuing prosperity and development as China's foremost priority upon taking office as Party General Secretary. However, the incoming helmsman moved swiftly instead to put in place a changed set of preferences and attendant strategies in which national security imperatives would assume far greater attention and authority under his watch. Although economic development remains of immense importance, a new national security–centric state is being forged that is markedly different from past administrations and has far-reaching implications for how the Chinese state views and engages with the international system, makes use of its technological capabilities, and manages its internal affairs.

Much of the foundations and superstructure of this national security state (NSS) were laid down during Xi's first term between 2012 and 2017. New institutional, doctrinal, and regulatory mechanisms have been established that include a powerful national security commission and expansive national security–related laws and regulations. There has been implementation at the same time of more assertive domestic and external security postures such as the building of fortified artificial islands in the South China Sea and the erection of an imposing public security and surveillance apparatus within the country.

This chapter examines the logic, origins, drivers, characteristics, and strategy behind the rise of the NSS under Xi. A number of major questions will be explored. Why did Xi make a hard turn toward national security when he assumed power despite the absence of any significant changes to the country's security environment? How different is national security viewed and managed under Xi's leadership? What were the main motivations behind the building of the NSS? How seriously did Xi take the threat of political grabs for power orchestrated by senior leaders of the Hu regime? What means were available to forge a powerful and effective NSS? What role, for example, has the creation of the Central National Security Commission (CNSC) played in the building of the national security edifice? What is the strategic vision girding the NSS, which is put forward by Xi in the Holistic National Security Concept (HNSC; 总体国家安全观, *Zongti Guojia Anquan Guan*)? What are the defining characteristics of this emerging NSS, such as its areas of responsibility, the nature of political control, and its representation at the top echelons of power? What is the relationship between the NSS and the techno-security state? What are the long-term prospects for the NSS and its domestic and international implications?

Before proceeding, the issue of what constitutes an NSS needs to be examined. The notion of an NSS has traditionally been associated with the garrison state, a concept coined by Harold Lasswell in the 1930s about the Sino-Japanese War in which he argued that military technological advancement would lead to military specialists eventually taking over control of the state.[1] Not surprisingly, the NSS has often been viewed in sinister terms, especially as a threat to democratic rule. Legal scholars, for example, have focused on the erosion of civil liberties and infringement of human rights in the US NSS that emerged after the terrorist attacks on September 11, 2001.[2] In the case of contemporary China, a small but growing number of Western studies have labeled the country a security state but without offering any explicit definitions of what that means beyond identifying the expansion, influence, and intensifying use of the security apparatus and the "securitization" of the state.[3]

The concept of the NSS is analytically useful in examining regimes that are primarily concerned with conflict or the threat of conflict and whose central objective is to safeguard national security. As this chapter looks specifically at both the domestic and external dimensions of how China thinks about and safeguards its national security, the definition that will be used focuses on the key characteristics and dynamics related to both. The NSS places national security considerations at the top of policy priorities, takes an expansive view of what constitutes national security, and gives privileged treatment and access to power, resources, and capabilities to organizations specializing in coercion and control. Moreover, the outside world is seen through a zero-sum and threat-based prism that requires the need for heightened preparations and proactive measures.

It is also important to differentiate between defensive and offensively minded national security regimes. In international relations theory, structural realism distinguishes between defensive and offensive realism.[4] Defensive realists see the anarchic international system as generally benign and assume that states are able to peacefully coexist with one another. Although states have to ensure their own security, this is primarily carried out in ways that are constrained and nonthreatening. Offensive realists, though, take a zero-sum view of the international system and seek security through domination and hegemony. Offensive realists take actions that can and occasionally do lead to conflict.

Applying the defense-offense framework to the NSS concept allows for a more nuanced understanding of what the intentions and capabilities of states are. The ideal-type defensive NSS engages in restrained positive-sum balancing behavior in which the main goal is to maintain the status quo and not to maximize power. These defensive states build their security through internal resource mobilization rather than outward expansion and focus mainly on domestic security and border defense, with only limited and temporary efforts at power projection. The ideal-type offensive NSS engages in zero-sum thinking and behavior that is coercive and relies heavily on preemptive or punitive use of military force beyond the state's immediate borders. They are also highly repressive internally and seek to mobilize their economies and societies to support their external policies. Offensive NSSs look to undermine or defeat their adversaries and annex their territory. States in reality do not fall neatly within these two categories and often combine both defensive and offensive attributes.

The National Security Turn under Xi Jinping

For most countries, especially democratic regimes, becoming an NSS is a herculean undertaking that requires intensive debate, bureaucratic shake-ups, and reordering of the political, security, economic, and social institutions and norms on which a country and its national identity is moored. Although China at the beginning of the 2010s was authoritarian and pro-statist, it nevertheless was firmly committed to economic development. Economic agencies and economic officials were the dominant political and bureaucratic constituencies in the policy process. Moreover, the previous several decades of reform and openness had led to the emergence of an increasingly tolerant and robust civil society with checks and balances that helped to set limits on the power of the party-state and allowed for restricted debate over policy choices.

No discernable public or even internal debate took place, though, over the adjustment of China's national security posture following Xi's accession. There were few signs that the new administration was even contemplating a profound shift toward national security as changes were being made. The first official indication that the key components of a new national security order were being put in place was a brief discussion of national security matters in the communiqué of the 18th Party Congress Third Plenum in November 2013. This was followed in April 2014 with the public unveiling of the CNSC, which was the green light that allowed for the gradual dissemination of articles and books that adhered closely to the official line but offered some additional insights as to why this momentous change from development to security was taking place.

In seeking to answer why China made this hard turn to national security, we need to examine the motivations, means, and circumstances involved. Additionally, how did the decision-making process take place? Was China already moving down this securitization path before Xi took charge and he only accelerated the effort, or did Xi carry out this shift against fierce resistance? What were the means employed to establish a national security state?

New Perspectives on National Security

For China's realist-minded security policymakers who were at the helm in the early 2010s, the country's national security situation was complicated but manageable and well understood. In his swan song address at the 18th Party Congress in November 2012, Hu Jintao (胡锦涛) said that "the world today is undergoing profound and complex changes," but the overall "balance of international forces is developing in a direction favorable for the maintenance of world peace, creating more favorable conditions for overall stability in the international environment."[5] Hu warned, though, that "the world is still very unstable" noting that "hegemony, power politics, and neo-interventionism have been on the rise, and local turmoil keeps cropping up."

Other authoritative security assessments at this time also offered the same cautious but generally favorable assessments of China's external security situation. The 2013 Chinese Defense White Paper noted that "China still faces multiple and complicated security threats and challenges," highlighting problematic relations with Japan, concerns with Taiwan, territorial sovereignty issues, natural disasters, and growing competition with the United States. However, nothing stood out as overly alarming.[6]

For Xi, these traditional realpolitik perspectives only painted a partial and far-too-rosy picture of China's actual security environment. He brought to office a very different set of assumptions and viewpoints as to what constituted the most worrying sources of dangers to the party and country and how they should be addressed. As a longtime provincial apparatchik, Xi's worldview was dominated by domestic and party concerns. Analysts who have examined Xi's track record running Fujian and Zhejiang Provinces in eastern China in the 1990s and 2000s found a "dogged supporter of party orthodoxy."[7] Even as Xi learned the reins of power, he remained focused on the perils confronting the Chinese Communist Party (CCP: 中国共产党, *Zhongguo Gongchandang*). Xi in particular spent considerable time studying the lessons emanating from the collapse of the Soviet Union.[8] Shortly after becoming paramount leader, Xi asked in a speech why the Soviet Union and the Soviet Communist Party had collapsed, and his answer was that "their ideals and beliefs had been shaken." Xi said that this was "a profound lesson for us. To dismiss the history of the Soviet Union and the Soviet Communist Party, to dismiss Lenin and Stalin, and to dismiss everything else is to engage in historical nihilism."[9]

Xi was determined that the CCP should avoid the same fate, even though China in the 2010s bore little resemblance to the decrepit Soviet regime in its twilight years. Xi's answer was a hand-in-glove strategy of hard-hitting ideological purification and building up a repressive NSS. This was signaled at the 18th Party Congress by Hu who previewed Xi's incoming policy agenda, stating that the emphasis in the security domain was on "improving the mechanisms for national security strategy and work, maintaining a high level of vigilance and resolutely guarding against the activities of separatism, infiltration, and subversion carried out by hostile forces, and ensuring national security." Xi added more detail to his new more holistic national security framework at a Central Military Commission (CMC: 中央军事委员会, *Zhongyang Junshi Weiyuanhui*) enlarged meeting following the party congress when, in his capacity as the new commander in chief, he told the assembled top brass that "we must guide officers and men in strengthening their awareness of unexpected developments and their sense of crisis."[10]

This need to prepare for danger in times of peace and to be ready for sudden incidents became important strands in the weaving of the HNSC tapestry. The HNSC has become the overarching conceptual framework for Xi's NSS. The country's first-ever national security strategy that was issued in 2015 is derived largely from the HNSC.[11] A central argument of the HNSC is that "China now faces the most complicated internal and external factors in [its] history."[12] At first glance, this statement would appear to be outlandish as China endured nuclear threats from the United States in the 1950s and border clashes with the Soviet Union that nearly escalated into full-scale conflict in the 1960s. However, the point being made by the HNSC is that the dangers imperiling China in the twenty-first century are not the gravest that it has ever faced but the most complex. From Xi's reconceptualization of national security, the most dangerous threats are internal, nontraditional, political, and emerging. From this vantage point, the world is a far darker and more menacing place that justifies the establishment of a strong NSS. The concrete security environment that China faced in the early 2010s had not radically deteriorated, but the way its new leaders perceived the situation had significantly altered.

What Motivated the Building of the National Security State?

The motivating factors behind the building of the contemporary Chinese NSS can be divided between threats and opportunities. Xi summarized the nature and extent of these challenges and openings in a pithy formulation that deputy chief of the People's Liberation Army (PLA) General Staff Admiral Sun Jianguo (孙建国) outlined in the authoritative party journal *Qiushi* (Seeking Truth) in 2015: the "Three Major Dangers" (三大趋势, *Sanda Qushi*) and the "Three Unprecedenteds" (三个前所未有, *Sange Qiansuo Weiyou*).[13] The three dangers were (1) threats from invasion, subversion, and splittism, (2) the undermining of reform, development, and stability, and (3) the interruption of China's socialist system. These three categories corresponded with the country's official core national interests of sovereignty, development, and security.

This first category of "invasion, subversion, and splittism" primarily concerns the external and internal dangers to the country's territorial integrity and sovereignty. The external dangers were over maritime sovereignty disputes in the South and East China Seas. China was engaged in heated confrontations with Japan over the Diaoyu/Senkaku Islands beginning in 2010, which flared up in 2012 after the Japanese government purchased the islands. Tensions became even more severe in the South China Sea after China began to expand the size of half a dozen islands and atolls in the disputed Spratly Islands and build large-scale military facilities such as runways and air defense fortifications. Territorial integrity was related to ensuring that Taiwan remained a part of China. Although cross-strait ties were improving when Xi took power, they worsened when the independence-leaning Democratic Progressive Party returned to power under Tsai Ing-Wen (蔡英文) in 2016 and have remained strained since then.

Splittism and subversion is tied to the ethnic unrest that China faces in its autonomous far western regions of Tibet and Xinjiang. There have been major upheavals in these two regions over the past couple of decades and Uighur separatists have been engaged in terrorist attacks in Xinjiang, other parts of China, and against Chinese targets overseas. Xi oversaw a significant ramping-up of efforts to build a massive coercive apparatus in Xinjiang beginning in 2014, which led to the detention of large numbers of local Uighur residents and the establishment of a pervasive and highly intrusive surveillance state. The enormous scale of this effort did not become apparent to the outside world until the late 2010s with the help of satellite imagery showing the building of detention camps and the leaking of official Chinese documents disclosing the Chinese leadership's role in managing this crackdown.[14]

The second category of dangers referred to the undermining of reforms, economic development, and stability. Mitigating social instability is a first-order priority for the Chinese authorities in the face of widening social inequality, pervasive corruption, deep-seated structural unemployment, and numerous other social problems. Sun points out that there are "frequent occurrences of social contradictions and accumulating social contradictions." The identification that the "undermining of reforms" poses a national security danger is unusual as this would equate opposition to Xi's reform agenda as a national security threat. Sun noted that "reforms were entering a critical period," which was a reference to the ambitious set of economic, social, and military reforms that were announced at the Third Plenum of the CCP Central Committee in November 2013.[15] There have been occasional reports in the official Chinese media indicating that Xi's reform policies have run into difficulties. A widely published commentary in the Chinese state media in August 2015 said the "scale of resistance" against Xi's reforms "is beyond what could have been imagined."[16] Much of this resistance to Xi's policies appears to be coming from entrenched political and bureaucratic interests that stand to lose from the changes, such as state agencies and state-owned corporations.

The third and most important cluster of dangers revolves around the Communist Party's hold on power, which Sun obliquely referred to as the danger of "China's socialist development being interrupted." The biggest concern for the CCP leadership is the threat to its continued rule, which it views as coming from numerous quarters domestically and externally. This includes a deeply held view among CCP leaders that the West is seeking regime change in China, which has only been reinforced in recent years by the spectacle of "colored revolutions" in Europe and the Arab Spring upheavals that swept the Middle East.

Closer to home, the CCP authorities were unnerved by the student-led political unrest in Hong Kong known as Occupy Central in 2014, which Sun described as the "Hong Kong version of the color revolution stage-managed meticulously by a small number of radical groups in Hong Kong incited and supported by external forces." The Chinese authorities became even more animated by the student-led protests in Hong Kong in 2019–2020, which led to a far-reaching and draconian crackdown and the imposition of a sweeping national security regime that effectively ended the One Country, Two Systems arrangement that had allowed Hong

Kong limited political autonomy after its return to Chinese sovereignty from British rule in 1997. Foreign "black hands" were identified as playing a central role in fomenting this unrest.[17]

One of the most important catalysts behind Xi's national security turn may have been in response to an apparent attempt to thwart his rise to power by a cabal of senior figures in the Hu regime, of which both the civilian and military components of the national security apparatus were deeply implicated. Xi and other senior members of his administration have spoken about attempted power grabs, splittist activities, and political conspiracies by more than half a dozen senior leaders in the Hu regime. In a speech at the Sixth Plenum of the 18th CCP Central Committee in October 2016, Xi said five senior civilian and military leaders of the Hu regime had all conspired in "political activities":

- Zhou Yongkang (周永康), a Politburo Standing Committee member and head of the domestic security apparatus, was arrested in 2013 and sentenced to life imprisonment.
- Bo Xilai (薄熙来), party secretary of Chongqing and a Politburo member, was arrested in 2011 and sentenced to a life term.
- Ling Jihua (令计划), the head of the CCP General Office, was arrested in 2014 and sentenced to life imprisonment.
- General Guo Boxiong (郭伯雄), executive vice-chairman of the CMC, was arrested in 2015 and given a life sentence.
- General Xu Caihou (徐才厚), a CMC vice-chairman, was arrested in 2014 but died before being sentenced.

Xi described these officials as being "politically ambitious, often agreeing in public but opposing in secret, and forming cliques for personal interests and engaging in conspiracy activities."[18] Xi was quoted elsewhere as saying that as Zhou, Bo, Ling, Xu, and another provincial leader, Su Rong (苏荣), rose higher up the political ladder and accumulated more power, "the more they ignored the party's political discipline and political rules, even to the extent of being completely unscrupulous and reckless."[19] They were all arrested shortly after Xi took power and initially charged for corruption offenses. These political crimes were only disclosed later on.

Wang Qishan (王岐山), one of Xi's top lieutenants and anti-corruption czar, has offered the same account of the political conspiracies against the paramount leader. Speaking at a meeting of the 12th Standing Committee of the Chinese People's Political Consultative Conference in October 2016, Wang said that Zhou, Bo, Guo, Xu, and Ling had "attempted to seize party and state power to realize their political ambitions, engaged in plots to split the party, and seriously threatened the nation's political security."[20] Yet another senior official, China Securities Regulatory Commission chairman Liu Shiyu (刘士余), speaking in 2017, added Sun Zhengcai (孙政才), Chongqing party secretary and Politburo member, to the list of conspirators plotting to seize power.[21]

The Chinese authorities have released few concrete details of the political crimes committed, but rumors about possible attempted coups and political intrigues have been reported by Western, Hong Kong, and non-mainland Chinese media organizations, especially after the arrest of Bo in March 2012.[22] The Chinese official media establishment has stayed silent and official censorship has been tight to prevent online discussion. But Chinese official news outlets did report on activities that hinted at this infighting, such as the dispatch of several thousand party cadre from the security apparatus to Beijing for ideological retraining and the absence of key figures such as Zhou from the public spotlight.[23]

Although little is known about the exact nature of this apparent attempted seizure of power, Xi has been clear in his public remarks that he regarded these actions as a very serious threat. Xi swiftly acted on taking office to arrest his foes and began a sweeping reorganization of the national security apparatus to centralize authority and oversight under his direct personal control. This shows that the national security turn was also strongly driven by Xi's personal motivations to secure his hold on power. Some analysts also argue that Xi's ability to consolidate his power at the beginning of his rule was primarily due to the widespread support that he received from the highest levels of the leadership, especially because of concerns that the regime was facing dire threats and required an all-powerful leader to take decisive charge.[24]

But was this split in the Chinese leadership so serious as to endanger the Communist Party's command of the country? Sheena Chestnut Greitens argues that authoritarian rulers like Xi face a "coercive dilemma" in which they have to defend themselves against two very different types of domestic dangers at the same time.[25] First are threats from their own populations, and second are dangers from the ruling elite, especially from those in charge of the coercive apparatus. Greitens says that in building a coercive apparatus, autocrats face an organizational trade-off between dealing with the risk of popular overthrow or coup-proofing against their political rivals. The former demands a unified security apparatus with inclusive intelligence networks, while the latter requires an internally fragmented and socially exclusive security force. For Xi, his choice has been to forge a tightly integrated and cohesive NSS, which would suggest that his greatest fears are of popular unrest rather than coup attempts from within the leadership ranks.

Besides the top-level leadership intrigues, the Xi administration has also regarded subversion within the ranks of the Chinese political and social systems as another serious national security threat. The CCP General Office issued a communiqué in April 2013, "On the Current State of the Ideological Sphere," also known as Document No. 9, that warned of seven perils subverting the party's grip on power. They included Western constitutional democracy, the promotion of universal values of human rights, Western notions of media independence, civil society, neoliberalism, and nihilist views of history.[26] These liberal ideas and reforms had been allowed to take root during the Jiang and Hu regimes, but the Xi administration launched major crackdowns on political, academic, legal, and media freedoms and against nongovernmental organizations promoting civil society and human rights.

At the same time as the Xi regime was taking drastic defensive steps to tackle what it perceived as a volatile threat environment, it also saw a golden opportunity for China to step forward and gain recognition as a leading global power. A key tenet of Xi's grand strategic vision, or China Dream, on taking office was that after decades of arduous economic catching-up, China was now sufficiently prosperous and powerful to assume a leading role in world affairs. This notion—that the time has finally come for China's arrival at the center of the global stage after a hiatus of several centuries—has become a powerful source for a more assertive national identity.

From a national security perspective, China enjoys a number of strategic advantages in becoming a world leader that Xi refers to as the "Three Unprecedenteds."[27] The first "unprecedented" is that China is approaching the center of the world stage in an unprecedented fashion. In other words, China's rapid economic development has caused disruption to the global balance of power. The second "unprecedented" signifies that China is approaching the goal of the great rejuvenation of the Chinese nation in an unprecedented manner. This success in China's nation building has been due to the central role of the Communist Party. The third "unprecedented" is that China now has unprecedented capabilities and confidence to achieve its objectives of becoming a great power. What this means is that a confident, capable, and socialist-led China should take advantage of the strategic opening made possible by its remarkable economic development to claim a leading spot in the international system.

But Chinese leaders point out that this window of opportunity for breaking through to the top is not open for long and China's ability to succeed faces fierce opposition by competitors led by the United States. Consequently, China will need to adopt a more assertive national security posture to meet these challenges. Sun Jianguo has argued that China will need to "struggle" (斗争, douzheng) to ensure that its vital interests are met: "It is impossible to have the United States respect our core interests. Without struggle, it is impossible to achieve cooperation and mutual benefit on a foundation of equality. And without struggle, it would be impossible to have today's favorable situation."[28] The implications for the building of the Chinese NSS in this era of strategic opportunity is that it will need to be more offensively oriented.

The Means of Forging the National Security State

Although Xi was keenly motivated to forge an NSS under his direct control, having the tools and means to accomplish this objective was a different matter. As a relative newcomer to the national political stage and with a thin background in national security affairs, Xi faced formidable obstacles. Past leaders had tried and failed in similar enterprises because of deeply entrenched political and bureaucratic interests. Jiang Zemin (江泽民), for example, had sought to set up a US-style permanent national security council in the 1990s, but fierce resistance from the national security bureaucracy forced him to eventually accept a much weaker ad hoc national security leading group.[29]

What means did Xi have at his disposal to allow him to succeed where his predecessors had not? Having apprenticed as Hu's deputy, Xi would have been well aware of the political stagnation, power struggles, rampant corruption, and policy paralysis that blighted Hu's rule. Upon taking office, Xi quickly went on the offensive—he went after his political opponents in order to begin to arrest the decline of the party and its hold on power. However, Xi was careful not to directly confront vested political and bureaucratic interests head-on and instead pursued a more indirect approach employing unconventional methods and targeting vulnerable points.

A no-holds-barred discipline enforcement campaign was the centerpiece of Xi's arsenal that consisted of several elements of which two were especially important.[30] The most well known was the sweeping anti-corruption crackdown, and a second key component was a political discipline campaign that focused on investigating senior party officials for violations of political discipline. Other initiatives were undertaken to support this discipline enforcement clampdown, such as a vigorous ideological rectification program that enforced a rigorous austerity regime on the spending activities of public officials.

The scale of the discipline enforcement crackdown far exceeded past campaigns, which meant that the Xi administration had to mobilize investigative resources that it could control and trust. The principal organization tasked with this responsibility was the Central Commission of Disciplinary Inspection (CCDI; 中央纪律检查委员会, *Zhongyang Jilu Jiancha Weiyuanhui*), a party entity that was put under the leadership of Wang Qishan. Special ad hoc central inspection teams were also formed with personnel seconded from the CCDI and the Party Central Organization Department to conduct special investigations. These entities were all outside of the traditional national security apparatus.

The anti-corruption campaign was the first part of the disciplinary enforcement initiative to be implemented. Running in parallel was a carefully crafted two-part plan put forward by Xi to comprehensively remake the national security system. The first stage was a revamp of the civilian national security apparatus, which would be followed in a second phase by a sweeping reform of the military high command. The civilian security apparatus that Xi inherited "does not meet the requirements of safeguarding national security," which means there is an urgent need "to build a strong and powerful platform" that would allow for a unified approach in carrying out national security work.[31] The elements of this revamped system would include (1) a new centralized command structure, (2) a new theoretical and strategic approach to thinking about national security that would greatly broaden and redefine what key threats were and where they came from, and (3) a new national security regulatory regime providing new laws and rules of the road to govern issues such as privacy and access to information. Altogether, this revamped national security model would be more intrusive, more centralized, and more expansive than anything in China's past, including the Maoist era.

The first step to realizing Xi's grand vision came at the Third Plenum of the 18th Party Central Committee, which stated that "setting up a national security commission has become urgent now in order to strengthen centralized, unified leadership over national security work." The primary duties of the new CNSC are to "formulate and implement a national security strategy, push forward the construction of national security legislation, formulate national security work principles and policies, and study and resolve major national security issues."[32]

The plenum statement provided the broadest of outlines of the proposed new national security setup that would rest on three legs: (1) the CNSC, which would be the powerful organizational anchor of the system, (2) a legal framework that would revolve around a new national security law, and (3) a doctrinal component that would provide a comprehensive threat assessment and identify the strategic and operational priorities for the new NSS to carry out its tasks. This new model is sometimes referred to as the three-in-one national security system (三位一体的国家安全体系, *sanwei yiti de guojia anquan tixi*).[33]

The CNSC was approved in January 2014 and resides at the apex of the new national security edifice. Its authority, power, and reach stems largely from its leadership structure with Xi as the chairman and the premier and the National People's Congress (NPC) chairman as deputy chairmen. The CNSC is a party organ that reports directly to the Politburo Standing Committee and is described as "the nerve center of the central authorities responsible for making decisions and coordination on national security affairs."[34]

Little is known about the activities of the CNSC, its internal organizational structure, and how it engages with the rest of the national security, party, and state apparatuses.[35] After the brief media coverage of the CNSC's first meeting in 2014, there was no more official reporting of its meetings and activities until four years later in April 2018 when the first meeting of the Post-19th Party Congress CNSC took place. There has been coverage of national security–related meetings, such as a National Security Work Symposium in February 2017, but the cloak of secrecy around the commission has been extremely tight.[36]

At the CNSC April 2018 meeting, Xi provided a tantalizing but brief overview of the commission's work in its first four years. He said that the CNSC had (1) built an "initial main framework," (2) developed a theoretical system, (3) improved the "strategic national security system," and (4) forged mechanisms for coordinating national security work. Xi also expressed satisfaction that the CNSC "has solved many tough problems that were long on the agenda but never resolved, and accomplished many things that were necessary but never got done." Although no details were provided, Xi said that the end result was that "national security has been comprehensively strengthened, and a firm hold has been kept on the initiative in the overall work of safeguarding national security."[37] Xi added that attention should also be focused on dealing with long-term challenges along with the need to improve social management capabilities. Liu Yuejin (刘跃进), a prominent national security scholar at the Ministry of State Security (MSS: *Guojia Anquan Bu,* 国家安全部)–affiliated College of International Relations, said that Xi's remarks on the resolution of many tough long-standing problems referred to the implementation of the anti-corruption and ideological rectification campaign, major military reforms, formulation of the HNSC, establishment of the CNSC, promulgation of the national security law, and development of a national security education program to enhance public awareness.[38]

The building of a sweeping legal framework is the second pillar of the national security system, which is anchored around the National Security Law (NSL: *Guojia Anquan Fa,* 国家安全法) that was passed in July 2015. The main intention of the law was to provide "a legal format for the Holistic National Security Concept," a *People's Daily* commentary explained.[39] Consequently, the law resembles a "Communist Party ideology paper and a call to arms aimed at defending the party's grip on power" more than a standard impartial legal text.[40] Previous national security legislation such as the 1993 NSL were far more narrowly focused on espionage matters.

The new NSL offers an expansive definition of national security as the "protection of the political regime, sovereignty, national unification, territorial integrity, people's welfare, and the 'sustainable and healthy development' of the economy and society." More specifically, the NSL identifies an extensive array of domains that include political security, homeland security, military security, economic security, financial infrastructure security, energy security, food security, cultural security, scientific and technological security, information security, ethnic security, religious security, anti-terrorism security, societal security, environmental security, nuclear security, and the security of outer space, deep seas, and polar regions. Along with other security-related legislation that has been passed during Xi's tenure such as the National Intelligence Law (2017), Counterespionage Law (2014), Counterterrorism Law (2015), Cybersecurity Law (2016), and Foreign Nongovernmental Organizations Management Law (2016), the Chinese NSS has unassailable legal authority to do anything it wants within its own borders and increasingly beyond.

The Strategic Vision behind the National Security State

When Xi assumed power, China's international and domestic security environments looked stable and manageable. The 2013 Chinese Defense White Paper assessed that "the balance of international forces is shifting in favor of maintaining world peace, and on the whole the international situation remains peaceful and stable." However, with the HNSC, Xi put forward a very different "socialist scientific" framework with which to view the national security landscape. The HNSC was attuned to a broader and different array of factors arising from nontraditional and political-ideological domains. Xi has described the HNSC as a "powerful ideological weapon for safeguarding and shaping the security of a big country with Chinese characteristics," which alludes to its essential political character. The HNSC became China's first-ever official national security strategy in January 2015 when the Politburo approved the National Security Strategy Outline (NSSO; 国家安全战略纲要, *Guojia Anquan Zhanlue Gangyao*).[41] The contents of the NSSO and HNSC are the same.[42]

At the heart of the HNSC are two related paradoxes that help to explain why China under Xi became a NSS despite enjoying a benign security environment. The first is that even though China has never been more prosperous, its national security has also never been more problematic. The second is that the brighter the future, the greater the need to be on alert and prepared for major challenges to China's security.[43] At the inaugural 2014 meeting of the CNSC, Xi pointed to these fundamental contradictions by decrying that China "faces the most complicated internal and external factors in [its] history."[44]

Xi has provided an overarching ideological guidance for the HNSC that revolves around the trinity of the nation, the people, and the Communist Party, although this is obfuscated behind dense Marxist terminology: "We must put national interests (国家利益, *guojia yili*) first, take protecting our people's security (人民安全, *renmin anquan*) as our purpose, and safeguard political security (政治安全, *zhengzhi anquan*) as our fundamental task." This formulation seeks to align the country's national interests closely with the Communist Party's ideological and political priorities within the HNSC rubric so that they are "organically unified." What this means is that China's approach and pursuit of national security at the very highest levels of policymaking is fundamentally defined and driven by ideological and political considerations. In other words, this is the politicization of national security.

What actually constitutes the national interest, the people's security, and political security as contained in the HNSC? Tsinghua University professor Yan Xuetong (阎学通) offers a broad definition of national interests that provides useful context for understanding Xi's thinking. National interest is "the common material and spiritual need[s] of all the people of a nation state. In material terms, a nation needs security and development. In spiritual terms, a nation needs respect and recognition from the international community."[45] These material and spiritual (or normative in Western social science parlance) needs that Yan identifies correspond to China's official core interests of sovereignty, security, and development.

Another perspective on the formulation of Chinese national interests that complements Yan's analysis is by US Naval Academy professor Yong Deng, who argues that factors related to national identity are central sources of influence. Although Yong's research dates to Chinese academic debates on national interest in the 1990s, his findings are still relevant in the Xi era because one of the dominant factors in shaping contemporary Chinese national identity is nationalism, especially a realpolitik version profoundly influenced by the narrative of humiliation and victimization suffered by China between the mid-nineteenth and mid-twentieth centuries. This has led to the forging of a national identity of an insecure state struggling with legitimacy and suspicions of international influence.[46] The crucial difference between the 1990s and the twenty-first century is that this lack of confidence and insecurity is juxtaposed by surging confidence and strength.

On the issue of core national interests, the balance between development, security, and sovereignty has been revised under Xi's tenure. From Deng to Hu, development was by far the most important national priority, but Xi has elevated security to the same level, if not higher. "We not only emphasize development issues but also security issues," Xi said at the CNSC meeting in April 2014.[47] Moreover, Xi said that national security and development are deeply intertwined. "Security and development are two sides of the same issue, two wheels in the same driving mechanism. Security guarantees development, and development is the goal of security."[48] What this means is that China needs to pursue a more proactive and assertive approach in shaping and protecting its security environment to promote development rather than its previously more reactive and low-key posture. Tsinghua University professor Hu Angang (胡鞍钢) says that Xi's efforts to rethink the nature and balance of the development-security relationship reflects "the changes of the times and China's new requirements for development."[49] This was also highlighted by Xi at a national security meeting in February 2017 when he said that national security planning "must consider the general background that China is in a period of important strategic opportunity for development."[50]

Within the HNSC trinity, "people's security" is a phrase that on the surface appears to have little purpose other than to extend Xi's guiding ideological thoughts into the national security realm. More precisely, people's security is the application of the people-centered development philosophy that is a cornerstone of "Xi Jinping Thought on Socialism with Chinese Characteristics for the New Era." Xi has pointed out that "we insist that national security is for the sake of the people," and consequently, "we persist in putting the people first and in the people-centric idea."[51] Marxism scholar Li Yongsheng (李永胜) explains that people's security is to "realize, safeguard, and develop the fundamental interests of the broad masses," and he further argues that the concept can be likened to the "soul" of China's national security.[52] This is because the purpose of people's security is to ensure the security and well-being of the Chinese people so that they are able to "live and work in peace under contentment of the leadership of the party and the socialist system." How this is accomplished is left to the operational components of the HNSC framework. A bleaker and more accurate interpretation of people's security is that it is the ideological construct of the Orwellian surveillance state that justifies the development of a vast monitoring and social control apparatus using any ideological pretext that the leadership deems appropriate.

Political security is the final element of the HNSC trinity and is the most important in the actual shaping and operationalization of national security policy and implementation. Political security is defined as the fundamental task of the HNSC, which means that its central objective is to safeguard the Communist Party's leadership and maintain the socialist system.[53] Some analysts also say that political security extends to the defense of the country's sovereignty and territorial integrity. Writing in the *Liberation Army Daily*, Central Party School analyst Yang Dazhi (杨大志) said that "the most basic aspect of maintaining political security is to safeguard the sovereignty and independence of the country and territorial integrity, to ensure that the sovereignty and territory of the People's Republic of China are not violated and the country is not divided."[54] Others argue that there is a separate "territorial security" (领土安全, *lingtu anquan*) concept that would be responsible for sovereignty and territorial integrity issues, although no such category is listed in the NSL. Some analysts argue that homeland security (国土安全, *guotu anquan*), which is one of these defined domains in the NSL, would include territorial security.[55] Political security is the main bridge between the HNSC guidance and the operational dimensions of Chinese national security strategy and policy.

In conclusion, the HNSC represents a markedly different lens with which the Xi regime views the external and internal security environments. Indeed, the starkly political nature of the HNSC is much more alarmist and prone to seeing far more threats and challenges. This increases the risks for misperceptions, faulty analysis, and poor decision making, which is especially worrisome in periods of high tension or crises that China may increasingly face domestically and externally.

The Characteristics of Xi's National Security State

The national security establishment that Xi inherited was a big and awkward behemoth. His goal has been to remake it into a strong, agile, cohesive, politically loyal, state-of-the-art twenty-first-century institution. These are not traits commonly associated with China's coercive institutions. The entrenched conservatism, insularity, and compartmentalization of the sprawling national security base are formidable obstacles to this reform effort, but in reviewing the progress made during his first term, Xi offered a positive appraisal, stating that "national security work has been strengthened in an all-round way."[56]

A number of major improvements have taken place to help move the needle from being big toward being strong. First is the top-down centralization of leadership authority. This has been principally focused on the establishment of the CNSC. But even though the overarching leadership authority of the CNSC is not in doubt, its ability to effectively oversee and operationally manage a sprawling, compartmentalized, decentralized, and fiercely competitive bureaucratic apparatus is. In the first few years of its establishment, Xi placed trusted political aides in key CNSC positions who had little national security expertise. This move is unlikely to have helped in the building of effective coordination mechanisms with the military, security, and intelligence apparatuses, and suggests instead that the CNSC is a personalistic symbol of Xi's command of the NSS.

Second is the imposition of tight party control at all levels of the national security hierarchy and across all parts of the country. As Xi is the core of the

party, this party control is also about ensuring his personal control. Xi has re-
peatedly stressed that "it is necessary to uphold the party's absolute leadership
over national security work and implement stronger leadership and coordination."[57] The CNSC is responsible at the national level, while party committees
are in charge at lower levels. At a CNSC meeting in April 2018, a party committee national security responsibility system was agreed on that required party
committees at all levels to strengthen supervision and inspection of the performance of national security duties.[58]

Third and related to the issue of political control is the expansion of the NSS's
areas of responsibility to include anti-corruption and ideological discipline, especially within governing institutions. This likely means that the newly established national supervisory system and existing discipline inspection system will
be closely tied into the national security establishment and used to police the
official establishment. Xi has used anti-corruption and discipline inspection as
important tools in his arsenal to address domestic threats to his rule, most seriously from high-level political opponents, and to crack down on ideological de-
cay and drift. This has made the anti-corruption and discipline systems an
indispensable component of the NSS, especially with the emphasis on political
security.[59]

The anti-corruption and discipline inspection systems, however, have historically not been part of the national security establishment but affiliated instead
with other parts of the party-state setup. The discipline inspection system belongs to the party, most closely with the Party Central Committee, Politburo,
and Politburo Standing Committee, while the anti-corruption apparatus is affiliated with the Supreme People's Procuratorate that is under the political-legal
(政法, zhengfa) system. The anti-corruption and discipline inspection systems
were combined in 2018 to form the National Supervision Commission (Guojia
Jiancha Weiyuanhui, 国家监察委员会), which reports to the NPC and is consti-
tutionally a fourth branch of the government.[60] Although the discipline inspection system reports to the supervisory commission, it continues to serve in its
original role as a party outfit but now has two reporting channels.

Adding the supervisory and discipline inspection apparatus to the organizational lineup of the NSS expands its security capabilities in the ideological
and disciplinary spheres but does not add to its bulk. This is because these two
institutions are small in scale compared to the principal public security and military organs. The CCDI, for example, has a workforce of not much more than a
thousand personnel.[61] One Hong Kong publication, quoting official Chinese media reports, said that the supervision and discipline inspection system might
have around thirty thousand specially appointed supervisory personnel.[62]

The main pillars of the NSS are as follows (see figure 2.1):

- Public security system: The public security apparatus is the domestic front line of the NSS and has a wide portfolio of responsibilities ranging from traffic management to cybersecurity. Personnel strength ranges from 1.6 million to 2 million, which, although large in absolute terms, is small as a ratio of the national population compared to other countries.[63]

- State security/intelligence and counterespionage system: The MSS is the country's principal state security organization and is chiefly responsible for intelligence and counterespionage.[64] The Ministry of Public Security (MPS: *Gongan Bu,* 公安部) and PLA also have significant intelligence capabilities. The MSS is a relatively young organization having only been created in 1983 and has had to compete for resources, manpower, and power with its much older, larger, and more powerful public security sibling. The creation of the MSS was an important move by the Chinese authorities to shift intelligence work from under the auspices of the party to a state agency, which has allowed the development of a more professional approach to intelligence operations.

- People's Liberation Army: The PLA is the largest, most capable, and politically most influential component of the NSS, but it has also been the most isolated from its civilian security and intelligence counterparts. The PLA has been primarily focused on meeting China's external security needs but has occasionally had to intervene domestically such as during the Cultural Revolution and to quell popular unrest in 1989, which seriously set back its military professionalism. The PLA is the world's largest standing armed forces with two million troops, of which less than half belong to the ground forces.[65] It also has considerable numbers of reserve units.

- People's Armed Police: The PAP has been the crucial link between domestic law enforcement and the military establishment ever since it was created in 1983. From its beginning to the late 2010s, the PAP reported to both the CMC and State Council.[66] This dual-hatted structure helped to mitigate the civilian-military gap that runs deep in the NSS. But as part of Xi's far-reaching reforms of the defense establishment, the PAP was brought exclusively under the CMC in January 2018.[67]

Although this reorganization would appear to go against Xi's general goal of promoting MCF and a more unified NSS, more important objectives are to significantly bolster the PAP's coercive capabilities, provide better war-fighting support

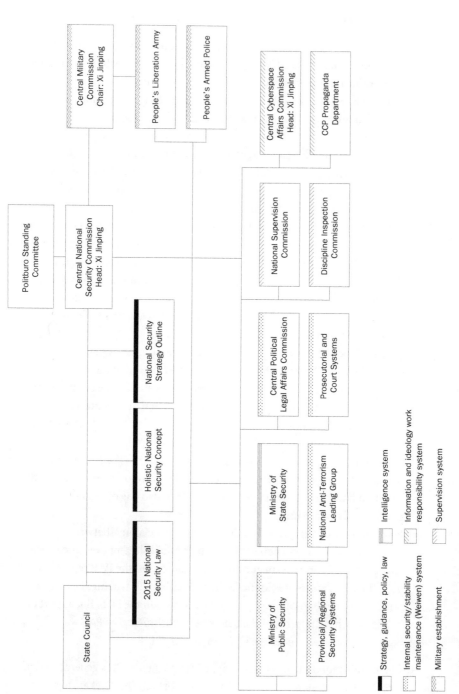

FIGURE 2.1. The Chinese national security state under Xi Jinping

Central Military Commission
Chair: Xi Jinping

People's Liberation Army

People's Armed Police

Central Cyberspace Affairs Commission
Head: Xi Jinping

CCP Propaganda Department

Politburo Standing Committee

Central National Security Commission
Head: Xi Jinping

National Supervision Commission

Discipline Inspection Commission

National Security Strategy Outline

Holistic National Security Concept

2015 National Security Law

Central Political Legal Affairs Commission

Prosecutorial and Court Systems

State Council

Ministry of State Security

National Anti-Terrorism Leading Group

Ministry of Public Security

Provincial/Regional Security Systems

Strategy, guidance, policy, law

Internal security/stability maintenance (Weiwen) system

Military establishment

Intelligence system

Information and ideology work responsibility system

Supervision system

to the PLA, and enhance the centralization of the PAP's control, which has traditionally been closely affiliated with provincial authorities. One key reform is the building of mobile and special operations forces that can be quickly deployed anywhere in the country. This includes establishing two major PAP mobile contingents (总队, zongdui). Another development is the beefing-up of the PAP's presence in Xinjiang by upgrading the PAP unit assigned to the Xinjiang Production and Construction Corps into a provincial-level force that would complement the existing PAP Xinjiang contingent.[68] Estimates of the size of the PAP range between eight hundred thousand to more than one million troops.[69] These numbers have steadily increased with the transfer of military personnel and the addition of the Coast Guard to the PAP in 2018.

- Political-legal affairs system: The Chinese party-state has developed an extensive domestic security apparatus to address rising social unrest and stability maintenance (维稳, weiwen) challenges. Yuhua Wang and Carl Minzner trace the securitization of the political-legal affairs system to the aftermath of the 1989 popular unrest that threatened to topple the Communist Party. There is a core political-legal affairs system that is made up of the public security, state security, judicial (courts and procuratorate), and party political-legal affairs apparatuses, as well as a broader comprehensive public security management system that includes dozens of state organizations such as the Ministry of Personnel, banks, and even the tourism board. Party political-legal affairs committees exist at many levels of the party bureaucracy and are in charge of this mobilized effort of domestic security management.[70] To underline the political importance of the political-legal affairs system, the head of the Central Political-Legal Affairs Commission has a seat on the Politburo Standing Committee.

A fourth improvement that has helped to strengthen the NSS is the elevation in the political status and clout of the national security bureaucracy and its leadership. Historically, the national security and intelligence agencies have not been fully trusted by their political masters and consequently have struggled for seats in the upper echelons of the political and policymaking apparatuses. Their representation in key bodies such as the Politburo Standing Committee and full Politburo has been limited. Under Xi's tenure, the national security community's presence in these bodies has grown significantly, both directly and indirectly. Five officials with national security–related portfolios were appointed to the twenty-five-member Politburo at the 19th Party Congress. They are Guo Shengkun (郭声琨), secretary of the Central Political-Legal Affairs Commission, Yang Xiaodu (杨晓渡), director of the National Supervision Commission, General

Zhang Youxia (张又侠) and General Xu Qiliang (许其亮), CMC vice-chairmen, and Zhao Leji (赵乐际), CCDI secretary and a Politburo Standing Committee member. Indirect representation refers to civilian officials with little background in security affairs who have been given appointments to the CNSC or other national security bodies. They include Premier Li Keqiang (李克强), NPC chairman Li Zhanshu (栗战书), and director of the CNSC General Office Ding Xuexiang (丁薛祥). However, the heads of the MPS and MSS have not yet been able to secure appointments to the Politburo.

Fifth is a gradual shift in the ingrained institutional culture of responding to security threats only when they have occurred to proactively preventing them from taking place or nipping them in the bud as quickly as possible. The public security bureaucracy has been the chief proponent of a reactive mindset. Xi, though, has strongly pushed for a more forward-leaning preemptive approach. At a risk mitigation workshop for provincial and ministerial-level cadres in January 2019, Xi talked about the need to be "highly vigilant against 'black swan' and guard against 'gray rhino' events."[71] This cultural change requires fundamental adjustments to operational practices, such as adopting information-based and intelligence-led approaches instead of "old-fashioned strategies based on 'gut suppositions'" that "require diverting resources away from traditional priorities such as manpower and equipment."[72]

Sixth is the sustainable growth in resource allocations to the military and domestic security establishments to prevent imposing an excessive financial burden that might affect economic development (see table 2.1). This has meant that even though officially declared national security spending has ramped up in absolute terms, it has held steady relative to overall national expenditures. Public security expenditures rose on average 12.6 percent annually between 2010 and 2018, although this fluctuated considerably from a low of 7.3 percent in 2014 to a high of 17.6 percent in 2016. Annual defense expenditures during this same period rose on average by 9.6 percent. Although these are significant growth rates, they originate from low base levels in the 1990s and early 2000s. Surprisingly, the average annual increase for public security and defense expenditures fell during the first six years of Xi's tenure (2013–2018) to 11.7 percent and 9.1 percent, respectively. This suggests that Xi's support for the building of a robust NSS is more equivocal from a resource allocation perspective than his policy positions. However, these official budget and expenditure figures lack transparency and exclude major funding sources that are normally counted in the expenditures of more open and accountable democratic regimes. For the defense budget, items such as spending on foreign weapons acquisitions and defense research and development are left out, while for the public security budget, it is very likely that intelligence spending is omitted. Official domestic security

TABLE 2.1 Chinese defense and public security expenditures, 2007–2018

YEAR	DEFENSE BUDGET	DEFENSE BUDGET PERCENTAGE INCREASE YEAR-OVER-YEAR	PUBLIC SECURITY EXPENDITURES (A: CENTRAL; B: PROVINCIAL)	PUBLIC SECURITY BUDGET PERCENTAGE INCREASE YEAR-OVER-YEAR	DOMESTIC SECURITY AS RATIO OF DEFENSE BUDGET
2007	355.5	17.6%	348.6	36.0%	98.1%
2008	417.9	18.5%	406.0	16.5%	97.2%
2009	495.1	7.7%	474.4	16.8%	95.8%
2010	533.3	7.7%	551.8	16.3%	103.5%
2011	602.8	13.0%	630.4	14.2%	104.6%
2012	669.2	11.0%	711.2	12.8%	106.3%
2013	741.0	10.7%	778.6	9.5%	105.1%
2014	829.0	11.9%	835.7	7.3%	100.8%
2015	908.8	9.6%	938.0	12.2%	103.2%
2016	976.6	7.5%	1,103.2	17.6%	113.0%
2017	1,046.0	7.1%	1,240.6 (A: 184.9; B: 1,061.2)	12.4%	118.6%
2018	1,128.0	7.8%	1,378.1 (A: 204.1 (14.8%; B: 1,174 (85.2%))	11.1%	122.2%

Sources: *China Statistics Yearbook*; Zenz, "China's Domestic Security Spending"; Greitens, "Rethinking China's Coercive Capacity"; and Yue Xie, "Rising Central Spending."

and defense expenditures each account for between 5 percent and 7 percent of overall government expenditures, which combined is around 12–13 percent of state spending. This is equivalent to between 2.5 percent and 3 percent of gross domestic product.

There are instances, though, where security spending has soared and could potentially destabilize this balanced equilibrium between security and development if left unchecked. The enormous expenses of the securitization of Xinjiang is the most obvious case of the runaway NSS. Xinjiang's domestic security spending increased nearly tenfold between 2007 and 2018 from RMB 5.45 billion (US$845 million) to RMB 57.95 billion (US$9.078 billion). A significant part of this increase was a 92.8 percent increase between 2016 and 2017, much of which went toward a massive security facility infrastructure building spree, especially of detention camps.[73]

The Relationship between the National Security State and Techno-Security State

When Lasswell first put forward the concept of the garrison state, he was addressing the impact that highly disruptive military technological developments would have on the relationship between the military and the state. For Lasswell in the late 1930s, it was about the revolutionary consequences of airpower. The need for technologically sophisticated soldiers, or what Lasswell termed specialists on violence, would lead to the rise of the NSS in which the military would be in control of state and society. In the high-technology age of the twenty-first century, the relationship between technology and the NSS is even more important and intertwined.

For China, the NSS's approach toward technology is a tale of two contrasting institutional cultures. The technology-intensive defense establishment has rushed to embrace technological innovation as central to its transformation. By contrast, the relationship between technology and the internal security apparatus has been more circumspect. The law enforcement and social stability–centered missions of domestic security organs have traditionally been more reliant on manpower than technology and have lacked, until recently, adequate resources to devote to technology investment.

The public security apparatus has made concerted efforts to build a more technologically capable system with public security informatization (公安信息化, *gongan xinxihua*) as the centerpiece since the early 2000s.[74] The principal initiative is the Golden Shield Project (金盾工程, *Jindun Gongcheng*) that began in 2003, which is aimed at moving the public security apparatus from the analog to the digital era in the collection, analysis, application, and diffusion of information with the goal of enabling "unified command, rapid reaction, and coordinated operations." Of particular focus is improving the sharing of information across the entire system in a timely fashion. This has involved the construction of a dedicated national trunk network, setting up of command centers to handle the data flow at the central, provincial, and municipal levels, establishment of large-scale information databases, and the development of integrated information platforms that allow information to be consolidated into a single mechanism for easier access. Edward Schwarck argues that Golden Shield "has fundamentally changed how public security authorities see data on a conceptual level" and has forced "a rewiring of the ministry's information management structures to ensure that data that was once siloed and scattered can now be pooled and analyzed coherently."[75]

The construction of the public security informatization system has allowed the MPS to significantly enhance critical capabilities, of which intelligence gathering and analysis is a prime example. The Big Intelligence System (大情报系统, Da Qingbao Xitong) has been built on top of the trunk network, which is composed of integrated intelligence departments located at the national, provincial, and municipal levels staffed by twenty-eight thousand analysts who collate and assess intelligence and information flows.[76] These sophisticated technological capabilities have allowed the MPS to pursue a more effective intelligence-led policing model. The experience and expertise acquired from this public security informatization project will be extremely useful to the MPS as it moves ahead with even more advanced and ambitious technological development projects such as mass surveillance and the utilization of artificial intelligence (AI)/machine learning capabilities.

The MSS has also stepped up the development of its technological capabilities, especially in computer network exploitation assets that have become the crown jewel of its intelligence-gathering system. The MSS has leveraged the civilian cybersecurity industry to support its innovation efforts since the 1990s. This has led to the forging of a network of public-private partnerships that analysts say has helped to obscure the role of the Chinese intelligence apparatus in cyber-espionage activities. One key public-private relationship, for example, is between Topsec Network Security Technology Company and China National Information Technology Security Evaluation Center.[77]

Chinese leaders are urging the national security apparatus to accelerate and deepen its embrace of technology and innovation. Xi has pointed out that "security in the field of science and technology is an important part of national security," and more effort is needed in the "overall planning and organization of major scientific and technological tasks that concern national security." Key priorities for the NSS that Xi highlighted include the construction of an early warning and monitoring system for scientific and technological security, especially focused on AI, genome editing, medical diagnosis, automated driving, unmanned aerial vehicles, cybersecurity, and robotics.[78] Xi has also called for the development of better safeguards and defense of the NSS, especially of its cybersecurity infrastructure.[79] The Edward Snowden revelations in 2014 of extensive US cyber operations and penetration of the Chinese political, economic, and security systems jolted the Chinese authorities into action.[80] The overlap between the Chinese national security and techno-security states is steadily growing.

Assessing the Nature of the Chinese National Security State

Shrouded in secrecy, the contemporary Chinese NSS remains a riddle. Little is known about how vital organs like the CNSC operate, how personally involved Xi is in decision making and policy implementation, or the relationship between key civilian, military, and intelligence power centers. But although information on the internal nuts and bolts of the NSS is closely guarded, there are plenty of insights available on the broader forces at play that shape its development, preferences, and institutional identity. They include the consequences of leadership engagement, the catalytic impact of threat perceptions, the detrimental effects of bureaucratic politics on institutional cohesion, how political ideology corrodes performance, the continuing influence of historical determinants on current developments, the importance of political economy issues such as resource inputs and budgets, the emphasis on the expansion and modernization of security capabilities, and the significance of external influences on domestic processes.

Moreover, the fledging comparative study of the coercive dimensions of authoritarian regimes offers additional perspectives, of which five will be discussed here. First, coercive security regimes that focus on the development of surveillance and preemptive capabilities rather than traditional brute force and indiscriminate capabilities are likely to be more effective in achieving their goals of preventing instability and challenges to the regime.[81] Second, autocrats construct coercive institutions according to the threats they perceive as most dominant at the time they come to power. Consequently, institutional inheritance and external influence are important but not decisive in shaping institutional development.[82] Third, intelligence plays a critical role, but the nature of the information autocrats need—and consequently the types of intelligence agencies required—vary according to their political and security interests and threat perceptions.

Fourth, autocrats face a coercive dilemma in that they face a fundamental trade-off between optimizing their internal security apparatuses to deal with popular grassroots threats and coup-proofing to defend against elite rivals.[83] If the top priority is preventing mass instability, a unified security force is required with embedded and socially inclusive intelligence networks. Guarding against coups demands the opposite: a deeply fragmented security apparatus in which different organizations are pitted against each other.

Fifth, when dictators gain personal control of security apparatuses, this is a giant step toward the personalization of rule, even in countries with a united military or disciplined ruling party. Although dictators seek personal control over internal security to protect themselves from ouster, this personalization of internal security also contributes to greater regime longevity and more stable dictator tenure. Even more worrisome is the finding that the personalization of dictatorial rule is associated with poor governance, more erratic and aggressive international behavior, and enhanced prospects for violence.[84]

In assessing the current state, continuing development, and future prospects of the Chinese NSS, a number of key questions will be examined. Is the leadership regime personalistic or institutionalized in nature? How cohesive and integrated is the national security enterprise? What are its primary threat concerns and opportunities? Are they more internally focused or becoming increasingly external? Finally, is China's security posture more defensively or offensively oriented?

Personalistic versus Institutionalized Rule

One gauge of the balance between personalistic and institutionalized control of the NSS is the composition of the top leader's inner circle for national security affairs. If political loyalists with little past experience in national security matters are appointed to many of the key slots, then personalistic rule is strong. However, if national security professionals are placed in these posts, then this will indicate institutionalization is taking place. In Xi's first term, three of the seven members of his national security inner circle were political loyalists (see table 2.2). This increased to five out of eight members in Xi's second term. This would indicate that Xi's personalistic rule has increased during his time in power.

Could the current NSS remain intact if Xi is no longer at the helm? Xi's departure would certainly leave a huge power vacuum, especially if he does not devise a clear succession plan beforehand. Xi's current deputies in charge at the CNSC and CMC would be unlikely to take over from him in anything more than a short-term caretaking capacity because they lack sufficient political clout and authority to succeed in a post-Xi leadership contest. Consequently, the long-term durability of a post-Xi national security setup would be in serious doubt.

TABLE 2.2   Members of the national security inner circle during the first two terms of Xi Jinping's leadership, 2012–2022

POSITION	XI'S FIRST TERM	XI'S SECOND TERM
Public Security Minister	*Guo Shengkun*	*Zhao Kezhi*
General Office Director, Central National Security Commission	**Li Zhanshu**	**Ding Xuexiang**
Discipline Inspection Committee Chair	**Wang Qishan**	**Zhao Leiji**
Central Military Commission Vice-Chairs	*Fan Changlong*; *Xu Qiliang*	*Xu Qiliang*; **Zhang Youxia**
People's Armed Police Commander	*Wang Jianping* (until 2016); **Wang Ning**	**Wang Ning**
Central Political-Legal Affairs Commission, Head	*Meng Jianzhu*	*Guo Shengkun*
National Supervisory Commission	Not established	**Yang Xiaodu**

Note: Names of political loyalists are in boldface; national security professionals are in italics.

Cohesion versus Fragmentation

One of the enduring characteristics of the Chinese national security apparatus from its inception to the present day is its deep-seated organizational fragmentation and an entrenched institutional culture of mistrust and politicization. This is because the raison d'être of the security apparatus—for both its civilian and military components—is to serve the Communist Party or, more accurately, the competing factions jockeying for power and leadership. When the Communist Party first established its security apparatus in the late 1920s, it was in the midst of shifting political loyalties, civil war, internal intrigue, and foreign invasion. Communist security and intelligence units proliferated and their purposes were as much to compete against one another and root out suspected spies and counterrevolutionaries within their own ranks as to fight against enemy forces.[85] These inward-facing responsibilities were self-evident in the names of some of these organs. The Committee for Eliminating Counterrevolutionaries was the first dedicated security body established by the Communist Party in 1928. Another was the Department of Eliminating Traitors, Spies, and Trotskyists, which was formed in the late 1930s, initially as a military entity, but was later brought under Communist Party control. Some of these entities continued to exist well after the Communist Party came to power. The First Bureau of the MPS was commonly known as the Bureau of Investigating Counterrevolutionaries until its merger with the MSS in 1983.

Besides these ominously named outfits, the primary security and intelligence agencies included the State Political Security Bureau that was set up in the 1930s and the Social Affairs Department and its Intelligence Department that was started in 1939 to serve as Mao's principal security and intelligence mechanism and subsequently became the MPS after 1949. There was also the Central Committee's Investigation and Research Commission that was formed in 1941 and the Central Guard Bureau and Unit 8341 responsible for protecting the central leadership.

These harsh political and coercive origins of the security apparatus profoundly shaped its institutional culture, its organizational structure, and its normative behavior. The security apparatus continued to be heavily involved in the political struggles and intrigues in the aftermath of the Communist Party's takeover of power. Even though the security apparatus wielded considerable power and was widely feared, it was also deeply distrusted. This is an important reason why the security apparatus has been kept on the sidelines of national politics with limited representation at the highest levels of decision-making authority.

The political legacy of the security apparatus has contributed significantly toward its divided nature and dysfunctionality. The intelligence system is a classic example of this fragmentation. The bureaucratic competition between the MPS and MSS has been fierce ever since the latter was created in 1983. Much to the chagrin of the MPS, its espionage and counterintelligence capabilities were absorbed into the MSS, which also incorporated the Investigations Department of the Party Central Committee. Although the MPS is primarily responsible for domestic law enforcement duties while the MSS is in charge of foreign intelligence and counterintelligence, there is considerable overlap in their activities. However, instead of cooperating, these "two ministries have usually competed . . . in the areas in which they share jurisdiction."[86] There have been efforts to improve coordination and overcome fragmentation by having joint oversight of security organizations, especially across the civil-military divide, such as with the PAP.

Internal, External, and Transnational Security

Before Xi's seismic shake-up of the Chinese national security order, a longstanding organizing principle was a strict partition between internal and external security. A primary reason for this compartmentalized approach was bureaucratic: internal security was the chief responsibility of civilian institutions while external security was handled by the military with a supporting role by the MSS. There were occasional efforts to bridge this divide driven by transnational and nontraditional security issues such as terrorism and crime, but they were limited and had marginal impact on overcoming the deeply held conventions of the change-averse security establishment.[87]

Pursuing an integrated holistic approach that emphasizes the linkages between internal and external security is a central plank of Xi's thinking on national security. His logic is derived from the ideological lens with which he views national security. The downfall of authoritarian and communist regimes around the world since the end of the 1980s through colored revolutions, Arab Springs, and other labels is seen by Xi as being instigated by hostile foreign forces led by the United States and its allies. In a speech to a military audience early in his tenure in July 2013, Xi said that "currently, struggles in the ideological field are extraordinarily fierce. The Western hostile forces are speeding up their 'peaceful evolution' and 'color revolution' in China. . . . What they want to see most is that China also suffers from turmoil and troubles, so they intensify the political strategies of Westernizing and splitting up China overtly and covertly."[88]

This theme of foreign elements behind Chinese internal security challenges has been a constant high priority throughout Xi's reign. In January 2019, Zhao Kezhi (赵克志), public security minister and head of the Central Political-Legal Affairs Commission, told participants at an annual public security conference that they must "stress the prevention and resistance of 'color revolutions' and firmly fight to protect China's political security." Zhao pointed to hostile foreign forces engaging in "all kinds of infiltration and subversive activities."[89]

Xi has highlighted three salient features of this blurring between internal and external security threats, which he has referred to as the Three Prominents (三个更加突出, Sange Gengjia Tuchu).[90] The first prominent trend is that traditional and nontraditional security threats are becoming increasingly intertwined. The second trend is that the transnational nature of security threats has become more prominent. The third trend is the broadening diversity of security threats that are borderless, especially cyber-related threats and financial and high-tech crimes.

An important consequence of this integrated national security perspective is that the geographical remit of Chinese security and intelligence agencies has broadened to allow them to increasingly conduct operations well beyond the country's borders against individuals and organizations.[91] Xi has called for a "global vision in national security work."[92] Targets have included Uighurs who have fled China because of the security clampdown in Xinjiang, exiled dissidents and other prominent critics of the Chinese party-state, Hong Kong booksellers, Falun Gong members, and officials and business executives who have fled from the Xi regime's anti-corruption crackdown. One indicator of the enormous scale and global reach of the Chinese NSS is Operation Skynet, which is the name of China's worldwide anti-corruption drive, that brought back to China more than seven thousand fugitives between 2013 and 2019.[93]

Overcoming the deeply entrenched internal-external security organizational divide is an extremely difficult challenge that is being addressed by a top-down strategy centered on Xi's personal authority and institutionally through the CNSC. As chairman of the CNSC, CMC, and Central Cyberaffairs Commission, Xi is able to override the vertical silos that the different security organizations work within. However, relying on Xi's personal intervention is risky because he

has limited bandwidth available and can only become involved on a highly selective basis.

Consequently, the role that the CNSC can play to mitigate the structural
internal-external security gap is crucial, but few details have been released to
show what concrete steps have been taken. Only the names of the chairman and
two deputy chairmen have been publicly released, and the rest of the leadership
lineup remains unknown. Some observers point to a high-level national security seminar that took place in February 2017 as a window into the makeup of
the CNSC leadership. Xi and the two deputy CNSC chairs, Li Keqiang and Zhang
Dejiang (张德江), attended the seminar, along with twenty other senior civilian
and military leaders.[94] Military representatives included one CMC vice-chair and
the heads of the CMC Joint Staff, Political Work, Joint Logistics, and Equipment
Development Departments. If these military officials are on the CNSC, then the
commission would be a credible interagency mechanism able to effectively coordinate and integrate internal and external security activities.

Defensive or Offensive Orientation—or Both?

China under Xi is seeking to establish itself as a leader on the international stage,
and the development of a more capable and assertive NSS is a critical component in this grand effort. This has meant that the country's national security posture is in transition from being primarily defensively minded to combining
both defensive and offensive elements. As discussed at the beginning of this
chapter, defensive NSSs view the world in benign terms and look to find cooperative solutions to ensuring their security without undermining those of their
neighbors or other related states. They are also focused inwardly on the development of national security capabilities.

From Deng to Hu, China would fall under this defensive rubric, but the same
argument cannot be made in the Xi era. In his international engagement, Xi talks
about pursuing a "new type of international relations with win-win cooperation
at its core," forging a "community of destiny for humanity" emphasizing peace,
shared security, and common prosperity, and taking the "road of peaceful development." But this open hand is enclosed in an iron glove as Xi has also maintained that China "absolutely cannot abandon our legitimate rights and interests,
nor can we sacrifice national core interests" in offering this shared approach to
peace and development.[95]

In contrast to this peaceful rhetoric, China's actual national security posture
is acquiring some of the attributes of offensive NSSs. The most obvious example
is engaging in zero-sum security behavior, most evidently in its enlargement and
fortification of islands in the South China Sea. The building-up and forward

deployment of China's military capabilities is another sign of the shift from a defensive to a more offensive posture, although China has been careful not to employ the actual use of force. But in overall terms, China has not yet become a fully-fledged offensive NSS, at least externally. The situation is different, though, in the domestic domain where a more convincing case can be made that China has become an offensive internal security state.

The National Security State, COVID-19, and US-China Relations

The Xi regime has touted the ramping-up of its national security apparatus as prescient in the face of the acute challenges that China has had to face simultaneously or near-simultaneously: from COVID-19, mass protests in Hong Kong, and rapidly deteriorating US-China relations. Indeed, one of the lessons that Beijing says it has learned is that even more investment should be made in fortifying the resilience, reach, and capabilities of the NSS.

In an assessment of how the Chinese national security system addressed the COVID-19 pandemic, Chen Wenqing (陈文清), CNSC General Office deputy director and State Security minister, proclaimed that China's tough response to controlling the pandemic "fully shows General Secretary Xi Jinping's foresight and vision, and demonstrates the theoretical power and practical character of the holistic national security concept."[96] Not surprisingly, there was no mention of the initial slow response during the first few weeks of the outbreak that highlighted the structural problems of the authoritarian top-down system in which bottom-up reporting is often neglected or is slow to percolate upward. But Chen said that the "People's War" against the virus was a testament to several crucial advantages of the socialist system, which include the ability to concentrate resources and efforts quickly, the highly centralized and coordinated leadership system, and the country's deep mobilizational experience and expertise.

These qualities will be much needed for dealing with the deepening and drawn-out across-the-board struggle with the United States that has intensified significantly with the pandemic. The NSS thrives when threats are severe, direct, and imminent, and the accelerating adversarial competition between the United States and China will be used by the Chinese national security apparatus to strengthen its already commanding position at the heart of the country's power structure. The Xi regime views the challenge posed by the United States as increasingly comprehensive in nature, which means externally on the global stage and also within and around China's borders.

3

THE PROMISE AND PERIL OF MILITARY-CIVIL FUSION

At the heart of the Chinese techno-security state is the grandiose idea of a strategic economy that seamlessly serves civilian and military needs that Xi Jinping has vowed to create. In a keynote address at the 19th Party Congress in 2017, Xi called for the building of an "integrated national strategic system" (一体化的国家战略体系, *yitihuade guojia zhanlue tixi*). This is a daunting challenge because of the long-standing and deeply entrenched separation between the civilian and defense sectors.

Past efforts at civil-military integration (CMI; 军民一体化, *junmin yitihua*)—or what the Xi administration refers to as military-civil fusion (MCF: *Junmin Ronghe*, 军民融合)—have produced an underwhelming track record. Deng Xiaoping diverted large segments of the defense industrial base from military to civilian production to support broader economic development in the 1980s. Jiang Zemin and Hu Jintao pursued an incremental ad hoc approach between the 1990s and 2000s of reducing barriers between the civilian and defense economies to promote an expanding overlap of economic activities, such as allowing civilian firms to compete for military orders and permitting defense firms to tap into the capital markets.

On taking office, Xi inherited a meandering MCF development effort that was strategically incoherent, lacked high-level leadership support, and suffered from a flawed misalignment of interests and interactions between the civilian and defense sectors. To address these deficiencies, Xi has sought a far more ambitious, expansive, and top-down approach to MCF. This chapter explores how the Xi regime is meeting this challenge of forging a tightly integrated military-civil strategic economy. What is the development vision and implementation strategy for MCF? How directly involved is Xi in this effort? How does MCF connect with the civilian and military systems, especially in the key areas of national development strategy and weapons and equipment research, development, and production? Who is paying for this expensive undertaking? What is the best way to evaluate progress in MCF implementation?

Defining Military-Civil Fusion

From its humble origins in the late 2000s as a mid-tier policy tool in the arcane world of Chinese defense industrial affairs, MCF was thrust into the spotlight of Chinese domestic and international attention from the mid-2010s. For China, MCF has become a prized strategy that Xi has personally taken ownership of that will unleash powerful forces to bring together the siloed military and civilian sectors to form an integrated and energized techno-security state. On the other hand, the United States and its allies view MCF as a sinister means to, as then US secretary of state Mike Pompeo said, "ensure that the People's Liberation Army has military dominance."[1] MCF has joined Made in China 2025 and the Thousand Talents Program as a source of deep suspicion by Western governments and become a major target for countermeasures from sanctions to calls to pursue similar dual-use innovation strategies.

Given the controversy surrounding MCF, having a clear and accurate understanding and definition of what it is—both as a guiding strategy and policy construct—is an essential starting point for informed analysis and policy. To provide necessary context and background, there first will be a short excursion into the history and evolution of the broader notion of CMI and how this specifically relates to MCF.

China's efforts to bring together the military and civilian economic and technological systems have their roots extending back to the early years of the People's Republic and have witnessed five stages of evolution that correspond with the different regimes that have been in power.[2] This has spawned a collection of sometimes ill-defined terms to describe efforts to promote CMI, which is the universally accepted technical term that covers this issue. A starting point to comprehending this confusing kaleidoscope of CMI labels is to sort them into two general categories: military-civil combination (MCC; 军民结合, *junmin jiehe*) and MCF. Chinese analysts point out that fusion is significantly different from the combining of military and civilian activities. Liu Zhiwei (刘志伟), an

MCF analyst at the Academy of Military Sciences, argues that "combining is relatively simple and extensive, while fusion is the penetration of elements and their close interaction at the micro-level."[3]

MCC refers to the complementarity of civilian and military economic and technological activities that, when brought together, may lead to incremental changes. There are four types of combination-style activities in this category. At the lowest level is defense conversion (军转民, *junzhuanmin*), which is the process of moving from military to civilian output. This is followed by spin-off (技术成果转移, *jishu chengguo zhuanyi*), which refers to military research and technologies being turned into civilian applications. The reverse process of civilian to military application is spin-on. At the third level is dual-use activity (军民两用, *junmin liangyong*), which includes science and technology (S&T), industrial research, and other programs that serve both defense and civilian outcomes. At the top of this category is locating military potential in civilian capabilities (寓军于民, *yujun yumin*) or the application of technology in the civilian sector for military purposes.

The second category, MCF, covers fusion-related activities, which involves the synthesis of military and civilian elements to generate new hybrid outcomes. Xi has described China as going through three stages of MCF (see figure 3.1). First is the preliminary (初步, *chubu*) stage, which Xi said the country emerged from in the mid-2010s and entered into a transitional (过渡, *guodu*) stage. The goal was to progress into a final deep (深, *shen*) stage by the beginning of the 2020s. Xi did not elaborate as to what he meant by these stages but did point out that the preliminary stage had "problems such as the lack of ideology and concepts, lack of top-level coordination and management systems, lagging policies, regulations and operating mechanisms, and insufficient implementation."[4]

Xi's explanation offers useful indicators as to how his administration defines these three stages and what steps need to be taken to advance along the fusion spectrum. Some of the key factors include organizational structure, governance, strategy and planning, implementation, and political oversight and intervention. Other crucial factors include market-related considerations such as access to financial capital, private sector participation, supply-demand dynamics, the role of the S&T system, and the participation of local administrations and actors. A more thorough examination of the critical factors in understanding MCF will be undertaken later in the chapter to evaluate its performance.

Some MCF analysts have sought to more precisely define the degree of China's MCF development (军民融合程度, *junmin ronghe chengdu*) by offering quantitative estimates. In its 2014 annual MCF development report, the Defense Economics Research Center at the National Defense University (NDU) judged

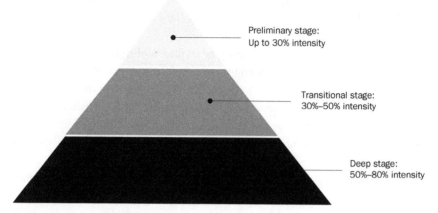

Preliminary stage:
Up to 30% intensity

Transitional stage:
30%–50% intensity

Deep stage:
50%–80% intensity

FIGURE 3.1. The stages of China's military-civil fusion development by intensity rate

China's MCF level at around 30 percent, which it said marked the country's advancement from an initial to a deep stage of integration. However, the fatal flaw in this assessment is that there was no explanation provided as to how this figure was calculated and what criteria were used. Another NDU scholar, Jiang Luming (姜鲁鸣), put the MCF level in the weapons and equipment research and production sector at between 36 percent and 40 percent in a 2017 study, but his justification was also flimsy.[5] Jiang's main evidence was that the number of People's Liberation Army (PLA) cadres trained in the national education system in recent years was around 30 percent. He also pointed to a lack of MCF advancement in the socialization of the PLA's logistics system compared to the United States, which enjoyed MCF rates of 80 percent in logistics and technical support. Jiang said that in overall terms, the level of MCF in key domains in China had not yet reached half of the rate of developed countries.

Although not explicitly spelled out, the long-term Chinese goal in the deep stage of MCF development appears to be to attain the 70–80 percent level achieved by the United States. Even though this target will likely take many years to accomplish, there are small pockets of the Chinese defense industrial system that have reportedly already reached this goal. An executive from the 701st Institute of the China Shipbuilding Industry Corporation, the systems integrator responsible for the construction of China's first indigenous aircraft carrier, said that most of the five hundred enterprises supplying major equipment for the warship were civilian contractors and the MCF rate was close to 80 percent.[6]

In a study on measuring the rate of MCF development, Yin Jun (尹君) and Tan Qingmei (谭清美) from the Nanjing University of Aeronautics and Astronautics criticize these methodologically deficient efforts at gauging MCF levels by pointing out that they focus on ad hoc individual attributes rather than providing a systematic examination of a broad array of factors that would give a more comprehensive and balanced picture.[7] Yin and Tan instead offer a business-oriented analytical framework to address this gap by measuring both the breadth and depth of the MCF implementation process. They argue that horizontal integration is primarily about the acquisition or merger of enterprises engaged in manufacturing operations, and so the key MCF-related factors involve product, standardization, and regulatory issues. Vertical integration refers to how military and civilian companies are able to find ways to cooperate along the acquisition process from research and development (R&D) to testing, production, and after-sales service support.

Viewing MCF from an economics-centric lens is especially relevant because the use of economic resources is a central goal of MCF. Jiang Luming offers an economic-driven definition by pointing out that MCF "aims to provide a common economic and technology base for the development of economic and defense capabilities through the overall planning of resources from the military and civilian sectors in accordance with the inherent requirements of achieving coordinated, balanced, and compatible development, so that limited social resources can be transformed into military combat effectiveness and productive forces. In other words, one type of input could result in multiple types of output. The core idea of MCF is to incorporate the strengthening of national defense and the armed forces into the system of social and economic development to realize their mutual promotion, interoperability, and shared support."[8] The key areas of emphasis in Jiang's definition are access to and the sharing of resources and finding economic compatibility between the civilian and military realms.

This discussion makes clear that MCF is a constantly evolving and sprawling concept with different technical, policy, and political layers. This complexity makes defining MCF a complex challenge. The definition offered here seeks to capture its essence rather than be exhaustive. Two dimensions are of central importance: MCF as a strategy and as a process. The definition of MCF employed here is as a national-level strategy that supports the goal of the complete and seamless integration of strategic and complementary civilian and military economic and technological domains. MCF is a broad bidirectional process involving the civil-military sharing of information, resources, and capabilities and is anchored around the opening of the defense science, technology, and industrial system to civilian, and especially market sector, participation.

The Origins and Making of Military-Civil Fusion

Under Hu's tenure in the first decade of the twenty-first century, the Chinese state's approach to CMI started to become more systematic and planned. This was when fusion replaced combination as the preferred approach to CMI. At the 17th Party Congress in 2007 that marked the beginning of his second and last term, Hu said it was time to "embark on a path of military-civil fusion with Chinese characteristics" (走出一条中国特色军民融合式发展路子).[9] This was the first time that MCF was used to describe CMI.

After Hu came out with the MCF label, new thinking and policies began to flow. The most important initiative was the "Opinions of the State Council and Central Military Commission on Establishing and Improving the *Junmin Jiehe, Yujun Yumin* Weapons and Equipment Research and Production System" (*Guowuyuan Zhongyang Junwei Guanyu Jianli He Wanshan Junmin Jiehe Yujun Yumin Wuqi Zhuangbei Keyan Shengchan Tixi De Ruogan Yijian,* 国务院, 中央军委关于建立和完善军民结合, 寓军于民武器装备科研生产体系的若干意见) or Document No. 37 as it was more widely known. This policy document sought to impose a more disciplined, coordinated, systematic, and long-term approach to MCF that was directly aimed at opening up the closed defense industry. As Document No. 37 was only issued halfway through Hu's final term in 2010, his administration had little time for implementation. One of the few policy recommendations that was successfully executed was the establishment of the Inter-Ministerial Coordination Group on *Junmin Jiehe, Yujun Yumin* Weapons and Equipment Research and Production System Construction (军民结合 寓军于民武器装备科研生产体系建设部际协调小组, *Junmin Jiehe Yu Yujun Yumin Wuqi Zhuangbei Keyan Shengchan Tixi Jianshe Buji Xietiao Xiaozu*). Overall, although Hu's approach to CMI was low key, belated, narrow, and focused on process, this approach was very helpful to Xi when he assumed power.

After Xi took office, he initially followed Hu's MCF road map. In the 18th Party Congress address that laid out the incoming agenda of the Xi regime, the brief passage on MCF simply affirmed that it would be pursued along the same lines as had already been taking place, although with more emphasis on "strengthening development strategy planning, system building, and laws and regulations," all of which was already advocated for in Document No. 37.[10]

It is unsurprising that Xi did not immediately tackle MCF issues from the start of his rule as he had his hands full with an overflowing policy and political agenda. There were occasional references by Xi and other officials that new ideas and approaches to MCF were being examined, but no substance was forthcoming. For example, the first time that Xi publicly talked about MCF was at a plenary meeting with PLA delegates at the National People's Congress (NPC) in March 2013 when he stressed the necessity to "coordinate economic construction and national defense construction, strive to achieve the integration of a rich country and a strong army," and "adhere to a state-led, demand-driven" approach.[11] These two themes would become major anchors of the MCF development strategy when it was eventually rolled out.

The first substantive policy reference to MCF came at the Third Plenum of the 18th Party Congress in November 2013, which offered a tantalizing hint of what might be contained in the prospective MCF development strategy. The plenum communiqué referred to the establishment of "mechanisms for unified leadership, coordination between the military and localities, and linking the needs and demands and resource sharing at the national level so as to promote the joint development of the army and the people." It also pointed to the requirement of "guiding superior private enterprises to enter into areas of military research, development, production, and maintenance."[12]

From a policy perspective, the making of a high-level MCF development strategy could not effectively take place until the Xi regime had drawn up its overarching strategies for economic development, technology and innovation development, national security, and military modernization. These are first-tier national-level strategies, whereas CMI has historically been a lower-tier sectoral strategy. The MCF community had to wait patiently as the Innovation-Driven Development Strategy (IDDS), the national security strategy, and the military strengthening guidance were being drafted in the opening years of Xi's rule.

Xi injected much-needed momentum to the glacial MCF formulation process in March 2015 by publicly announcing at the NPC that he was elevating MCF to the status of a national strategy. Xi called this step a "major achievement in our efforts of exploring the law of effecting well-balanced development of economic construction and national defense building over a long period and is a major policy decision based on the overall requirements of the national security and development strategies."[13] Although this elevation puts MCF on par with economic development, innovation, national security, and military strengthening strategies, the reality was that MCF both as a strategy and also in institutional terms lacked the political or bureaucratic standing, clout, and even critical mass to take advantage of the opening presented by Xi. It would take considerable time and effort for MCF to become a credible national strategy and for the fledgling MCF community to become a recognized player in the domestic bureaucratic process.

Shortly after the IDDS was issued in May 2016, the first major MCF policy document was jointly released by the Communist Party Central Committee, State Council, and Central Military Commission (CMC) in July 2016. The "Opinions on the Integrated Development of Economic Construction and Defense

Construction" (关于经济建设和国防建设融合发展的意见, *Guanyu Jingji Jianshe He Guofang Jianshe Ronghe Fazhande Yijian*) spelled out an aspirational security-driven, and seamless approach to MCF and its role in China's development as a techno-security state.[14] The rationale for a fundamentally different way of pursuing MCF compared with prior administrations was that the relationship between economic development and national security had significantly altered. The Xi regime now viewed military/security priorities as equally, if not more, important as economic priorities. The opinions point this out by emphasizing the necessity of pursuing balanced, coordinated, and compatible economic and military development.

In bringing the civilian and defense sectors closer together, a key objective of the new MCF approach is to establish what the opinions call "a deep development pattern" that encompasses "all factors, multiple domains, and is highly efficient" (全要素, 多领域, 高效益, *quanyaosu, duolingyu, gaoxiaoyi*).[15] The terminology employed here seeks to incorporate economic and military concepts.[16] Jiang Luming defines "all factors" as referring to the breadth of integration, "multiple domains" to the scope of integration, and "high efficiency" as the effects of integration.[17]

"All factors" applied in the economic context has connotations with total factor productivity, which is an economic concept used to determine what factors account for the portion of output not explained by the amount of inputs used in production, of which technology and innovation is often cited as the most important factor.[18] Military effectiveness is the counterpart military concept to total factor productivity, and is defined as the process by which armed forces convert resources into fighting power.[19] Integrated together, "all factors" refers to the application of tangible and intangible civilian productivity and military effectiveness factors that can be fused to work together. This includes technology, human talent, infrastructure, capital, information, norms, governance regimes, and standards.

"Multiple domains" refers to the expanding array of domains that MCF occurs within. The opinions point to six systems, which is two more than originally identified by the Hu administration.[20] They can be sorted into two groupings. The first category includes systems that are engaged in conducting advanced research, development, and production of advanced strategic, defense, and dual-use high-technology capabilities:

- Advanced Defense Science, Technology, and Industrial System: This is the largest and most powerful of the six systems but is also the most resistant in accepting MCF reform because of its long-standing closed monopoly structure dominated by a small number of state-owned corporations.[21] The advanced label would suggest that this system is selective and includes only high-end entities and domains engaged in strategic, core, and emerging cutting-edge defense research and production and excludes those focused on conventional activities. The opinions also reference participation in the development of strategic emerging industries. Xi has particularly emphasized the development of the space, maritime, and cyberspace sectors because these domains have become the PLA's top areas of military concern and opportunity.

- Civil-Military Science, Technology, and Innovation Collaboration System: This system consists of civilian and military universities, research institutes, and laboratories engaged in basic and applied R&D that have or may have dual-use purposes.[22] There have been growing efforts to integrate these separate systems through the establishment of key entities such as national laboratories as well as information sharing platforms, which is being accelerated under the MCF development strategy. Emerging technology areas highlighted for special attention include biology, new energy, and artificial intelligence.

- Human Talent Cultivation System: This system includes leading PLA, civilian, and defense science, technology, and engineering higher educational institutions that feed top talent into the military-civil domain as well as the proliferating number of civilian and military human talent recruitment programs.[23] Many of the 135 universities that are part of the World First-Class University and First-Class Academic Discipline Construction Initiative (世界一流大学和一流学科建设, *Shijie Yiliu Daxue He Yiliu Xueke Jianshe*), otherwise known as the Double First-Class University Initiative (双一流, *Shuang Yiliu*), are likely to be prime members of this system. They include five institutions affiliated with the PLA or defense industrial system: Beijing Aeronautics and Astronautics University, Beijing Institute of Technology, Harbin Institute of Technology, National University of Defense Technology (NUDT), and Northwestern Polytechnical University.

The second category covers systems that provide basic and essential support for military-civilian activities:

- Fundamental Infrastructure and Key Resources System: This system is comparable to what the US government defines as the critical infrastructure and key resources system that covers sixteen sectors of the US economy ranging from transportation and critical manufacturing to financial services, communications, information technology, defense, industrial, and energy sectors.[24] In addition, Chinese analysts include the governance regime within this system, especially related to standards setting. The Chinese fundamental infrastructure and basic resources system does not include the defense industrial base, which falls under a separate category.

- Military Socialized Support and Logistics System: The logistics apparatus has been a pioneer within the PLA in leveraging the civilian economy for its needs since the 1990s.[25] This outsourcing of goods and services has been concentrated in noncombat support areas such as catering support, commercial services, barracks support, transportation, medical services, clothing supply, petroleum and oil supplies, and the employment of civilian workers.[26] Guidelines on promoting MCF in military logistics were issued in 2017.[27]

- National Defense Mobilization and Emergency Management System: The defense mobilization system is firmly anchored in the intersection between the defense and civilian spheres, so it has had to constantly adapt to the ebb and flow of CMI initiatives.[28] This has meant the defense mobilization system has undergone regular revamps since the early 1990s, of which the most recent was the elevation of the organizational importance of mobilization matters in the far-reaching overhaul of the PLA high command in 2016 with the creation of the CMC National Defense Mobilization Department.[29] The increased attention and clout given to mobilization by the PLA leadership and civilian authorities is being translated into the incorporation of military requirements into the development and running of the civilian economy, especially in critical infrastructure construction, urban air defense, and the management of strategic reserves.[30]

An important goal for MCF is the maximization of military, economic, and social benefits, which is why "high efficiency" is included here as a key concept. Bringing together military and civilian capabilities is intended to lead to economies of scale and avoidance of waste and duplication caused by segregation and fragmentation. It will also allow more optimal allocation of capabilities for both the civilian and military sectors. The overall end result is the establishment of a strategic system that is vertically and horizontally fused across multiple domains and is highly efficient and effective. The opinions anticipated that the foundations of this system would be largely completed by 2020, which would then allow the MCF process to move from a transitional phase to deep integration. These goals appear to have been largely met, although an official clampdown on any mention of MCF beginning in 2020 means that there is no official acknowledgment that the MCF development process has now shifted to the deep stage of integration.

The opinions also put forward a number of key principles and observations. First was the dominant importance of the Communist Party in guiding MCF. "Party leadership is the greatest advantage of the Socialist system," the opinions emphasized. Second, concerning the relationship between the state and the market, the state would play the leading role while market demand would be the key driver. Third, there should be much better utilization of the market economy, especially tapping private firms and financial markets as sources for investment, innovation, and goods. This should be a "state-led, demand-driven, and market-oriented work system" (国家主导, 需求牵引, 市场运作相统一的工作运 行 体系, *guojia zhudao, xuqiu qianyin, shichang yunzuo xiang tongyi de gongzuo yunxing tixi*).

Although the opinions provided the overarching guidance, goals, and strategic design for China's MCF development, it did not deal with policy implementation. This was covered in the "Economic Construction and Defense Construction Integrated Development 13th Five-Year Plan" (经济建设和国防建设融合发展"十三五" 规划, *Jingji Jianshe He Guofang Jianshe Ronghe Fazhan "Shisan Wu" Guihua*) spanning from 2017 to 2020 that was issued by the CMC and State Council at the end of 2016.[31] The plan has not been officially released, but media reports and speeches of senior officials have offered a few tidbits of information.

The plan had a lengthy list of 101 key tasks of which several of the most important have been disclosed.[32] The first and most important task has been to pursue twenty-one major MCF pilot demonstration projects that would provide insights and lessons on how to effectively carry out MCF. These demonstration projects have in particular focused on industrial and information technology domains such as electric batteries, cybersecurity, strategic early warning, nuclear security, integrated industrial telecommunications simulation platforms, and MCF integrated service platforms. A second high-priority task has been to support the Science and Technology Innovation (STI) 2030 Plan, of which around half of the projects are deemed to be defense related, according to former Ministry of Industry and Information Technology (MIIT) minister Li Yizhong (李毅中). Megaprojects that Li highlighted included aircraft and marine engines, deepsea stations, and the earth-space integrated information network. A third key task focused on deepening MCF between the defense industry and manufacturing, especially in offshore engineering equipment, high-end semiconductor chips, unmanned equipment, robots, large-scale integrated circuits, large-sized passenger aircraft, and specialized new materials.

The opinions and the special 13th Five-Year Military-Civil Fusion Science and Technology Plan (13th MCF S&T Plan: 十三五科技军民融合发展专项规划, *Shisan Wu Keji Junmin Ronghe Fazhan Zhuanxiang Guihua*) together provided a detailed programmatic road map to inject new momentum into the MCF system so that it could have a reasonable chance of accomplishing the goal of completing its transitionary phase by 2020. However, as these MCF plans were only rolled out in the second year of the 13th Five-Year Plan, time was short for their implementation. What undoubtedly helped bolster this effort was the establishment of the Central Military-Civil Fusion Development Commission (CMCFDC; 中央军民融合发展委员会, *Zhongyang Junmin Ronghe Fazhan Weiyuanhui*) in January 2017.

With the MCF reform and implementation drive kicking off in 2017, the MCF development strategy was approved in March 2018 by the CMCFDC. Officially known as the Military-Civil Fusion Development Strategy Outline (军民融合发展战略纲要, *Junmin Ronghe Fazhan Zhanlue Gangyao*), the development strategy was not publicly released and there has been scant reporting of its contents. However, its general points are detailed in an article by Jin Zhuanglong (金壮龙), the executive deputy director of the CMCFDC, in *Qiushi*, an authoritative Communist Party mouthpiece, in July 2018.[33] Jin makes clear that the MCF development strategy is a product of Xi's thinking that "systematically answers the fundamental, directional, and overall issues as to why, what, and how to achieve military-civil fusion." The development strategy "clarifies the major significance, strategic status, overall goals, requirements of the new era, and key domains and methods of conducting MCF development."

The MCF development strategy represents a crucial link in Xi's efforts to coordinate between national security, economic development, and technological innovation. The strategy is the last piece in the jigsaw puzzle of national strategies that Xi has drawn up from the IDDS to the Holistic National Security Concept (HNSC). Xi has made clear that security and development are of equal importance as core national interests, so MCF development should reflect this balanced relationship. The primary challenge is to have these national strategies coordinate and converge with each other rather than operate on parallel but separate tracks as has traditionally been the case.

Hand in hand with the promotion of MCF as a national strategy is its political elevation. With Xi in personal charge of MCF affairs, the MCF community has access to and the attention of the highest levels of leadership, which it has not previously enjoyed. Moreover, MCF has been enshrined in the party constitution as a national priority, which means that it will likely retain this status for the duration of Xi's rule.

The overall goal of the MCF development strategy is to build an integrated national strategic system with corresponding capabilities, Jin points out. This reiterates what Xi said in his 19th Party Congress speech, but there is no detailed explanation of what such a strategic system is meant to be. Is it the sum total of the systems detailed in the opinions and MCF plans, or is it referring to an even more ambitious and expansive techno-security system at the very heart of the Chinese state over the long term?

Jin also points to the geostrategic and military context that the MCF development strategy was drawn up under. It was shaped in response to "dealing with complex security threats and to develop major measures to win national strategic advantage." The MCF development strategy should take into account Xi's ideology of military strengthening, the Military Strategic Guidelines, and the HNSC.

In conclusion, the formulation of the MCF development strategy took more than five years and steadily grew bolder and bigger over time. This can be largely attributed to Xi's increasing interest and involvement in MCF-related matters. At the beginning of his tenure, Xi was keenly interested and engaged in military modernization, national security, and science, technology, and innovation. As he intensively worked on these domains, he came to appreciate the role that MCF would play as a crucial link between these topics. This learning experience led Xi to become more actively involved in MCF policymaking and strategic thinking from the mid-2010s onward, which can be measured in the additional policy attention paid to MCF issues and in Xi's participation in MCF-related activities. From being viewed as an awkward, difficult orphan at the outset of Xi's reign, MCF is now warmly embraced and seen as vital in bringing together the civilian and military sectors to form a seamless integrated national system of systems. Although the aspirational vision is clear, can the Xi regime actually carry out this daunting task?

Obstacles to Military-Civil Fusion

Even though Xi and his administration command enormous power and authority, realizing the vision of a truly integrated techno-security state will be a titanic and prolonged struggle with the eventual outcome far from clear. The obstacles to the remaking of the economic and national security contours of the Chinese state come from some of its most privileged, protected, and politically powerful constituencies whose opposition will be fierce and relentless even as they pay lip service to following top-level orders.

The obstacles that stand in the way of pursuing MCF are fundamental, wide ranging, and numerous. In a speech to PLA delegates at the NPC in March 2015, Xi pointed out that "there is still a lack of ideas and concepts to keep up with the development of military-civil fusion, a lack of top-level coordination and management systems, a lag in policies, laws and regulations, a lack of operational mechanisms, and insufficient implementation."[34] Although this list is far from comprehensive, it highlights a potent cocktail of structural, normative, institutional, and operational barriers. Additional major obstacles worth highlighting include the absence of an MCF political and bureaucratic support base and the powerful entrenched defense-industrial corporatist interests that maintain a tight monopolistic grip on the defense and dual-use sectors.

Chinese MCF analysts such as Jiang Luming argue that the most salient barrier to MCF development has to do with the interrelationship between systemic arrangements (体制, *tizhi*) and mechanisms (机制, *jizhi*).[35] *Tizhi* can be understood narrowly as referring to a system of organizations but in combination with *jizhi* should be more broadly interpreted to cover organizational systems and social institutions such as rules, regulations, norms, and customs. This analytical perspective equates academically with the New Institutional Economics school of analysis. Jiang points to bureaucratic fragmentation as one of the root causes that has stymied the nurturing of formal institutional arrangements such as regulations, laws, and routines dealing with MCF as well as informal institutions like shared norms, customs, and conventions. A 2016 assessment by the NDU Defense Economics Research Center, a leading MCF research outfit, said that although some progress had been made in developing a body of MCF laws and regulations, they were "mostly departmental regulations or normative documents. The long-awaited comprehensive laws regulating military-civil fusion have not yet been introduced."[36] This may help to explain why one of the first priorities for the CMCFDC after its establishment was to begin passing regulations, policies, and official guidances.

Formulation of MCF-related legislation, however, has proven to be problematic and time consuming. According to Zhang Jiantian (张建田), a former official in the CMC Legal Affairs Bureau, a serious lack of qualified and experienced legal experts on MCF issues has meant that many of the laws that have been issued are "not sufficiently comprehensive or specialized." Moreover, some of the laws promulgated in the 1980s and 1990s are now obsolete, and the drafting of new legislation such as a comprehensive MCF law has been excessively slow and "can take decades to come into effect."[37] Without an adequate and transparent legal framework, civilian firms have been hesitant to engage in MCF-related activities because the military establishment is largely outside of the civilian legal system.

More broadly, there is an absence of legal norms that would be considered essential to the development of a robust and independent legal order. This includes notions of judicial independence, political intervention, due process, and questions of fairness and favoritism, such as between state and private actors. There had been efforts in the 1980s and 1990s to implement broad legal reforms to establish a more independent and rigorous legal system that selectively embraced

Western legal norms, but this came to an end in the early twenty-first century and there was, as Carl Minzner has argued, a turn against law and the reemphasis of politics in command, a trend that has only become more pervasive under Xi.[38] Besides legal norms, other normative concepts that would be important pillars in shaping the social construction and routine interactions of the MCF system but have struggled to be accepted include openness and fair competition.

The tightly closed nature of the defense industrial base is another huge impediment to MCF implementation. State-owned defense industrial conglomerates have enjoyed monopolies in their assigned sectors ever since they were created as state ministries in the early years of the People's Republic. Consequently, they have deeply vested interests in preserving this status quo. These corporations have also suffered harsh experiences from past CMI initiatives, such as when they were forced to switch from military to civilian production from the late 1970s as part of the country's pivot from militarization to economic development. This conversion process between the 1980s and 1990s led to widespread layoffs and a deep and brutal culling of many enterprises. It is not surprising that these defense conglomerates view Xi's MCF development strategy warily, since the goals are to open up much of the defense industrial sector to private sector competition and to revamp the ownership structure of these behemoths from a wholly state-owned model to a mixed-ownership arrangement.

A chronically weak implementation track record is yet another threat to the prospects for the establishment of a vibrant MCF ecosystem. The assessment by the National Defense Economics Research Center was that even though government agencies were keen to support MCF initiatives, the functional offices and departments that were assigned the responsibility for implementation displayed a lack of enthusiasm. This is known as the "two hot ends but a cold middle" (两头热, 中间冷, liangtou re, zhongjian leng) phenomenon. Supervising entities lack credible disciplinary measures to tackle this implementation deficit. There is no target responsibility system for units and progress on MCF implementation is not included in the all-important personnel performance evaluation reports that determine promotion for officials.[39]

A key structural reason for this lack of enthusiasm in promoting MCF interests is the absence of the development of a dedicated MCF professional workforce and institutional interests. Tightly sandwiched between the defense and civilian domains, MCF has long been an ignored orphan without access to high-level political and bureaucratic attention and support until the Xi era. The MCF community has historically been small in size, struggled to gain stature and influence, and lacked a coherent institutional identity. The bulk of personnel assigned to MCF-related responsibilities are seconded from the civilian and military systems and rotated in and out of assignments. Until Xi's reforms led to the establishment of a high-level MCF leadership apparatus, the most senior dedicated MCF officials were mid-level bureaucrats and military officers in charge of departments and offices scattered across the state and military bureaucracies. In the absence of a sizable dedicated and experienced cadre of MCF professionals that enjoy high-level support, China's efforts to develop its MCF capabilities will always struggle to meet its objectives.

Evaluating the Implementation of the Military-Civil Fusion Development Strategy

The opaqueness of the MCF process will mean that much of the intensifying efforts to establish an independent and fully fledged Chinese MCF ecosystem will occur in the shadows, making timely and accurate evaluation a daunting challenge. Compounding this difficulty is the absence of up-to-date methodological thinking on CMI that could help to mitigate information gaps with more creative, sophisticated, and targeted research insights learned from studying other countries. The scholarly and policy examination of CMI matters have been mostly neglected in the past couple of decades and the overwhelming bulk of research conducted on CMI-related issues date to the end of the Cold War in the 1990s when discussion revolved around how to restructure the United States and global defense industrial bases for peacetime. Although policy interest in CMI in the United States has begun to gradually pick up again since the mid-2010s with the focus on nurturing the national security innovation base to support great power competition with China and Russia, little new research has so far been generated.[40]

Casting a wider net to other fields of study, there is research involving issues that are comparable and relevant to understanding MCF. One such topic is the implementation of jointness in the armed forces. Jointness refers to the integration of the capabilities, doctrines, manpower, and operations of single service arms into a joint force of two or more services. Jointness has plenty in common with MCF as they both seek to bring together fiercely independent institutions to operate collaboratively in a tightly integrated manner. The United States and other Western armed forces such as Australia, Canada, and the United Kingdom have been engaged in building joint capabilities since the second half of the twentieth century with varying degrees of success. Although the theoretical research on how to evaluate jointness is limited, some useful insights have emerged. A 2018 Australian defense study sought to develop a theoretical model of joint military activities and identified the need for four constituent elements: operational requirements and tasks, establishment of new organizational joint structures, a dedicated educational apparatus, and the crafting of joint doctrines.[41]

Another study in the early 2000s that reviewed progress in implementing jointness in the US military since the passing of the 1986 Goldwater-Nichols Act found that although there was success in the development of war-fighting concepts and in the planning and execution of joint warfare, there was little jointness in the creation of a joint force or in the development of capabilities to support joint war-fighting needs.[42] This was because there was an absence of a joint warfare profession—that is, a dedicated body of personnel working their entire careers in the joint space. These insights show that successfully implementing jointness or fusion is far more than the top-down implementation of strategies and plans but requires deep institutionalization, nurturing new norms, and forging a dedicated profession.

The broader study of the development of China's defense innovation system also offers pertinent insights into determining the key factors and dynamics involved in evaluating the success of MCF implementation. These include the crucial role played by major external threats and opportunities, governance factors such as legal and regulatory issues, and the importance of high-level leadership intervention and support.[43]

The voluminous studies of MCF by Chinese analysts and scholars also offer some nuggets of insights. However, the bulk of this published output has simply been to repeat and justify Xi's thinking with little critical analysis. This is because MCF development strategy has become ideological orthodoxy, as demonstrated by its incorporation in the party constitution in 2017.

From the insights gleaned from these various areas of study, eight key criteria can be identified as being especially useful in evaluating China's MCF implementation efforts:

- Establishing an independent but coordinated organizational ecosystem: The creation of a new MCF organizational structure and ecosystem that is truly independent and coequal to its civilian and military peers, but at the same time maintains close coordination and deep ties with these other systems, is an essential prerequisite to successful MCF implementation. This includes a leadership apparatus that has high-level representation and access to the top channels of power and policymaking authority.
- Building a comprehensive and robust institutional system: Hand in hand with the creation of the organizational ecosystem is the forging of a governance regime consisting of norms, laws, regulations, and routines that contribute to the cultivation of a well-defined institutional culture, practices, and professional identity. This includes the development of a

regulatory regime with a comprehensive set of regulations, laws, and standards. Key norms include risk taking, adherence to rules, intellectual property protection, openness, and competitiveness.

- Proactive top-level leadership engagement and intervention: Active and sustained engagement and intervention from party, state, and military leadership at the highest levels combined with strong and competent management at the operational level is especially important in the early stages of MCF implementation. This provides political protection and much-needed support to overcome entrenched bureaucratic interests.
- Constructing an integrated innovation and acquisition system: One of the biggest challenges in MCF implementation is to merge complementary parts of the civilian and defense science, technology, and industrial systems so that they will be able to operate interactively. This will require fundamental and often painful systemic reforms of the acquisition system, the R&D system, the corporate ownership system, and other related systems.
- Creating a dedicated and permanent MCF personnel workforce and institutional identity: The cultivation and training of new generations of personnel who will spend the bulk of their careers working on MCF issues will be important to ensuring that MCF implementation is deep and permanent. The lack of a dedicated MCF professional track means that personnel who are assigned to work on MCF issues are transitionary in nature and expertise and institutional memory is often lost once they are rotated elsewhere.
- Implementing local-level MCF demonstration technology zone projects: As China pursues MCF with limited knowledge, expertise, and experience, carrying out trial-and-error pilot and demonstration experiments will be an important approach to identifying the most suitable and effective paths forward. The application of MCF innovation demonstration zones at local levels and of major MCF technology and engineering projects will be useful real-time indicators in measuring the progress of MCF implementation.
- Facilitating access to resources and equitable resource sharing: The lifeblood of the new MCF system will be access to and the management and sharing of resources, which include financial, economic, human, technological, informational, raw material, and numerous other material elements. Investment resources are the most important, especially the cultivation of new funding channels from the financial markets as access to state resources are finite and fiercely contested.

- International reach and impact of MCF: The fledging MCF system is facing profound external security threats and technological challenges that could act as powerful catalytic impetuses in promoting its development. The threat comes from deepening geostrategic and geoeconomic competition with the United States and its allies that is leading to diminishing access to advanced Western technologies and markets. The challenge is the intensifying global revolution in commercial and military technologies creating breakthrough opportunities in a diverse array of domains that especially encourage dual-use applications.

A detailed examination of these eight factors will now be undertaken. In doing so, a major focus will be on three of the six systems at the center of the MCF development strategy: the advanced defense science, technology, and industrial system; the military-civil science, technology, and innovation collaboration system; and the human talent cultivation system.

Establishing an Independent and Coordinated Organizational Ecosystem

The establishment of a strong, independent, and deeply rooted MCF leadership and management system has been one of the foremost priorities since implementation of the MCF development strategy began (see figure 3.2). The prior absence of a coherent and effective organizational structure at the top of the Chinese system had been a crippling barrier to the promotion of CMI. The occasional ad hoc interventions by top leaders prior to Xi into CMI matters were largely ineffectual.

The forging of the MCF leadership and management system began with the creation of the CMCFDC, which is headed by Xi and has a roster of twenty-six high-level leaders in charge of many of the country's most powerful party, state, and military entities. They include the Politburo Standing Committee and three party departments and commissions, the State Council and ten government commissions and ministries, and the CMC and three of its executive agencies. A key organizational goal was to put the CMCFDC at or near the same level as the CMC and State Council, which would be essential for balanced military-civilian coordination. The CMCFDC reports directly to the Politburo Standing Committee.

In its first two years of existence between 2017 and 2018, the CMCFDC met twice a year in plenary session. These meetings were extremely busy and productive with an extensive number of major policies and regulations passed, according to media accounts. In its first meeting in June 2017, the CMCFDC was

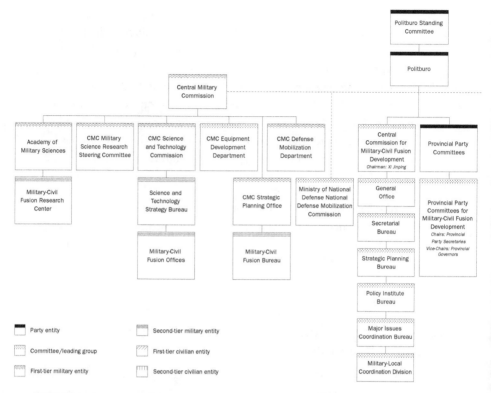

FIGURE 3.2.   Organization chart of the Chinese military-civil fusion ecosystem

primarily engaged in finalizing internal work arrangements and establishing a national network of provincial leadership and management organs. In its second meeting in September 2017, the CMCFDC approved a long list of measures that included the 13th Five-Year MCF S&T Plan, Opinions on MCF in the defense industry and military logistics system, and regulations on the management of economic projects with defense utilization.

This active pace of policymaking was maintained in 2018, but public reporting on the CMCFDC's activities stopped beginning in 2019. With the accelerating momentum in MCF policymaking and implementation, it is extremely unlikely that the CMCFDC has ceased its activities. The more plausible explanation is that its activities are now classified because of growing international scrutiny of China's MCF activities.[44] There were media reports of meetings of provincial MCF development committees being convened in early 2019, although this coverage also ceased after spring 2019.[45]

Although its high-powered membership lineup has turned the CMCFDC into the country's authoritative decision-making center for MCF-related issues, does

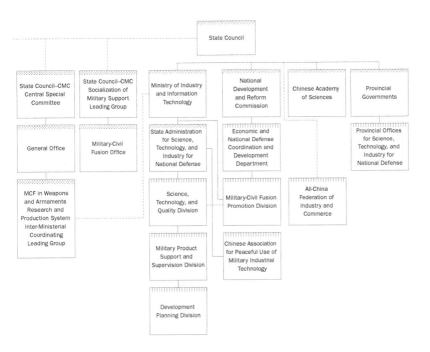

this extend to its institutional capacity to effectively carry out policy implementation? Media reporting for the first several years of the CMCFDC's permanent administration, which is centered on its general office, shows that it has been active and has become the center of bureaucratic gravity for the fledging MCF ecosystem. An important source of the general office's high status and influence is that it is headed by a Politburo Standing Committee member, who is between one and three administrative ranks higher than counterparts in the party, CMC, and State Council general offices and other similar commissions.[46]

Besides being responsible for the daily administration of the CMCFDC, the general office appears to have considerable policymaking authority. Outside of its biannual plenary sessions, the CMCFDC has been able to "promulgate and implement" a sizable number of initiatives. In 2017, for example, this included the 13th Five-Year MCF S&T Plan, special MCF programs for people's air defense and economic mobilization, and MCF plans for at least twenty provinces.[47] The CMCFDC has also organized leading groups to address special topics, such as the Defense Science and Technology, Weapons, and Equipment Collaboration and

Innovation Leading Group (国防科技和武器装备协同创新领导小组, *Guofang Keji He Wuqi Zhuangbei Xietong Chuangxin Lingdao Xiaozu*).[48] Zhang Gaoli, the inaugural head of the CMCFDC General Office, said that ad hoc small groups (专项小组, *zhuanxiang xiaozu*) would play a key supporting role in the work of the CMCFDC.[49]

Another indicator of the CMCFDC's expanding reach is the establishment of provincial CMCFDC organs across the country. By the end of 2017, all of the country's thirty-one provincial party committees had established MCF development committees and/or general offices.[50] This quick response raises the question of how credible and effective these provincial MCF entities will be in serving as local agents for the central MCF system.

Eric Hagt argues that there is wide variation in the nature of MCF institutional arrangements at the subnational level and in the alignment between local and central interests in MCF.[51] He identifies at least three contrasting MCF models. The first is the state-dominant Mianyang Inland model that applies to legacy "third line" (三线, *sanxian*) provinces in the western interior. Hagt points out that a wide mismatch in productive capacity and technological sophistication between the underdeveloped local civilian economies and advanced defense facilities located in these areas means that MCF complementarity is low. Mianyang, one of the traditional centers of strategic defense innovation in China, is a good example of an advanced defense technological and industrial base with a surrounding underdeveloped civilian economy.

The second model is represented by Shenzhen on China's southern coast, which is almost the polar opposite of Mianyang. In Shenzhen, the role of the state is limited and the civilian sector is far more advanced than its defense counterpart. Hagt argues that this market-led corporatist model is a handicap for MCF integration as the military becomes primarily a customer rather than a partner with ease of access to technology supplies. The third approach is the Beijing model, which Hagt says is the most important because it occupies a central position in the country's access to political, scientific, educational, and defense industrial inputs. The Beijing model highlights all the pluses and minuses of engaging in MCF, and the overall result is substantial MCF activity that is highly inefficient. Although there are many strands of MCF activity, the Beijing model is in general "piecemeal, ad hoc, top-down, and fragmented rather than broad-based, institutionalized, and bottom-up."[52]

The CMCFDC superstructure was placed on top of an existing rickety MCF apparatus that reflected the pedestrian and ad hoc MCF efforts of past administrations. The principal government agency in charge of overseeing the management of the MCF ecosystem until the creation of the CMCFDC was the

Military-Civil Integration Promotion Department (MCIPD; 军民结合推进司, *Junmin Jiehe Tuijin Si*) under MIIT.[53] A major responsibility of the MCIPD was to support the work of the Inter-Ministerial Coordination Group on *Junmin Jiehe Yujun Yumin* Weapons and Equipment Research and Production System Construction, which was the chief pre-CMCFDC mechanism to coordinate MCF issues across the central government. This coordination group is housed under the MIIT, and the MIIT minister heads the group. There have been only six publicly disclosed plenary meetings of this coordination group between 2011 and 2017, which calls into question whether this entity is still active. However, a MIIT review of the coordination group's activities in 2017 painted a glowing assessment that included helping to set up several batches of national MCF industrial demonstration bases.[54] The CMCFDC General Office works most closely on MCF affairs with the National Development and Reform Commission (NDRC: 国家发展和改革委员会, *Guojia Fazhan He Gaige Weiyuanhui*), especially its Economic and Defense Coordination Development Department (国家发改委经济与国防协调发展司, *Guojia Fagaiwei Jingji Yu Guofang Xietiao Fazhansi*), and the CMC Strategic Planning Office. These three entities are described as providing a "unified leadership" on MCF matters.[55]

One intriguing MCF-related organization is the State Council–CMC Central Special Committee (CSC) General Office (国务院中央军委专门委员会办公室, *Guowuyuan Zhongyang Junwei Zhuanmen Weiyuanhui Bangongshi*), which MCIPD director Yin Weijun (尹卫军) referred to in a discussion of his department's work plans for 2017. Yin pointed out that the MCIPD would undertake liaison service work with the CSC General Office and other "relevant leading agencies in the national defense field."[56] In many ways, the CSC, especially its earlier version dating to the 1960s and 1970s, is the forerunner to the CMCFDC as it engaged in bringing together military and civilian capabilities to support strategic and defense S&T programs. (There is more detailed analysis of the CSC in chapter 5.)

Leadership Engagement and Intervention

Establishing a high-level MCF leadership and management institutional structure is necessary but insufficient to ensure that it will successfully become accepted as coequal with the military and civilian systems. To ensure that this fledging apparatus has credible political authority and clout, Xi has placed himself at the helm along with a critical mass of the inner circle of the country's leadership elite. Xi has also been an active participant in the CMCFDC's affairs, chairing all of the four plenary sessions that have been publicly reported and providing plenty of detailed policy guidance. As long as Xi remains actively involved, chances are good that the MCF system will successfully develop into an influential and capable actor.

Although the membership of the CMCFDC is a who's who of China's most powerful policymaking elite, how deeply engaged and supportive they are is up for debate. The party is represented by four of the seven members of the Politburo Standing Committee, which includes Xi and six Politburo members. The state presence consists of the premier, one vice-premier, two state councillors, and ten state ministers or party secretaries. For the military, in addition to Xi as CMC chairman, there are two CMC vice-chairmen, and three CMC members. At least eight of these members are especially important and relevant because of their institutional affiliations: (1) the Politburo Standing Committee member who also serves concurrently as CMCFDC General Office director; (2) the vice-premier responsible for industrial and defense industrial affairs; (3) ministers in charge of the NDRC, Ministry of Finance, MIIT, and Ministry of Science and Technology (MOST); and (4) the CMC vice-chairman responsible for military modernization matters and the CMC representative who is also director of the Equipment Development Department (EDD).

Although Xi is the pivotal figure in the making or breaking of the CMCFDC specifically and the development of the MCF ecosystem more broadly, the roles of the CMCFDC General Office director and executive deputy director are also critical because they are in charge of operational implementation. As the CMCFDC General Office director is a Politburo Standing Committee member, it is unlikely that they can participate in the management of the general office's affairs in more than a limited capacity. Consequently, the overwhelming burden of work falls to the deputy director who has been Jin Zhuanglong since the establishment of the CMCFDC. Jin is a missile engineer by training, has served his entire career in the defense industry, and has an experienced track record in MCF-related affairs.[57] As a former State Administration for Science, Technology, and Industry for National Defense (SASTIND) deputy director and the head of a major state-owned corporation, Jin's CMCFDC status would likely be equivalent to a ministerial or vice-ministerial rank, which would make him the country's most senior official in daily charge of MCF policy.

Jin's strong professional background and senior administrative status suggests that the CMCFDC has been organized for effective policy implementation. The short track record since its establishment shows that the CMCFDC General Office has been a proactive and consequential player in MCF affairs. The general office regularly convenes workshops and issues administrative guidance and has been steadily building an organic policy research and support capability, such as with a strategic planning bureau.

Building a Comprehensive and Robust Institutional System

The lack of a robust institutional system has been identified as a critical weakness in the efforts to forge an MCF ecosystem. The nascent MCF leadership apparatus has been addressing this problem by issuing a growing volume of policy regulations, guidelines, and plans. The number of MCF-related policy documents annually issued jumped from one to two between 2008 and 2012 to ten in 2013, twenty-six in 2015, sixty-four in 2017, and fifty-eight in the first nine months of 2018 (see figure 3.3). But as PLA MCF analysts point out, the total number of MCF-related policy documents "is already very large, but the prominent problem is that they are not systematic, the coverage is incomplete, and there are missing gaps." They argue in particular that the lack of central-level "laws that regulate MCF development has led to an unclear definition of what MCF is in terms of its scope, rights, and responsibilities."[58]

Consequently, one area to evaluate and measure progress in MCF implementation is the passing of national-level legislation on MCF matters. One of the most important pieces of draft legislation is a comprehensive MCF law that is slowly winding its way through the legislative process. The revision of existing national and defense-specific legislation to take into account MCF-related matters is another way to measure progress in MCF institutional development. Analysts point out that key legislation will need to be modified including the National Defense Law and the Government Procurement Law, the latter of which deals with civilian and military procurement issues but does not have any provisions with military-civil applications.

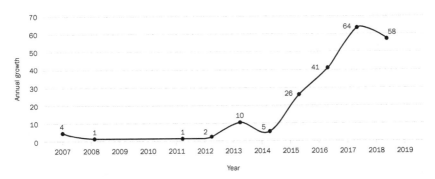

FIGURE 3.3. Annual growth in the issuance of military-civil fusion policy documents, 2007–2018

Forging an Independent and Dedicated Military-Civil Fusion Profession

Educating and training a dedicated professional cadre of MCF personnel is another important foundational pillar in the building of a robust MCF ecosystem, but this does not appear to be a high priority for the Chinese authorities. One structural reason is that the Chinese workforce system has been traditionally siloed with the overwhelming majority of personnel spending their entire careers within a single vertically integrated functional or geographic system or *xitong* (系统) with little opportunity for horizontal transfers. This means that unless a new independent MCF system is established, the vast majority of personnel working for entities dealing with MCF that are scattered across the civilian, military, and defense industrial systems will only serve short-term assignments (see table 3.1).

One comparative case study that may offer some insights into the MCF's dilemma is the PLA's efforts to achieve jointness among its service arms since the beginning of the twenty-first century. An assessment of the PLA's track record in developing a joint force by RAND analyst Mark Cozad offers a mixed picture. Although "the PLA has made progress in joint operations, and its ability to perform many joint functions is better today than it was in 2001 when these programs were initiated, the repeated reintroduction of reform initiatives to address longstanding problems strongly suggests that there are significant impediments to progress."[59] One of the biggest obstacles to jointness was the long-standing dominance of the ground forces, which required a herculean effort by Xi to overcome by lowering its status to the same level as other service arms. The lesson here is that the MCF system will struggle to be a viable actor if it cannot overcome the dominance of the military and civilian systems.

Under Xi's tenure, momentum and intensity toward jointness has grown, as demonstrated by the 2016 organizational reforms of the high command that established joint theater commands and joint CMC departments. But overall progress has been incremental and will take time to show definitive results.

There appears to be no plans to establish an MCF-dedicated training and educational apparatus that would be a lynchpin in the cultivation of an MCF institutional culture and esprit de corps. Xi has said that "it is necessary to build a pattern of institutes with joint operations institutes as the core, specialized armed services as the foundation, and military-civil fusion training as the supplement."[60] Xi's remark indicates that cultivating an MCF professional corps through education is a secondary priority. However, the NDRC in conjunction with the CMC Strategic Planning Office announced that one of its goals in 2018 was to build a bureau-level management cadre training platform that would be

TABLE 3.1 Organizations affiliated with the military-civil fusion ecosystem

PRINCIPAL INSTITUTION	SUBORDINATE ENTITIES
National Development and Reform Commission	Department of Economic and Defense Coordination
Ministry of Industry and Information Technology	State Administration for Science, Technology, and Industry for National Defense
	MCF Promotion Bureau
Ministry of Science and Technology	
State-Owned Asset Supervision and Administration Commission	
China National Intellectual Property Administration	
Ministry of Finance	
Central Military Commission	Strategic Planning Office
	Equipment Development Department
	National Defense Intellectual Property Office
	National Defense Mobilization Department
	Science and Technology Commission
	Strategic Support Force
People's Liberation Army	Military Academic Institutions: Academy of Military Sciences, National Defense University, National University of Defense Technology
	Provincial Military Districts
Central Cyberspace Commission	
Ministry of Education	
Ministry of Civil Affairs	
Ministry of Transportation	
Ministry Human and Social Affairs	
Ministry of Public Security	
State-Owned Defense Corporations	
Private Sector	

administered by NDU to provide special training courses on MCF for the growing numbers of personnel serving in MCF-related positions.[61]

In assessing the prospects of success of the nascent MCF system, it is worth pointing out that new organizations have periodically emerged and survived the cutthroat bureaucratic competition within the Chinese system to become important players. Two cases of institutional innovation in the military realm offer some clues: the creation of the General Armament Department (GAD) in 1998 and the formation of the PLA Strategic Support Force in 2016.[62] These two entities owe their accomplishments to two key factors. First, they were established through the merger of already existing substantial organizations that allowed them to have a critical mass from the very beginning as opposed to new small organizations that grow organically. Second, their portfolios were clearly defined, specialized, and of high priority, which justified the need for a dedicated institutional solution. The MCF apparatus has the latter of these factors, but not the former.

Carrying Out Military-Civil Fusion Proof-of-Concept Demonstration Projects

Much of the work to advance MCF by the Xi regime in its first term was concentrated on policy, administrative, and reform issues, and there was limited effort devoted to on-the-ground execution of projects. As the new MCF edifice took shape, Xi was eager to pivot toward implementation and called for carrying out "dragonhead projects" (龙头工程, *longtou gongcheng*) that referred to leading-edge programs that would showcase the spoils of MCF.[63]

This need for demonstrative effects was clearly articulated in the 13th Five-Year MCF S&T Plan that emphasized the launch of a raft of pilot and demonstration initiatives.[64] Two categories of demonstration programs were highlighted: technology and engineering-focused major MCF demonstration projects (军民融合重大示范项目, *junmin ronghe zhongda shifan xiangmu*) and MCF innovation demonstration zones (军民融合创新示范区, *junmin ronghe chuangxin shifanqu*). For the former group, twenty-one major technology demonstration projects were chosen across a broad range of areas and appear to have been selected because they were already well under way in their development.[65]

For the demonstration zones, the 13th Five-Year MCF S&T Plan called for the building of a number of strategic and comprehensive MCF collaborative innovation platforms in different parts of the country of which one of the most important was the National Military-Civil Fusion Innovation Demonstration Zone (国家军民融合创新示范区, *Guojia Junmin Ronghe Chuangxin Shifanqu*). These national-level zones are intended to be microlevel experimental field tests of the deeply integrated military-civil industrial, technological, financial, support, and mobilization systems advocated by Xi.[66] Since the CMCFDC approved the National MCF Innovation Demonstration Zone Construction Implementation Plan in March 2018, there has been intensive lobbying by provinces to be selected for one of those zones because they would be lucrative engines of economic growth.[67] One of the first zones approved was the Guzhenkou MCF Innovation Demonstration Zone in Qingdao (青岛古镇口军民融合创新示范区) on China's east coast.[68]

These national-level MCF demonstration zones are a major upgrade from the proliferation of local MCF-style development bases that have been established since the end of the 2000s. MIIT helped to pioneer the creation of local MCF industrial zones with the setting-up of National New-Type Industrialization Demonstration Bases (国家新型工业化产业示范基地, *Guojia Xinxing Gongyehua Chanye Shifan Jidi*) beginning in 2009. Thirty-two of these industrial demonstration bases have so far been set up across twenty-two provinces, with eleven bases in eastern China, nine bases in central China, and twelve bases in western China.[69] The largest and most consequential of these bases in terms of economic output are Harbin Economic Development Zone in Heilongjiang Province and Mianyang Science and Technology City, with a cumulative industrial output value of more than RMB 200 billion (US$30.86 billion) each. Several other types of local MCF-style bases include mobilization centers and support bases (动员中心和保障基地, *dongyuan he baozhang jidi*), MCF industrial parks (产业基地或园区, *chanye jidi huo yuanqu*), and MCF strategic cooperation framework agreements (战略合作协议, *zhanlue hezuo xieyi*) between local governments and military and defense industrial agencies.[70] The development fortunes of these local MCF demonstration bases, especially the latest MCF innovation demonstration zones, offer a convenient proxy to monitor and measure the performance of the national MCF system.

Constructing an Integrated Military-Civil Fusion Innovation and Industrial System

MCF policymakers see the establishment of a fully integrated military-civil innovation and industrial system as the golden key to unlocking China's vast techno-security potential. The defense innovation and industrial system consists of two intertwined but distinct complexes that have different structural and institutional approaches and interests toward MCF. The defense innovation ecosystem is primarily oriented toward R&D and has established close working ties with its civilian counterpart, especially in areas such as basic and emerging research where much of the leading-edge work has dual-use applications. By contrast, the more traditional and closed defense industrial system has been far more reluctant to open up and engage in MCF, in particular the applied development, engineering, testing, and production segments of the system that are under the monopoly control of the country's state-owned defense corporations and are subject to tight secrecy restrictions.

Several plans and guidances have been specifically drawn up to implement MCF in the defense innovation and industrial systems. The most important include the Opinions of the State Council General Office on Promoting the In-Depth Development of Military-Civil Fusion in the Defense Science and Technology Industry (国务院办公厅关于推动国防科技工业军民融合深度发展的

意见, *Guowuyuan Bangongting Guanyu Tuidong Guofang Keji Gongye Junmin Ronghe Shendu Fazhan De Yijian*), also known as Document No. 91, issued in November 2017, and the 13th Five-Year MCF S&T Plan.[71]

Document No. 91 was issued shortly after the 19th Party Congress in 2017 to reiterate to state and local agencies, state-owned enterprises, and other entities associated with the defense innovation and industrial systems that they should "earnestly implement the decisions and arrangements" made by the Communist Party Central Committee and the State Council to deepen defense industrial reforms and "build an integrated national strategic system with capabilities." The document stressed the importance of a lengthy number of policy measures. First was the need to expand the opening-up of the defense industry by requiring monopoly defense corporations to increase cooperation with the private sector, encouraging private capital to participate in the shareholding reform of defense companies in their transition from state to mixed ownership, widening access to the defense acquisition system for private firms, and promoting competition in weapons and equipment production, especially for subsystems and support equipment.

A second goal was to reconfigure the layout of the civilian and defense innovation systems to allow for increased cross-sharing of R&D infrastructure and the building of new collaborative facilities such as research laboratories, innovation centers, regional innovation bases, and testing facilities. Moreover, the document highlighted the need to form defense technology innovation alliances between academia, industry, military, and state entities. The third goal was to develop a robust military-civil governance regime that proactively sets the conditions allowing for seamless integration, such as through the setting of universal military-civilian standards, information sharing platforms, common testing, inspection, and evaluation agencies, and providing better protection and distribution of intellectual property rights.

A fourth priority was to enhance the development of the military-civilian human talent pool by drawing up a talent development plan, supporting the building of joint defense-oriented universities and laboratories, encouraging close educational and research cooperation between higher education institutions, the PLA, and the defense industry, and fostering innovation teams. Fifth was emphasizing the space, cyberspace, and maritime domains through the pursuit of large-scale military-civil technology and engineering projects. Of particular importance was the development of satellite remote sensing, deep-space exploration, network security and electromagnetic spectrum resource management systems, deep-underwater stations, nuclear-powered offshore floating platforms, and polar research vessels.

Sixth was the promotion of domestic regional MCF development with an initial focus on the Beijing-Tianjin-Hebei region, Yangtze River economic belt, northeast China rust belt, and inland western provinces. A seventh target was the opening-up of external export markets to sell dual-use products. The Belt and Road Initiative is one of the main conduits for this effort with export promotion campaigns for nuclear power plants, aviation equipment, and space technology such as the BeiDou navigation system and satellite remote sensing services.

Many of the focus areas in Document No. 91 are also covered in the 13th Five-Year MCF S&T Plan, which set the target of "basically" establishing a military-civil science and technology collaborative innovation system by 2020 that would then allow for deep MCF to begin based on the "total factor, multi-domain, and high-efficiency" approach. This plan outlined an ambitious list of sixteen major tasks to be implemented across seven areas:

1. Closer S&T coordination and collaboration between the military and civilian sectors from technical and policy exchanges to the drafting of long-term plans at both the central and subnational levels
2. Strengthening MCF science, technology, and innovation capability building by developing mechanisms to enable joint MCF research in basic and cutting-edge topics, especially intelligent unmanned S&T, biotechnology, advanced electronics, quantum technology, future networks, advanced energy, new materials, and advanced manufacturing; and common operating practices and compatible standards
3. Developing joint basic research platforms with national laboratories and national engineering centers to the implementation of strategic megaprojects associated with the MLP and STI 2030
4. Promoting the two-way flow of technology and knowledge through the creation of dual-use technology trading centers, information exchanges, and other mechanisms
5. Carrying out pilot MCF demonstration projects with the establishment of MCF zones and regions, research institutes, and financial services platforms such as the setting-up of an MCF S&T achievement transformation government guidance fund
6. Enhancing MCF human talent development through the development of joint innovation teams and attracting talent into the MCF sphere domestically and internationally
7. Improving the MCF policy system through the building of a robust regulatory and legal system and intellectual property protection apparatus and nurturing an MCF-centric institutional culture

Two initiatives are worth scrutinizing as they represent the cornerstones in the building of the new MCF edifice. The first is the glacial opening-up of the defense acquisition system to the participation of civilian companies. The second is the establishment of large-scale advanced joint military-civil research and engineering facilities.

Efforts to allow civilian firms to take part in the defense acquisition process have been occurring since the end of the 1990s. The central authorities have moved cautiously, though, in the face of strident resistance from incumbent defense conglomerates that are deeply worried that this reform initiative will threaten their lucrative sources of income or guaranteed "iron rice bowl." There are several prominent features in this effort to pry open the shuttered gates of the defense industrial citadel that represent notable departures in established practices, behavior, and norms.

A first distinguishing characteristic is that the nascent MCF industrial system has been extremely active in reaching out and engaging with the civilian sector through exhibitions, trade fairs, informational workshops, and many other two-way exchanges. This outreach began in 2014 with the launch of a regular large-scale flagship MCF exhibition of high-tech achievements (军民融合高科技成果展览, *Junmin Ronghe Gaokeji Chengguo Zhanlan*) in Beijing that attracts hundreds of private high-tech firms as well as academic and research institutes. Five of these exhibitions were held between 2014 and 2020 and top-ranking civilian and military leaders have thrown their political weight behind this mobilization effort. Xi brought the entire Politburo Standing Committee to the second exhibition in 2016 while the entire CMC leadership attended the fourth exhibition in 2018.[72] There are also numerous regional and sectoral MCF exhibitions held across the country.

A second feature is the opening-up of the defense procurement market to civilian enterprises and research organizations. The primary means of entry into this lucrative but highly protected arena is through the issuance of weapons and equipment research and production licenses (WERPL; 武器装备科研生产许可证, *wuqi zhuangbei keyan shengchan xukezheng*) and equipment contractor certificates (ECC; 装备承制单位资格证, *zhuangbei chengzhi danwei zigezheng*) that allow entities to bid for contracts. The licensing system is jointly administered by SASTIND and the PLA armaments bureaucracy and consists of several licenses covering confidentiality and qualification requirements.[73] SASTIND is responsible for managing the WERPL process, while the EDD is in charge of the ECC process. The WERPL allows enterprises or research entities to conduct research, development, testing, and production of approved military products and projects, while the ECC allows entities to undertake scientific research, production, testing, repair, and various technical support services.

There are three levels of licenses.[74] Category 1 licenses are awarded to companies that perform the most complex, classified, core, and combat-related activities, such as systems integrators that are responsible for putting together the finished products that come off the production line. In addition, contractors that research and manufacture important subsystems such as engines are in this category. The big state-owned defense firms have maintained an iron grip on licenses in this domain. Category 2 licenses cover special equipment and general support products that are primarily for non-war-fighting purposes but can be used for such needs if required, such as transportation equipment. This means that confidentiality and qualification requirements are less stringent. Category 3 licenses are for off-the-shelf civilian products that military units can use such as food, clothing, fuel, and other logistics supplies.

The number of civilian firms that have received WERPLs and ECCs has steadily grown since the beginning of the 2000s when they first began to receive them, although precisely how many is unclear. SASTIND announced in 2016 that more than one thousand private enterprises had obtained WERPLs, which was a 127 percent increase compared to the end of the 11th Five-Year Plan in 2010.[75] This would mean upward of 450 private firms had obtained WERPLs in the first ten years of the opening-up of the licensing scheme. Other studies from PLA analysts indicate there were a total of around nine hundred civilian firms with WERPLs in 2008, which included state-owned and private firms.[76]

Not surprisingly, civilian firms with little defense expertise are overwhelmingly concentrated in categories 2 and 3 of the licensing system. There are unverified reports in the Chinese news media and in stock brokerage reports on the defense industry in the 2016–2017 period that around fifty civilian enterprises had received category 1 licenses by 2017, which would constitute between 3 percent and 5 percent of the civilian licensed community.[77] These companies specialized in areas such as unmanned systems, nano, and micro-miniature-scale technologies.[78] The size of the ECC community is considerably larger than its WERPL counterpart, most likely because of its inclusion of repair services, which is a lower technical barrier of entry for civilian firms compared to the research and production-focused WERPL. According to Tan Yungang (谭云刚), a retired PLA acquisition expert, there were 1,800 civilian entities with ECCs in 2018 compared to 1,189 with WERPLs.[79]

In addition to allowing more civilian firms into the acquisition system, the tight controls on what types of military contracts are allowed for competitive bidding has also been steadily relaxed. SASTIND and the EDD publish a Weapons and Equipment Research, Development, and Production License Catalog (武器装备科研生产许可目录, Wuqi Zhuangbei Keyan Shengchan Xuke Mulu) that lists all key military-related projects and contracts to be offered for tender. Because of the highly classified nature of these projects, only firms with category 1 licenses are usually allowed access to the catalog and bid for work. However, the contents of the catalog have been gradually pared down since the 2000s, and more defense projects and technologies have been opened up to contract tenders without being included in the catalog. There have been five revisions to the catalog since the beginning of the 2000s of which the largest reduction in scope and restrictions occurred with the 2018 edition, which saw the number of listings shrink by 62 percent from 755 in the prior 2015 catalog to 285 items.[80] However, these remaining items are related to programs that have "important impact on national and strategic security as well as social and public security," which almost certainly means they account for the lion's share of the defense procurement budget.[81]

A third characteristic is encouraging acquisition transparency, information sharing, and accessible means of business transactions through the use of online portals. This is the opposite of the segregated, opaque, and paper-based approach to information management that the legacy defense industrial base has traditionally practiced. This move into the online era began with the establishment of the Weapons and Equipment Acquisition Information Network (WEAIN; 全军武器装备采购信息网, *Quanjun Wuqi Zhuangbei Caigou Xinxi Wang*), which was set up in 2015 by GAD. General Zhang Youxia said that WEAIN was a test case for MCF implementation and a weather vane for the reform of the PLA's approach to armament management.[82]

WEAIN passed this test with flying colors with its rapid and widespread use across the military establishment and among civilian enterprises. Between its establishment and October 2019, WEAIN had more than 29,000 registered users and more than 170,000 procurement requests had been disseminated on the portal with transactions totaling hundreds of billions of renminbi.[83] The portal has both open and classified sections as well as physical offices in more than thirty locations across China to handle highly classified information. There are also other online portals such as the State Military-Civil Fusion Public Service Platform (国家军民融合公共服务平台, *Guojia Junmin Ronghe Gonggong Fuwu Pingtai*) hosted by MIIT and the Military Procurement Network (军队采购网, *Jundui Caigou Wang*) operated by the CMC Logistics Support Department.

The opening-up of the defense acquisition system to civilian participation in the first two decades of the twenty-first century has been a slow and tortuous journey. Although this pace has noticeably picked up under Xi's tenure, the MCF outreach campaign has touched only a tiny segment of the national economy. With more than 130,000 civilian small- and medium-sized technology firms, the approximately three thousand firms that have been signed up into the defense acquisition system represent a participation rate of just 2.3 percent. While some of the leading private technology firms like Huawei, Alibaba, and Dajiang Innovations Science and Technology Co., Ltd. (DJI) are likely to be within this recruited pool, this is still an underwhelming achievement for twenty years of effort. Measuring this uptake rate of civilian entities into the MCF system both in terms of quality and quantity will be a useful gauge for evaluating the effectiveness of MCF implementation over the long term along with other indicators such as the cumulative numbers of WERPL and ECC licenses issued to civilian, especially private, firms and how they are divided across the different acquisition categories.

The second key initiative at the vanguard of MCF advancement into the defense innovation sector is the establishment of large-scale advanced joint military-civil research and engineering facilities, which are playing a central role in transforming the Chinese S&T system from an absorption-based development model to an original innovation-focused approach. National laboratories are one of the main organizational vehicles used here. The Xi regime considers the formation of a system of large-scale comprehensive national laboratories an essential platform to accelerate fundamental and applied research, especially for big science, strategic, and military-civil-related endeavors. Xi has pointed out that "national laboratories are important vehicles in which developed countries seize the high ground in technological innovation."[84]

Even though China has been building national laboratories since the early 1980s, they have been single-purpose small-scale facilities with workforces numbering in the hundreds compared to the large-scale comprehensive facilities in the United States and other advanced countries that employ thousands of scientists and engineers.[85] Ten national laboratories were set up between 1983 and 2003 specializing in areas such as synchrotron radiation, high-energy physics, tandem accelerator nuclear physics, materials science, condensed matter physics, information science, and optoelectronics. Another ten laboratories followed in 2006 with specializations in marine S&T, magnetic confinement fusion, clean energy shipbuilding and ocean engineering, microstructures, major disease research, protein science, aeronautical S&T, rail transportation, and modern agriculture.

The Chinese authorities are looking to model the Chinese national laboratories on US and European multidiscipline facilities such as Argonne and Helmhortz. The 13th Five-Year Science, Technology, and Innovation Plan states that national laboratories are "at the strategic commanding positions that have promise to lead future development."[86] However, although Xi has strongly advocated for this comprehensive national laboratory initiative since the mid-2010s, implementation has been painfully slow because of entrenched resistance, bureaucratic fragmentation, and unresolved questions about how they should be organized and funded.[87] Only the Qingdao Marine Science and Technology Pilot National Laboratory (青岛海洋科技试点国家实验室, *Qingdao Haiyang Keji Shidian Guojia Shiyanshi*) had been established as a test case by 2020,[88] although another half a dozen had been approved as national research centers (国家研究

中心, *guojia yanjiu zhongxin*) and marked as in preparation to become national laboratories. The 14th Five Year Plan has stated that national laboratories will be established in at least six emerging and core technology areas that include quantum information, photonics, network communications, artificial intelligence, biotechnology, and modern energy systems.[89]

The defense science, technology, and industrial apparatus has also set its sights on establishing comprehensive national-level laboratories since at least the late 2000s. A senior Commission for Science, Technology, and Industry for National Defense (COSTIND) official said in 2007 that demonstration work was being carried out for a defense national laboratory focused on "major basic research, strategic high-technology, and systems integration research."[90] Little more was heard, though, until the mid-2010s when the building of national laboratories reappeared on the national agenda and SASTIND signaled its continuing interest in this goal. At its 2016 annual S&T work conference, SASTIND said that it would "actively coordinate with MOST and strive to establish a national laboratory in the defense science and technology field."[91] Although no authorization has so far been granted for a defense S&T national laboratory, SASTIND had been actively building up a significant apparatus of at least sixty defense S&T key laboratories (国防科技重点实验室, *guofang keji zhongdian shiyanshi*) and defense S&T key subject laboratories (国防科技重点学科实验室, *guofang keji zhongdian xueke shiyanshi*) by 2019.[92]

When joint military-civil national laboratories finally emerge, it will mark a major milestone in the formation of an MCF integrated innovation system. This is because strategic, defense, and dual-use innovation is heavily driven by a state-led, top-down, big science approach. The lack of such a cutting-edge innovation standard bearer is a major gap in China's techno-security ambitions and capabilities.

Another important but painstakingly slow reform initiative taking place within the defense innovation system since the late 2010s to open up to civilian participation is the restructuring of the ownership status of research institutes belonging to or affiliated with major state-owned defense conglomerates. Even though these institutes are a core component of the R&D capabilities of the defense firms, they are designated as "government-affiliated institutions" (事业单位, *shiye danwei*), which means they are subject to state ownership restrictions and cannot be restructured into listed entities. Many defense research institutes have developed lucrative advanced technologies and are viewed as "cash cows" by their parent defense corporations. For example, 30 percent of the profits of the China Shipbuilding Industry Corporation in 2014 came from its twenty-eight research institutes.[93]

The restructuring of defense research institutes is viewed as critical to overall efforts to reform the defense industry and improve its innovation capacity.[94] In

2016, SASTIND began drafting a number of proposals to reform the defense research institute system. They included the "Scheme on Classification of Defense Research Institutes," "Defense Research Institutes Classified Reform Implementation Plan," and "Supporting Policies on the Restructuring of Defense Research Institutes under Public Institution Reform." In the third document, SASTIND drafted a total of thirty-one policies on party building, personnel placement, income distribution, social welfare, and security and secrecy issues.[95] In addition, defense research institutes were divided into three categories to determine the nature of their ownership structures.[96] A thicket of thorny issues dragged out this reform effort, which included asset management, personnel placement, income distribution, social welfare, taxation, and secrecy considerations.

In 2018, though, a list of forty-one defense research institutes were chosen for a pilot initiative to convert them from wholly state-owned entities into mixed-ownership enterprises that would allow them to participate in asset securitization (AS). Only one institute belonging to the China Ordnance Equipment Group Corporation was given initial approval to undertake a partial switch to a mixed-ownership structure. The reform of the remaining forty research institutes was delayed until the beginning of the 14th Five-Year Plan beginning in 2021. Their restructuring is tied to a three-year action plan passed by the State Council at the end of 2020 to significantly overhaul the state-owned enterprise system by encouraging mixed private-public ownership of subsidiaries and allowing firms more opportunity to tap the capital markets through AS and other investment instruments.[97] The revised goal is to complete the pilot program to reform the forty research institutes by the end of 2021 and then allow the rest of the defense research institute system to be restructured by 2023.[98] Moreover, this action plan will also involve accelerating the AS process in defense sectors that have been lagging in this effort, such as ordnance and space.

Access to and Utilization of Financial Resources

As China pushes hard to develop a highly capable and seamless MCF ecosystem, its access to financial resources, especially market-sourced investment, to bankroll this expensive endeavor will play a decisive role in determining how fast, expansive, and effective the outcome will be. A key mantra of the MCF development strategy put forward by the Xi Jinping regime since the mid-2010s is that it should be "state-led, demand-driven, and market-oriented." What this means is that (1) party and state agencies provide the strategic guidance, leadership support, and regulatory oversight of the institutional regimes set up to raise and manage investment capital; (2) market demand from end users drives the pace, scale, and direction of development; and (3) market requirements—that is, profitability—are of primary consideration. In reality, in China's statist system, national security and political determinants usually take precedence over market considerations.

Extensive effort has been made since the early 2010s to develop linkages that would allow China's insular defense industrial complex to access lucrative investment capital from the financial markets to supplement state funding for techno-security priorities. Two types of initiatives have been especially important: AS (资产证券化, *zichan zhengquanhua*) and government guidance funds (GGFs; 政府引导基金, *zhengfu yindao jijin*).

ASSET SECURITIZATION

AS has been used extensively by the Chinese defense industry to leverage the resources of the domestic stock market and state investors to support its expansion. With plenty of orders coming from the PLA, a bulging pipeline of new generations of equipment under development, and fervent leadership support, the defense industry has attracted strong domestic stock investor interest.

The Chinese authorities began preparing state-owned defense industrial enterprises to tap into the capital markets from the mid-2000s by establishing a regulatory framework to ensure a secure and orderly process. An initial round of deals was allowed to take place in 2007 in the shipbuilding and aviation sectors,[99] but this initiative was curtailed by the 2008–2009 global financial crisis. It resumed in 2013 when SASTIND began to permit firms to issue share placements using military assets as securitization.[100]

Opening up the defense industry to investment from the capital markets is part of a broader initiative by Chinese authorities to forge closer integration between the S&T system and financial markets. Premier Li Keqiang said in 2014 that "it is necessary to increase the efficiency of science and technology innovations with institutional innovation . . . and let the market decide allocation of innovative resources. We should intensify financial support, guide more enterprises and social capital to increase input in research and development. We should pay particular attention to activating stock assets and enhance capital usage efficiency."[101]

The first defense AS deal was done in 2013 by the China Shipbuilding Industry Corporation (CSIC), which undertook an RMB 8.5 billion (US$1.38 billion) private share placement with ten Chinese parties to acquire production facilities to manufacture warships. More than one-third of funds, or RMB 3.275 billion (US$533 million), was earmarked for the acquisition of medium- and large-sized surface warships, conventional submarines, and large landing ships, while RMB 2.66 billion (US$433 million) was designated for arms trade-related undertakings and civil-military industrialization projects. The remaining RMB 2.54 billion (US$413 million) was set aside as working capital.[102] CSIC explained that the funds would "satisfy the development and manufacture of a new generation of weapons and equipment," adding that "we need urgent large-scale technological improvements and need to expand our financing channels."[103] Dalian Shipyard, one of the CSIC facilities that received proceeds from the share placement, built the country's first domestically designed aircraft carrier. Subsequently, all other defense conglomerates began issuing public and private equity offerings and bond issuances, although at widely varying levels of intensity.

The average AS rate among defense conglomerates reached 56.9 percent by the end of 2020 (see figure 3.4 and table 3.2). Aviation Industry Corporation of China (AVIC) led the way with an AS ratio of 83.14 percent. In second place was China South Industries Group Corporation (CSGC) with a ratio of 70.1 percent, closely followed by China State Shipbuilding Corporation (CSSC) with an AS rate of 69.3 percent. This showed that the aviation, shipbuilding, and ordnance sectors have warmly embraced AS as a key source of fundraising.

By contrast, the defense electronics and space and missile industries have been far more tentative in leveraging the capital markets. CASIC had the lowest AS rate in 2020, at 14 percent, while the China Aerospace Science and Technology Corporation's (CASC) ratio was 20.8 percent as of 2019. China Electronics Technology Corporation (CETC) had an AS rate of 31.8 percent in 2020, which was still well behind the leading pack. The ordnance sector is split down the middle: whereas CSGC has been very keen, China North Industries Group Corporation (CNGC) has been far more conservative, with an AS rate of only 29.35 percent by 2020.

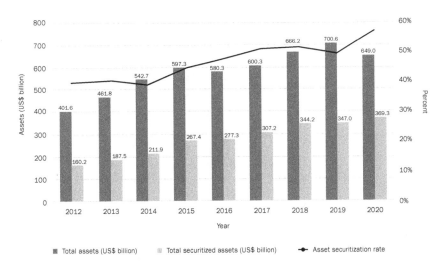

FIGURE 3.4. Asset securitization trends in the Chinese defense industry, 2012–2020

TABLE 3.2 Asset securitization trends in the Chinese defense industry, 2012–2020

	2012	2013	2014	2015	2016	2017	2018	2019	2020
Total assets	401.6 (2,534)	461.8 (2,840)	542.7 (3,343)	597.3 (3,751)	580.3 (3,859)	600.3 (4,058)	666.2 (4,417)	700.6 (4,841)	649 (4,478)
Total securitized assets	160.2 (1,011)	187.5 (1,153)	211.9 (1,305)	267.4 (1,679)	277.3 (1,844)	307.2 (2,077)	344.2 (2,282)	347 (2,398)	369.3 (2,548)
Year-on-year increase of securitized assets		27.3	24.4	55.5	9.9	29.9	37	2.8	22.3
Asset securitization rate	39.9%	40.6%	39%	44.8%	47.8%	51.2%	51.6%	49.5%	56.9%

Note: Amounts are in US$ billion; amounts in parentheses are in RMB billion.

Some Chinese analysts have noted that the AS ratio for US defense prime contractors is between 70 percent and 80 percent and suggest this should be the overall target for the Chinese defense industry. AVIC, CSGC, and CSSC have already reached this level, but the remaining state-owned defense corporations still have some distance to go.

The ten principal state-owned defense corporations raised a combined RMB 2.548 trillion (US$369.3 billion) between 2012 and 2020, or RMB 283.1 billion (US$41 billion) on average annually. There has been considerable variation in the amount of funds raised year-over-year (see figure 3.5 and table 3.3). In 2015, AS deals totaled RMB 357 billion (US$56.8 billion), but this dropped to just RMB 18 billion (US$2.6 billion) worth of transactions in 2019 before rebounding to RMB 143.5 billion (US$20.8 billion) in 2020. Over the next five years, AS could allow the Chinese defense industry the capacity to raise upward of another RMB 1 trillion (US$154 billion).

The pace, scale, and reach of AS among Chinese defense enterprises is expected to significantly pick up in the first half of the 2020s, boosted by the three-year reform plan of the state-owned enterprise (SOE) sector by the Chinese government that began in 2020.[104] One of the central goals of this reform initiative is to promote mixed ownership of SOEs, especially by encouraging private-public ownership of subsidiaries and allowing firms more opportunities to tap the capital markets through AS and other investment instruments. Although this reform effort covers all SOEs, the defense industrial sector will be a major beneficiary, especially companies that have so far lagged behind in the implementation of the AS process.

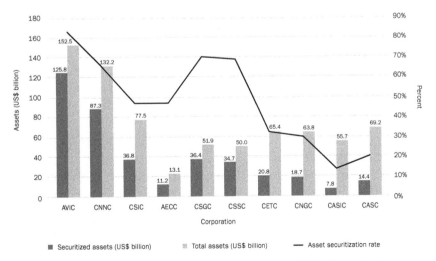

FIGURE 3.5. The state of asset securitization among China's principal defense industrial corporations in 2020

TABLE 3.3 The state of asset securitization among China's principal defense industrial corporations in 2020

	SECURITIZED ASSETS US$ BILLION (RMB BILLION)	TOTAL ASSETS US$ BILLION (RMB BILLION)	ASSET SECURITIZATION RATE
Aviation Industry Corp. of China (AVIC)	126.8 (874.6)	152.5 (1052)	83.1%
China National Nuclear Corp. (CNNC)	87.3 (602.1)	132.2 (912.3)	66%
China Shipbuilding Industry Group (CSIC)	36.8 (253.6)	77.5 (534.5)	47.5%
Aero Engine Corp. of China (AECC)	11.1 (76.4)*	23.1 (159.3)*	48%*
China South Industries Group Corp. (CSGC)	36.8 (254)	51.9 (358.4)	70.1%
China State Shipbuilding Corp. (CSSC)	34.7 (239.4)	50 (345.1)	69.4%
China Electronics Technology Group Corp. (CETC)	20.8 (143.5)	65.4 (451.6)	31.8%
China North Industries Group Corp. (CNGC)	18.7 (129.1)	63.8 (439.9)	29.4%
China Aerospace Science and Industry Corp. (CASIC)	7.8 (53.8)	55.7 (384)	14%
China Aerospace Science and Technology Corp. (CASC)	14.4 (99.5)*	69.2 (477.5)*	20.8%*

*Figures are for 2019.

GOVERNMENT GUIDANCE FUNDS

GGFs along with other industrial investment funds have been the second major pool of financial capital flowing into the MCF system since the early 2010s. GGFs are investment vehicles in which central and local government agencies make investments that are combined with private venture capital and SOEs in areas of strategic importance.[105] The government portion of the fund is usually small, officially capped at between 20 percent and 30 percent but is often closer to between 5 percent and 15 percent, which allows for considerable leveraging of non-state and state corporate assets.[106]

GGFs offer a competing mix of strengths and weaknesses.[107] Positive attributes include (1) allowing the state to leverage the market for investment resources and best practices, (2) offering "patient" capital that is stable with long-term investment horizons, and (3) being complementary rather than competitive with other industrial policy instruments like AS. The disadvantages and drawbacks of GGFs are that (1) many of the funds that are raised have not yet been invested in projects, in large part because there is a deficit of suitable investment opportunities,

(2) GGFs often raise much less money than their stated targets,[108] (3) there are too many GGFs, which has led to excessive redundancy and low efficiency, (4) management quality of many funds is poor, (5) there is plenty of corruption, rent seeking, and other malpractices that create extensive waste and misuse of resources, (6) there is only limited investment in early-stage start-ups and much of the resources goes instead to mature ventures,[109] and (7) GGFs often fail to attract private sector capital, and many of the funders and stakeholders are government agencies and SOEs.

Although GGFs were first established in the early 2000s, they did not take off in general popularity and scale until the mid-2010s when the Xi regime began to actively encourage their use.[110] The 13th Five-Year Science, Technology, and Innovation Plan, for example, said that it would "expand the scale of entrepreneurial investment and government entrepreneurial investment guidance funds."[111]

The growth of the GGF sector since the second half of the 2010s has been rapid. According to an assessment by ChinaVenture Group, a Chinese investment advisory group specializing in the private equity and venture capital investment industry, the number of GGFs grew annually between 2012 and 2018 by 39 percent, while the total amount of funds increased annually by 69 percent.[112]

There were an estimated 1,741 GGFs with total targeted and actual fund sizes of RMB 11 trillion (US$1.59 trillion) and RMB 4.76 trillion (US$690 billion), respectively, by the first quarter of 2020, according to Zero2IPO.[113] A ChinaVenture assessment pointed out though that the rate of growth in funds had significantly decelerated since 2017, and the GGF industry had entered a "fund winter."

GOVERNMENT GUIDANCE FUNDS FOR MILITARY-CIVIL FUSION

MCF-related GGFs represent a small subset of the GGF industry and can be divided into two categories. First are what can be termed as MCF-dedicated funds whose chief purpose is to invest in MCF-specific activities tied to the national security and defense-related technological and industrial domains. Second are MCF-lite funds, which are GGFs that make limited investments in sectors that may have defense, dual-use, and broader strategic technology applications such as satellite navigation and integrated circuits and/or also have defense industrial corporations or PLA-affiliated entities as stakeholders.

A careful review of Chinese investment databases, financial media, corporate, and central and local government websites reveal eighty-three MCF-dedicated and MCF-lite funds that were established between 2010 and 2019 (see table 3.4).[114] Although there was substantial reporting of MCF-related GGF activities between 2010 and 2019, this information flow has since dried up and there has been no public announcements of any new MCF-related funds since the beginning of 2020.

TABLE 3.4   State of military-civil fusion–related government guidance funds, as of the end of 2019 (based on 2019 exchange rate)

FUND CATEGORY	NUMBER OF FUNDS	TOTAL VALUE OF FUNDS RMB BILLION (US$ BILLION)	GEOGRAPHIC LEVEL OF FUNDS
MCF-dedicated funds	39	238.5 (34.5) Actual raised	National funds: 8
		671.5 (97.2) Targeted	Subnational funds: 31
MCF-lite funds	44	633.8 (91.7) Actual raised	International funds: 1
		911.4 (131.9) Targeted	National funds: 11
			Subnational funds: 32
Total	83	872.3 (126.2) Actual raised	International funds: 1
		1,583 (229.1) Targeted	National funds: 19
			Subnational funds: 63

The publicly available data on MCF GGFs also suggests a similar trajectory to its civilian counterparts: rapid growth in the mid-2010s followed by a sharp retreat in the late 2010s. MCF-related fundraising peaked in 2016 and then posted moderate drops in 2017 and 2018. A far sharper fall took place in 2019. This apparent decline in the fortunes of the MCF GGF sector, though, is almost certainly due to a tight information clampdown on MCF funding activities by the authorities, rather than a pullback in investment demand. This is because as this falloff in MCF fundraising was supposedly occurring from 2017, the central authorities were giving the green light for a major ramp-up in market-based investment capital going into the defense industrial and MCF sectors. The State Council General Office issued an opinion in November 2017 promoting the flow of social capital for defense and dual-use investment, especially to support reforms allowing for mixed public-private ownership of military industrial enterprises.[115] The document called for "expanding investment and financing channels for MCF development, creating a national defense science, technology, and industry MCF industrial investment fund, and encouraging and supporting local governments and qualified institutions to set up related industrial investment funds."[116]

China's flagship MCF fund is the National Defense Science, Technology, and Industry MCF Industrial Investment Fund (国家国防科技工业军民融合产业投资基金, *Guojia Guofang Keji Gongye Junmin Ronghe Changye Touzi Jijin*), or Defense S&T MCF Investment Fund. Established in July 2018 by SASTIND in conjunction with CETC and the Fujian Provincial Economic and Informatization Commission, there has been very little public reporting about its activities.[117] The absence of information on such an important MCF funding vehicle means that there are significant gaps in understanding the nature and scale of the development of China's MCF funding efforts.

What is the volume of funds raised from GGFs? Caution is required in calculating the investment figures advertised by funds as different numbers are sometimes given for different purposes. Many funds provide an overall target of the amount of capital they seek to raise, but these goals are often overly optimistic.

A more realistic indicator of the role played by MCF-related GGFs is what has actually been raised in initial rounds of fundraising (see table 3.5 and figure 3.6). The figures for initial batches of capital raising by all MCF funds up to the end of 2019 was RMB 872.3 billion (US$126.2 billion), while total targeted investment was RMB 1.583 trillion (US$229 billion). Although the total of eighty-three MCF funds is equivalent to 4.8 percent of the total number of GGFs, their RMB 872.3 billion (US$126.2 billion) in raised fund holdings accounted for 18 percent of the total value of GGFs, which was valued at RMB 4.76 trillion (US$690 billion) in the first quarter of 2020. Sixty-three of the MCF funds, or 76 percent of the total number, are subnational funds, but they accounted for only RMB 251.6 billion (US$36.4 billion), or 28.8 percent, of total MCF funds that were raised in initial rounds. This underscores that MCF funds primarily serve central needs even though a growing number of provinces and municipalities are seeking to become MCF bases.

Among MCF-dedicated funds, thirty-nine have an aggregate value of actual funds raised of RMB 238.5 billion (US$34.5 billion) as of the end of 2019. Thirty-one of the funds, or 82 percent in total, were subnational funds either at the provincial or county/municipal level, while seven were national-level funds. MCF-dedicated subnational funds raised as of the end of 2019 totaled RMB 141 billion (US$20.4 billion), or 59 percent of all MCF-dedicated funds, while national funds totaled RMB 97.6 billion (US$14.1 billion).

Among MCF-lite funds, forty-four held a total value of RMB 752.8 billion (US$108.9 billion), of which thirty-two are subnational in origin and focus, eleven are national level, and one is a cross-national Sino-Russian fund. One example of an MCF-lite GGF is the RMB 139 billion (US$20.1 billion) National Integrated Circuit Industry Investment Fund. One of this fund's stakeholders is CETC, which held a tiny 0.9 percent stake with an RMB 35 million (US$5 million) investment.

An important caveat to the figures compiled here is that there was no financial information for nineteen of these funds, of which eleven were MCF-dedicated and eight were MCF-lite funds. This means that the actual size of the MCF funds sector is considerably larger than the statistics reported here.

Efforts by other Western and Chinese analysts to gauge the size of the Chinese MCF fund sector have produced considerably different results. This is due in part to definitional issues concerning what constitutes an MCF fund. In an October 2019 report, Audrey Fritz and Scott Kennedy of the Center for Strategic and International Studies identified forty-two MCF funds of which two were

TABLE 3.5 MCF funds raised annually, 2010–2019

	2010	2011	2012	2013	2014	2015	2016	2017	2018	2019
Total initial investment raised, RMB billion (US$ billion)	24 (3.5)	5 (0.8)	5.3 (0.8)	0	139.4 (22.6)	13.3 (2.1)	241.3 (36.3)	261.7 (38.7)	67.6 (10.2)	18.5 (2.7)
Total targeted amount to be raised, RMB billion (US$ billion)	24 (3.5)	5 (0.8)	5.3 (0.8)	0	139.4 (22.6)	29 (4.6)	471.3 (70.8)	388.3 (57.4)	355.1 (53.5)	60 (8.7)

Note: Exchange rates are based on specific years.

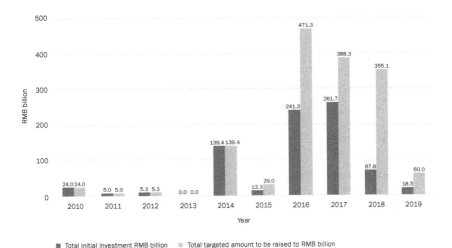

FIGURE 3.6.   Military-civil fusion funds raised annually, 2010–2019

national funds, twenty-seven were created by localities, and thirteen were set up by companies. These funds collectively totaled at least US$73 billion. They define MCF funds as encapsulating the concept of China's MCF strategy, which is a vague definition.[118] Another analysis of the MCF fund sector by ChinaVenture Institute (投中研究院) that was published in March 2019 identified twenty-three dedicated MCF funds.[119]

EXAMINATION OF THE TOP TEN MILITARY-CIVIL FUSION GOVERNMENT GUIDANCE FUNDS

Although there are more than eighty MCF-related GGFs, the ten largest actual or planned funds account for the lion's share of financial assets. These top ten funds had raised US$82 billion (RMB 566 billion) by 2019, which is 65 percent of all funds raised by MCF GGFs (see table 3.6). Overall fund targets issued by the top ten MCF GGFs by the end of 2019 totaled RMB 1.24 trillion (US$179 billion), or 79 percent of the combined target of all MCF GGFs. There is an even five-to-five split between MCF-dedicated and MCF-lite funds, although the latter category had by far the largest share of raised funds accounting for four of the top five slots.

The largest MCF-related fund is the China Structural Reform Fund Corporation Ltd. (CSRF), which accounts for 15 percent of all actual MCF funds raised. CSRF qualifies as an MCF-lite fund because one of its shareholders, CNGC, is a leading defense industrial conglomerate, and its broad investment scope includes defense and strategic technology and resources.[120] However, the overwhelming proportion of the investment portfolio of CSRF in its first few years of operation was in the civilian domain, such as airlines, electric power infrastructure,

TABLE 3.6 The ten largest military-civil fusion government guidance funds

No. 1: China Structural Reform Fund Co., Ltd. (中国国有企业结构调整基金)

Date of establishment/National or subnational status: September 2016/National

MCF intensity: Lite

Fund size: Overall goal of RMB 350 Bn (US$52.6 Bn based on 2016 exchange rate); RMB 131 Bn (US$19.7 Bn) of initial funds raised

Ownership: 10 central-level state-owned corporations including China Chengtong Holdings Group Co., Postal Savings Bank of China, China North Industries Group Corp., Sinopec, and China Mobile

Areas of investment focus: Third-generation nuclear power, internet of things, big data, new energy; support high-value international mergers and acquisitions, SOE globalization; defense and military, strategic material reserves, oil and gas backbone pipe network, power grids, communications infrastructure, and strategic mineral resources development

No. 2: National MCF Industry Investment Fund (国家军民融合产业投资基金)

Fund size: Overall goal of RMB 150 Bn (US$22.6 Bn); RMB 50 Bn (US$7.5 Bn based on 2018 exchange rate) of initial funds raised

Date of establishment/National or subnational status: December 2018/National

MCF intensity: Dedicated

Ownership: Ministry of Finance; Aviation Industry Corp. of China, Ltd.; China Electronics Technology Corp.; China Nuclear Industry Corp.; China Shipbuilding Industry Corp.

Areas of investment focus: Prime focus is investment in MCF projects directly and through subfunds with special attention on Jilin Province

No. 3: National Integrated Circuit Industry Investment Fund (国家集成电路产业投资基金)

Fund size: Overall goal of RMB 139 Bn (US$22.6 Bn); RMB 139 Bn (US$22.6 Bn based on 2014 exchange rate) raised

Date of establishment/National or subnational status: October 2014/National

MCF intensity: Lite

Ownership: Eight state-owned corporations and financial institutions including China Development Bank Capital Co., Ltd., China Tobacco Corp., China Mobile Communications Corp., Shanghai Guosheng (Group) Co., Ltd., and China Electronics Technology Corp.

Areas of investment focus: Integrated circuit chip manufacturing, chip design, packaging and testing, equipment, and materials industries

No. 4: China Innovation Fund (中央企业国创投资引导基金)

Fund size: Overall goal of RMB 150 Bn (US$22.2 Bn); RMB 113.9 Bn (US$16.8 Bn based on 2017 exchange rate) of initial funds raised

Date of establishment/National or subnational status: May 2017/National

MCF intensity: Lite

Ownership: Eight state-owned corporations, financial institutions, and local governments including China Aerospace Investment Holdings Ltd., Guoxin International, Industrial and Commercial Bank of China, Shanghai Pudong Development Bank, and Beijing Municipal Government

Areas of investment focus: MCF, 3D printing, aerospace, biological medicine, clean energy, high-speed rail, information technology, nuclear energy, power grid, quantum communication, robotics, and shipping industries

No. 5: Shanxi Provincial Government Investment Fund–Shanxi Taihang Industry Fund (山西省级政府投资基金-山西太行产业基金)

Fund size: Overall goal of RMB 105 Bn (US$15.5 Bn based on 2017 exchange rate); RMB 20 Bn (US$3 Bn) of initial funds raised

Date of establishment/National or subnational status: September 2017/Subnational

MCF intensity: Lite

Ownership: Key stakeholders include Shanxi provincial government, China Resources Capital Management Co., Ltd., and Taiyuan branch of Shanghai Pudong Development Bank

Areas of investment focus: New energy, Strategic Emerging Industries, innovation, small and medium enterprises, MCF; fund acts as a "mother fund" to invest in other industry-related funds

No. 6: Guangdong Provincial Industry Development Fund (广东省产业发展基金)

Fund size: Overall goal of RMB 50 Bn (US$7.4 Bn based on 2017 exchange rate); RMB 50 Bn (US$7.4 Bn) raised

Date of establishment/National or subnational status: December 2017/Subnational

MCF intensity: Lite

Ownership: More than a dozen Guangdong-based state-owned corporations, banking and financial institutions, and technology companies including Guangdong Yuecai Investment Holding Co., Ltd., Industrial and Commercial Bank of China Limited Guangdong Branch, Bank of China Limited Guangdong Branch (中国银行股份有限公司广东省分行), Agricultural Bank of China Limited Guangdong Branch, TCL Corp., Giant Ship Intelligent Equipment Co., Ltd., and Shenzhen Innovation Investment Group Co., Ltd.

Areas of investment focus: Next-generation information technology, high-end equipment manufacturing, low carbon emissions and environmental protection, biomedicine, digital innovation, new materials, industrial internet; support companies participating in One Belt, One Road, SOE reform, and MCF fields

No. 7: Haiying MCF Fund (海银军民融合基金)

Fund size: Overall goal of RMB 100 Bn (US$15.1 Bn based on 2018 exchange rate); No information on initial funds raised

Date of establishment/National or subnational status: March 2018/Subnational

MCF intensity: Dedicated

Ownership: Haiyin Wealth Management Co., Ltd.

Areas of investment focus: Investment in key industries to support MCF as well as investing in enterprises and projects with potential for military veterans to start their own businesses

No. 8: Shandong MCF Fund (山东军民融合产业基金)

Fund size: Overall goal of RMB 100 Bn (US$15.1 Bn based on 2018 exchange rate); No information on initial funds raised

Date of establishment/National or subnational status: March 2018/Subnational

MCF intensity: Dedicated

Ownership: Qingdao MCF Development Group Co., Ltd. and Qingdao West Coast New Area Private Enterprise Allied Investment Group Co., Ltd.

Areas of investment focus: Investment for defense industry, communications, new materials, new energy, and environmental protection

No. 9: Aviation Industry Investment Fund (航空工业产业投资基金)

Fund size: Overall goal of RMB 50 Bn (US$7.2 Bn based on 2019 exchange rate); RMB 12 Bn (US$1.7 Bn) of initial funds raised

Date of establishment/National or subnational status: July 2019/National

MCF intensity: Dedicated

Ownership: AVIC Capital, AVIC Rongfu, Guoshou Guangde (Tianjin) Equity Investment Fund, and Zhenjiang Dingqiang Intelligent Manufacturing Investment Partnership

Areas of investment focus: Investments within the aviation industry

No. 10: Henan Provincial MCF Industry Investment Fund (河南省军民融合产业投资基金)

Fund size: Overall goal of RMB 50 Bn (US$7.4 Bn based on 2017 exchange rate); RMB 50 Bn (US$7.4 Bn) raised

Date of establishment/National or subnational status: October 2017/Subnational

MCF intensity: Dedicated

Ownership: Six Henan-based corporations, financial institutions, and local governments including Luoyang municipal government, Henan Investment Group, and Henan Zhongqin Huirong Fund Management Co., Ltd.

Areas of investment focus: MCF industries, Luoyang National MCF Demonstration Zone, and Henan Provincial MCF Industry Base telecommunications, environmental protection, energy conservation, and financial technology.[121] Other large-sized MCF-lite funds such as the National Integrated Circuit Industry Investment Fund and the China Innovation Fund are also in a similar position to CSRF—that is, largely focused on civilian investment with a very small exposure to defense and dual-use activities.

CASE STUDY OF THE NATIONAL MILITARY-CIVIL FUSION INDUSTRY INVESTMENT FUND CO., LTD.

An examination of the top nine MCF-dedicated funds provides additional insights into the nature of China's MCF funding landscape. These nine funds account for three-quarters of the total amount of funds raised by MCF-dedicated funds (see table 3.7). Six of the nine funds are national-level funds, of which three are sector specific (two aviation, one shipbuilding), and the other three are general. The three provincial-level funds are intended for Shandong, Henan, and Jiangsu, which highlights the active presence of eastern coastal provinces in the MCF process.

A window into how an MCF-dedicated fund is structured, owned, and operationally oriented can be glimpsed through the National Military-Civil Fusion Industry Investment Fund Co., Ltd. (National MCF Fund; 国家军民融合产业投资基金有限责任公司 *Guojia Junmin Ronghe Changye Touzi Jijin Youxian Zeren Gongsi*). This fund was established in 2018 with a first investment round of RMB 50 billion (US$7.5 billion) and an ultimate goal of RMB 150 billion (US$22.6 billion). The fund's biggest shareholder is the Ministry of Finance, which invested

TABLE 3.7 Top nine military-civil fusion–dedicated funds

RANK	FUND NAME	PLANNED FUND SIZE/ACTUAL FUNDS RAISED (RMB BILLION)
1	National MCF Industry Investment Fund (国家军民融合产业投资基金)	150/50
2	Shandong MCF Fund (山东军民融合产业基金)	100/NA
3	Haiying MCF Fund (海银军民融合基金)	100/NA
4	Aviation Industry Investment Fund (航空工业产业投资基金)	50/12
5	Henan Provincial MCF Industry Investment Fund (河南省军民融合产业投资基金)	50/50
6	Sino MCF Industry Development Fund (国华军民融合产业发展基金)	30.2/30.2
7	Jiangsu MCF Industry Development Alliance Fund (江苏省军民融合产业发展联盟基金)	30/10
8	AVIC Industry Investment Fund (中航工业投资基金)	20/20
9	China Shipbuilding Industry Corp. MCF Industry Investment Fund (中船重工军民融合产业投资基金)	20/5
	Total size of planned funds/actual funds raised	**550.2/177.2**

RMB 8 billion (US$1.2 billion) for a 14.3 percent stake, followed by two defense corporations, CETC and AVIC, and a private firm, Beijing Zhongwang Investment Development Corporation, each with an 8.93 percent stake.[122]

Another two defense firms, CNNC and CSIC, and a municipal government–affiliated entity, Beijing Municipal Government Investment Guidance Fund, each have a 7.14 percent holding. In addition, there are twenty-four other companies with investment stakes of between 0.09 percent and 5.35 percent, of which nine are closely affiliated with the defense industry.

AVIC is the lead organizer of this fund even though the Ministry of Finance has the largest stake. In addition to the 8.93 percent stake that AVIC's parent company has in the fund, AVIC Capital Co., Ltd., the financial investment arm of the country's aviation industrial monopoly, has a 1.79 percent stake, giving AVIC a combined 10.72 percent share of the National MCF Fund. The fund is managed by Huihua Fund Management Co., Ltd., which was set up by AVIC Capital Co., Ltd. in partnership with CETC, CNNC, Zhongwang, and Tus Holdings.[123] Huihua is majority owned by AVIC Capital Co., Ltd. and is a major investment vehicle being used by AVIC to develop its business presence in the MCF domain.[124]

One of the stated goals of the National MCF Fund is to promote MCF development in Jilin Province even though seven other provinces are also shareholders with stakes equal to or larger than Jilin's meager 0.89 percent investment.[125] Many of the initial investments by the fund are in aviation-related areas, especially in the aero-engine sector.

Comparing Asset Securitization and Government Guidance Funds

In comparing the amount of funds that have been raised so far by AS and GGFs (see table 3.8), the AS process has been by far the most lucrative and impactful. Between 2012 and 2020, an average of RMB 283.1 billion (US$41 billion) were raised annually through AS funds, more than double the RMB 120.8 billion (US$17.5 billion) of average annual funds raised by MCF-related GGFs over the same period.

The investments raised from AS and GGFs are complementary and address different needs of the MCF and defense and dual-use ecosystems. GGFs are concentrated on funding start-ups and nonlisted companies, while AS funds go more to meeting current operational needs.

Besides AS and GGFs, bank loans and debt issues are also being used by the defense industry to tap into the capital markets. All of these mechanisms will likely be in heavy demand during the 2020s and beyond to support a significant acceleration in the development of the MCF ecosystem and PLA modernization. Whether there will be sufficient market appetite to meet the increasing investment

TABLE 3.8 A comparison of funds raised by military-civil fusion government guidance funds and defense-related asset securitization funds, 2012–2020 (exchange rates based on specific years)

YEAR	MCF GOVERNMENT GUIDANCE FUNDS RAISED, US$ BILLION (RMB BILLION)	ASSET SECURITIZATION FUNDS RAISED, US$ BILLION (RMB BILLION)
2012	0.8 (5.3)	160.2 (1011)
2013	0	46.9 (288.4)
2014	22.6 (139.4)	27.3 (168.4)
2015	2.1 (13.3)	61 (383)
2016	69.2 (460.3)	10.3 (68.3)
2017	38.7 (261.7)	30.5 (206.3)
2018	10.2 (67.6)	38.5 (255.3)
2019	2.7 (18.5)	2.8 (19.3)
2020	NA	22.3 (153.9)
Annual average funds raised	17.5 (120.8)	41 (283.1)

needs of the defense and dual-use sectors is a big question mark, although the interest generated so far suggests there is extensive public and market interest in defense and dual-use-related investment offerings.

The International Reach of Military-Civil Fusion

MCF is predominately focused on the reconfiguration and integration of the domestic Chinese civilian and defense economies, but there are important global dimensions and implications to this process. Three functional and geographical issues are especially worth highlighting. Two address the role of MCF in supporting the expansion of China's external geostrategic and geo-economic influence and presence through defense and dual-use exports, especially in new and emerging technologies, and across the vast expanse of the Belt and Road (一带一路, *Yidai Yilu*) Initiative (BRI). The third area of examination involves the role of MCF as a source of external technological and knowledge acquisition and the intensifying international controversy that this is generating, especially in the United States.

On the role of MCF in China's defense and high-technology exports, the November 2017 State Council General Office "Opinions on the In-Depth Development of Military-Civil Fusion" pointed out that an important task of MCF is to support the expansion of military trade and international cooperation that could be achieved by promoting advanced high-technology products being made by MCF-affiliated sectors. The opinions highlighted technologies such as civilian nuclear equipment, aviation and space technologies, and advanced ships, but in addition to these mature large-scale technologies, there are several new and emerging dual-use technologies with highly promising export potential, of which unmanned aerial vehicles (UAV) and surveillance technology stand out.

The Chinese UAV industry has grown rapidly since the beginning of the 2010s in both the military and civilian sectors. In the defense domain, the monopoly state-owned defense aviation and aerospace corporations are the leading producers of high-end strike-capable drones such as the Rainbow (彩虹, *Caihong*) series by CASC and the Wing Loong (翼龙) by AVIC's Chengdu Aircraft Industry Group. According to an analysis by the Center for Strategic and International Studies of Chinese military drone exports between 2008 and 2018, China was the world's third leading global military drone supplier with 163 drones sold, a third of which were Rainbow and more than half were Wing Loong UAVs.[126] The biggest purchasers were from the Middle East led by the United Arab Emirates and Saudi Arabia.[127] A requirement of some of these sales was the establishment of joint drone production and maintenance facilities. Saudi Arabia signed a deal to acquire three hundred Chinese UAVs in 2017 after China agreed to set up a manufacturing and servicing plant in Saudi Arabia for Wing Loong UAVs.

The Chinese commercial UAV industry has grown even more quickly than its military counterpart. There was reportedly a tenfold increase in the number of Chinese civilian drone producers between 2012 and 2018 from around 120 to more than 1,200. Chinese firms held upwards of an 80 percent share of the global drone market in the late 2010s. DJI is the runaway leader and has enjoyed a 70 percent share of the global market annually since the mid-2010s with its inventory of retail consumer-based products.[128] Although the vast majority of DJI drones are used for civilian purposes, a small number have been used by frontline US Army units for tactical surveillance missions. However, the employment of these drones was banned by the US Army in 2017 over concerns that the information they collected could be transmitted to Chinese authorities.[129]

Chinese commercial drone manufacturers and operators in the business, academic, logistics, and industrial sectors have been actively engaged in developing MCF collaborations with PLA and defense industrial entities. The military and national security market is lucrative but extremely difficult and costly for commercial drone firms to penetrate because of the extensive barriers to entry into the acquisition system. There has been no shortage of firms, though, that are willing to make the effort to sell to military customers because of the cutthroat competition in the civilian market.[130] Some drone firms that have had some MCF success include Xian Aisheng Technology Group, which is also known as the UAV Research Institute of Northwestern Polytechnical University. Three types of Aisheng UAVs participated in the PLA's ninetieth-anniversary parade in 2017 and the research institute is the country's only key special UAV technology laboratory.[131]

Another leading civilian MCF player is Shenzhen-based AEE Technology Co., Ltd., which was the only civilian drone firm to participate in the drafting of UAV standards by the PLA and Ministry of Public Security. AEE's small drones are used by military and public security units for aerial surveillance because of their extended endurance capabilities.[132] After a flare-up in China-India border tensions in 2017 in the Doklam region, thirty sets of AEE drones were sent to the front line to carry out military and law enforcement missions.[133] Although these civilian drone makers appear to have limited their MCF business activities to Chinese national security customers so far, the global dual-use marketplace represents a golden opportunity ripe for exploitation as the case of the DJI drones in US military service underscores.

The second important geographical dimension in MCF's emerging international profile is the growing role that dual-use technology and infrastructure is playing in supporting the expansion of China's geostrategic and geo-economic presence, of which the BRI is a central gateway. Chinese analysts argue that the BRI and MCF go hand in hand because of overlapping economic, investment, strategic, trade, and technological interests. The State Council General Office Document No. 91 in 2017 pointed out that as part of the implementation of the BRI, emphasis should be given to promoting nuclear power plants and nuclear equipment, aviation and aerospace equipment, and the construction of a BRI "space information" corridor (空间信息走廊, *kongjian xinxi zoulang*).

The development of this ambitious BRI space information corridor is being led by SASTIND and NDRC, who issued a joint "Guiding Opinions on Accelerating the Construction and Application of the 'Belt and Road' Space Information Corridor" in 2016. The aim of this ten-year project is to utilize China's growing space-based satellite assets to provide an integrated information system for countries along the BRI served by Chinese weather, communications, navigation, data relay, and remote sensing satellites.[134] This system would require China to build ground stations and information networks in many of these countries to be able to receive, process, and use the data. This space information corridor would be closely linked to China's global BeiDou Navigation Satellite System (北斗卫星导航系统, *Beidou Weixing Daohang Xitong*) and the Earth-Space Integrated Information Network project, which is one of the sixteen strategic programs in STI 2030.

Hand in hand with the development of the space information corridor is the establishment of a digital version of BRI in which Chinese firms, closely overseen by the Chinese government, are building a comprehensive cyber-secure digital information infrastructure that covers much of the maritime belt and continental road. This includes international optical cable systems, international submarine cable lines, broadband network infrastructure, internet of things projects, and 5G network infrastructure. As of late 2019, sixteen countries had joined the BRI Digital Economy International Cooperation Initiative, including Egypt, Saudi Arabia, United Arab Emirates, Serbia, Thailand, and Turkey.[135]

In the nuclear field, the Chinese nuclear industry has been extremely active in promoting the export of its civilian nuclear capabilities, and many of the countries that have expressed interest and signed deals are associated with the BRI.[136] Pakistan has been China's biggest customer so far and the only country where Chinese-built nuclear power stations are in operation. China has exported six reactors to Pakistan of which four CNP-300s are already in operation at Chasma. Another two advanced Hualong One reactors are being built near Karachi. China has also signed agreements and memorandums of understanding to build or refurbish nuclear power plants in the United Kingdom, Turkey, Kenya, Egypt, Iran, Sudan, South Africa, Armenia, and Kazakhstan. However, several of these transactions are in doubt because of geostrategic tensions, such as the deal with the United Kingdom.[137] A long-running deal for China to build a nuclear power plant in Romania was canceled in June 2020 because of misgivings by the Romanian government over funding and other issues.[138] Argentina has also been in advanced negotiations with China for nuclear power stations, although it is not geographically part of the BRI. Chinese analysts estimate that 80 percent of around 240 nuclear power stations that are forecast to be built globally by 2030 will take place along the BRI, and China is seeking to build at least thirty of these units.[139]

The third international dimension is the role of MCF as an instrument for acquiring foreign technology and knowledge. This feature has become a prominent part of international perceptions that MCF poses a serious national security and economic threat, especially with the United States and its allies. One area that has received elevated attention is the role of MCF in academic engagement between Chinese military and civilian universities and counterparts in the United States, Australia, and other Western states. The Chinese MCF authorities make no secret of their desire to engage in international academic cooperation on MCF. The 13th Five-Year MCF S&T Plan is keen to "encourage cooperation with internationally renowned scientific research institutions, establish research and development institutions overseas, build a number of international cooperation platforms such as joint research centers, technology transfer centers, technology demonstration and promotion bases, and science and technology parks with countries with innovative advantages in related fields, and create innovative development models for military-civil fusion."[140]

Some analysts argue that the central purpose of this collaboration, much of which is covert and masterminded by the CCP, is to acquire technology and know-how to support China's military modernization. Alex Joske, an analyst at the Australian Strategic Policy Institute, is a leading proponent of MCF as an intelligence conduit. He argues that MCF is important in enabling Chinese civilian universities to pursue international research collaboration with its foreign counterparts and to recruit foreign talent to support China's military modernization efforts, especially through programs such as the Double First-Class University Plan that he says is tied to MCF.[141] Sixty-eight universities are identified as "parts of the defense system or are supervised by" SASTIND. Among academic institutions under this "supervision" are some of the country's premier entities including Peking University, Tsinghua University, Zhejiang University, and Nanjing University. There is no definition of what "supervision" means, but the implication from the report is that Chinese civilian universities are inextricably increasing their integration with the country's defense and national security, especially intelligence, apparatuses. One of the conclusions that Joske makes is that there is "a growing risk that collaboration" with Chinese universities can be leveraged by the PLA or security agencies "for surveillance, human rights abuses, or military purposes."

Although plenty of robust evidence has been uncovered by Joske and others about the deepening relationship between Chinese universities and MCF,[142] there are serious weaknesses with the analysis, especially imprecision and a lack of context. In these assessments, MCF is viewed as an effective enterprise that has a long-running and successful track record, and any ties uncovered between defense/military agencies and civilian academic institutions mean that these latter entities should be considered part of the MCF system. Moreover, there is no effort to provide comparative context to show that the deep defense-academia relationship in China is not unique. The United States is the most obvious comparison, with the Pentagon and national security community fostering expansive long-term relationships with many institutions of which some of the most prominent are the Massachusetts Institute of Technology, Stanford University, and Johns Hopkins University.[143] The high point of these ties was during the Cold War, but they remain broad and deep in the twenty-first century.[144]

Western governments, led by the United States under the Donald Trump administration, have made use of these assessments to target MCF as a clear and present danger to their national security. Mid-level US policymakers such as Christopher Ford, assistant secretary of state for International Security and Non-Proliferation Affairs in the Trump administration, began to talk about the threat posed by MCF in 2019.[145] Ford offered a number of assertions about the nature and implications of MCF:

- MCF is "nothing like what normal countries do," which is to "seek to encourage innovation and growth in their economies."
- MCF has meant that China is taking "technology-seeking to unprecedented levels" and applying "heavy-handed coerciveness."

- MCF "now constitutes a major national security challenge" for the United States, China's neighbors, "and any country with a stake in the open international order historically underpinned by US leadership."
- MCF "is backed by the full force of national law and the coercive powers of the state, leaving no one within Beijing's reach any choice but to comply with its dictates."[146]

This ideological narrative that MCF is an unprecedented, coercive, deviant technology-stealing threat to the United States and its democratic allies became the accepted dogma of the Trump administration and only further justified an earlier determination in the 2017 National Security Strategy and 2018 National Defense Strategy that China was its biggest long-term strategic challenge. US defense secretary Mark Esper said in January 2020 that "President Xi Jinping's elevation of the 'Military-Civil Fusion Strategy' to a national level puts our exports for peaceful, civilian use at risk of transfer" to the PLA.[147] The White House in May 2020 issued a statement on efforts to protect the United States from Chinese attempts to steal technology and intellectual property and pointed out that "China's MCF strategy is an attempt to develop the most technologically advanced military in the world by any means necessary, including by co-option and coercion. Through China's MCF strategy, the People's Liberation Army is using certain Chinese students and researchers to steal American technological secrets and innovations. President Trump has issued a proclamation to block certain graduate level and above Chinese nationals associated with entities in China that implement or support China's Military-Civil Fusion (MCF) strategy, from using F or J visas to enter the United States."[148] US congressional legislators across the political spectrum have joined in these efforts to restrict China's access to the US academic and research system by drafting laws to curb or ban Chinese students and researchers from entering the United States to study or conduct research in the sciences, technology, engineering, and mathematics fields.[149]

For the US political and policy communities, MCF has conveniently emerged to represent all that is evil and threatening about the Chinese Communist party-state: a dark-of-the-night boogeyman seeking to fatally undermine the American way of life. Although there are certainly aspects of MCF that warrant concern and careful scrutiny, it is a very long way from posing an existential danger to the United States and its allies. There will be a detailed discussion of the strategic and security implications of the rise of MCF and the Chinese techno-security state, for the United States and the world, in the concluding chapter.

This US-led scrutiny and demonization of MCF led the Chinese authorities to begin to conceal MCF activities in 2019. There has been no official reporting of the meetings of the CMCFDC since late 2018. There was little mention of MCF at the NPC annual meeting in May 2020, and there has been a decline in media coverage of MCF activities.[150] MCF was not mentioned in the 14th Five-Year Plan, although there is abundant reference to CMI-focused activities and priorities. Although MCF activities have played a major role in the Chinese state's response to the COVID-19 pandemic, Xi has avoided mentioning MCF and has instead talked about military-civil unity (军民团结, *junmin tuanjie*) to describe civil-military cooperation.[151] Increasing secrecy and controversy about MCF presents a considerable deterrent to its future development because it undermines the importance of transparency and access to information and greatly amplifies the geopolitical risks for civilian companies considering the pros and cons of becoming involved in MCF activities.

Xi's Vision of an Integrated National Strategic System

The herculean efforts to implement MCF is the result of the investment of considerable time, effort, and political capital by Xi Jinping. Without his personal involvement in this issue, MCF would have remained a floundering mid-tier policy initiative lacking political support that would occasionally receive passing leadership attention. The elevation of MCF to a national-level development strategy in 2015 was quickly followed by consequential structural, regulatory, and policy initiatives as well as significant resource flows and commitments.

In 2017, Xi put forward the next grand step for his MCF vision, which was the goal of gradually establishing a civil-military integrated national strategic system with capabilities. He put forward this idea at the inaugural plenary meeting of the CMCFDC, but media reports offered no details to describe what he actually meant.[152] Xi repeated this vague notion of an integrated national strategic system (INSS) in his 19th Party Congress keynote address, and the Chinese MCF policy community has scrambled to come up with explanations of INSS as well as offer policy ideas for its implementation.

In a review of the initial policy debate by MCF policy scholars after Xi's 19th Party Congress speech mentioning INSS, NUDT scholars Huang Chaofeng (黄朝峰) and Ma Junyang (马浚洋) argued that Xi's idea was a "major strategic proposition" to tightly integrate the national security and national development systems.[153] This would considerably broaden the scope of MCF beyond just the military and civilian spheres to the national security and national development domains. A number of prominent MCF scholars agreed that this was the intention of Xi's remarks. NDU academics Jiang Luming and Wang Weihai (王伟海) said that the fundamental goal in building the INSS was to "reshape the national security and development strategy systems under the framework of integrated economic and defense construction," which would significantly enhance China's innovation capacity, military deterrence effectiveness, and global economic competitiveness.[154]

Policy research on the INSS concept is in its infancy, but the topic will almost certainly command high priority for policymakers and the MCF policy research community that will have to come up with the rationales, strategies, and implementation plans based on Xi's guidance. The rise in importance of the securitization of the Chinese economy since the late 2010s is one area with plenty of scope for complementarity and coordination with the development of the INSS framework.

Another techno-industrial program that could also be brought under the INSS umbrella is the strategic emerging industries (SEIs; 战略性新兴产业, *zhanluexing xinxing chanye*) initiative. SEIs have been mentioned in passing in MCF development strategies and plans such as the July 2016 "Opinions on the Integrated Development of Economic Construction and Defense Construction" but have not received detailed policy attention. The SEI initiative was originally a technology and industrial policy initiative from the Hu administration in 2010 in response to the global financial crisis but received little leadership attention after Xi took power.[155] The initiative, though, was subsequently revived and enlarged by the Xi regime in the 13th and 14th Five-Year Plans. The main areas of focus of the SEI initiative are in five so-called pillar industries that include biotechnology, information technology, green and low-carbon industry, high-end manufacturing, and the digital and creative industries.[156]

MILITARY STRENGTHENING

The Maoist adage that power flows from the barrel of a gun is at the very core of Xi Jinping's approach to propelling the country to the pinnacle of the global techno-security order. The possession of a strong, vibrant, and technologically advanced military and defense economic apparatus is pivotal to Xi's project of national rejuvenation and the forging of a potent techno-security state. Xi's thinking on the building of China's military power is formally known as Military Strengthening in the New Era (新时期的强军, *Xinshiqide Qiangjun*) and is codified and enshrined in the Chinese Communist Party (CCP) constitution as part of a more extensive collection of "Xi Jinping Thoughts on Socialism with Chinese Characteristics in the New Era."[1]

Xi's guiding thoughts on military strengthening calls for a three-step transformation of Chinese military power to the middle of the twenty-first century.[2] The first step was to achieve the mechanization of the People's Liberation Army (PLA) by 2020 along with making major progress in the development of "informatization" and strategic capabilities. This has been largely accomplished. The second, more ambitious phase is to "basically" complete defense modernization by 2035, which would mean that the PLA and the defense science, technology, and industrial base would have finally caught up with the world's top tier of advanced defense countries. The third and most challenging stage is for China to become a comprehensive world-leading military power by 2050 in which it would begin to compete to overtake the United States in global superiority.

Half a dozen issues will be addressed in this chapter that are essential to understanding the relationship between Xi's strategic thinking on military strengthening and the Chinese techno-security state. First is the crystallization of Xi's thinking on military strengthening since coming to power. Second is the nature and relationship between China's national military strategy, or what is known as the Military Strategic Guidelines (MSG: 军事战略方针, *Junshi Zhanlue Fangzhen*), and the strategies and policies guiding the country's development of its weapons and defense equipment. Third is the PLA's ability to foster military technological innovation and armament development. Fourth is the efforts of the defense industrial base to reform and modernize its capabilities to ensure that it keeps up with the demands of military end users. Fifth is assessing the array of defense technology and weapons development programs directly responsible for the modernization of the PLA's combat capabilities that includes the 995 New High-Technology Project, Defense Medium- and Long-Term Science and Technology Development Plan, and five-year plans. Finally, an effort to measure the progress in China's military strengthening drive is conducted through an analysis of the generational upgrading of the PLA's frontline arsenal between the end of the 1980s and the end of the 2010s.

Xi's Strategic Thinking on Military Strengthening

One of the chief purposes of the Chinese techno-security state is to enable the development of a strong, technologically advanced and politically reliable military establishment that is able to meet an expanding portfolio of missions and responsibilities. However, the PLA has rarely had the luxury of enjoying high-end military technological self-reliance, which is a basic requirement for any aspiring great power. The development of strategic nuclear and ballistic missile deterrent capabilities in the 1960s and 1970s was one of those occasional moments when self-sufficiency was achieved in advanced military capabilities. However, for the most part the conventional weapons system has struggled mightily because of chronic early dependence on imported Soviet technologies and know-how and deep-seated structural barriers that stymied coordination and development.[3]

There is rising optimism and expectation within the contemporary Chinese defense establishment that this dismal state of affairs is coming to a decisive end and the country will soon be able to join the world's advanced defense industrial powers at the global technological frontier. The overarching objective of Xi's military strengthening guidance is to catch up and then lead as quickly as possible. This requires close coordination and collaboration between the military strengthening guidance, the Innovation-Driven Development Strategy (IDDS), national security strategy, and military-civil fusion (MCF) development strategy. Whether by accident or design, these four strategies combine to form a comprehensive and cohesive interlocking development approach. They were all drawn up during Xi's first term and his hands-on involvement in the making of each of these strategies is the glue that binds them closely together.

Xi began to put forward his ideas and thinking on military strengthening immediately on becoming party general secretary and Central Military Commission (CMC) chairman at the 18th Party Congress in November 2012. At an expanded CMC meeting following the congress, the new commander in chief instructed the assembled military chiefs that the PLA needed to step up its deterrent and combat readiness, be prepared for military struggle, and embrace a revolution in military affairs with Chinese characteristics.[4]

Xi has expended enormous time and effort on formulating and promoting his military strengthening guidance. One measure of this investment is Xi's numerous visits and inspections of military and defense science, technology, and industrial facilities and his attendance at key military and defense science and technology (S&T) meetings. Between 2012 and 2020, Xi conducted around 120 military and defense S&T-related visits, meetings, and conferences that were publicized, or the equivalent of thirteen visits annually (see figure 4.1).[5]

One of the most high-profile ways in which Xi has shown off his paramount military authority has been his participation in large-scale military parades between 2015 and 2019. In his first decade in power, from 2012 to 2021, Xi took the salute at five parades, compared to just one each for Deng Xiaoping, Jiang Zemin, and Hu Jintao during their tenures.[6] The fifth and largest was an October 2019 parade in Beijing to mark the seventieth anniversary of the founding

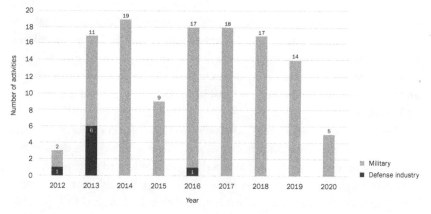

FIGURE 4.1. Xi Jinping's military and defense science, technology, and industry engagements, November 2012–2020

of the People's Republic of China. This level of engagement is a clear political signal by Xi about the indispensable importance of the military to his rule.

Although these public demonstrations of Xi's role as commander in chief provide for good propaganda, the actual implementation of his military strengthening guidance has been a far more complex and challenging undertaking. This is because the highly conservative military establishment has jealously guarded its professional autonomy from its party masters, especially from civilian leaders with limited military experience.[7] To bend the powerful PLA hierarchy to his will, Xi launched a two-pronged shock-and-reform campaign beginning in 2013. The shock component consisted of a sweeping ideological discipline and anti-corruption campaign that targeted senior levels of the officer corps.

The military corruption crackdown has been unprecedented in its breadth, scale, and duration. More than one hundred generals at or above the grade of corps-level commanders were punished in Xi's first term and another thirteen thousand PLA and People's Armed Police (PAP) officers at or above the regiment level were audited at the height of the campaign between 2013 and 2017.[8] A sizable number of senior officers have also been caught in the anti-corruption campaign during Xi's second term, most prominent of which was General Fang Fenghui (房峰辉), the chief of the CMC Joint Staff between 2012 and 2017, who received a life sentence in 2019, and General Zhang Yang (张阳), the head of the CMC Political Work Department from 2012 to 2017, who committed suicide shortly after stepping down.[9]

The political discipline campaign was undertaken because Xi had worried that the party's grip over the PLA had steadily declined during the reform era and there were serious ideological problems within the officer corps that cast a shadow over their political loyalties. In November 2014, Xi used the eighty-fifth anniversary of the 1929 Gutian Conference to host a second version of the namesake meeting to address PLA political work in which more than four hundred generals attended.[10] The first Gutian meeting was a seminal moment when Mao Zedong was able to enshrine the principle of Communist Party control of the military as a core party doctrine that has set the tone for the PLA's political work ever since. The goal of this second Gutian political disciplinary undertaking was to provide "strong political guarantees for realizing the party's goal of military strengthening in the new situation." Officers were required to undertake intensive political reindoctrination courses to reinvigorate their revolutionary spirit, which centered on promoting total allegiance to Xi.

This crackdown allowed Xi to assert sweeping authority over the military establishment. The PLA leadership became politically and professionally acquiescent, allowing Xi to embark on the second prong of his campaign to implement his military strengthening initiative focusing on overhauling the operational and war-fighting side of the PLA. Of particular importance was updating military strategies and associated plans, revamping the organizational command and control system, and pursuing high-end armament and technological development and innovation.

The Relationship between Military Strategy and Weapons Development Strategy

The application of Xi's high-level military thinking into the duties, missions, and responsibilities of the military establishment is the domain of the MSG, which constitutes the PLA's "programs and principles for planning and guiding the overall situation of war in a given period," or how the PLA would prepare to fight a future war.[11] The technological, economic, industrial, and innovation-related means available for war fighting fall within the scope of the Weapons and Equipment Development Strategy (WEDS; 武器装备发展战略, *Wuqi Zhuangbei Fazhan Zhanlue*) and its associated implementation plans. As the MSG and WEDS are classified, any examination of their nature and contents is limited to circumstantial evidence.

The formulation of the MSG is overseen by the CMC and carried out in coordination with numerous PLA units.[12] The MSG addresses a multiplicity of factors including external threat perceptions, likely contingencies, geostrategic assessments, and domestic concerns, and identifies tasks crucial for determining the likely nature of future wars. Four are especially relevant to the examination of the relationship with techno-security innovation. The first is the identification of the strategic opponent (战略对手, *zhanlue duishou*). This is based on an assessment of the international security environment and consideration of threats to China's national interests. The United States was the principal enemy between the 1950s and early 1960s, followed by the Soviet Union from the mid- to late 1960s to the end of the 1970s. Chinese military authorities have not publicly identified their principal strategic opponent since the 1980s, but some internal PLA writings suggest that the United States became China's principal strategic opponent (but not enemy) beginning in the 2000s.

One prescient assessment of the regional security environment by Chinese military analysts affiliated with the Academy of Military Sciences (AMS) in 2011 argued that "the United States does not want to see big powers like China and Russia to grow stronger, and it particularly fears that China's rapid rise would hurt its own status as the global hegemon. Therefore, the United States sees China as its potential strategic opponent."[13] The study detailed that what was especially worthy of attention was the fact that

> the United States has already shifted the focus of its military prevention, containment, and strike on China. The United States has sped up its advancement of the building of its strategic missile defense system; used the war against terrorism as an excuse to establish a military presence in Central Asia; wooed India to expand its military influence in South Asia; further increased its troops deployment in the Asia-Pacific region and turned Guam into a front support point for strategic delivery and strategic strike; supported Japan's effort to break free from the "defense only" restriction so as to have Japan play a role in Asia; sped up its effort to advance its military ties with its Asia-Pacific allies, such as establishing bilateral U.S.-Japan, U.S.-Republic of Korea, U.S.-Philippines, and U.S.-Australia military alliances, and helping its allies adopt U.S. military structures and staffing, weapons and equipment, technical standards, and command process to realize interconnection and communication with its allies' military information systems and to realize intelligence and information sharing. All of those, though done with multiple considerations and multiple levels of strategic goals in mind, point to the main strategic target: China.[14]

PLA analysts say China "must absolutely" respond to these US moves with the development of "strategic balancing capabilities" capable of breaking through this perceived containment and encirclement. They argue that "if China does not have this kind of military capability, then it will become a colossus with feet of clay."[15] They are aware, though, that such responses may lead to an "intense arms race."[16]

A second concept is the main strategic direction (MSD; 主要战略方向, *zhuyao zhanlue fangxiang*), which refers to the geographic focal point for potential conflict and provides the basis for the prioritization of resource allocations. The MSD is a contingency-based assessment that informs wartime operations and peacetime war planning for "worst-case" scenarios to develop forces and capabilities and make deployment decisions. Only one MSD is permitted at any time, although multiple secondary strategic directions are allowed. The MSD has shifted extensively over the course of the history of the People's Republic of China, initially focused on threats from its east between the early 1950s and early 1960s in the direction of the United States and regional allies such as Japan and Taiwan. The MSD pivoted to China's north and northwest from the mid-1960s to the mid-1980s to face off against the Soviet Union. There was a lull between the mid-1980s and early 1990s when there was no major state-based threat, but

Taiwan became the MSD from the early 1990s and has continued to occupy this position at the beginning of the 2020s, although the threat aperture has likely widened to include the role of the United States in any Taiwan contingency. The third component is the "basis of preparations for military struggle" (军事斗争准备的基点, *junshi douzheng zhunbei de jidian*), which is concerned with the nature and form of future war (total, local, conventional, or nuclear) that China will need to fight and the patterns of operations that will need to be conducted.

The fourth component is army construction and development (军队建设发展, *jundui jianshe fazhan*), which is concerned with all aspects of the PLA's modernization, development, and reform efforts. The MSG guidance on construction and development provides the broad priorities and parameters for the detailed formulation of near-, medium-, and long-term implementation plans. One of the most important of these programs is the "Outline of the Five-Year Plan for Army Construction and Development" (军队建设发展规划纲要, *Jundui Jianshe Fazhan Guihua Gangyao*), which comes out at the same time as the national five-year development plan. The outline of the 13th Five-Year Plan for Army Construction and Development was the first to be prepared and issued during Xi's rule in 2016 and heavily reflects the priorities and goals of the MSG.[17] An extensive array of construction, development, and reform tasks are covered, which include (1) ideological and political work, (2) force structure, (3) weapons and equipment, (4) logistics, (5) information infrastructure, (6) military training, (7) defense mobilization, (8) international military cooperation, (9) defense technological innovation, (10) military theory and regulations, (11) battlefield support, and (12) MCF. The outline emphasizes that priority should be placed on military struggle preparations.

The MSG dates back to the early years of the People's Republic of China and has been continually adjusted and updated on a rolling basis to take into account constantly changing security dynamics.[18] Taylor Fravel has identified nine iterations of the MSG from 1956 to the mid-2010s that he divides into two baskets depending on whether the changes to their content were minor or major in nature. Three versions in 1956, 1980, and 1993 had major changes, which Fravel defines as requiring the PLA to "change how it prepares to fight future wars."[19] Six other adjustments (1960, 1964, 1977, 1988, 2004, and 2014) involved only minor modifications.

The 1993 "Winning Local Wars under High-Technology Conditions" MSG was the PLA's post–Cold War baseline military strategy and marked a far-reaching break from its Maoist past. One of the major changes was the elevation of S&T to the forefront of the PLA's priorities. The 2004 and 2014 editions produced what appeared to be only incremental updates to the PLA's thinking about waging future wars. The 2004 MSG titled "Winning Local Wars under Informatized Conditions" emphasized the importance of informatization, which continued to be the prime focus in the 2014 MSG with the label of "Winning Informatized Local Wars." Although the title change appears prosaic, some PLA analysts argue that this adjustment is significant because informatization has shifted from being important to becoming the dominant factor in a future war.[20]

Whereas Fravel dates the most recent MSG to 2014, the Chinese government issued a 2015 defense white paper on "China's Military Strategy" that amounted to a de facto public outline of the MSG. The white paper spelled out noteworthy adjustments to the country's military strategy, especially the need for heightened preparations for maritime conflict, information-era warfare, and the prioritization of the oceans, outer space, and cyberspace as the new "critical security domains."[21] The document is circumspect in mentioning the United States in its assessment of intensifying global defense technological competition and its implications for China's national security. "The world revolution in military affairs is proceeding to a new stage. Long-range, precise, smart, stealthy and unmanned weapons and equipment are becoming increasingly sophisticated."

The white paper provided an assessment of the global strategic environment that highlighted several significant technological trends. The first was that the global revolution in military affairs was at a new stage and "posing new and severe challenges to China's military security." A second feature of the rapidly evolving technological landscape was the emergence of new domains of which outer space and cyberspace are emphasized as the "new commanding heights in strategic competition." A third accelerating trend was a fundamental change in the nature of warfare toward informatization, which refers to the information age and the rise of information-related processes and capabilities. The white paper pointed out that it was the "major powers"—primarily referring to the United States—that are in the vanguard of this process and are "speeding up their military transformation and force restructuring."

Moreover, the white paper stressed the importance of "maritime military struggle" in future preparations for military struggle. This signaled that the PLA Navy now stands at or near the top of priorities among the service arms. There was also an important change in naval strategy that added "open-seas protection" (远海护卫, *yuanhai huwei*) to the list of the PLA Navy's chief missions alongside its traditional "offshore defense" strategy. By comparison, the 2010 and 2013 defense white papers had only mentioned that the PLA Navy was developing "open-sea" capabilities.[22]

Whereas a strict military interpretation of the post-1993 MSGs would show more continuity than change in the PLA's perspectives on future war, a broader and more holistic examination of the MSG going beyond narrow war-fighting parameters would yield a different and more complex picture of accelerating and disruptive change in the nature and thinking of Chinese military power and the evolving state of war in the twenty-first century. One argument that can be made is that the 2014 MSG should be regarded as a short-term placeholder for a more far-reaching and comprehensive revision that will occur in the coming years. The drafting of the 2014 MSG took place in the early years of the Xi administration and ahead of the completion of the major innovation, national security, and military strengthening strategies. All of these strategies point out that the 2010s are a transitionary stage of development and more deep-seated and transformative improvements will only materialize from the 2020s onward.

Several of the key components of the 2014 MSG show signs of major change that cumulatively point to a far more consequential change to China's thinking and approach to future war than the assessment offered by Fravel. First is the concept of military struggle. From solely a war-fighting prism, the 2014 MSG made what appears to be a modest amendment from winning local wars under informatized conditions to winning informatized local wars. However, some Chinese military analysts argue that the Xi regime introduced an important shift by broadening the scope of the meaning of military struggle to incorporate other dimensions of geostrategic struggle. In an article examining the 2014 MSG, Senior Colonel Luo Derong (骆德荣), an associate professor at the PLA Nanjing Political Science Academy, pointed out that China should "combine military struggle with political and diplomatic struggle."[23] In addition, Luo points out that the 2014 MSG includes references to the Holistic National Security Concept that views China's national security more expansively to cover economic and domestic affairs. Moreover, China has embraced the use of so-called grayzone tactics that blur the civilian-military divide.

Second is the identification of the strategic opponent. At the time that the 2014 MSG was being drawn up, the military-strategic competition between the United States and China was still in its infancy and the two countries continued to pursue cooperative working relations. From the mid-2010s, however, and especially with the arrival of the Trump administration in 2016, the pace, scale, and intensity of bilateral military rivalry escalated across the defense spectrum from defense technological competition to contested forward military deployments in the Asia-Pacific region and major adjustments in force structures directly targeting the other side. For example, the US Marine Corps announced in 2020 that it would undergo a far-reaching revamp to become lighter and mobile so that it would be better able to contest against Chinese forces in the Asia-Pacific region.[24]

The PLA had been very careful in its official public assessments of the United States as a military and strategic threat, but this began to change in the second half of the 2010s. Whereas the 2015 Chinese defense white paper made only mild and indirect comments about the United States, the 2019 version is more pointed and direct in identifying the United States as the main culprit in undermining stability and challenging China's national security through "growing hegemonism, power politics, unilateralism, and constant regional conflicts and war."[25] The white paper adds that the United States "has provoked and intensified competition among major countries, significantly increased defense expenditures, pushed for additional capacity in nuclear, outer space, cyber, and missile defense, and undermined global strategic stability."

Third is the army construction and development component. A number of subcomponents have undergone considerable adjustments that include ideological and political work, force structure and organizational reforms, defense technological innovation, MCF, and weapons and equipment development. Xi summed up the far-reaching extent of these changes in a speech to celebrate the ninetieth anniversary of the founding of the PLA when he declared that "the People's Army now has a new system, a new structure, a new pattern, and a new look."[26]

The Weapons and Equipment Development Strategy

Whereas the MSG provides broad strategic principles and general guidelines on weapons requirements and acquisition issues, the detailed nuts and bolts of programmatic management, strategic design, planning, and implementation is the responsibility of the WEDS and its attendant Weapons and Equipment Construction Plans (WECPs; 武器装备建设规划, *Wuqi Zhuangbei Jianshe Guihua*). These planning documents represent the near-, medium-, and long-term visions and road maps for implementation of the Chinese defense establishment's S&T development for its weapons and equipment capabilities and have witnessed profound changes over the last several decades.

Not surprisingly, the WEDS and WECP are highly classified, and there are only occasional references to their role and importance in guiding the PLA's technological modernization. However, in an article marking the reorganization of the General Armament Department (GAD) into the CMC Equipment Development Department (EDD) as part of the restructuring of the PLA high command in 2016, *China Military Industry News* (中国军工报, *Zhongguo Jungong Bao*), the GAD's official news mouthpiece, disclosed for the first time that one of its accomplishments was to establish "scientific planning of long-term defense science and technology and weapons and equipment development through a twenty-year development strategy, ten-year construction outline, and three five-year plans."[27]

The WEDS provides the overall strategic rationale for the country's armament development. It offers long-term planning stability and provides an integrated approach involving input from across the entire defense establishment. Moreover, it is a rigorous assessment that looks at regional and global strategic, military, and technological trends, and the nature of future war and compares these dynamics with China's national, military, economic, industrial, and technological capabilities to support armament research and development (R&D). As one PLA study noted, "In the formulation of military equipment development plans, it is necessary to use a military equipment development strategy as the foundation. Chiefly, this means considering the country's situation for a relatively long period of time in the future, and the country's military strategic policies, as well as analyzing and making predictions for the international strategic environment, the security environment on the country's periphery, and the military equipment needs of the country's troops in future military conflicts."[28]

The WEDS comes in two categories: a national-level version and service-level variants. The national-level WEDS is produced by the EDD and is a comprehensive and integrated strategy for the PLA and defense S&T establishment. The WEDS is described as "subordinate to and serves" the MSG and also takes into account the country's national development strategy and S&T plans.[29]

The national-level WEDS appears to have been introduced in the first half of the 2000s, which is relatively recent when compared to the MSG, which dates back to the mid-1950s. An October 2002 article in the PLA's official media mouthpiece, the *Liberation Army Daily*, on weapons modernization mentioned that the PLA was in the process of implementing a "weapons and equipment development strategy" along with the 2001–2005 10th Five-Year "Weapons Construction Plan" (装备建设计划, *Zhuangbei Jianshe Jihua*), which had been formulated by the CMC and PLA general headquarters.[30] This would suggest that the WEDS was issued around 2002 or 2003.

Beginning around this same time, the Commission for Science, Technology, and Industry for National Defense (COSTIND) was standing up efforts to formulate a long-term defense S&T development plan that would parallel a similar national planning effort. It took three years for the Defense Science and Technology Medium- and Long-Term Development Plan (DMLP; 国防科技工业中长期科学和技术发展规划纲要, *Guofang Keji Gongye Zhongchangqi Kexuehe Jishu Fazhan Guihua Gangyao*) and its civilian companion to be finished and approved in 2006. Both cover a period of fifteen years to 2020. It would make considerable sense for the WEDS to be aligned with the DMLP as there is almost certainly extensive overlap and complementarity between these two programs. There is fragmentary evidence to suggest these two development strategies and plans run parallel to each other. In regulations issued by the State Administration for Science, Technology, and Industry for National Defense (SASTIND) in 2010 on managing basic scientific research, one of the provisions stated that the defense industrial regulatory agency would set up expert groups to conduct research on development strategies according to the WEDS and DMLP.[31]

A major reason why the PLA was a latecomer in putting together an overarching weapons development strategy is that it did not establish a high-level unified armament decision-making and policy-planning system until the formation of the GAD in 1998. Prior to the GAD's existence, COSTIND was in charge of the defense S&T portfolio. It had devised a long-range defense S&T strategic road map in the second half of the 1980s titled "China's Defense Science and Technology to the Year 2000." This strategic guidance was much longer than the WEDS and was a consensus document reflecting the input of more than two thousand military and civilian experts.[32] At the same time, military units such as AMS and the PLA Navy also produced development strategies for the PLA and their service arms.

The fledgling PLA armament community in the 1980s and 1990s sought to capitalize on the experience gained from these ad hoc strategy and planning exercises and turn them into regularized processes. The PLA Navy appears to have been the first service in the mid-1980s to identify the importance and need for long-range weapons and equipment development strategies and implementation plans. This was due to the influence of the navy commander between 1982 and 1987, Admiral Liu Huaqing (刘华清), who was a strong advocate of long-term armaments planning.[33] The WEDS process played a critical role in allowing the PLA Navy to think longer term and push ahead with large-scale capital projects such as aircraft carriers and nuclear submarines that otherwise would not have been possible with the conventional five-year planning timelines.

The PLA armament apparatus developed the conceptual designs and frameworks for drawing up WEDS and other related planning and implementation mechanisms. The general nature and composition of the WEDS is outlined in authoritative PLA armament studies and consists of a number of key elements:[34]

- Analysis and forecasting of the international strategic environment: This is the starting point in the formulation of the WEDS and involves the assessment of global strategic trends and threats as well as the identification and examination of China's principal global military competitors and opponents.
- Assessing China's regional security periphery: The focus here is on the security situation and dynamics between China and its neighbors in Northeast Asia as well as with countries in South and Southeast Asia. The most pressing priority is the safeguarding of China's sovereignty and territorial integrity, which means cross-strait relations and maritime security flash points in the South and East China Seas. Other issues that warrant extensive scrutiny include the tense security situation on the Korean Peninsula, in particular North Korea's nuclear weapons

program and Japan's desire to become an increasingly prominent member of the regional security order.

- National conditions and national development strategy: The guiding principle here is to find an appropriate balance between economic development and national security. This means that the WEDS will need to take into account the pace and direction of long-term national development and the nature of China's evolving national development model.
- Review and coordination of the MSG with the WEDS: A clear hierarchy exists in China's military strategies and plans, of which the MSG is the overarching guidance issued by the CMC. The WEDS is subordinate to the MSG and one of the core principles is that the planning and development of weapons and equipment must meet the long-term requirements of China's military struggle. The overriding importance of end-user demand may appear obvious, but China's armament development has historically been driven by technology push.
- Military armament requirements in future conflicts: Understanding what the most likely forms of future war the PLA will be engaged in is of pivotal importance in shaping the technological and armament requirements. Will military conflict be localized or total in nature? Will China fight defensive or offensive campaigns? What will be the dominant domain? What are the equipment requirements for conducting local informationized wars, especially in terms of command, control, communications, computers, intelligence, surveillance, and reconnaissance systems, electronic warfare systems, integrated command automation networks, and satellite-based navigational positioning systems?
- Assessing the strengths and weaknesses of China's armament capabilities: Such an assessment would cover the state of the R&D system, training and human talent cultivation and management, the effectiveness of the acquisition system, the organizational structure of the armament development and support apparatus, and the development of a modern governance regime with appropriate rules, regulations, and norms.
- Long-term science and technology development and trends: The Chinese authorities attach considerable importance to examining long-term global S&T trends and their potential impact on China. In the defense S&T domain, the foremost concern is what the Chinese authorities see as an accelerating pickup in the pace of the global revolution in military technological affairs.

The WECP is responsible for the implementation of the strategic requirements and tasks that are set out in the WEDS (see figure 4.2). There are different versions of the WECP based on duration (ten, five, or one year) and organizational level (national or service arm). At the pinnacle is the national-level Long-Term Weapons and Equipment Construction Plan that extends over a ten-year planning period and covers the entire defense establishment. This plan is "primarily used to direct the formulation of military equipment development plans and the implementation process of significant policy decisions and to indirectly guide specific management actions. The [long-term] military equipment development plan holds a dominant position among military equipment development plans: that of the foundation of other military development planning work."[35] Operational implementation is carried out by a five-year Medium-Term Weapons and Equipment Construction Plan and a one-year Short-Term Weapons and Equipment Construction Plan. The Medium-Term Weapons and Equipment Construction Plan parallels the five-year planning cycles undertaken by the national economy and the PLA. The Medium-Term Weapons and Equipment Construction Plan is responsible for the direct formulation and guidance of defense S&T-related research, development, acquisition, maintenance, and resource allocations, while the Short-Term Weapons and Equipment Construction Plan is a detailed implementation plan focused on specific projects.

Whereas the WEDS by design is meant to be broad in focus, provide a panoramic strategic vision, and offers only general principles, the contents of the weapons and equipment construction programs and plans are far more detailed and address the nuts and bolts of requirements, acquisition, implementation, and program management matters. Areas that the long-, medium-, and short-term WECPs cover include the following:

- Guiding ideology on equipment development
- Global military S&T and weapons development trends
- Global and regional military-strategic assessments
- Development trends in the Chinese economy and S&T
- Overall conception of each type of equipment to be developed
- Funding requirements and fund distribution
- Equipment scientific research plans
- Purchasing plans
- Maintenance plans

Applying these top-level development strategies and implementation plans into detailed operational requirements for specific weapons programs is the responsibility of specialized armament and equipment research institutes belonging to the

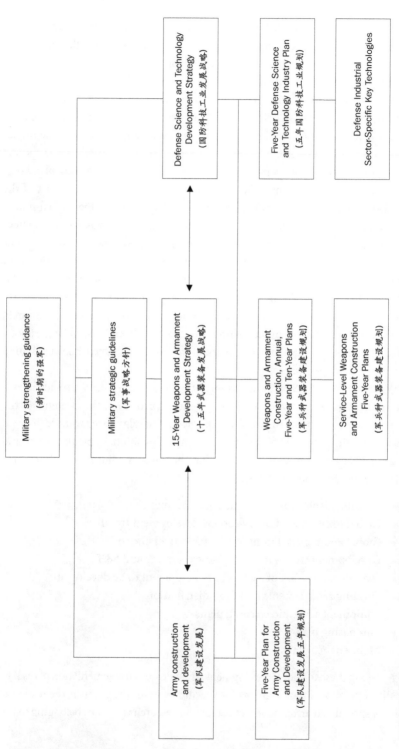

FIGURE 4.2. China's strategies and plans for short-, medium-, and long-term weapons and equipment development

CMC EDD and service equipment departments.[36] They include the likes of the PLA Navy Research Institute (海军研究院, *Haijun Yanjiuyuan*) and Navy Equipment Demonstration Research Center (海军装备论证研究中心, *Haijun Zhuangbei Lunzheng Yanjiu Zhongxin*), and its counterparts in the other service arms.

The Chinese military authorities are tightly guarded over the exact contents of these armament strategies and plans but occasionally do offer broad hints about their general principles. In an article in the China Military Industry News shortly after Xi took office, GAD executive deputy director Lieutenant General Li Andong (李安东), a prime architect of the armament modernization effort between the early 2000s and mid-2010s, talked about the need to strengthen the strategic guidance for the country's armament building.[37] Li highlighted a number of key points:

- Importance of unified central leadership and joint weapons development: Li said that a top requirement for the PLA high command is to strengthen armament integration between the air force, ground forces, and navy. This means, "raising the level of coordination and combination and preventing the establishment of separate stand-alone systems." Li also hinted at the fierce interservice rivalry on armaments development and how disruptive it could be to the armament planning process. He said that it was important to "resolutely safeguard the authority and binding force of the plans. Once the armament building plans are approved, no one can change them freely or act in their own way."
- Prioritizing the building of offensive capabilities: For much of the PLA's history, the focus has been on developing defensive capabilities to deter against invasion and encroachment of its territorial integrity. This has shifted decisively in the past one to two decades with the country's development and expanding external interests. The priority now, Li pointed out, is to "lay stress on the development of offensive weapons according to the requirement of combining offense and defense."
- Establishing credible strategic deterrence capabilities: The development of a credible strategic deterrence force has been one of the PLA's foremost priorities in the aftermath of the 1999 Belgrade embassy bombing. Li pointed out that the PLA should ensure that its strategic deterrence capabilities are operationally tested and deployed so that an "effective and credible deterrence can be guaranteed."
- Promoting asymmetric development: One of the foremost priorities in the PLA's armament building since the late 1990s has been the development of asymmetric capabilities targeted at the vulnerabilities of a stronger opponent, of which the foremost candidate is the United States.

Li stressed that "what we should do is to concentrate on developing our unique armaments that can effectively overpower the enemy through systems sabotage against the vital parts and system weaknesses of the opponent." Likely key areas include precision missile capabilities such as anti-ship ballistic missiles, kinetic and nonkinetic anti-satellite assets, and cyber tools.

- Selective development of advanced armaments: The principle of selectivity was first put forward by Deng Xiaoping in the 1980s during a period of scarce resource allocations for defense modernization. However, with surging funding and strong end-user demand, this guidance appears to have been largely ignored as the PLA and defense industry pursue an ever-lengthening list of weapons projects. Tied with this selectivity requirement is a stress on the pursuit of advanced capabilities, especially doing so by "leaps and bounds." Li points out that "we should develop key defense technologies and weapons that will play a decisive role in future wars . . . and spare no effort to achieve successful results in these crucial projects." This priority on high-end innovation at the global technological frontier has benefited the development of capabilities such as stealth aircraft, hypersonic air vehicles, aircraft carriers and carrier-borne combat aircraft, precision missiles, and high-performance computers.

- Striving for indigenous innovation: Li urged the defense establishment to foster homegrown innovation to limit foreign dependence, but he was aware that there were competing bureaucratic interests on this issue. The defense industry was especially keen to promote technological self-reliance, as they benefited from resource allocations. The PLA, and especially its war fighters, want the best available capabilities as soon as possible, which would mean sourcing from foreign suppliers. Li noted that although self-reliant innovation is critical, "we should grasp opportunities and actively carry out international cooperation." The prime focus of this foreign engagement is with Russia.

- Pursuing MCF: The PLA armaments apparatus is one of the principal proponents for integration of the civilian and defense economies, and Li points out that the emphasis should be on encouraging civilian entities to participate in research, development, and production along with repair, maintenance, and other support services. Li also says that MCF would help to promote market competition by establishing a competitive procurement process.

Li's instructions offer some useful insights into the contemporary state of China's armaments strategies and plans. First, a major focus of China's armament development is on how to counter a stronger adversary, primarily the United States, through credible deterrence and asymmetric capabilities. Second, armament development is making solid progress, and the Chinese defense S&T system appears to be making a decisive shift from engaging in absorption and the making of technologically limited products to the development of more innovative capabilities, especially in meeting the PLA's more demanding requirements. Third, despite the progress being made, the structure and process of armament development continues to suffer from deep-seated problems such as compartmentalization, weak institutionalization, and reliance on foreign technologies.

The Coming Together of the MSG and WEDS

When Xi took the reins of power, he paid considerable attention to defense technology, innovation, and armament issues. A topic that very likely would have been on Xi's initial agenda is whether the WEDS needed to be revised or replaced. A key rationale for conducting such a review was that the MSG was going through an update not long after Xi came to power. There are indications that a review of the WEDS was undertaken at the same time as the MSG reappraisal. In January 2014, GAD director Zhang Youxia said in reference to the revamping of the MSG that this "will certainly bring about profound adjustments in our military's construction and development."[38]

At the All-Army Armament Work Conference in December 2014 in which the country's armaments leadership met to review the current state of, and future prospects for, weapons development, Xi gave a keynote speech that offered a clear sign that a revision of the WEDS was taking place. He pointed out that in the "face of the new situation and new tasks, the strategic guidance for armament building must adapt to the times." Xi added that "the present time and for a period to come mark a window of strategic opportunity for our military's armament building and also a crucial stage for making leapfrog development."[39]

Not surprisingly, other parts of the PLA establishment also appeared to be embarking on the revision of their weapons development strategies and plans. At a PLA Navy Party Committee plenary session in January 2015, then PLA Navy chief Admiral Wu Shengli (吴胜利) said that the Chinese navy was in a "critical period of strategic transformation" with a major expansion of missions and tasks and also facing important reforms. To cope with these changes, Wu said there was a real need to "revise and perfect" the PLA Navy's development strategies, especially to "scientifically formulate plans for military struggle preparation and building, optimize and perfect combat operation plans, and promote the entry of military strategic guidance into the practice of navy building and military struggle preparations."[40] Wu added that Xi had been playing an active leadership role in this endeavor and was "personally involved in making decisions and promoting major issues on naval building and development."

In the search as to what a new Chinese long-term WEDS would look like, the 2019 defense white paper offers some intriguing clues.[41] In an assessment of the state of global military technological competition, the white paper points out that "the United States is engaging in technological and institutional innovation in pursuit of absolute military superiority." This marks a change from previous defense white papers that have been more circumspect in explicitly identifying the United States as a major source of concern or threat.

Addressing technological trends, the white paper said that driven by the technological and industrial revolutions, the development of emerging cutting-edge technologies is "gathering pace" and are having a significant impact on future warfare. Technologies with military applications include AI [artificial intelligence], quantum information, big data, cloud computing, and the internet of things." Additionally, new and high-tech information technology–based military technologies are also developing rapidly. In the military domain, the white paper noted that the "prevailing trend" is the development of long-range precision, intelligent, stealthy, and unmanned weapons and equipment. In peering deep into the crystal ball, the white paper believed that "war is evolving in form toward informationized warfare, and intelligentized (智能化战争, *zhinenghua zhanzheng*) warfare is on the horizon."[42] The PLA is investing considerable time and effort on examining military intelligentization. The rising importance of intelligentization can be seen from its inclusion in key texts such as the *Science of Strategy*, which is an authoritative Chinese perspective on military strategy produced by AMS. Influential Chinese military analysts argue that the shift toward military intelligentization is inevitable and will eventually become the dominant face of warfare.[43]

The white paper praised the "great progress" that China has so far made in the pursuit of the revolution in military affairs but pointed out that this effort was insufficient to close the combat gap with the world's leading defense technological powers. The white paper said that the PLA had yet to complete the first stage of its three-step modernization drive by accomplishing mechanization and was "in urgent need of improving informationization." This somber assessment stands in contrast to the more upbeat views offered by PLA leaders. The white paper warned that "the PLA still lags far behind the world's leading militaries" and needs to make "greater efforts to invest in military modernization to meet national demands." This means that China is vulnerable to "technology surprises and a widening technology generational gap." This was a classic bureaucratic call for increased funding.

The People's Liberation Army's Ability to Promote Technological Innovation and Armament Development

The clamor within China for an advanced military establishment equipped with cutting-edge technological capabilities has been ramping up since the 1990s against the backdrop of rapid technological advances by the United States and other leading military powers. No one has been more emphatic that the PLA should become a leading military technological champion than Xi, who has demanded that "our sights should be set on seizing the strategic commanding heights in future military competition."[44] The problem for Xi on coming to office was that the defense establishment was not well organized, well suited, or well led to get ahead of the technology and innovation curve and identify, develop, and deploy state-of-the-art capabilities.

The PLA and the attendant defense science, technology, and industrial system has had a checkered record in the making and management of armament and military technological innovation programs.[45] Although the PLA has been engaged in the design, engineering, test and evaluation, production, operation, and support of weapons and equipment since the 1950s, acquisition was subordinate to war fighting, political discipline, and logistics. The acquisition system was divided between two competing systems. One portion was manned by serving military officers working within the PLA General Staff Department as well as in armament management entities at the service level. The competing component was comprised of civilians and uniformed personnel and attached to COSTIND. This bifurcated arrangement was a product of the socialist central planning system that managed the Chinese economy between the 1950s until the 1990s. It led to constant and often bitter bureaucratic infighting because these two groups had widely divergent interests. As the consumer, the military wanted weapons that could be produced on time, meet its specifications, and be cost effective. However, the defense industry had little incentive to meet the PLA's requirements because it faced little competition.

It was not until 1998 that the GAD was created as an equal-level entity alongside other PLA general headquarters departments. The establishment of the GAD led to a far-reaching reorganization of the acquisition system. A crucial change was that the GAD assumed primary responsibility for acquisition matters, while the defense industry was relegated to a supporting role. This change did not happen overnight, though, and met considerable resistance because of the entrenched control that the defense industry had long enjoyed over the acquisition process.

Although the GAD prevailed over the civilian defense industrial regulatory system, it was less successful in dealing with bureaucratic infighting within the military system. The GAD's responsibilities were limited to managing the armament needs of the ground forces and PAP.[46] The navy, air force, and strategic missile forces had their own armament bureaucracies and competed fiercely with one another for resources. This bureaucratic fragmentation intensified parochial interests that hampered efforts to promote joint undertakings. There were also coordination gaps and rivalries between the GAD and the General Staff and General Logistics Departments in areas such as policy planning, resource allocations, and drafting longer-term development plans.[47] Overall, the PLA armament acquisition and management system in the early 2010s was competent and had a good track record, but inherent structural limitations called into question whether it could meet the needs of an increasingly technologically demanding military establishment. GAD director Zhang Youxia highlighted this predicament in a speech in 2014 when he said that structural and process problems have become such an obstacle that the primary "bottleneck issue for armament development is no longer the shortage of funds or technology. Instead, institutional systems and mechanisms have become the greatest hurdle to armament building and development."[48] Zhang added that if these impediments cannot be removed, future progress in weapons development "may just be empty talk."

These concerns were shared by Xi when he took office, although not just in the armament domain but more broadly across the PLA high command. However, Xi had to proceed cautiously with pushing forward major reforms because of the powerful political autonomy that the military top brass had long enjoyed. Xi's intention to conduct a sweeping overhaul of the upper echelons of the PLA was telegraphed in the 18th Party Congress Third Plenum communiqué in November 2013, which talked of "deepening the adjustment and reform of military structures and personnel allocation." More specifically, the communiqué spelled out the need to "move leadership and management structure reform forward, optimize the deployment of leadership organ functions and the organic deployment of the Central Military Commission and the General Headquarters, perfect leadership and management structures for all service branches" and "accelerate the unified management of informatized construction and centralization."[49]

The reform planning effort began in earnest in March 2014 when the CMC established a leading group on national defense and military reform. This group was headed by Xi and acted as the command headquarters for designing reform plans, coordinating work among different departments, and policy implementation.[50] After fifteen months of investigation, a reform plan titled "Proposal on Deepening Defense and Military General Reform Plan" was approved at a leading group meeting in July 2015. The plan was subsequently released at the CMC Work Conference on Military Structural Reforms in November 2015, which marked the formal start of the implementation of the most far-reaching structural reform of the PLA in its history.[51] PLA officials explained that these reforms were badly needed because the global revolution in military affairs had made the high command system "out of date and in need of change." Moreover, there were serious shortcomings in the existing apparatus, including "bloated" leadership organs, "imprecise operational command functions," and an "incomplete joint operations command structure."[52] These criticisms also applied to the armament acquisition and management system. At the CMC reform conference, Xi stressed the importance of "giving full play to innovation in driving development" and "fostering new growth points in combat power."[53] To achieve these goals, Xi said it was incumbent on the PLA to select the right points to achieve breakthroughs, strengthen the ability to conduct forward-looking and exploratory R&D into new technologies and concepts, and actively seek advantages in military technological competition.

This long-awaited military reform drive was launched at the beginning of 2016 and led to a far-reaching overhaul of the high command centered on the integration and reorganization of the PLA general headquarters apparatus directly under the CMC, replacement of military regions with theater commands, establishment of a separate army command, and the fostering of a joint operations model[54] (see figure 4.3). The armament acquisition and management system also underwent a sweeping reconfiguration with the implementation of several especially important reform measures. First was the reorganization of the GAD into the CMC EDD, which was intended to turn the EDD into a truly joint organization able to meet the needs of joint operations. The EDD is in a better position to carry out the mandate of providing credible centralized management of the armament system than its predecessor. The structural bias toward the ground forces that was baked into the GAD has been mitigated with the establishment of an army EDD under the new army headquarters. This allows the CMC EDD to focus more on military-wide and joint issues.

The transition from the GAD to the EDD went relatively smoothly and was helped by having extensive continuity of duties and staffing. General Zhang Youxia became the EDD director for its first eighteen months before being promoted to a CMC vice-chairmanship in October 2017.[55] A review of the EDD's early performance between 2016 and mid-2017 in the *Liberation Army Daily* highlighted several achievements.[56] The first was the EDD's success in establishing a market access system that was described as "smooth, effective, standardized, orderly, and secure." Second was the setting up of an open and fair competitive environment especially related to market pricing mechanisms, an MCF-based specialized services mechanism, defense intellectual property rights, and the building of an integrated civil-military standards system. A third heralded success was the setting up of a dedicated testing and evaluation organization that was

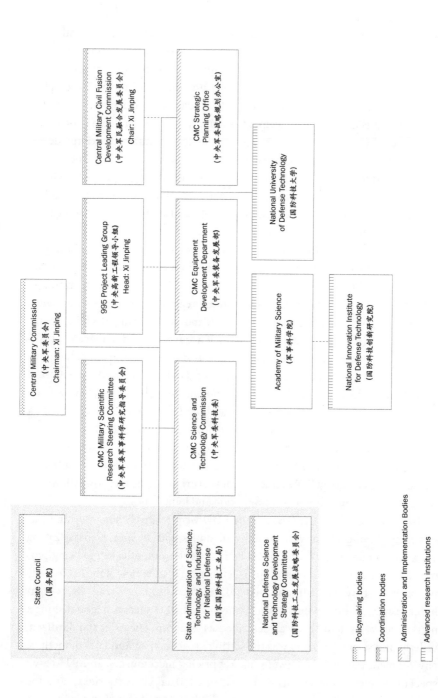

FIGURE 4.3. Top-level organizational layout of the Chinese military and defense science, technology, and industrial armament and innovation system since the late 2010s

more rigorous and disciplined and closed gaping holes in the testing process. This has apparently led to significantly improved testing and evaluation results for weapons and equipment. A fourth noteworthy accomplishment was the overhaul in the process of distributing weapons and equipment to theater commands that better correspond to their strategic requirements. Adjustments that have been made include the prepositioning of equipment and supplementing existing arsenals with additional resources. A fifth signature achievement was the launch of the Weapons and Equipment Acquisition Information Network in 2015 to disseminate information for contract tenders, primarily through an online portal.

A second major reform effort was the elevation of the GAD Science and Technology Committee to a commission-level rank reporting directly to the CMC. The upgrading of the CMC Science and Technology Commission (CSTC) demonstrated that the Chinese military authorities, and especially Xi, were serious about engaging in higher-end science, technology, and innovation activities and establishing a high-level coordinating mechanism through CSTC to provide operational leadership and guidance. Lieutenant General Liu Guozhi, who was the GAD Science and Technology Committee director, took charge of CSTC. Liu is the role model soldier-scientist that the PLA was keenly looking for. He has spent much of his career engaged in high-technology R&D, has a PhD in physics from Tsinghua University, is a Chinese Academy of Sciences (CAS) academician, and has technical expertise in accelerator physics and high-power microwave technology.[57]

The CSTC has been tasked with a number of key responsibilities. They include (1) strengthening the strategic management of defense S&T efforts, (2) the promotion of indigenous innovation, and (3) advancing MCF in the S&T arena. In a 2016 interview, Liu said that the key missions and tasks of the CSTC were to "enhance our forward-looking, exploratory, pioneering, and disruptive efforts in major technological research and new concept research, and actively seek competitive advantages in military technology."[58] Liu's statement makes clear that the primary missions of CSTC are in emerging, disruptive, and large-scale S&T research.

Although CSTC is a wholly military-controlled and staffed organization that is located deep within the high command hierarchy, it does have elements of an operating style that are comparable with foreign counterparts such as the US Defense Advanced Research Projects Agency and Defense Innovation Unit. One is the leveraging of research capabilities of the civilian academic system through annual research competitions. This is managed by the CSTC's Technology Innovation Bureau. A 2016 solicitation covered a wide range of emerging dual-use technological sectors including information technology, computing, advanced materials, biotechnology, and environmental and manufacturing technology.

The CSTC also signed a five-year cooperation agreement in 2016 with the National Natural Science Foundation on MCF-related basic research.[59]

A second innovation in the CSTC's operating style is the creation of defense science, technology, and innovation rapid response small groups (国防科技创新快速响应小组, *guofang keji chuangxin kuaisu xiangying xiaozu*) stationed in high-technology-intensive regions of the country to be able to gain speedy access to advanced commercial technology with potential military relevance. The first was established in Shenzhen in 2018 with an initial call for projects in maritime intelligent target recognition technology and intelligent human-machine interaction. In its first two years of operation, this small group issued seven batches of solicitations.[60] By 2020, small groups had also been set up in Dalian and Chongqing, and many more can be expected.[61]

A third major plank in the reform of the PLA armament and innovation system has been to significantly enhance military academic and policy research capabilities that support military decision making, especially in areas such as emerging and long-range exploratory research on new technologies, concepts, and theories. One of the primary ways this reform is being carried out is through the transformation of AMS. This venerable institution has been the PLA's leading think tank on military-strategic issues since the 1950s, although its traditional center of attention has been on matters related to military strategy and operations, foreign military study, political work, and military history.[62] Research on science, technology, innovation, and engineering matters was left to entities that specialized in these fields such as the National University of Defense Technology (NUDT) and service counterparts. In 2016, NUDT president Lieutenant General Yang Xuejun (杨学军) was appointed as AMS commandant and given the task of broadening and recentering the research focus onto emerging, core, frontier, and long-range S&T issues. As one of China's leading supercomputing scientists, Yang had the scientific credentials to turn AMS into the PLA's leading hub for strategic high-technology research and has a direct line to the highest levels of the Chinese military leadership.

There has been large-scale hiring of new generations of young military scientists to join new research enterprises that have been established at AMS. In its first recruitment campaign in 2016, AMS brought in more than 120 researchers, 90 of whom had doctorates. A second recruitment drive yielded an additional influx of more than one hundred research scientists.[63] Many of these researchers have been assigned to work in the newly established research centers. The flagship entity is the National Innovation Institute for Defense Technology (国防科技创新研究院, *Guofang Keji Chuangxin Yanjiuyuan*), whose leading research priorities include AI, unmanned systems, and frontier cross-domain technologies.[64] Centers have been set up in each of these domains to organize research activities. The AI center specializes in intelligent algorithms, robotics operating systems, intelligent computing chips, big data, and cognitive radio and communications. The Unmanned Systems Technology Research Center (无人系统研究中心, *Wuren Xitong Yanjiu Zhongxin*) concentrates on the integration, verification, and application of intelligent unmanned systems and systems of systems. The Frontier Cross-Disciplinary Technologies Research Center (前沿交叉研究中心, *Qianyan Jiaocha Yanjiu Zhongxin*) is engaged in a diverse array of early-stage and next-generation topics such as neurocognition, quantum technologies, and flexible electronics.

AMS is also cultivating research expertise in applied and advanced engineering, especially addressing cutting-edge, complex, and large-scale engineering challenges. The Systems Engineering Research Institute (系统工程研究院, *Xitong Gongcheng Yanjiuyuan*) leads this work, leveraging expertise across the defense innovation ecosystem. In April 2018, for example, the Systems Engineering Research Institute joined with the China Aerospace Academy of Systems Science and Engineering to coestablish the Qian Xuesen Military Systems Engineering Research Institute (钱学森军事系统工程研究院, *Qian Xuesen Junshi Xitong Gongcheng Yanjiuyuan*). This institute is likely to be focused on engineering work related to missile and space technology issues.[65]

The reform of AMS is also tied to a broad restructuring of the PLA's academic research and educational system that took place in July 2017.[66] This involved a nearly 40 percent reduction in the number of academic institutions from seventy-four to forty-four. At the top level, there has been a clearer distinction in the areas of responsibility of the three leading entities.[67] Besides AMS, NUDT oversees the education of science, technology, engineering, and support personnel and conducts advanced research in key defense and dual-use high-technology areas such as satellite innovation, optic fibers, lasers, high-performance computing, and hypersonics. The primary mission of the National Defense University is to train military personnel in joint operations.

The rapid evolution of AMS into a high-powered, technology-intensive research institute with direct access to the country's national and military leaderships has made it a powerhouse of authoritative influence on defense science, technology, and innovation policy in the Chinese techno-security state.[68] The CMC did stand up a Steering Committee on Military Scientific Research (中央军委军事科学研究指导委员会, *Zhongyang Junwei Junshi Kexue Yanjiu Zhidao Weiyuanhui*) in 2017, which appears to have a role in overseeing AMS, NUDT, and other military academic research organizations, but no information has so far been released about the makeup and responsibilities of this entity.[69] AMS has amassed a highly impressive concentration of young scientific talent that is second to none not only in China but in the rest of the world. The cost, though, is likely a significant brain drain from other parts of the military scientific research enterprise. Moreover, the cohorts of traditional military strategists appear to have been pushed to the sidelines in favor of a younger generation of technologically minded researchers with scientifically precise answers.[70] This approach is representative of the centralized top-down mobilization model that is the hallmark of China's S&T development, which has been pushed to an even greater extent by Xi.

Strengthening the Defense Industrial Economy

The defense industrial sector is an integral part of the military strengthening drive, but its approach to reform, upgrading, and modernization is more incremental and low-key compared to the big bang restructuring strategy pursued by the PLA. This is because the enterprise-driven development model that the defense industry has adopted since the turn of the twenty-first century has performed remarkably well so far. Industry-wide profits and revenues have been surging annually, a broad and deep array of advanced weapons and equipment is coming off the production lines, and the research, development, and engineering pipeline is bulging. However, deep-seated structural problems such as monopolies, compartmentalization, and corruption continue to impede efficiency and hamper innovation and stand in the way of the goal of transforming the defense industry from a catch-up development model into a truly advanced original innovation leader by the 2030s.

The defense industrial base is pursuing a number of initiatives and reforms intended to be forward leaning and able to adapt to the fast-changing security, economic, technology, and innovation landscapes. At the strategic policy planning and regulatory levels, these adjustments have been modest in scope because the role and authority of the state institutions overseeing the defense industrial economy have been steadily downgraded in rank and influence since the late 1990s. COSTIND was the dominant actor in overseeing defense science, technology, and industrial affairs during the 1980s and 1990s but was pushed to the sidelines by the PLA at the end of the 1990s in the management of the defense research, development, and acquisition system. COSTIND's standing and clout suffered another heavy blow in 2008 when it was downgraded two levels from a super ministry to a lowly state administrative agency (SASTIND) and placed under the Ministry of Industry and Information Technology (MIIT). A constant turnover of leadership, especially at the director level, has meant that SASTIND has at times appeared rudderless and with a weak bureaucratic voice in the interagency process.

A key role that COSTIND played during its heyday was to draw up long-term defense S&T development strategies. It helped to pioneer this more disciplined and rigorous planning approach in the 1980s, which was subsequently adopted by the PLA with its WEDS framework. COSTIND was also responsible for the formulation and implementation of the 2006–2020 DMLP. There has been very little public reference to the DMLP since its introduction, which has called into question whether the DMLP specifically and the long-term development planning model more generally have gone out of favor. SASTIND's announcement in June 2015 that it would establish a National Defense Science and Technology Development Strategy Committee (NDSTDSC; 国防科技工业发展战略委员会, *Guofang Keji Fazhan Zhanlue Weiyuanhui*) demonstrated that it was keen to remain engaged and have a say in long-range defense technology and innovation planning.[71]

The general role of the NDSTDSC is to conduct research and provide policy input that will help the country's leadership in its decision making on defense S&T R&D over the next twenty to thirty years. Specific initial tasks of the committee include the following:

- Support the implementation of the Communist Party leadership's strategic decisions and plans, especially the IDDS and the MCF development strategy.
- Focus on conducting strategic, comprehensive, and forward-looking studies.
- Provide policy recommendations and consultation on defense S&T development and innovation.
- Draw up a blueprint for the reform and development of the defense industry during the 13th Five-Year Plan.
- Provide policy analysis on the National Defense Science and Technology Industry Strong Foundation Project 2025 (国防科技工业强基工程 2025, *Guofang Keji Gongye Qiangji Gongcheng*), which is the defense industry's equivalent of the Made in China 2025 plan.

The NDSTDSC has several dozen members drawn from across the government, PLA, academic and scientific institutions, and the corporate sector. The head is the SASTIND director and its members include ten academicians from CAS and the Chinese Academies of Engineering (CAE), and senior representatives from the National Development and Reform Commission (NDRC), Ministry of Education, Ministry of Science and Technology, Ministry of Finance, and PLA armament units. The presidents of CAS and CAE serve as senior scientific advisers. There were media reports of the committee's first two annual plenary meetings in June 2015 and July 2016, but there has been no subsequent open reporting of its activities.[72] Committee officials, though, actively participate in defense industry events, which is an indicator that it remains active and prominent.[73]

The NDSTDSC appears to have briefly eclipsed the Science and Technology Committee (科技委, *Kejiwei*) belonging to SASTIND between the late 2000s and 2010s. The Science and Technology Committee had originally been a highly influential advisory body under COSTIND and was headed by legendary defense scientific leaders such as Qian Xuesen.[74] The Science and Technology Committee disappeared from sight after the establishment of SASTIND, but after a ten-year hiatus, a new committee was set up in November 2018.[75] There is considerable overlap in the tasks and membership between the SASTIND Science and Technology Committee and the NDSTDSC, although the former appears to be more focused on nearer term applied operational tasks while the latter is concentrated on longer range basic research issues.

The Science and Technology Committee reports to SASTIND's party group and was assigned three areas of initial work: (1) helping to promote MCF in the defense industry, (2) supporting indigenous innovation and development through involvement in programs such as the Strong Foundation Project 2025, and (3) assisting in the building of a robust defense innovation ecosystem, especially on issues such as the cultivation of human talent, advising on the drafting of regulations and laws to enhance the governance regime, and helping to evaluate projects and performance metrics. The Science and Technology Committee is chaired by a SASTIND deputy director and its membership is heavily populated by corporate representatives, including the heads of many of the major defense conglomerates, as well as scientists and engineers from CAS, defense universities, the China Academy of Engineering Physics, government ministries, and PLA representatives.

The center of gravity of the defense industrial strengthening initiatives and reforms has been focused on the state-owned defense corporations that dominate the defense industrial economy. Between the 1950s and end of the 1990s, they became formidable obstacles to innovation because of their role as all-powerful state bureaucracies that protected their institutional interests by preserving the central planning system that had allowed them to flourish. It was not until the beginning of the 2000s that the central government decided to undertake major reforms to transform these entities from chronic loss-makers into more market-driven enterprises. Since then, these corporations have been slimmed down, allowed to shed heavy debt burdens, and given access to new sources of investment, especially from the capital markets. They are now engaged in ambitious expansion strategies to become global arms and strategic technology champions.

Combined with a strong pickup in defense and civilian orders, these corporations have become profitable since the mid-2000s. The annual profitability of

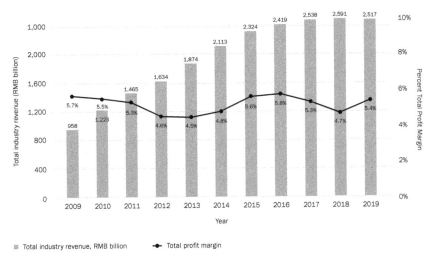

FIGURE 4.4. Financial performance of China's defense corporations, 2009–2019

the Chinese defense industry between 2009 and 2019 has hovered in a narrow range of between 4.5 percent and 5.8 percent (see figure 4.4). Around two-thirds of the defense industry's annual revenue comes from civilian operations, such as automobiles and white goods like washing machines and refrigerators. The aviation, space/missile, defense electronics, and naval sectors have been the chief beneficiaries of this rising tide of defense procurement, while the ordnance industry has enjoyed considerable success from sales of civilian products such as motor vehicles.[76]

These defense industrial behemoths have found strong and sustained political support from the highest levels of the civilian and military leaderships since the end of the 1990s for their efforts to significantly expand and upgrade their scientific, technological, and industrial capabilities. This has been translated into the elevation of defense industrial issues to the top of government priorities, significant increases in the allocation of financial, human capital, and other resources, enactment of a range of regulations, policies, and plans to support defense industrialization and innovation, and active leadership intervention to tackle structural obstacles that have often stymied progress.[77]

One of the thorniest issues, though, for the defense corporations in their long-term relationship with the Chinese government concerns monopolies. Little competition exists in the awarding of contracts for major weapons systems and defense equipment because each of the country's six traditional defense industrial sectors are closed to outside competition and dominated by one or two state-owned defense industrial corporations. Contracts are typically given through single sourcing mechanisms to these corporations. Competitive bidding and tendering usually only takes place for noncombat support equipment, such as logistics supplies.

An effort in 1999 to inject more competition by splitting corporations that monopolized their sectors into two separate entities did little to curb monopolistic practices because these firms focused on different areas of business in their domains and there was little direct rivalry. These powerful defense firms have sought to reverse this effort at demonopolization by finding ways to remerge or collaborate, which has met with success. In 2008, the aviation industry reintegrated its two post-1999 entities back into a single monopoly structure. This was followed by the consolidation of the nuclear and shipbuilding sectors in the late 2010s. In 2020, the two principal state-owned space and missile corporations, the China Aerospace Science and Industry Corporation and the China Aerospace Science and Technology Corporation, signed a strategic cooperation agreement that could finally lead to their merger.[78] If this consolidation does take place, it leaves only the ordnance sector with a duopoly structure.

This return to monopolization goes against the expressed desire of the Chinese government to encourage full-fledged market-driven competition in the defense industrial economy. This objective is outlined in high-level policy documents such as the July 2016 "Opinions on the Integrated Development of Economic Construction and Defense Construction" and the November 2017 "Opinions of the General Office of the State Council on Promoting the In-Depth Development of Military-Civil Fusion in the Defense Science and Technology Industry," which stressed the need to open up the defense industry to the private sector, allow for growing competition in weapons acquisition, and support the transition in the state ownership of defense firms into mixed ownership structures. State-owned monopolies have so far successfully limited meaningful implementation of these market-opening measures.

The Chinese government is also seeking to chip away at the stranglehold of the long-standing defense industrial giants by establishing new functional monopolies in critical high-technology sectors that have been inadequately served by existing entities. The prime example was the creation of a new aero-engine conglomerate called Aero Engine Corporation of China (AECC; 中国航空发动机集团有限公司, *Zhongguo Hangkong Fadongji Jituan Youxian Gongsi*) in 2016 in which forty of the engine-related research, development, and production outfits belonging to Aviation Industry Corporation of China (AVIC) and the space and missile firms were put under this new structure.[79] Even though AVIC is a major shareholder, it has little involvement in the operational management of AECC.

To improve the defense industrial economy's capacity for innovation, many of the major state-owned defense corporations have set up defense S&T industrial technology innovation centers (国防科技工业技术创新中心, *Guofang Keji Gongye Jishu Chuangxin Zhongxin*) as anchors to drive advanced research, development, and engineering across the entire defense industrial ecosystem starting in 2016. This has led to the formation of at least fourteen of these centers by the beginning of the 2020s (see table 4.1).

There are two types of these centers. The first are industry-wide system design innovation centers (系统设计类创新中心, *xitong shejilei chuangxin zhongxin*) that provide defense, macroeconomic, and technological advice related to their industrial sectors such as the drafting of technology development and application strategies and systems innovation plans. They are also intended to be national and global technology leaders in their industrial domains. To help them achieve these ambitious goals, these centers are able to leverage resources and leading personnel from across their industrial sectors.[80] The inaugural head of the Defense Science and Technology Industrial Aviation Technology Innovation Center, for example, was Yang Wei (杨伟), one of the leading military aircraft designers at AVIC. The head of the center's expert committee was Sun Cong (孙聪), another leading military aircraft designer.[81] Besides the Aviation Technology Innovation Center, another five centers fall into this category, such as the maritime defense, space technology, nuclear power, and strategic rocket centers.

The second type of industrial innovation center is more limited in scope and focuses on the development of specialized technologies including fire explosives, intelligent weapons, optical precision machinery, computer numerical control (CNC) machinery, and automated charging technology. Some of these centers, such as the Efficient CNC Machine Technology Innovation Center, were previously or are still concurrently engineering centers or laboratories that are focusing more on innovation in their research and engineering work.[82]

The formation of high-level expert advisory committees and industry-level innovation centers are promising but represent only initial steps in the defense industry's evolution into a modern and sophisticated ecosystem. As the Chinese defense industry lays down the foundations for its long-term development into the 2030s and beyond, having access to high-quality research and independent expert opinion will be invaluable for decision making. However, there are concerns about the quality and analytical rigor of these think tanks and advisory committees. An assessment of defense S&T think tanks by researchers from the National Defense Technology Information and Management Research Center argued that there was still "a big gap" in the quality and research capabilities of the new generations of think tanks and what the defense industrial system requires from them.[83] This is because of the lack of core competence in these think tanks, their poor positioning within the defense industrial system, lack of key connections and access, and deficiencies in their internal organization and management,

TABLE 4.1 List of defense science and technology industry technology innovation centers

INDUSTRIAL INNOVATION CENTER	SPONSORING INSTITUTION
Defense Science and Technology Industry Strategic Rocket Innovation Center (国防科技工业战略火箭创新中心)	China Academy of Launch Vehicle Technology (subsidiary of China Aerospace Science and Technology Corp.)
Defense Technology Maritime Innovation Center (国防科技工业海洋防务技术创新中心)	China Shipbuilding Industry Corp.
Defense Science and Technology Industry Aviation Technology Innovation Center (国防科技工业航空技术创新中心)	China Aviation Research Academy (subsidiary of Aviation Industry of China Corp.)
Defense Science and Technology Industry Aero Engine Innovation Center (国防科技工业航空发动机创新中心)	China Aviation Development Research Institute (affiliated with China Aviation Power Institute, China Aero Engine Research Institute, and China Aero Engine Turbine Institute that are subsidiaries of Aviation Industry of China Corp.)
Defense Science and Technology Industry Fire Explosive Preparation Process Technology Innovation Center (国防科技工业火炸药制备工艺技术创新中心)	China North Industries Group
Defense Science and Technology Maritime Safety System Innovation Center (国防科技工业海洋安全体系创新中心)	Systems Engineering Research Institute (subsidiary of China State Shipbuilding Corp.)
Defense Science and Technology Industry Nuclear Material Technology Innovation Center (国防科技工业核材料技术创新中心)	China Institute of Atomic Energy (subsidiary of China National Nuclear Corp.)
Defense Science and Technology Industry Space Technology Innovation Center (国防科技工业空间技术创新中心)	China Academy of Space Technology (subsidiary of China Aerospace Science and Technology Corp.)
Defense Science and Technology Industry Nuclear Power Technology Innovation Center (国防科技工业核动力技术创新中心)	China Nuclear Power Research and Design Institute (subsidiary of China National Nuclear Corp.)
Defense Science and Technology Industry Optical Ultra-Precision Machine Technology Innovation Center (国防科技工业光学超精密加工技术创新中心)	China Academy of Space Technology (subsidiary of China Aerospace Science and Technology Corp.)
Defense Science and Technology Industry Aerospace Defense Innovation Center (国防科技工业空天防御创新中心)	Second Academy (subsidiary of China Aerospace Science and Industry Corp.)
Defense Science and Technology Industry Automated Charging Technology Innovation Center (国防科技工业自动装药技术创新中心)	Automation Institute (subsidiary of China South Industries Group)
Defense Science and Technology Industry Intelligent Weapons Technology Innovation Center (国防科技工业智能兵器技术创新中心)	China Ordnance Science Research Institute, NORINCO Automatic Control Technology Research Institute, and NORINCO No. 208 Institute (subsidiaries of China North Industries Group)
Defense Science and Technology Industry Efficient CNC Machine Technology Innovation Center (国防科技工业高效数控加工技术创新中心)	Beijing University of Aeronautics and Astronautics

such as the use of outdated administrative processes and insufficient funding support. These are challenging structural problems and will require high-level leadership attention and ample resources to overcome.

Even as the Chinese defense industry has made strong progress in its development since the beginning of the twenty-first century, there are serious fundamental weaknesses and constraints that if left unaddressed will undermine its quest to become a truly world-class technological and industrial powerhouse.[84] These inherent problems stem in part from its historical foundations and the uncertain efforts to overcome this corrosive legacy. The institutional and normative foundations and workings of the Chinese defense industry were copied from the former Soviet Union's command economy and continue to exert a powerful influence today.

Another serious weakness of the Chinese defense industrial system is bureaucratic fragmentation. This is a common characteristic of the Chinese organizational system,[85] but it is especially virulent within the large and unwieldy defense industrial sector. A key feature of the Soviet approach to defense industrialization that China imported was a highly divided, segmented, and stratified structure and process. There was strict separation between the defense and civilian sectors as well as between defense contractors and military end users, compartmentalization between the conventional defense and strategic weapons sectors as well as among the different conventional defense industrial subsectors, and division between R&D entities and production units. This excessive compartmentalization was driven by an obsessive desire for secrecy and the powerful influence of the deeply ingrained Chinese model of vertical functional systems (条条, tiaotiao) that encouraged large-scale industries like those in the defense and supporting heavy industrial sectors, such as iron and steel and chemicals, to become independent fiefdoms.

This severe structural compartmentalization is a major obstacle to the development of innovative and advanced weapons capabilities because it requires consensus-based decision making carried out through extensive negotiations, bargaining, and exchanges. This management by committee approach is cumbersome, risk averse, and results in a lack of strong ownership, which is critical to ensuring that projects are able to succeed in the thicket of bureaucratic red tape and cutthroat competition for funding.

The research, development, and acquisition system also suffers from compartmentalization along many segments of the acquisition process. Responsibilities for R&D, testing, procurement, production, and maintenance are in the hands of different units, and underinstitutionalization has meant that linkages among these entities tend to be ad hoc in nature with major gaps in oversight, reporting, and information sharing.[86] The fragmented nature of the acquisition process helps to explain why Hu Jintao was apparently caught by surprise by the first publicized test flight of the J-20 fighter aircraft that occurred during the visit of US defense secretary Robert Gates in January 2011.[87]

Yet another major weakness is that the PLA continues to rely on outdated administrative tools to manage projects with defense contractors in the absence of the establishment of an effective contract management system. The PLA did implement the use of contracts on a trial basis in the late 1980s with the introduction of a contract responsibility system.[88] These contracts are administrative in nature, however, and have few legal rights because of a lack of a developed legal framework within the defense industry. Consequently, contracts are vague and do not usually define contractual obligations or critical performance issues such as quality, pricing, or schedules. Contracts for complex weapons projects can be as short as one to two pages, according to PLA analysts.[89]

Moreover, the PLA acquisition apparatus is woefully backward in many of the other management approaches and tools it uses compared to its counterparts in the United States and other advanced military powers. It has yet to adopt total life-cycle management methods, for example, and many internal management information systems are on stand-alone networks that prevent effective communication and coordination.

The lack of a transparent pricing system for weapons and other military equipment is another serious weakness that contributes to a deficit of trust between the PLA and defense industry. The existing armament pricing framework is based on a "cost-plus" model that dates to the planning economy in which contractors are allowed 5-percent profit margins on top of actual costs.[90] There are a number of drawbacks to this model that hold back efficiency and innovation. One is that contractors are incentivized to push up costs since it also drives up profits. Another problem is that contractors are not rewarded when they find ways to lower costs such as through more streamlined management or cost-effective designs or manufacturing techniques. Contracts rarely include performance incentives, which discourages risk taking and any willingness to adopt new innovative approaches. Yet another issue is that contractors are dissuaded from making major investments in new technological capabilities or processes because of the low 5-percent profit margin.

To address this long-standing problem, the PLA, Ministry of Finance, and NDRC held a high-level meeting on armament pricing reform in 2009 that concluded that the outdated pricing system had seriously restricted weapons development and innovation.[91] A number of reform proposals were put forward that (1) provide incentives to contain costs, (2) switch from accounting procedures that focus on ex post pricing to ex ante controls, and (3) expand from a single pricing methodology to multiple pricing methods. Some of these ideas were incorporated in a document issued after the meeting titled "Opinions on Further Pushing Forward the Reform of Work Concerning the Prices of Military Products."

At the beginning of 2014, GAD announced that it would conduct and expand pilot projects on equipment pricing. These reforms included the strengthening of pricing verification of purchased goods, improving cost controls, and shifting from singular to plural pricing models, from "after-purchase pricing" to "whole-process pricing," and from "individual cost pricing" to "social average cost pricing."[92] These represent modest steps in the pricing reform process, but the PLA will continue to face fierce opposition from the defense industry on this issue.

Lastly, a huge impediment is corruption, which has thrived with the defense industry's uncertain transition from centralized state planning to a more competitive and indirect management model. PLA leaders have highlighted the defense acquisition system as one of a number of high-risk areas in which corruption can flourish. At the PLA's annual conference on military discipline inspection work in January 2014, CMC vice-chairman General Xu Qiliang (许其亮), who heads the PLA's anti-corruption efforts, pointed out that armament research, production, and procurement was one of two areas that required "better oversight."[93] The other area was construction projects.

There has been little public reporting on corruption in the defense industry and acquisition system—many cases involve classified weapons programs—which means that the full magnitude of the problem is impossible to assess. However, occasional cases have been disclosed that hint at the scale of this problem in the defense industry. One of those instances was when the Central Discipline Inspection Commission sent a team to investigate SASTIND for two months in the spring of 2016. SASTIND was required to set up a "comprehensive rectification program" covering one hundred measures and the investigation led to two officials being subject to party punishment, fourteen officials being verbally admonished, three officials being moved from their positions, and ten officials being given letters of criticism.[94]

Another cluster of reported defense industrial corruption cases relates to the China Shipbuilding Industry Corporation (CSIC). Several of the corporation's most senior executives have been arrested on corruption charges since the late 2010s. The most prominent was Hu Wenming (胡问鸣), the corporation's chairman and Communist Party chief during much of the 2010s.[95] A second top-level executive was Sun Bo (孙波), CSIC's general manager, who received a twelve-year prison sentence in 2019.[96] Sun was in charge of the refurbishment of the Liaoning aircraft carrier, and although he was targeted for corruption, there were media reports that Sun's real crime was espionage. Other senior CSIC executives picked up for malfeasance include Jin Tao (金焘), former research head of CSIC's No. 712 Research Institute, Liu Changhong (刘长虹), CSIC's head of discipline inspection and chief anti-corruption investigator, and Bu Jianjie (卜建杰), a former director of another CSIC research unit.[97] There is no public information to suggest that other defense firms have suffered a similar degree of endemic corruption, but the CSIC case does show that corruption occurs in the Chinese defense industry and can reach to the highest levels and spread widely.

Military Strengthening through Medium- and Long-Term Development Programs

As Xi began to issue his strategic thinking on military strengthening on taking office, he was able to capitalize on the dawning of a golden age in Chinese defense modernization that began under his predecessor. The qualitative performance of the defense research, development, and production system has posted significant gains since the beginning of the twenty-first century and is steadily narrowing the gap with the global technology frontier despite its many internal problems. There are many explanations to account for this major improvement in performance, but the focus here is on three key defense technology and weapons development programs: the DMLP that is focused on basic research and long-range objectives, the 995 New High-Technology Project aimed at critical weapons and equipment programs, and the Five-Year Defense Science and Technology Development Plan, which is an essential planning mechanism in bridging immediate and near-term (one- to three-year) operational needs and longer-term (ten- to fifteen-year) requirements.[98]

The Defense Medium- and Long-Term Science and Technology Development Plan

The DMLP was drawn up in the first half of the 2000s by COSTIND in tandem with the Medium- and Long-Term Science and Technology Development Plan (MLP) with the shared objective of overcoming the technological gap with the world's leading technological powers by 2020. The DMLP focused on guiding defense-related basic and applied R&D and improving the conditions for innovation. A summary of the DMLP outline issued by COSTIND in 2006 highlighted nearly two dozen issues of focus, of which the most important are as follows:[99]

- Enhancing the capacity for indigenous innovation and building up the defense innovation system: This would be carried out by accelerating the reform of the defense R&D system through initiatives such as expanding the number of high-quality defense laboratories engaged in basic research, building technology application centers, establishing closer linkages with leading civilian universities and research institutes, developing a robust service support apparatus to enable activities like technology transfers and commercialization, and allowing defense industrial enterprises to play a more involved role in innovation.

- Creating a favorable environment to promote innovation: The authorities recognize the importance of developing a robust governance and norms-based regime to cultivate practices, behaviors, and established rules of the road that promote and safeguard innovation. This includes promoting and strengthening incentives for innovation, such as the building up of an intellectual property rights protection system, improving planning and coordination to overcome entrenched compartmentalization, constructing a comprehensive defense standards apparatus, forging a rigorous evaluation system, and reforming management procedures and the innovation cultures of R&D organizations that have long been accustomed to a state-dependent "iron rice bowl" mentality to make them more responsive to market and end-user requirements.

- Increasing the scale and channels of investment in defense science and technology: State funding for defense R&D has been growing strongly since the late 1990s, but the DMLP sought to broaden the sources of this investment flow by requiring defense enterprises and research institutes to invest at least 3 percent of their sales revenues in R&D and also allowing them to tap the capital markets for fundraising through public and private offerings, bonds, and bank loans. The DMLP also promised to establish preferential investment policies, such as tax breaks and land use rights.

- Improving the ability of the defense S&T system to leverage foreign sources of technology and knowledge transfers: Although the DMLP was avowedly techno-nationalist and emphasized the overriding importance of self-reliant innovation, it also balanced this objective with the need to look overseas to absorb advanced technologies and know-how and find opportunities for international R&D cooperation, including encouraging defense enterprises and research institutes to set up joint research centers and laboratories.

- Meeting the PLA's requirements for advanced weapons and equipment: The DMLP pointed to the importance of adhering to the armament needs of the PLA as set out in the MSG, which included advancing R&D from the late industrial age to the information era.

- Promoting civil-military integration (CMI): Finding ways to bring about CMI was strongly encouraged, especially with the goal of making breakthroughs in industrial bottlenecks. A top priority was advanced manufacturing.

- Cultivating a capable scientific and engineering workforce: An Achilles' heel of China's defense S&T modernization has been the lack of well-trained and experienced scientists and engineers. The DMLP called for the establishment of various initiatives to address these manpower shortages, such as through talent training plans, special priority for critical disciplines, and the establishment of defense science, technology, and innovation teams.

Additional details about the DMLP were disclosed by COSTIND director Zhang Yunchuan (张云川) in a speech at a COSTIND work conference in May 2016:

- Top-priority sectors for defense development were nuclear and new energy, aerospace, aviation, electronic and information dual-use technology, shipbuilding, and ocean engineering.[100]
- Integrated innovation was identified as the "key direction" (重点方向, *zhongdian fangxiang*) for building China's indigenous innovation capabilities, while reinnovation "is an important way," and original innovation is the foundation. Zhang referred to integrated innovation as the extensive absorption and adoption of new technologies, processes, and materials that would drive leapfrog development.
- Long-standing structural problems that have been major barriers to innovation would be investigated, although solving them would not be easy. They included the pricing mechanism for military products and the protection of defense intellectual property rights.
- The implementation of major special projects was a top priority, especially in weapons and equipment technology, MCF, and advanced manufacturing. Specific projects included large-sized aircraft, advanced pressurized and gas-cooled nuclear reactors, manned spaceflight, high-resolution earth observation systems, and lunar exploration projects.
- Major reform of the military research institute system was highlighted as a top, but controversial, priority. Zhang noted that it was an "issue of widespread concern," in part because institutes employed large numbers of research and administrative staff. However, Zhang pointed out that "it is absolutely necessary for the state to maintain a lean, efficient, and relatively complete" research apparatus, which meant supporting key strategic outfits, especially those engaged in basic science research, and allowing applied research and engineering-oriented institutions to be taken over by commercial enterprises.

The public unveiling of the DMLP was a noteworthy step forward in Chinese defense transparency as these types of defense S&T programs have rarely been disclosed or even officially acknowledged. This candor, though, was short-lived as public news about the DMLP dried up within a couple of years of its introduction. One possible reason for this dalliance with openness was that COSTIND was downgraded in 2008 and a new leadership team was brought in to manage the successor agency, SASTIND. As the DMLP was an ambitious high-level program that required the support and protection of a powerful agency, SASTIND lacked those credentials. Some of the policy priorities in the DMLP were entrusted to other state organs. Responsibility for the promotion of CMI, for example, was placed under MIIT, which also became the parent agency for SASTIND. Although the DMLP was no longer visible, it may very well have continued to be implemented within the classified walls of the Chinese technosecurity state as such large-scale programs are notoriously difficult to shut down in China. In any case, much of the contents and goals of the DMLP have become the core tenets of the country's defense science, technology, and industrial system's modernization drive.

Whereas the Hu administration drafted separate defense and national long-term S&T development plans and disclosed them publicly, the Xi regime has been far less open. There is no public mention of a successor to the DMLP. One revealing indicator of this selective transparency approach is the case of Made in China 2025. Whereas the national plan has been published, the defense variant known as the Defense Science and Technology Industry Strong Basic Engineering Project 2025 has been kept under wraps. This program includes a defense industrial intelligent manufacturing special action plan (军工智能制造专项行动计划项目, *jungong zhineng zhizao zhuanxiang xingdong jihua xiangmu*) that focuses on nearly two dozen research topics aimed at the development of a defense intelligent manufacturing base.[101]

The 995 New High-Technology Project

One of the most important but least known Chinese plans promoting defense S&T development is the 995 New High-Technology Project (高新技术工程, *Gaoxin Jishu Gongcheng*). It is more commonly called the 995 Project in reference to the US bombing of the Chinese embassy in Belgrade in May 1999, which was the spark for the establishment of the project.[102] The Chinese authorities are reticent to mention the existence of this plan, but it is occasionally acknowledged in media reports, military journals, résumés of Chinese scientists and engineers, and project listings of university laboratories and companies engaged in defense-related work.[103] A valedictory message by the GAD upon its reorganization into the EDD at the end of 2015 officially confirmed the existence of the 995 Project by noting that one of the outstanding contributions of the GAD in its seventeen-year history was the "organization and implementation of phases 1, 2, and 3 of the New High-Technology Project." The reference to these three phases suggests that the 995 Project is organized in five-year cycles.[104]

The Chinese leadership's reaction to the Chinese embassy attack in Belgrade was to sharply intensify efforts to develop strategic weapons systems, or what the PLA terms *Shashoujian* (杀手锏) capabilities.[105] According to General Zhang Wannian (张万年), who was the CMC executive vice-chairman during the Belgrade embassy crisis, the CMC convened an emergency meeting immediately after the bombing, and one of the key decisions made was to "accelerate the development of *Shashoujian* armaments."[106]

Zhang pointed out that then–CMC chairman Jiang Zemin was especially insistent on the need to step up the pace of development of *Shashoujian* megaprojects, saying that "what the enemy is most fearful of, this is what we should be developing."[107] Although the enemy's identity was not made explicit, it was clearly the actions of the United States, and Jiang's guidance to the Chinese defense S&T system was to focus on the R&D of asymmetric capabilities targeting US vulnerabilities.

Selectivity was one of several core guiding principles that Jiang gave in the development of the *Shashoujian* projects and that very likely was also written into the 995 Project.[108] The actual guidance was to "do some things but not others (有所为有所不为, *you suowei, yousuo buwei*), and concentrate on developing arms most feared by the enemy." The "do some things but not others" guidance was raised by Jiang on a number of occasions in his discussion of strategic technology developments while he was in power.[109] What this meant was to be highly selective and focus on the development of asymmetric capabilities.

Jiang also put forward a number of other guiding principles:

- "Significantly boost science and technology innovation and make breakthroughs as soon as possible": This emphasis on higher-end innovation meant adopting a more risk-taking R&D model.[110]
- "Assassin's mace weapons should become the vanguard of the PLA's combat capabilities": The development and deployment of advanced high-technology weapons is the PLA's foremost priority.
- "Adhere to self-reliance, but actively introduce and digest advanced foreign weapons and technology": This meant stepping up efforts to acquire foreign technology transfers by whatever means available.

One of the most revealing descriptions of the 995 Project came in a public talk in 2012 by Major General Yao Youzhi (姚有志), a recently retired but influential AMS strategist. Yao confirmed that the 995 Project was established in response to the US bombing of China's Belgrade embassy and its purpose was to accelerate the R&D of new weapons systems.[111] "Without 995, the PLA would not have been able to get new generations of weapons developed as quickly as was achieved," Yao said, and he referred to the 2009 National Day military parade in which forty types of new weapons were displayed as evidence of the impact. "Who should we be ultimately thankful for" in enabling the PLA to make such progress, Yao asked rhetorically. "We should be grateful to the Americans." This remark suggests that the 995 Project was primarily aimed at the United States.

Yao's comments indicate that the 995 Project is enormous in scale and has had a profound impact on China's development of its weapons capabilities, but there is a paucity of information to make any nuanced assessments. A 2017 study of China's defense innovation and weapons development by a PLA professor observed that the introduction of the 995 program had led to a massive increase in defense R&D investment in the twenty-first century.[112] The study pointed out that total Chinese defense R&D investment between 1999 and 2009 (the first ten years of the 995 program) was more than all the investment in defense R&D in the prior fifty years. Another data point hinting at this project's huge scale is that there were on average nearly one hundred thousand workers participating in 995-related projects in Shaanxi Province alone in the mid-2010s, according to a Shaanxi labor union.[113]

To ensure that these major weapons projects receive high-level attention, the CMC established a New High-Technology Project Leading Group (995 Leading Group) in 1999 with the CMC chairman as its head. This coordinating body is responsible for providing top-level unified leadership and management of the development of high-technology weapons systems, and appears to have similar characteristics and roles as the Central Special Committee, which was established in the early 1960s to manage the development of the country's nuclear weapons and strategic launch capabilities.[114] The activities of the 995 Leading Group are rarely disclosed, but *China Aviation News* reported in December 2014 that there was a 995 Leading Group meeting that was attended by Xi that took place in conjunction with the All-Army Armament Work Conference.[115]

Besides the CMC chairman, there is no information available as to other members of the 995 Leading Group. Membership would likely include senior leaders from CMC headquarters departments and the PLA armament system, high-level strategic and technological institutions like AMS and SASTIND, and representatives from government ministries with direct involvement in the project such as the Ministry of Finance, MOST, and MIIT.

The 995 Project also has subordinate-level leading groups at the provincial level. For example, a brief notice issued by the Heilongjiang Provincial

Government in August 2005 reported on the adjustment of the provincial "High-Technology Project Leading Group."[116] The membership of the Heilongjiang 995 Leading Group included the governor, three deputy governors, and the directors of the provincial economic committee, S&T department, finance department, land and resources department, construction department, information industry department, defense science, technology, and industry department, transportation department, and taxation department. Others in the group included the director of the Harbin Railway Bureau, general manager of the provincial airport management company, general manager of the provincial electric power company, heads of the provincial branches of the Industrial and Commercial Bank of China and China Construction Bank, director of Harbin Customs, and the mayors of Harbin, Qiqihar, Mudanjiang, and Jiamusi. This leading group has a permanent office located in the provincial defense science, technology, and industry office, whose director also serves as the leading group's office head. The deputy head of this 995 leading group in 2005 was Li Zhanshu (栗战书), who is a close political ally to Xi and became a Politburo Standing Committee member at the 19th Party Congress in 2017.

The high-level makeup of this leading group is one indicator that there is a substantial 995 Project presence in the province. This is not surprising as Heilongjiang is home to a significant concentration of defense science, technology, and industrial facilities.[117] The provincial defense science, technology, and industry office issued a directive in December 2001 as the overall 995 Project was getting under way to inform local government offices to prepare for the arrival of work related to this program and to provide assistance. The directive pointed out that "our province occupies an important position in the scientific research and production of defense weapons and equipment and undertakes important construction tasks for the New High-Technology Project."[118] The participation of four mayors on the 995 Leading Group suggests that their cities are the locations for 995 projects. Some of the province's leading universities that conduct extensive defense-related research are reportedly involved in 995-related research. Harbin Engineering University was reported to have received an RMB 500 million (US$61 million) contract in 2005, which is likely related to naval research projects.[119]

Five-Year Plans

Five-year plans are the work horses of the Chinese planning process. This is especially the case for the military armament and defense science, technology, and industry systems where much, if not most, of the projects they manage stretch over multiple years. Each of these systems has its own five-year planning approaches. The PLA armament system has the five-year Medium-Term Weapons and Equipment Construction Plan, which is a core component of the PLA-wide Five-Year Plan for Army Construction and Development. The defense industry has its five-year defense S&T development plan that has numerous specialized five-year subplans for specific sectors and technologies. The stand-alone 995 Project also has a five-year planning cycle.

These plans are classified, so there is very little public information of their contents. Official mentions of these plans are very broad and vague. The description of the goals of the 13th Five-Year Plan for Army Construction and Development that spanned 2016–2020 demonstrates the Chinese propaganda art of saying something without disclosing anything:[120]

- The PLA will have achieved the second stage of a three-step development strategy guiding the modernization of the defense establishment by 2020. This second step means accomplishing mechanization and making extensive progress in informatization building, especially cultivating a robust capability of winning informatized warfare. This development strategy was revised in 2017 and this original second 2020 phase became the first stage of a new three-step strategy that extended to 2035 for the second step and 2050 for the final phase.
- The PLA will launch a number of major unspecified construction and engineering projects that are defined to be of pivotal strategic significance during the 2016–2020 period with the purpose of meeting the "urgent needs" for "military struggle" preparedness.
- The PLA will complete the far-reaching organizational reforms to the PLA high command, military services, and regional theater commands that were started at the end of 2015. This includes ensuring the recentralization of authority and oversight to the CMC, overhauling the political work system so that it is better able to safeguard the ideological loyalty of the PLA to the Communist Party, and establishing an effective disciplinary and supervisory system to tackle corruption.

In parallel, the state defense industrial bureaucracy formulated new strategies and plans for a less ambitious but still significant adjustment to the defense industry as well as to chart its medium- and long-term transformation. One of these key plans is the 13th Defense Science, Technology, and Industry Five-Year Plan (国防科技工业"十三五"规划, *Guofang Keji Gongye "Shisan Wu" Guihua*) which had several broadly defined tasks to achieve over its five-year life-span. First was the task of achieving "leapfrog" development in weapons and military equipment. Second was the enhancement of innovation capabilities in turnkey areas. Third was the optimization of the structure of the defense industry and the vigorous promotion of MCF. Fourth was the stepping up of weapons exports efforts.[121]

Compared to its predecessors, the 13th Defense Science, Technology, and Industry Five-Year Plan had a stronger focus on the development of high-technology weaponry and MCF. It also signaled a significant shift in the direction of defense industry development from absorption and reinnovation to original innovation. The 13th Defense Science, Technology, and Industry Five-Year Plan also shows that China is seeking to build on the inroads it has been steadily making in the international arms market. Chinese arms sales almost doubled during the 12th Defense Science, Technology, and Industry Five-Year Plan, according to the Stockholm International Peace Research Institute, with China supplying arms to nearly forty countries, with three-quarters of the exports within the Asia-Pacific region.[122]

In addition, many other defense industrial sectors, provinces, and S&T domains have developed their own five-year plans. Even though SASTIND is in charge of coordinating this planning process, how effectively this is carried out is unclear, especially given its diminished bureaucratic status. On rare occasions, brief outlines of such plans are publicly released, which was the case with the 13th Five-Year Special Plan for Science and Technology Military-Civil Fusion in 2016. By comparison, most national and civilian plans are fully publicized.

These plans, programs, and projects can be expected to grow in importance and size in Xi's techno-security state because they are the lifeblood of a top-down, statist development model. Their suitability, however, for the original innovation-driven approach that Xi is pushing is debatable. The Xi regime regards state intervention as vital in the nurturing of emerging and core technological sectors, especially for capabilities deemed essential to national and military security, which is increasingly becoming a catch-all phrase. State involvement under Xi is not the same, however, as the ham-fisted central planning methods employed in the Maoist era but instead represents a blended approach combining state- and market-oriented instruments. This expanding tool kit of dominant conventional planning, development, and acquisition approaches supplemented with hybrid and more commercially based mechanisms represents incremental improvement in what can be called the "soft" process-related dimension of the defense innovation model, which contrasts with the "hard" technology domain that is striving for disruptive leaps forward.

Assessing Military Strengthening by the Numbers

From an examination of the inputs, processes, and implementation efforts of the military armament and defense innovation systems, the final area of analysis is assessing the outcomes of these efforts. This will be undertaken through a quantitative generational analysis of the quality of the PLA's frontline arsenal over a three-decade cycle between the end of the 1980s and the end of the 2010s. This extended time frame allows for a comparison of trends before and during the Xi era.

General estimates of Chinese combat equipment frontline strengths are readily observable and captured by annual order of battle publications issued by Western security-orientated think tanks. The most consistent, reliable, and informed is the *Military Balance* produced by the London-based International Institute for Strategic Studies. One methodological problem, though, is that there is no universal agreement among defense analysts about what constitutes a technological generation for weapons systems. This includes disagreement on when to start counting the beginning of modern generations of weapons and how long each generation should be measured. This is not surprising as the rates of technological change vary widely across different domains. The Western military fighter aircraft community has a generational definition for jet fighters that begins from World War II when the first models of jet-powered fighter aircraft were developed and entered into service. The latest and most advanced generation of jet fighters are designated as fifth generation and refers to fighters that were developed since the late 1990s and embody technologies such as stealth and networked data fusion. Generational change for fighter aircraft occurs around every ten to fifteen years. Chinese definitions of its fighter aircraft generations lag by one generation compared to Western benchmarks.

Some analysts in the warship community define generations beginning with the introduction of the turbine-powered, ironclad big-gun battleship known as the Dreadnought at the beginning of the twentieth century and extending to the fifth-generation distributed operations and directed energy warships appearing in the 2010s.[123] Generational change for warships is around every twenty to thirty-five years. There is even less consensus within the international tank community about generational definition. The Russian tank community counts tank generations beginning from 1920 while Western countries such as Canada start from the post–World War II era.

These differences are too wide to be bridged, so the approach taken here is to begin the generational clock at the end of World War II in 1945 and count every ten years as one generation. Chinese weapons and equipment will be identified in generational terms by the dates that these platforms first entered into operational service (see figures 4.5–4.10):[124]

- First Generation, 1945–1954: J-5 fighter aircraft, H-5 and H-6 bombers, T-34 main battle tank, Chengdu-class (成都级) frigate, and Anshan-class (鞍山级) destroyer

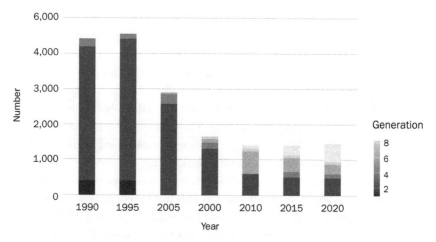

FIGURE 4.5. Generations of Chinese weapons systems: Fighter aircraft

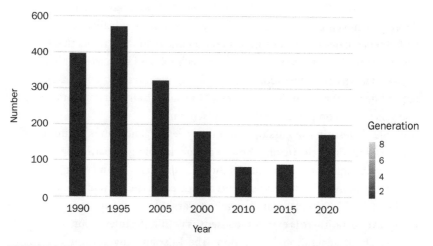

FIGURE 4.6. Generations of Chinese weapons systems: Bomber aircraft

- Second Generation, 1955–1964: J-6 and J-7 fighter aircraft, Q-5 ground attack aircraft, Type 59 main battle tank, and Romeo-class conventional submarine
- Third Generation, 1965–1974: Han-class (汉级) nuclear attack submarine, Ming-class (明级) conventional submarine, Jiangnan-class (江南级) frigate, Luda-class (旅大级) destroyer, and Dongfang (DF, 东风)-3 ballistic missile
- Fourth Generation, 1975–1984: Type 69, Type 79, Type 80, Type 85, and Type 88 main battle tanks, J-8 fighter aircraft, Jiangdong (江东)- and Jianghu-class (江湖级) frigates, Kilo-class (基洛级) conventional subma-

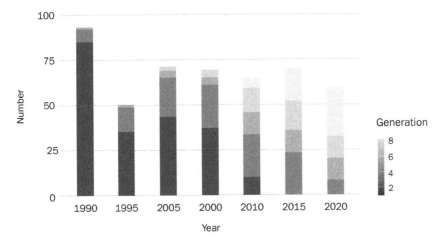

FIGURE 4.7. Generations of Chinese weapons systems: Submarines

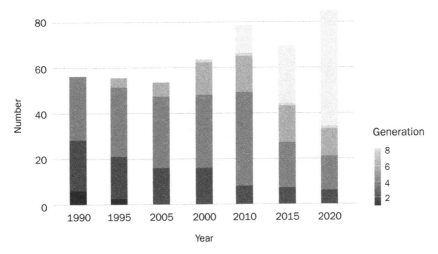

FIGURE 4.8. Generations of Chinese weapons systems: Surface warships (frigates and destroyers)

rine, Hangzhou-class (杭州级) destroyer, DF-4, DF-5, and DF-7 ballistic missiles

- Fifth Generation, 1985–1994: Type 96 main battle tank, JH-7 fighter aircraft, Xia-class (夏级) ballistic missile submarine, Jiangwei-class (江卫级) frigate, Su-27 fighter aircraft, Luhu-class (旅沪级) destroyer, and DF-11, DF-15, and DF-21 ballistic missiles
- Sixth Generation, 1995–2004: Type 98A and Type 99 main battle tanks, Song-class (宋级) conventional submarine, Luhai-class (旅海级) destroyer, and J-11 and Su-30 fighter aircraft

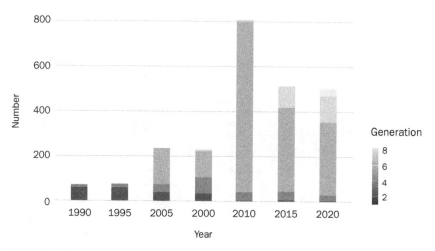

FIGURE 4.9. Generations of Chinese weapons systems: Ballistic missiles

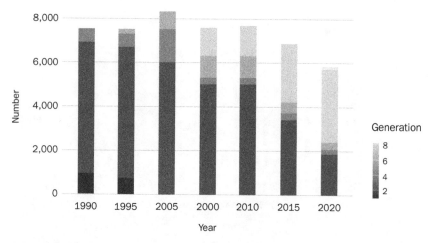

FIGURE 4.10. Generations of Chinese weapons systems: Battle tanks

- Seventh Generation, 2005–2014: J-16, J-10, and Su-35 fighter aircraft, Qing (清)- and Yuan-class (元级) conventional submarines, Jin-class (晋级) ballistic missile submarine, Shang-class (商级) nuclear attack submarine, Jiangkai-class (江凯级) frigate, Luyang II- and III-class (旅洋级) and Luzhou-class (旅州级) destroyers, and DF-16 and DF-31 ballistic missiles
- Eighth Generation, 2015–2024: DF-26 ballistic missile, J-20 fighter aircraft, Renhai-class (刃海级) cruiser, Type 093B nuclear attack submarine, and Type 096 nuclear ballistic missile submarine

This generational analysis offers a number of pertinent insights. First, in quantitative terms, only the aviation-related sectors show a significant decline in overall numbers from the end of the 1980s to the end of the 2010s. There were more modest declines between 1989 and 2019 for tanks and submarines. Overall numbers increased from 1989 to 2019 for surface warships and most dramatically for ballistic missiles.

Second, in qualitative terms, the most significant improvements in generational makeup are in surface warships, ballistic missiles, and submarines, where the composition of fourth-generation and higher technologies is most pronounced. The balance between older and newer generations is more distributed in fighter aircraft and main battle tanks, while the bomber force (B-6) remains based on early-generation technology but heavily modernized with regular incremental improvements.

A detailed examination of naval industrial and generational development trends offers additional perspectives. According to the US Department of Defense (DoD) and US Office of Naval Intelligence (ONI), much of the improvement in the PLA Navy's frontline arsenal since the beginning of the twenty-first century has been in the modernization of technological capabilities, while the overall numbers of vessels have only increased modestly (see table 4.2).[125] For the PLA Navy's submarine force (diesel, nuclear attack, and nuclear ballistic missile), the total number of vessels increased by four in the first two decades of the twenty-first century from sixty-two in 2000 to sixty-six in 2020.[126] There was a significant increase in seventh-generation platforms such as the Jin-class ballistic missile submarine, Shang I and II nuclear attack submarines, and Yuan- and Song-class diesel submarines. The DoD forecasts that two types of eighth-generation nuclear submarines will begin to be built from the early 2020s: the Type 096 nuclear ballistic missile submarine and the Type 093B nuclear attack submarine.[127] Furthermore, the Pentagon expects that the PLA Navy will replace older submarines with the latest generations on a "near one-to-one basis." This means that the PLA submarine force will be thoroughly modernized and overwhelmingly equipped with advanced and highly capable vessels.

For major surface warships, which cover aircraft carriers, cruisers, and destroyers, the size and quality of the PLA Navy's inventory has shown a much greater pace of expansion. In 2000, ONI calculated that the PLA Navy had a force of nineteen major surface warships consisting entirely of destroyers. By 2020, this had more than doubled to forty-three vessels made up of two aircraft carriers, several cruisers, and nearly twenty-five destroyers, almost all of which are of seventh- or eighth-generation technological standards. The production of PLA Navy warships is on a scale and pace usually associated with wartime levels of large-scale output.[128] ONI forecasts the number of major surface warships to increase

TABLE 4.2   The numerical size of the PLA Navy, 2000–2030

	2000	2005	2010	2015	2020	2025 PROJECTED	2030 PROJECTED
Ballistic missile submarines	1	1	3	4	4	6	8
Nuclear attack submarines	5	4	5	6	7	10	13
Diesel attack submarines	56	56	48	53	55	55	55
Aircraft carriers, cruisers, destroyers	19	25	25	26	43	55	65
Frigates and corvettes	38	43	50	74	102	120	135
Other noteworthy platforms (auxiliary and support ships)	1	91	89	92	149	154	149
Total size of PLA Navy battle force	**120**	**220**	**220**	**255**	**360**	**400**	**425**
Total size of US Navy battle force	**318**	**282**	**288**	**271**	**297**	**NA**	**NA**

Notes: These figures for the Chinese naval battle force come from information submitted by the US Office of Naval Intelligence to the US Senate Armed Services Committee. Battle force ships is a term employed by the US Navy to count the types of vessels that make up the quoted size of the navy. China's fast-growing inventory of missile-armed patrol craft are not included in this table. Although the total numerical size of the PLA Navy surpassed the US Navy in 2020 by a sizable margin, the bulk of the PLA Navy's numerical strength is in smaller warships such as frigates, corvettes, and diesel submarines as well as auxiliary and support vessels, while the US Navy has significantly more aircraft carriers, cruisers, destroyers, and nuclear submarines. O'Rourke, *China Naval Modernization*, 32.

further to sixty-five vessels by 2030, almost all of which will be the latest generations of warship design.

Third, the overall trends in weapons modernization show modest improvements in the 1990s, but a noticeable acceleration takes place in the rate of change from the beginning of the twenty-first century that continues and even picks up additional momentum in the 2010s. This trendline is most pronounced for ballistic missiles and fighter aircraft, while for submarines the pickup in its development rate is from the mid-2000s. For main battle tanks and surface warships, the rate of technological change has ramped up since the beginning of the 2010s.

One conclusion from this output analysis is that the stepped-up efforts at armament modernization and defense innovation starting from the mid-1990s required at least a decade or more before showing measurable progress. The development of strategic power projection capabilities such as ballistic missiles and submarines led the way, which may be explained by the enhanced treatment they received from special mechanisms such as the 995 Project.

The military component of the techno-security state can be expected to enjoy privileged support and ample access to resources as long as Xi is in charge. Although extensive internal barriers and weaknesses still exist and could impede this modernization drive, the Chinese armament and defense science, technology, and industrial systems are making strong and sustained progress. The prospects of China becoming a highly capable defense technological power that can comprehensively challenge the United States for global leadership within the next two to three decades are steadily improving, but the United States remains in the ascendancy and will be able to maintain an overall superiority as long as it steps up to forcefully compete with China. This US-China race for global techno-security dominance will be intense, hugely expensive, drawn out, and dangerously destabilizing not only for the participants but also for the rest of the world.

CHINA'S EFFECTIVE MODEL OF TECHNOLOGICAL ADVANCEMENT

In its pursuit of technological advancement and national security, the Chinese techno-security state has coveted the development of triumphalist projects to showcase what it touts as the superiority of the Chinese socialist system. A top-down statist approach has produced an impressive and growing list of signature achievements beginning with the atomic bomb in 1964 and progressing to hypersonic missiles half a century later. Xi Jinping (习近平) has enthusiastically embraced this approach by promoting bigger, bolder, and breakthrough initiatives that would catapult China to the forefront of the global innovation order by the middle of this century.

Can China achieve this audacious goal and what is its formula for success? The preceding chapters detailed the strategies, plans, and programs that have been formulated to guide the techno-security state's development. The focus of this chapter is on the high-level techno-security development model that leverages the core strengths of the country's political, economic, social, defense, and technological systems. These assets include a formidable mobilization system, an imposing authoritarian leadership structure, a determined absorption and innovation apparatus, and a disciplined approach to project selection and implementation. This is commonly known in China as the Two Bombs, One Satellite phenomenon in reference to the development of nuclear weapons, ballistic missiles, and space capabilities between the 1950s and 1970s (see introduction).

This book labels this approach to the development of critical strategic technology capabilities as Selective Authoritarian Mobilization and Innovation (SAMI) to identify the model's prime attributes. The story of the rise and evolution of the SAMI model illustrates the relationship between innovation and industrialization in the making of China's strategic technological capabilities. What these core features tell us is that even though innovative thinking and advanced research and development (R&D) capabilities are important, the main drivers responsible for China's successful outcomes so far in large-scale, complex, multiyear technological projects are sustained high-level leadership attention and engagement coupled with whole-of-nation support and mobilization.

As China becomes more developed and wealthier, its capacity for both original innovation and advanced industrialization is growing, and this presents a golden opportunity for the Xi regime to pursue transformational technology projects, especially in new and emerging areas. The Chinese state is adapting the SAMI model to the twenty-first century, seeking to combine the underlying strengths of the socialist system with more market and globalist attributes. Although the reinnovation component in the SAMI framework remains important, the focus is now on original indigenous innovation.

Defining the SAMI Model

China's techno-security state is immensely proud of its track record of successfully developing highly complex and advanced strategic technology capabilities in trying circumstances. The Two Bombs, One Satellite saga has assumed a heroic, near-mythical status and is held up by Chinese leaders as an ideological role model that emphasizes the fundamental importance of techno-nationalist self-sufficiency.

Beyond its propaganda value and nationalist appeal, Two Bombs, One Satellite provides an overarching framework for how the Chinese authorities prepare, organize, manage, and support the development of large-scale, complex, sophisticated, and strategically important technology programs. The key interlocking attributes at the heart of the Two Bombs, One Satellite approach are selectivity, authoritarianism, mobilization, and absorption/innovation, and they are derived from the specific circumstances of the Chinese political, economic, strategic, societal, and technological systems.

Selectivity means that only a limited number of projects deemed to be of the utmost national importance are chosen for fast-track development. Selection of these projects is normally contained in special long-term science and technology (S&T) plans. Authoritarianism refers to the highly centralized top-down nature of the authoritarian political and bureaucratic system in which leadership and management authority of the selected projects is often carried out by shadowy high-level special entities.

Mobilization involves the leveraging and concentration of material, human, and institutional resources to support projects. This is a daunting task because of the deeply fragmented, underdeveloped, and decentralized nature of the Chinese system. Mobilization drives were easy to justify and undertake when China was on a war footing and faced acute external security threats during the height of the Cold War. However, in more peaceful times, mobilization requires a very different approach.

These first three elements address the political, organizational, and decision-making aspects of the SAMI model. The fourth component, innovation, deals with the technology development process and is concerned with how the state gains access to the knowledge and technology used for its projects. The concept of innovation that is used here can be divided into two types.[1] First is innovation as the recombination of existing knowledge, technology, and processes that results in improved or new output. The second meaning of innovation is novel discovery and invention that leads to the introduction of brand-new products or processes.

China's experience with the pursuit of innovation, especially in the context of the SAMI model, reflects this differentiated approach between recombination and novel innovation. For most of its existence, the SAMI model has predominantly been concerned with the assimilation of foreign sources of technology supported by domestic R&D to adapt to Chinese requirements and to produce incremental improvements. This combination of absorption and innovation is what the Chinese authorities define as reinnovation (再创新, *zaichuanxin*). This version will be known as the SAMI-A model.

The original catalyst behind the Two Bombs, One Satellite programs in the 1950s was the pressing need to build the indigenous strategic innovation system to compensate for a lack of Soviet help in critical strategic areas. Under Xi's rule, the focus is pivoting increasingly toward original discovery-driven domestic innovation. This second version will be labeled as the SAMI-B model (see figure 5.1).

There are also other significant traits of the SAMI model. First is the love affair with mega-sized projects or what Xi has referred to as big things. Megaprojects were first pioneered by the United States in World War II with its Manhattan Project to build the atomic bomb and subsequently became a defining characteristic of the rise of US strategic and technological power through undertakings such as its space program and an expansive range of defense technology projects.[2] Although megaprojects can be found in many sectors of the Chinese economy, the strategic innovation system is a breeding ground for them.

Second is the exploitation of latecomer advantage to catch up through rapid industrialization and absorption of foreign know-how and capabilities. This is

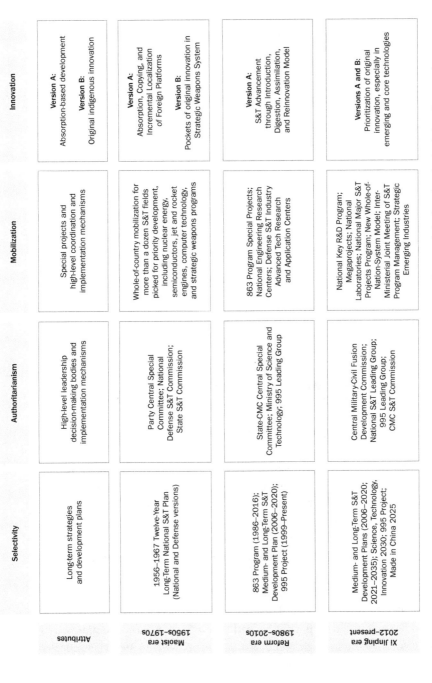

FIGURE 5.1. China's selective authoritarian mobilization and innovation model of technological development

an approach that China's regional neighbors such as Japan, South Korea, and Taiwan pursued in the second half of the twentieth century, although they were primarily engaged in civilian industrialization and absorption in contrast to China's militarized path. However, all of these states shared a similar top-down state-led development model.[3] Third and closely related to the latecomer approach is a techno-nationalist mindset that emphasizes the nurturing of homegrown indigenous industrial and innovation capabilities, although this is carefully balanced with leveraging foreign assistance. Techno-nationalist thinking has been a powerful influence in shaping the technological development of countries regardless of regime type as shown by the roll call of its adherents that include the likes of the United States, China, and Japan.

To sum up, the SAMI model is tailored to the specific characteristics of the Chinese regime, and especially the techno-security state, but there are important features that are not China-specific. Other authoritarian states with similar security concerns have established their own versions of the SAMI model such as North Korea and Iran.[4] Attention now will turn to the origins and evolution of the SAMI model and will focus on the roles of selectivity, mobilizational support, authoritarian leadership, and absorption versus innovation beginning from the Cold War in the 1950s to the 1970s.

The Two Bombs, One Satellite Original SAMI Model

The SAMI model originated in response to the pressing challenge of how China would build nuclear weapons and ballistic missiles to defend itself against the very real possibility of nuclear attack from the United States in the 1950s. The Communist Party and the People's Liberation Army (PLA), skilled in protracted guerilla warfare, had very little experience or in-country expertise to guide them in the development of strategic weapons capabilities. The notion that an impoverished, war-ravaged, agrarian society could follow in the footsteps of the United States, Soviet Union, France, and the United Kingdom and construct an independent nuclear deterrent seemed ludicrous at the time. However, the upstart communist regime had a propensity for hubris that was most disastrously demonstrated by the Great Leap Forward campaign of the late 1950s, which was a vain attempt to catch up with the world's most advanced economies within fifteen years. In the strategic sector, at a meeting in January 1955 that gave the go-ahead for the building of the country's nuclear apparatus, Mao Zedong (毛泽东) declared that "as long as we have people and resources, any miracle can be created."[5] So although the question of whether the country should embark on strategic weapons development was resolved, the issue of how still had to be answered.

Although the Soviet Union had been generous in helping to build the Chinese conventional military-industrial base, it was far less willing to assist with strategic, especially nuclear, technologies. Moreover, there were competing institutional interests within the Chinese governing system. The conventional military-industrial base was the leading contender because it was the most advanced component of the Chinese industrial economy and enjoyed considerable political clout. However, its calamitous track record with the Great Leap Forward allowed proponents of a fledging strategic innovation system to successfully make their case to be in charge.[6]

This strategic innovation system laid down the organizational foundations and governing principles and norms that became the basis of the SAMI model. This developmental framework was dictated by the harsh operating conditions of its formative years: scarce resources, a paucity of expertise, little external access, and fierce bureaucratic competition. To maximize its limited start-up capabilities, the strategic innovation system emphasized the importance of selectivity, mobilization, hands-on top-level leadership engagement, and combining absorption with indigenous innovation.

Selectivity

Selectivity was crucial to ensuring that the nascent Chinese S&T system did not spread itself too thin or have to constantly adjust course because of changing political and resource priorities. Even though the acquisition of nuclear weapons and ballistic missiles was of paramount priority, this required the development of an extensive range of underlying and enabling technologies. The authorities decided in the mid-1950s to draw up a comprehensive extended range S&T plan that would provide a definitive development road map, which was called the 1956–1967 Twelve-Year Long-Term National Science and Technology Plan (十二年科学技术发展远景规划, *Shier Nian Kexue Jishu Fazhan Yuanjing Guihua*).[7]

After extensive policy deliberation, fifty-five scientific and technological fields were earmarked as "important national scientific and technological tasks." However, a more select list of a dozen technologies was determined to be of top priority. A classified defense version of the plan also listed these same technologies for fast-track development. Prominence was given to five technologies, known as the five golden flowers (五朵金花, *wuduo jinhua*), which were deemed to be of the utmost strategic importance: nuclear energy, semiconductors, jet and rocket technology, computer technology, and automation technology.[8]

Mobilization

Mobilization allowed the strategic innovation system to leverage whatever resources and capabilities were deemed necessary to achieve its goals. It was able "to 'steal' personnel, gather resources, and raid other bureaucratic systems" to meet its needs.[9] At its apex in the late 1960s, the strategic weapons system controlled more than one hundred research institutes with a workforce of more than 130,000. Many of these research institutions specialized in nuclear and missile-related research, especially applied research.

The strategic weapons bureaucracy also maintained close ties with an extensive network of S&T organizations in the civilian sector, including universities under the Ministry of Education system and the Chinese Academy of Sciences (CAS).[10] This extensive civil-military interaction was the exception in a country where the defense and civilian domains were separated. Laboratories and departments belonging to civilian universities conducted a significant proportion of the basic research in fields such as optical physics, nuclear physics, hydrodynamics, electronic technology, and radiation chemistry.[11]

Authoritarian Leadership

Active support and participation from the very highest levels of the authoritarian political system was viewed as essential by the strategic innovation system to ensure access to resources and to overcome barriers. Their political masters concurred because they regarded the possession of strategic deterrence capabilities as crucial in guaranteeing China's national security and independence.[12] A three-person central group (中央三人小组, *zhongyang sanren xiaozu*) of senior military and civilian leaders made up of Chen Yun (陈云), Nie Rongzhen (聂荣臻), and Bo Yibo (薄一波) was placed in initial charge of overseeing the strategic weapons programs in the late 1950s.[13] As these projects expanded in size, complexity, and urgency as the international environment grew more threatening, the need increased for a more robust and authoritative oversight mechanism. In December 1962, a fifteen-member Central Special Committee (CSC; 中共中央专门委员会, *Zhonggong Zhongyang Zhuanmen Weiyuanhui*) was set up that was designed to overcome entrenched bureaucratic compartmentalization. This high-level body was given wide-ranging decision-making authority and reported directly to Mao and the Politburo Standing Committee. The CSC represented an unprecedented institutional innovation by the Chinese leadership in the face of serious external security threats to find ways to navigate around deep-rooted structural deficiencies of the Chinese system.[14]

The CSC was established to take over the management of the nuclear, ballistic missile, and other strategic weapons and innovation programs that were already in full swing. In creating this committee, Liu Shaoqi (刘少奇), who was the country's state president at the time, pointed out that "cooperation among different organizations is very important. The Communist Party should establish a special structure to strengthen the leadership [of these strategic programs]."[15] The entity reflected a number of key organizational principles, some of which continue to have relevance today:

- Civil-military integration: The membership of the CSC was intended to foster close interaction between the party, state, and PLA. Members included seven vice-premiers, several of whom were senior military commanders, and seven senior officials from the State Council, key industrial ministries, and the Central Military Commission (CMC). A permanent secretariat to the CSC was housed in the State Council National Defense Industry Office, a civilian body that oversaw the conventional defense industry. The head of this office was General Luo Ruiqing (罗瑞卿), a Long March veteran.
- Party dominance but state administration: The CSC was a party organization that reported to the Politburo, but Zhou Enlai (周恩来) was explicitly chosen as its head because he was premier, which gave him oversight of the economy, especially the heavy industrial sectors.
- Enhancing coordination and promoting science, technology, and industrial mobilization: One of the overriding goals in establishing the CSC was to facilitate coordination across fragmented bureaucratic and science, technology, and industrial systems. The development of the nuclear weapons program, for example, required the involvement of twenty-six government ministries, twenty provinces and cities, and more than nine hundred factories, research institutes, and specialized academies.[16]
- Interactive leadership-scientist coordination: The CSC maintained close two-way working ties with the scientific community. Senior scientists and engineers had direct and regular access to Zhou and CSC members and briefed them regularly on the status of their projects.
- Streamlined and authoritative decision making: The CSC was allowed wide-ranging authority by the party leadership to make major policy and operational decisions to ensure the rapid development of strategic weapons projects.
- Top-down command and control: A military-style hierarchical command-and-control system was established to allow the CSC to issue orders that

would be required to be swiftly implemented by the large number of organizations involved in these strategic projects located across the country.

- Institutionalization of personalistic policymaking: The CSC was an attempt to institutionalize the highly personalistic style of policymaking and governance during this period, especially to develop formal and robust linkages between high-level decision making and policy implementation.

The CSC flourished under the dynamic and hands-on leadership of Zhou. Between 1962 and his death in 1974, Zhou chaired more than sixty major CSC meetings and another five hundred smaller work sessions.[17] Although the development of the atomic and hydrogen bombs was of foremost priority in the CSC's early years, it also provided leadership guidance on numerous other major defense and strategic technology projects such as nuclear submarines, satellites, and civilian nuclear reactors. The CSC's permanent office was moved from the National Defense Industry Office to the Commission of Science and Technology for National Defense in 1967, which was a higher-level defense industrial administrative organ responsible for strategic weapons projects.

After Zhou's passing, the CSC became less active and steadily became marginalized in decision making. Hua Guofeng (华国锋) took over as CSC head after Zhou, but his brief tenure as the country's paramount leader coincided with rapidly diminishing leadership interest and appetite for strategic weapons projects and other expensive big-science programs.[18] When Deng Xiaoping (邓小平) replaced Hua in 1978, he also assumed the leadership of the CSC but appears to have paid little attention to its work.[19] Without a chief patron, the CSC was eventually dissolved in 1982 with the establishment of the Commission for Science, Technology, and Industry for National Defense (COSTIND), which assumed its responsibilities.

Reinnovation

Both absorption and innovation played vital roles in the initial development of China's strategic weapons capabilities. The primary reason for China's Two Bombs, One Satellite odyssey was its inability to access critical nuclear technological and engineering knowledge from the Soviet Union. When Beijing asked Moscow for help in nuclear arms-related R&D in the early 1950s, it was initially given assistance for only civilian nuclear power projects. The Soviets did eventually provide help on uranium enrichment, plutonium reprocessing, and warhead design and production in the late 1950s, which allowed China to lay the foundations of a nuclear industrial base. However, Moscow did not deliver on its promise to provide Beijing with a working atomic bomb, which became a major contributing factor in the breakdown of Sino-Soviet ties in 1960. This led to the almost overnight departure of Soviet nuclear experts.

Even though the abrupt termination of Soviet assistance for the Chinese nuclear weapons program was a serious blow, it was far from fatal. Nie Rongzhen, who was in charge of China's strategic weapons programs during this period, offered a candid analysis to Mao Zedong in July 1960 when Soviet nuclear scientists were pulling out of China. He said that "the Soviet side's stranglehold on us on the crucial issue of key technology is really infuriating. But indignation is useless. We are just going to have to show them. Maybe this kind of pressure will instead become the impetus for developing our science and technology, so we strive even more resolutely for independence and autonomy and self-reliance in science and technology, rather than counting on foreign assistance."[20] Chinese scientists and engineers were able to effectively build on what they had learned from the Soviets and conducted an atomic bomb test within four years of the rupture in relations.

The official story that Two Bombs, One Satellite was a triumph of Chinese indigenous S&T with little or no foreign help is a propagandistic narrative. It was the absorption of Soviet knowledge and technology in combination with homegrown Chinese innovation that drove success. General Zhang Aiping (张爱萍), who was one of the principal architects in the building of China's armaments apparatus between the 1950s and 1980s, has called the "digestion and absorption" of imported technologies a "force multiplier."[21]

The SAMI Model from Deng Xiaoping to Hu Jintao

The golden era of grand strategic technology development ended with a whimper in the late 1970s when Deng ascended to power and pivoted away from national security to economic development. As external threat assessments of imminent all-out nuclear conflict were downgraded to peaceful coexistence, the pressing need to maintain a militarized state and society and support expensive strategic and conventional weapons bases evaporated. Defense budgets shrunk, and there was a lengthy hiatus in the pursuit of strategic S&T programs.

By the mid-1980s, senior scientists and engineers from the strategic innovation system became so concerned that their R&D capabilities would be irretrievably lost that they wrote to Deng to plead for a restoration in funding to allow for the resumption of critical strategic programs. This lobbying effort came as the United States launched a highly ambitious space-based missile defense program to mitigate the threat of nuclear missile strikes from the Soviet Union and other rivals like China. Deng approved a new initiative to support strategic S&T projects that became known as the 863 Program to commemorate the date of its establishment in March 1986.[22]

While the 863 Program began to stir the strategic innovation system from its deep slumber, a key question was whether the SAMI approach was still appropriate in a peacetime environment focused on economic development. Even though selectivity was even more imperative in a resource-constrained environment, the ability of the strategic innovation system to mobilize what it needed across the Chinese system and to receive sustained top-level leadership attention and support was unlikely as their national security missions no longer ranked high in national priorities.

Selectivity

Selectivity was an important factor in the drawing up of strategic S&T development plans that resumed with the 863 Program. These long-term planning efforts to support R&D of nascent strategic technology capabilities had mostly lapsed after the 1956–1967 Twelve-Year Long-Term National Science and Technology Plan was concluded ahead of schedule in the early 1960s.[23] As technological innovation grew in importance in the 1990s, both for economic competitiveness and national security reasons, more long-term strategic technology development programs were established, such as the 995 New High-Technology Project, which focused on the development of strategic defense technologies at the beginning of the twenty-first century, and the 2006–2020 Medium- and Long-Term Science and Technology Development Plan (MLP).

The 863 Program had grand intentions but shoestring budgets in the 1980s and 1990s, which meant that only a few areas of research could be properly funded. Openly disclosed civilian allocations to the 863 Program in its first fourteen years from 1987 and 2000 totaled around RMB 5 billion, or a paltry average of RMB 360 million annually (US$780.8 million and US$52 million, respectively, based on 2021 exchange rates).[24] The PLA also provided funding as it jointly managed some dual-use and defense-focused 863 Program projects, but the scale of this support is unknown. Funding went into eight technology areas: laser technology, space, biotechnology, information technology, automation and manufacturing technology, energy, and advanced materials. Of these, lasers and space technology appear to have received the most attention and resources because they were directly managed by COSTIND. Other 863 Program projects that had significant defense and dual-use applications included optoelectronics, super-large-scale integrated circuits, information technology, and new materials.

The 863 Program enjoyed a major and sustained increase in funding from the beginning of the twenty-first century, which meant that the number and size of projects grew rapidly. In the information technology industry, for example, projects have covered the development of optical electronics, telecommunications, artificial intelligence (AI), and computing. There was also more attention paid to technology application and commercialization rather than simply fundamental R&D.

When Hu and Wen Jiabao (温家宝) took office in 2002, one of their early priorities was to examine the formulation of a large-scale initiative to accelerate and expand the scale of the country's S&T development, especially in critical strategic areas. Under Wen's direction, planning began in 2003 on what became known as the MLP.[25]

The MLP was meant to be both wide ranging and selective, much like its predecessor twelve-year plan from the late 1950s. There was intense debate among drafters as to whether the plan should be more of a decentralized bottom-up approach favored by the scientific community or the more traditional centralized top-down framework. Those who advocated for the "small science" approach said that pursuit of large-scale projects diverted resources from more original and innovative investigator-driven projects.[26] However, those in favor of the Two Bombs, One Satellite–inspired "big science" model could count on high-level political support, and they eventually prevailed.

One of the MLP's signature initiatives was the development of sixteen megaprojects deemed critical for enhancing national competitiveness. Thirteen were publicly disclosed, but another three went unnamed because they involved classified activities (see table 5.1). A sizable number of the open projects have dual-use applications, which was one of the guiding principles in the selection of many of these programs. Civilian entities and the PLA or the State Administration for Science, Technology, and Industry for National Defense (SASTIND) jointly managed four projects: major new drugs, prevention and control of major infectious diseases, high-resolution earth observation systems, and manned space flight and lunar exploration. Several other projects had dual-use applications such as high-grade numerically controlled machine tools, core electronic components and high-end universal chips, nuclear power stations with large-scale advanced pressurized water reactors and high-temperature and gas-cooled reactors, and single-aisle commercial airliners. In 2017, Ministry of Science and Technology (MOST) officials said that ten of these projects were purely civilian or *minkou* (民口) in nature, and the rest were defense or dual use. Setting aside the three classified projects, the three publicly disclosed defense or dual-use projects would

TABLE 5.1 The thirteen disclosed megaprojects of the 2006–2020 Medium- and Long-Term Science and Technology Development Plan

PROJECT NAME	STATE AGENCY IN CHARGE
Core electronics, high-end general chips, basic software	Ministry of Industry and Information Technology
Ultra-large-scale-integration manufacturing technology and complete sets of technology	Beijing, Shanghai governments
Next-generation broadband wireless mobile communication	Ministry of Industry and Information Technology, Datang Electronics Corp., Chinese Academy of Sciences Shanghai Institute of Microsystems, China Putian Corp.
High-end CNC machine tools and basic manufacturing technology	National Development and Reform Commission, Ministry of Industry and Information Technology
Large-layer oil and gas fields and coal bed methane development	China Petroleum, China United Coalbed Methane Corp.
Large-scale advanced pressurized water nuclear reactor	Ministry of Science and Technology, National Energy Bureau, Tsinghua University
Water pollution control and treatment	Ministry of Environmental Protection
Genetic transformation breeding of new plants	Ministry of Agriculture
Major new drugs	Ministry of Science and Technology, Ministry of Health, People's Liberation Army General Logistics Department
Prevention and control of major infectious diseases	Ministry of Science and Technology, Ministry of Health, People's Liberation Army General Logistics Department
High-resolution earth observation system	China National Space Administration, State Administration for Science, Technology and Industry for National Defense
Large passenger aircraft	Ministry of Industry and Information Technology, Commercial Aircraft Corp. of China
Manned space flight and lunar exploration project	People's Liberation Army General Armament Department (Now Equipment Development Department), State Administration for Science, Technology and Industry for National Defense, Chinese Academy of Science, China Space Technology and Industry Corp.

likely be the manned space and lunar program, high-resolution earth observation system, and either the high-end computer numerical control (CNC) machine tools and basic manufacturing technology or large commercial airliner projects.[27]

The performances of these megaprojects have been mixed. Those with top-level leadership attention and the support of powerful bureaucracies such as the

PLA and the defense industrial base have performed well because of ample access to resources, such as the space and aviation-related projects. Those that are civilian focused with little or no security spillover such as health care and environmental pollution have struggled.[28]

Mobilization

The mobilization component of the SAMI model underwent a far-reaching makeover in the post-1978 reform era. The Two Bombs, One Satellite wartime system was mothballed and major parts of it converted for civilian use in the 1980s and early 1990s as the country demilitarized and concentrated on economic development. Lip service was paid to the need to maintain a credible military production capacity in case the country was under serious threat again, but few resources were allocated to support these pronouncements.

Deng, for example, put forward a sixteen-character strategic guidance on restructuring the techno-security state soon after he took charge of the country that had two principles related to mobilization. One was the civil-military integration (CMI) requirement to combine military and civilian activities. This principle became the foundation for efforts to overcome the deep compartmentalization of the civilian and defense economies through the process known as defense conversion. In the 1980s and much of the 1990s, CMI focused on converting large segments of the defense industrial base for civilian application.

The second principle was the need to integrate peacetime and wartime preparations (平战结合, *pingzhan jiehe*). This guidance, though, was largely overlooked during the 1980s as China enjoyed a benign security environment. However, the importance of preparing for wartime mobilization began to gain leadership attention as external security concerns grew from the early 1990s because of rising tensions across the Taiwan Strait.[29] In 1994, a State National Defense Mobilization Committee was established to coordinate the building of a new national mobilization apparatus, although this focused on building civil defense ties with provincial and local counterparts rather than on technology-related matters.[30]

At around the same time, the defense industrial bureaucracy and strategic innovation system were making their case that the 1990–1991 Gulf War had shown how technologically backward China was militarily compared to the United States and its allies. For the techno-security establishment, mobilization had two dimensions: internal and external. On internal mobilization, the strategic innovation system and its related components within the defense industrial base—namely, the nuclear and space and missile sectors—had built up an extensive infrastructure during the Cold War, but much of it had been mothballed or converted to commercial civilian applications in the reform era. Their argument was that there was a need not only to preserve these existing facilities from the encroaching defense conversion process but also to rebuild atrophied capabilities, which was made more pressing by the deteriorating cross-strait security dynamics and the need to strategically deter US military intervention. CMC executive vice-chairman General Liu Huaqing (胡锦涛), who oversaw the running of the defense economy during most of the 1990s, said in 1994 that "as the focus of the country's agenda has shifted onto economic construction, many old military industrial enterprises have begun to produce civilian goods. In consideration of the country's needs, we must still retain some of these essential enterprises."[31] On external mobilization, the issue of how to tap into an increasingly advanced civilian economy for defense and strategic applications through CMI initiatives began to be raised from the late 1990s.

The arguments for enhancing internal and external strategic innovation and industrial mobilization capabilities grew stronger as Taiwan's push for independence intensified throughout the 1990s and the United States flexed its military muscle in the face of Chinese saber rattling. Any lingering debate ended in 1999 following the US bombing of the Chinese embassy in Belgrade, which led to the establishment of the 995 Project and the beginning of a sharp and long-term ramp-up in the development of strategic deterrence capabilities.

Authoritarian Leadership and the Return of the Central Special Committee

The demise of the CSC lasted throughout the 1980s, but it was eventually reestablished in 1989. A key reason was that the central authorities had begun to renew their interest in strategic technologies as shown by the establishment of the 863 Program. The management of the 863 Program projects, especially those related to defense, dual-use, and large-scale strategic issues such as space were in the hands of government entities such as COSTIND and the State Science and Technology Commission (which became MOST in 1998) as well as elements of the PLA to oversee. However, it became apparent after a few years that these organizations lacked the political clout and organizational expertise to coordinate across bureaucratic systems to implement some of the larger projects. The reintroduction of strategic big-science technology programs provided an important rationale for the revival of the CSC to help oversee their development.

Another impetus for restoring the CSC was China's cutoff from foreign defense and high-technology transfers following the 1989 Tiananmen Square crackdown. In his memoirs, Liu Huaqing, who was a CMC vice-chairman at the time, said that he and COSTIND director Ding Henggao (丁衡高) met with Premier Li Peng (李鹏) in August 1989 to discuss the state of the country's defense industrial modernization, especially the problems associated with speeding up weapons development. One of the issues brought up was the need to strengthen the macromanagement and macroregulation of the defense industry, especially between the State Council and CMC.[32] Two months after this discussion, it was quietly announced that the CSC would be reestablished.[33]

The new CSC was different from its Cold War predecessor in a number of significant ways. First, the committee was no longer a party institution but instead came under the joint leadership of the State Council and the CMC. Second, it became an advisory and coordinating organ, losing the sweeping decision-making powers that it had enjoyed in its former life. Third, the authorities downplayed the public profile of the new CSC, unlike the earlier body that received extensive attention and was lauded for its track record. There was little official reporting of the activities of the reestablished CSC and it rarely appeared on any official government or defense-related organization charts.

When the State Council announced the lineup of its organizations in 1998 and 2003, the CSC was listed in the category of "advisory and coordinating organs." These mostly ad hoc institutions were comparatively low ranking with limited influence.[34] They included the State National Defense Mobilization Committee, State Frontier Defense Committee, State Flood Control and Drought Relief Headquarters, State Science, Technology, and Education Leading Group, and numerous other organs. However, the CSC disappeared from this list of advisory and coordinating organs beginning in 2008.[35] Instead, there was an obscure State Council notice in that same year announcing an "adjustment" in the CSC without providing any further details. A rare public reference to this notice was posted on a Hubei county government website.[36]

However, there were some important continuities between the new and old CSCs that suggested that its formal standing did not reflect its actual policy influence and bureaucratic authority:

- High-level leadership lineup: The head of the CSC was the premier and the rest of its membership was comprised of senior civilian and military officials with high-level bureaucratic standing. They included the CMC vice-chairman responsible for the defense science, technology, and industry portfolio, the vice-premier in charge of industrial affairs, and the defense minister.[37] Other reports suggested that several senior PLA officials served on the CSC, including the heads of the PLA General Staff, Logistics, and Armament Departments (see figure 5.2).[38] Moreover, the permanent administrative office of the CSC was located within COSTIND (subsequently SASTIND after 2008) and the SASTIND director was its office head.[39]

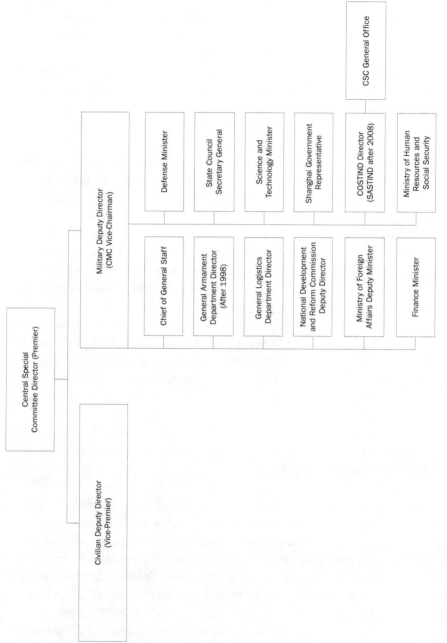

FIGURE 5.2. Organizational chart of the Central Special Committee in the 1990s

- Forging CMI: The CSC was a leading organ promoting dual-use technology development. Whereas most of this effort during the 1990s and 2000s was on specific projects, this appears to have shifted in the late 2000s to guiding broader CMI policy.

- Civilian leadership with military cooperation: The CSC continued to promote the idea that national-level strategic S&T projects should be under civilian control to allow them to serve national interests and prevent them from becoming militarized. This is a lesson that the Chinese authorities learned from countries such as the United States that have placed key strategic technology programs, such as their space and nuclear weapons agencies, under civilian bureaucracies.[40]

- Direct top-level political access: Although the CSC was no longer a party organ, it had direct access to the upper echelons of the party leadership, including the Politburo Standing Committee as well as the CMC.

- Coordination and decision-making authority: Although the CSC was formally defined as a coordinating organ by State Council regulations, it also was described as having decision-making authority in official and media reporting. A *Xinhua News Agency* dispatch on the Tiangong-1 and Shenzhou 8 space projects in December 2011 noted that the CSC had on "many occasions researched and undertaken decision making on major issues" related to these two programs.[41]

- Personal authority of the CSC director: The CSC was lightly institutionalized and its authority and influence in policymaking and coordination depended heavily on its director and committee members. The CSC had three directors between 1989 and 2012. Li Peng was perhaps the most prominent and influential during his tenure from 1989 to 1998, including playing an instrumental role in its revival. Zhu Rongji (朱镕基) did not appear to have been active or very interested in the CSC's affairs during his five years at the helm from 1998 to 2003, which is not surprising as he had little experience in science, technology, or defense issues and spent most of his time engaged in economic reform matters. Wen appears to have more closely followed in Li's footsteps and played an active role as CSC director, in part because he took keen interest in S&T affairs, especially in the development of major megaprojects that dovetailed with the CSC's portfolio of responsibilities, such as the manned and lunar space programs.

Responsibilities and Activities of the Central Special Committee

At the beginning of the 2010s, the CSC sought to find new areas of policy responsibility to justify its continuing existence, and military-civil fusion (MCF) became a top area of focus. The State Council promulgated a policy document in 2010 known as Document No. 37 laying out a long-term strategy for MCF implementation.[42] The document pointed out that one of the principal organs for MCF macro-coordination and guidance was the CSC's permanent administrative office. This was the first time that the CSC office has been tasked with this role. To carry out this responsibility, the CSC office appears to have been assigned the MCF Promotion Office that belongs to the Ministry of Industry and Information Technology (MIIT).[43]

Although the CSC has played a prominent role in major defense programs, there is very little official reporting about the committee's activities in these matters. In his memoirs, Liu pointed out that the CMC and CSC jointly approved the go-ahead for the R&D of a new generation of nuclear submarines in 1994.[44] The CSC has also been involved in assessing China's military aviation industry. In April 1990, the Aviation Industry Corporation of China reported that the CSC held a two-day meeting on military aircraft research and development issues.[45]

There has been some publicity detailing the CSC's involvement in the development of space launchers, which have both civilian and military uses. This began in the early 1990s with evaluations of the Long March Series 2F rocket in 1992 and continued with the Long March Series 5 since the late 2000s.[46] Although there is no public information to link the CSC with the development of the ballistic missile variants of these Long March rockets, its Cold War predecessor played an active role even toward the end of its tenure in the late 1970s and early 1980s in guiding the R&D of the country's first- and second-generation intercontinental ballistic missiles such as the Dongfang-5. The old CSC was also interested in other defense-related high-technology projects with potentially disruptive innovation capabilities such as high-powered lasers. At a 1979 CSC meeting on laser weapons, Deng was quoted as saying "that we have to add more power and strength to the lasers. We will certainly need to rely on them in the future for our defense, to strike at aircraft and tanks."[47]

Case Study of the Central Special Committee and the Shenzhou Manned Space Program

The Shenzhou manned space program offers an insightful case study to understand how authoritarian top-down leadership was applied to the management of major defense and strategic projects in the 1990s and 2000s, as the CSC was closely associated with this program. The committee was given the responsibility to evaluate whether the manned space program should be allowed to move from research into full-scale development in the early 1990s. After a series of meetings, the CSC met in August 1992 and gave the green light for the project to proceed and at the same time put forward a three-stage road map for the development of the Chinese manned space program to 2020. To ensure collective responsibility, Li Peng asked all CSC members to sign the document titled "Regarding the Request for Instructions on the Engineering Development of China's Manned Spacecraft" to show that they personally backed the decision. The document was then sent to the State Council, CMC, and Politburo Standing Committee.[48]

The Politburo Standing Committee met a month later to give the final approval for the project based largely on the prior CSC decision.[49] Following this go-ahead, Jiang Zemin (江泽民) asked the CSC to organize the leadership group for the project. Operational project management was placed in the hands of COSTIND and the PLA General Staff Department. The General Armament Department (GAD) took over full control of the program following its establishment in 1998.[50] The CSC continued to monitor the Shenzhou program and was briefed ahead of every mission launch.[51]

Operational responsibility for the detailed management of the project was entrusted to the PLA, and specifically to the GAD that established the 921 Project Office. Because of the project's political and technological importance, the GAD director was put in charge. A separate project leading group comprised of senior technical experts provided regular oversight and review. The CSC built on this expertise in the space sector to become involved in other major space technology programs, of which its last one appears to have been the Chang'e lunar project.[52]

The Multistep Process of Introduction, Digestion, Assimilation, and Reinnovation

As efforts to revive the techno-security state began to pick up in the second half of the 1980s, a huge obstacle standing in the way was that years of neglect had left the original innovation component of the overall reinnovation engine broken. This meant that the burden of technological advancement rested on the SAMI-A absorption platform.

The strategic and especially the conventional defense innovation and industrial bases had become adept at technological and industrial absorption during the 1950s because of the influx of Soviet know-how and technology. However, this expertise atrophied after the rupture in relations with Moscow that largely cut off China from foreign technology sources for nearly the next two decades. When access to foreign technology markets was restored in the post-1978 reform era, China had to relearn its absorption skills. Long Guoqiang (隆国强), a senior researcher in the Foreign Economic Relations Department of the State Council Development Research Center, pointed out that "China emphasizes the introduction of technology but does not pay attention to its absorption."[53] A popular saying describing this anemic absorption process is "introduce, fall behind, reintroduce, fall behind again" (引进, 落后, 再引进, 再落后, *yinjin, luohou, zai yinjin, zai luohou*).[54] Long distinguishes between the acquisition and absorption of foreign technology. The importation of external hardware or knowledge is just one step in the complex multistage process of absorption.

Absorptive capacity is a widely studied concept in the business world because it is extensively utilized by enterprises. Shaker Zahra and Gerard George provide an insightful framework of analysis that identifies the different elements that make up absorptive capacity, which they define as a dynamic capability embedded in a firm's routines and processes, is geared toward effecting organizational change, and is strategic in nature as it defines a firm's path of development and evolution.[55] Although their focus is at the enterprise level, this can also be applied at the state level. They observe that absorptive capacity has four dimensions that can be grouped into two categories. First is that potential absorptive capacity allows organizations to be receptive to the absorption of external sources of knowledge, but it does not mean that they will be able to successfully exploit this knowledge. There are two key components of potential absorptive capacity:

- Acquisition signifies the capability to identify and acquire externally generated knowledge that is critical to operations.
- Assimilation refers to the routines and processes that allow organizations to analyze, process, interpret, and understand the information obtained from external sources.

The second category is realized absorptive capacity, which is the ability of an organization to turn its potential absorptive capacity into actual output. There are two key attributes:

- Transformation denotes a capability to develop and refine the routines that facilitate combining existing knowledge and the newly acquired and assimilated information.
- Exploitation allows organizations to refine, extend, and leverage existing competencies or to create new ones by incorporating acquired and transformed knowledge into its operations.

The Chinese authorities began to reconstitute a credible national absorption apparatus in the 1990s, although some analysts argue that serious efforts did not start until the beginning of the twenty-first century. Tsinghua University political economist Hu Angang (胡鞍钢) believes that it was not until China's accession to the World Trade Organization in 2001 that China "greatly increased its ability to import foreign technology, fully utilizing its ability to reinnovate technology (including imported innovations, copied innovations, and integrated innovations)."[56] Chinese expenditures on the acquisition of foreign technology and in-house assimilation of technology show state support for absorption grew gradually from the 1990s, although it only picked up pace from the early to mid-2000s as S&T development gained high-level attention. By comparison, the techno-security state's efforts to develop its introduce, digest, assimilate, and reinnovate (IDAR) system can be traced back to the early 1990s as it sought to take advantage of opportunities presented by the collapse of the Soviet Union.

Reinnovation became formally recognized as the centerpiece of China's near-to medium-term innovation strategy in the mid-2000s with the adoption of the MLP. Even though the plan made clear that China's ultimate goal was to develop a robust original innovation (原始创新, *yuanshi chuangxin*) capacity that would allow the country to be technologically self-sufficient, this was an aspirational objective that would take several decades to achieve. The reality for the next one to two decades would be to continue to rely heavily on foreign sources for technology and knowledge, although these foreign sources would be combined with increasing levels of domestic input. The MLP defined reinnovation as consisting of the multistep process of introduction (引进, *yinjin*), digestion (消化, *xiaohua*), and assimilation (吸收, *xishou*) that leads to reinnovated (再创新, *zaichuangxin*) output.[57] This can be concisely referred to as the IDAR strategy (see figure 5.3). These four stages roughly correspond with the four categories in the Zahra-George potential and realized absorptive capacity framework.

The IDAR strategy is most clearly articulated in a supplementary document to the MLP that called for encouraging the introduction of advanced foreign technology that could be digested and absorbed for reinnovation.[58] The document, titled "Opinions to Encourage Technology Transfer and Innovation and Promote the Transformation of the Growth Mode in Foreign Trade," was issued by a group of eight powerful government economic, financial, and planning agencies that included the National Development and Reform Commission (NDRC), Ministry of Finance, and Ministry of Commerce.

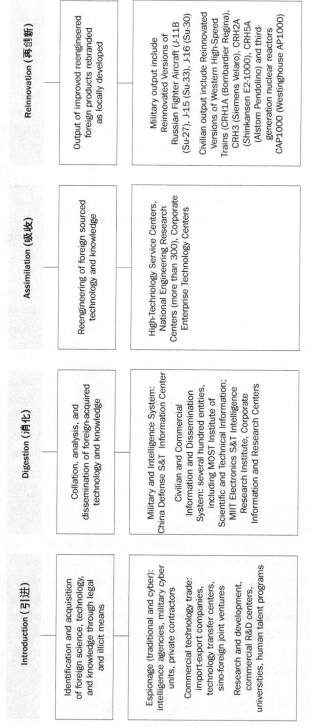

FIGURE 5.3. IDAR: China's absorptive model of technological development

Introduction (引进)	Digestion (消化)	Assimilation (吸收)	Reinnovation (再创新)
Identification and acquisition of foreign science, technology, and knowledge through legal and illicit means	Collation, analysis, and dissemination of foreign-acquired technology and knowledge	Reengineering of foreign sourced technology and knowledge	Output of improved reengineered foreign products rebranded as locally developed
Espionage (traditional and cyber): intelligence agencies, military cyber units, private contractors Commercial technology trade: import-export companies, technology transfer centers, sino-foreign joint ventures Research and development, commercial R&D centers, universities, human talent programs	Military and Intelligence System: China Defense S&T Information Center Civilian and Commercial Information and Dissemination System: several hundred entities, including MOST Institute of Scientific and Technical Information; MIIT Electronics S&T Intelligence Research Institute, Corporate Information and Research Centers	High-Technology Service Centers, National Engineering Research Centers (more than 300), Corporate Enterprise Technology Centers	Military output include Reinnovated Versions of Russian Fighter Aircraft (J-11B (Su-27), J-15 (Su-33), J-16 (Su-30) Civilian output include Reinnovated Versions of Western High-Speed Trains (CRH1A (Bombardier Regina), CRH3 (Siemens Velaro), CRH2A (Shinkansen E2-1000), CRH5A (Alstom Pendolino) and third-generation nuclear reactors CAP1000 (Westinghouse AP1000)

The Rise of the Techno-Security IDAR System

Once the techno-security state began to shift from survival to rebuilding mode in the mid- to late 1980s, it invested early and heavily to build a robust and comprehensive IDAR apparatus. This undertaking began modestly at first because of limited resources, restricted access to Western technology, and a fledgling absorption base, but these efforts ramped up significantly from the early 1990s because of a sharp deterioration in the external security environment and rich opportunities presented by the fall of the Soviet Union and its satellite states. By the beginning of the twenty-first century, the techno-security IDAR base had turned into a formidable absorption champion and has become progressively stronger and more capable ever since. Examination will now turn to the forging of this techno-security absorption system through its key components of introduction, digestion, assimilation, and reinnovation.

Introduction

Gaining access to external knowledge is vital for the Chinese techno-security state to compensate for the gaps and inadequacies of its R&D apparatus and in order to meet ambitious development targets. There are a variety of acquisition and technology transfer mechanisms and channels that include technology and equipment imports, foreign direct investment and direct (explicit technology transfer agreements) and indirect (transfer of governance and other types of less tangible soft skill sets) spillover effects, espionage through traditional industrial and information-era cyber operations, open-source information collection and analysis, establishment of foreign R&D centers, and human capital transfers and exchanges.[59] The most important of these channels are arms and defense technology-related imports, espionage, and open-source information collection and analysis.

China is one of the world's largest arms importers and exporters. The Stockholm International Peace Research Institute estimates that China was the world's biggest arms importer between 2003 and 2007 with a global share of 12 percent, second between 2009 and 2013 with a 4.8 percent share, and sixth from 2014 to 2018 with a 4.2 percent share.[60] A large majority of these imports have come from Russia, and the nature of these imports have evolved over time to reflect the changing technological priorities of the Chinese techno-security state.[61] In the first ten years of the resumption of the Sino-Russian arms trade relationship between the beginning of the 1990s and late 1990s, the bulk of Chinese acquisitions were of completed weapons systems that could be quickly fielded. This shifted from the late 1990s to the present day to absorption-related activities such as the purchase of specific components and subsystems that could be integrated into locally designed platforms or licensed local production of complete systems.

The PLA established a large and well-developed joint civilian-military bureaucracy to manage this arms trade. On the military side, the GAD (subsequently the Equipment Development Department [EDD] after 2016) is the principal responsible agency involved in the process. The GAD's Equipment Technology Cooperation Bureau (装备技术合作局, *Zhuangbei Jishu Hezuo Ju*) and Military Trade Office (军贸处, *Junmao Chu*) managed this portfolio.[62] On the government side, COSTIND (subsequently SASTIND after 2008) was the chief agency in charge through its Military Trade and Foreign Affairs Department (军贸与外事司, *Junmao Yu Waishi Si*). Other government agencies involved include MIIT and the Ministry of Commerce. Commercially, there are around half a dozen specialized trading firms responsible for the import-export activities of the ten major state-owned defense corporations. The PLA relies on China Poly Group Corporation (中国保利集团公司, *Zhongguo Baoli Jituan Gongsi*) for its arms trade activities, especially arms imports from Russia.

In the face of long-term international restrictions on defense-related technology transfers, two of the primary mechanisms that the Chinese defense S&T system employs to mitigate these limitations are open-source information collection and espionage activities. For open-source information collection, China has built a substantial infrastructure that dates back to the 1950s and was initially created to support the country's construction of its strategic nuclear weapons and ballistic missile capabilities. Information collection is an integral element of the information analysis and dissemination (IAD) system, which will be assessed in the next section on assimilation.

Espionage also plays an important and growing role in China's defense acquisition efforts, although its precise value is difficult to gauge because of the lack of transparency. It comes in two forms: industrial espionage and computer network exploitation or cyber espionage. Traditional industrial espionage has been the bread and butter of China's spying efforts since the founding of the communist republic, but its impact on improving the Chinese defense S&T system appears to have been limited and episodic until the beginning of the 1990s because of the country's economic and technological isolation from the global economy.

An important turning point in China's industrial espionage efforts took place in the early 1990s with the collapse of the Soviet Union. This allowed China to take advantage of the economic chaos in Russia and former Soviet republics and gain access to their defense industrial facilities and scientific and engineering personnel. Hundreds of Russian defense scientists and engineers were recruited and brought over to China to provide expert advice.[63] There has also been a proliferation of cases that show intensive Chinese intelligence-gathering activities taking place in the former Soviet Union. Yevgeny Livadny, the head of intellectual property for Rostec, Russia's state-owned conglomerate for arms exports, said in December 2019 that there had been five hundred cases between 2002 and 2019 of "unauthorized copying of our equipment abroad." Livadny singled out China, saying that "China alone has copied aircraft engines, Sukhoi planes, [aircraft carrier] deck jets, air defense systems, portable air defense missiles, and analogs of the Pantsir medium-range surface-to-air systems."[64] For example, the Russian chief executive of a rocket and missile company was imprisoned for illegally providing missile design information to China Precision Machinery Import-Export Corporation in 2007.[65] In another case also involving missile technology, two Russian academics from Saint Petersburg's Baltic State Technological University were jailed in 2012 for selling classified information on the Bulava, Russia's latest generation intercontinental ballistic missile, to representatives of Chinese military intelligence.[66]

A key role for defense S&T organizations is to provide technical targeting requirements to guide the work of collection units. Little information is known about how this targeting process works, but the notoriously hierarchical and compartmentalized nature of the Chinese defense establishment suggests that targeting requests by S&T organizations would go up through their respective chains of command. Entities affiliated with the defense industry would report to SASTIND, while PLA units would go through their own departments and service arms. Requirements by military units belonging to the armaments system, for example, will go up through the EDD hierarchy and its service arms counterparts. For cyber espionage, military targeting requests are likely to be overseen by the Network Systems Department of the PLA's Strategic Support Force, which is in charge of carrying out computer network exploitation operations.[67] The effective management of these coordination and transmission channels is crucial to the performance of the acquisition process. Entities that are likely to play influential roles in providing targeting requirements include the EDD, CMC Science and Technology Commission, SASTIND, and each of the major state-owned defense industrial corporations.[68]

Digestion

In the digestion of foreign technology and knowledge, a key mechanism that the techno-security state has cultivated since the 1950s has been an S&T IAD apparatus.[69] A key rationale for the historical development of the IAD system was to provide information on global S&T developments to civilian and military S&T and academic organizations that were largely isolated from the outside world between the 1950s and 1970s. The output of this system consisted of not only the acquisition, collation, and translation of foreign S&T literature but also of specific technical information that was of direct utility to R&D organizations, especially for nuclear, space, and computational outfits.[70]

The IAD system consists of around four hundred analysis and diffusion centers with around fifty thousand personnel, according to a 2006 assessment.[71] However, only around thirty-five belong to central government agencies; the rest are affiliated with provincial or lower level institutions.[72] A number of major IAD entities were established within the S&T system, including the Institute of Scientific and Technical Information of China, which belonged to the State Science and Technology Commission (now known as MOST), and the Electronics Science and Technology Intelligence Research Institute, which is affiliated with MIIT.

The vast majority of the external information that IAD organizations analyze comes from open sources such as media, the internet, academic research, and trade fairs.[73] The classified intelligence collected by PLA intelligence agencies is likely only available for the military component of the IAD system, which is centralized under the China Defense Science and Technology Information Center (CDSTIC; 中国国防科技情报中心, *Zhongguo Guofang Keji Qingbao Zhongxin*), which is affiliated with the EDD. CDSTIC has grown rapidly over the past few decades, especially since the end of the 1990s, to cope with intensive demand for its S&T information and analysis services from the defense innovation system, military organizations, and the country's leadership.[74]

Concerted efforts have been made to improve the ability of the IAD system to assimilate and disseminate information in a timely and organized fashion. This includes the development of internet-based and closed intranet S&T databases and information retrieval networks. CDSTIC, for example, operates an engineering technology information network, an all-army equipment S&T information network, an S&T intelligence network, and an online digital library.[75]

Another important aspect of digestion is learning, and the Chinese national and defense S&T systems have built up an extensive apparatus of research universities, vocational colleges, laboratories, and research institutes to study and improve on the acquired foreign technology and knowledge as well as to educate and train new generations of scientists and engineers. Although the country's higher educational system is able to produce sufficient quantities of science and engineering graduates to satisfy demand from both the civilian and defense sectors, the quality of this talent pool is mixed.

The number of science and engineering (S&E) graduates from Chinese higher education institutions has surged since the late 1990s. In 1998, there were around 250,000 S&E bachelor's degree graduates, but this increased to 1.7 million by 2015, of which nearly 70 percent were engineering-related degrees. By comparison, the United States produced around 800,000 S&E graduates in 2015, or less than half of the Chinese output.[76]

An even better gauge of advanced educational quality that contributes to innovative capacity is the number of doctoral degrees awarded, as this group is predominately engaged in R&D activities. The United States leads the world with forty thousand S&E doctoral degrees awarded in 2018, compared with China, which came in second with thirty-four thousand.[77] By comparison, China issued nineteen hundred doctorates in 1993.[78] Around one-third of US S&E doctoral degrees awarded, however, were to non-US citizens, of which Chinese nationals accounted for the largest number. Of the 210,000 US S&E doctoral degrees awarded between 2000 and 2017, Chinese nationals accounted for 66,700 or 32 percent. However, an overwhelming, if gradually declining, majority of Chinese doctoral degree holders stay in the United States for at least five years or longer. The stay rate was around 92 percent in 2003, but this had fallen to around 82 percent by 2017.[79]

Assimilation

Assimilation is the third step of the IDAR process and represents the engineering to manufacturing stage. One of the highest priorities of the techno-security state and the Chinese state in the reform era has been to upgrade its extensive but outdated labor-intensive engineering and manufacturing base to narrow the wide gap with state-of-the-art global levels. Key assimilation approaches to achieving this objective include reverse engineering, acquisition of advanced automation machine-building equipment, and the encouragement of foreign firms to establish engineering and manufacturing outposts in China to share their know-how and hardware with local partners.

The development of advanced manufacturing capabilities has featured prominently and consistently in China's five-year and longer-term S&T development plans over the past several decades. Automation and manufacturing technology was one of the select few technology sectors to be included in the 863 Program. The acquisition and development of computer-integrated manufacturing systems such as computer-aided design and computer-aided manufacturing hardware and software has been a top priority for the defense and civilian production bases since the 1980s. The aviation industry is especially keen on using computer-aided design and computer-aided manufacturing processes because they could significantly shorten the development time for military aircraft projects.[80] In the 2000s, the focus of 863 Program manufacturing projects turned to more advanced CNC machine tools, informatization, and the ability to use advanced and new materials in production processes, especially composite and specialized metals such as titanium.[81] In the MLP, two of the sixteen megaprojects were on engineering and manufacturing: ultra-large-scale integration manufacturing technology and high-end CNC machine tools and basic manufacturing technology. One of the sixteen major special projects contained in the Science, Technology, and Innovation (STI) 2030 program is on intelligent manufacturing and robotics.

The Chinese civilian and defense authorities have invested heavily in building up an extensive technology and engineering ecosystem to support efforts to combine digested foreign and local technologies. In the civilian domain, this includes the establishment of an extensive array of entities such as national engineering research centers (国家工程研究中心, *guojia gongcheng yanjiu zhongxin*), national-level enterprise technology centers (国家级企业技术中心, *guojiaji qiye jishu zhongxin*), state key laboratories (国家重点实验室, *guojia zhongdian shiyan shi*), national engineering laboratories (国家工程实验室, *guojia gongcheng shiyan shi*), national engineering technology centers (国家工程技术研究中心, *guojia gongcheng jishu yanjiu zhongxin*), national technology transfer centers (国家技术转移中心, *guojia jishu zhuanyi zhongxin*), and technology service centers (科技服务中心, *keji fuwu zhongxin*). Chinese authorities have also prioritized the recruitment of foreign technical experts through organizations such as the State Administration of Foreign Experts Affairs (国家外国专家局, *Guojia Waiguo Zhuanjia Ju*).

National engineering research centers have been an important mechanism in turning acquired and digested external technology into manufacturing output. They were first established in 1991 and came under the supervision of the NDRC. According to government regulations issued to manage these centers, their main purpose is to act as engineering and commercialization bridges between the R&D system and the industrial economy by helping to speed up the translation of research into actual production output, implement "engineering and system integration of major scientific and technological achievements with major market value," and enhance "indigenous innovation by digesting and assimilating technologies introduced from abroad and re-creating new technologies through the development of international cooperation and exchanges."[82]

There were 131 national engineering research centers at the end of 2017 of which the overwhelming majority were focused on civilian technologies. At least eleven of these centers are involved in dual-use-related activities or are located

TABLE 5.2 National engineering research centers engaged in dual-use activities or affiliated with defense industrial entities

NATIONAL ENGINEERING RESEARCH CENTER	PARENT COMPANY
National Engineering Research Center for Communication Software and Special Integrated Circuit Design (通信软件与专用集成电路设计国家工程研究中心)	China Electronics Technology Group Corporation, No. 54 Institute (中国电子科技集团公司第 54 所)
National Engineering Research Center of New Power Supply (新型电源国家工程研究中心)	China Electronics Technology Group Corporation, No. 18 Institute (中国电子科技集团公司第 18 所)
High-End CNC National Engineering Research Center (高档数控国家工程研究中心)	Shenyang Institute of Computing Technology, Chinese Academy of Sciences (中国科学院沈阳计算技术研究所)
National Engineering Research Center for Ship Design Technology (船舶设计技术国家工程研究中心)	Shanghai CSSC Ship Design Technology Co., Ltd. (上海中船船舶设计技术公司)
National Engineering Research Center for the Application of System Simulation Technology in Economics (经济领域系统仿真技术应用国家工程研究中心)	China Aerospace Science and Industry System Simulation Technology Co., Ltd. (航天科工系统仿真技术公司)
National Engineering Research Center of Small Satellites and Their Applications (小卫星及其应用国家工程研究中心)	Aerospace Dongfanghong Satellite Co., Ltd. (航天东方红卫星有限公司)
National Engineering Research Center for Computer Virus Prevention Technology (计算机病毒防治技术国家工程研究中心)	National Computer Virus Center (国家计算机病毒中心) Beijing Ruike Corp. (北京瑞科等)
National Engineering Research Center for Shipbuilding (船舶制造国家工程研究中心)	Dalian Shipbuilding Industry Co., Ltd. (大连船舶制造有限公司)
National Engineering Research Center for Ship Navigation System (船舶导航系统国家工程研究中心)	Dalian Ship Navigation System Co., Ltd. (大连船舶导航系统有限公司)
National Engineering Research Center for Mobile Communications (移动通信国家工程研究中心)	China Electronics Technology Group Corp., No. 7 Institute (中国电子科技集团公司第 7 所)
Engineering Research Center for Unmanned Aerial Vehicle Systems (无人机系统国家工程研究中心)	Northwestern Polytechnical University (西北工业大学)

within the defense industrial apparatus (see table 5.2). In addition, there were 346 national engineering technology research centers, which were overseen by MOST, 217 national engineering laboratories, 1,276 national-level enterprise technology centers, and hundreds of joint national-local engineering research centers.[83]

The defense establishment has built up its own substantial engineering assimilation apparatus. A key institutional platform is the Defense Science and Technology Industry Advanced Technology Research and Application Centers (国防科技工业先进技术研究应用中心, *Guofang Keji Gongye Xianjin Jishu Yanjiu Yingyong Zhongxin*), which were established in the late 2000s with a key goal of "transforming scientific and technological achievements into enterprise productivity."[84] When the first wave of these research and application centers were established, they focused on specialized manufacturing processes rather than specific technologies. The first two centers, which were set up as pilot projects to test the validity of this platform, were dedicated to welding automation and precision casting. Subsequent centers were dedicated to forging technology, electrical equipment, refractory materials processing, and special manufacturing technology.[85] A prime function of these centers is to operate as accelerated technology and engineering transfer conduits between universities and research institutes and defense industrial enterprises.

In addition to these research and application centers, there are several other types of defense institutions engaged in the assimilation process. Defense S&T laboratories (国防科技重点实验室, guofang keji zhongdian shiyan shi) are more focused on the basic research pipeline. There are also military and defense industrial engineering universities and their affiliated research organizations. They include entities such as Beijing Aeronautics and Astronautics University, Beijing Institute of Technology, Harbin Institute of Technology, Harbin Engineering University, Nanjing Aeronautics and Astronautics University, Nanjing Institute of Technology, and Northwestern Polytechnical University.

This heavy investment in and active pursuit of assimilation efforts led to a major improvement in Chinese civilian and defense engineering and manufacturing output between the 1990s and 2010s. As a share of global manufacturing value-added output, China grew from 3.6 percent in 1980 to becoming the world's biggest manufacturer with a 28.8 percent share by 2018.[86] In terms of technological quality, China has steadily moved up the ladder from a low-level manufacturing power in the 1980s to mid-level status in the twenty-first century and is now seeking to enter the elite global club of Industry 4.0 advanced manufacturing states by the late 2020s to mid-2030s.

Reinnovated Output

The final stage of the IDAR process is the manufactured output coming out of the introduce-digest-assimilate pipeline. The nature of the products can be classified according to how much of their content is composed of technologies directly copied or imported from foreign sources, locally modified but based on foreign intellectual property, or wholly developed domestically. There are eight categories in this imitation-to-innovation typology of which four come under the IDAR rubric and will be addressed in this section. The remaining four correspond with original innovation and will be examined later in this chapter.

First is duplicative imitation, which refers to products acquired from foreign sources that are closely copied with little or no technological improvements. This was the starting point of industrial and technological development for China when the Communist Party took power in 1949. The process begins with transfers of foreign technology and components that are assembled or produced with no local technology input. The overwhelming bulk of weapons output from the Chinese conventional defense industry in the early to mid-1950s falls into this category.

The second level is creative imitation that represents a more sophisticated form of imitation that generates largely copied products but with improved performance features. Domestic research input begins to find its way into modest improvements in components in noncore areas. The development process begins to take shape with limited but growing work done in the technology development and engineering and manufacturing stages. The bulk of work is primarily on how to integrate domestic components into foreign-acquired platforms. Much of the production activities of the Chinese conventional defense industry transitioned into this category in the late 1950s to early 1960s and the strategic innovation system would have started its initial R&D work pursuing creative imitation approaches at around the same time.

The third rung of the imitation ladder is creative adaptation or advanced imitation, which is what the IDAR process was set up to achieve. Products in this category are inspired by existing foreign-derived technologies but differ significantly in design, content, and performance. One of the primary forms of creative adaptation is reverse engineering. Creative adaptation requires considerably more research, especially in product or concept refinement, and significantly more effort to combine higher levels of domestic content and a foreign-derived platform. Since the 1990s, the conventional and strategic defense innovation and industrial systems as well as the national innovation system and industrial economy became firmly established at this level. Sizable portions of the Chinese techno-security state are at this level of advanced imitation.

The poster child of creative adaptation in the defense realm is the Shenyang J-11B fighter aircraft, which is the Chinese unauthorized adaptation of the Russian Sukhoi Su-27. The "IDARization" of the Su-27 fighter into the J-11B took place between the late 1990s and early 2000s. The Chinese and Russian governments signed a license agreement in 1995 for the assembly and eventual manufacturing of the Su-27 aircraft by Shenyang Aircraft Corporation, one of the country's most advanced military aviation enterprises. A first production run of around one hundred aircraft took place between the late 1990s and mid-2000s. Chinese engineers initially struggled to fully master the advanced manufacturing and industrial management methods needed to produce an aircraft that was a generational leap in technology. Shenyang Aircraft Corporation was eventually able to absorb the processes and lift output to its maximum rate by the early 2000s.[87]

As the two sides negotiated for another production round in the early 2000s, the Chinese side was discovered to have been secretly reverse engineering the aircraft, which they called the J-11B.[88] This led to a major rupture in the two countries' defense S&T cooperation as Russia demanded that China halt such intellectual property rights infringements and guarantee not to further engage in these practices.[89]

China, however, pushed back and claimed that the J-11B was a brand-new aircraft with significantly improved avionics, used composite materials, and had more advanced weapons systems. As the dispute continued into the late 2000s, China was found to have cloned two more Sukhoi fighter models. The first was the Su-33, which was an improved naval carrier version of the Su-27. The Chinese version was named the J-15. This project was not as big an irritant in China-Russia relations, though, because China had acquired a prototype from Ukraine in the early 2000s. The second reverse-engineering project was the Su-30 fighter aircraft, which was transformed into the J-16.

Beijing and Moscow eventually put their differences aside in the early 2010s, which allowed for the resumption of negotiations for major weapons packages. This access to former Soviet defense technology may have helped select portions of the Chinese defense industry to advance by at least one or more generations. The most significant contributions have been in fighter aircraft programs, air-to-air missiles, radars, fire-control systems, aircraft carriers, and other naval systems, and manned space flight.

The fourth step is crossover innovation, which is the transition from imitation to original homegrown innovation. This process refers to products that are jointly developed by Chinese and foreign partners with significant technology and knowledge transfers to the local side that result in the creation of an R&D base able to conduct independent and original innovation activities. However, there is still considerable reliance on foreign countries for technological and managerial input to ensure that projects come to fruition. Crossover innovation projects began to appear in small but steadily growing numbers from the end of the 1990s and especially since the beginning of the twenty-first century. One of the most prominent is the development of the Comac C919 airliner, which is China's first indigenously developed medium-sized narrow-body commercial aircraft. Around 30 percent of the C919's technologies are imported, including most of its most critical hardware such as engines and avionics systems, but the fuselage, wings, and other airframe components are designed and developed by the Chinese aviation industry.[90]

From SAMI-A to a Bigger, Better, Bolder SAMI-B in the Xi Jinping Era

In a keynote speech on science, technology, and innovation policy to the assembled ranks of China's leading scientists and engineers in 2016, Xi offered his thoughts as to the critical attributes of the Chinese state and society that would catapult the country to the top of the global S&T league under his watch. Most of the components of the SAMI model figured prominently. He explained how China's socialist system was a "magic weapon" (法宝, *fabao*) that allowed great scientific and technological endeavors to be accomplished. "Our greatest advantage is that under our socialist system, we can concentrate our efforts (集中力量, *jizhong liliang*) on doing big things (办大事, *ban dashi*)," Xi declared.[91] Xi said these socialist characteristics were responsible for the most spectacular S&T achievements since the establishment of the Chinese communist state.

Xi told the scientific elite this centralized top-down state-driven approach should continue to be the principal path to be taken in the pursuit of new, transformational S&T breakthroughs. "We should depend today on this magic weapon to promote a leap forward in science, technology, and innovation and form a new mechanism [新机制, *xin jizhi*] to concentrate our efforts on doing big things under the socialist market economy," Xi urged the audience. In alluding to the need for a new mechanism, Xi said that "we must give better play to the government's role in unifying and coordinating, exert ourselves to conduct coordinated innovation. . . . We must grasp the big, the cutting edge, the basic, thereby forming a powerful combined force to spur indigenous innovation."[92]

Xi's clear message to the S&T community was that he wanted the pace, scale, and reach of China's technological development to be faster, bigger, and bolder. He has also made the same demands to the country's techno-security apparatus. At a military parade celebrating the PLA's ninetieth anniversary in 2017, Xi said that it was necessary for the defense establishment to set their sights on leapfrogging to the forefront of the global defense S&T frontier by "speeding up strategic, cutting-edge, and paradigm-shifting technology development."[93]

The SAMI model is one of Xi's principal instruments in his policy and organizational toolkit. However, he has sought to make major adjustments to SAMI so that the model and its key components can more effectively step up to the challenge of meeting his goals, which are far more ambitious compared to his predecessors. Chief among these changes is emphasizing original innovation over reinnovation, reconfiguring the relationship between the state and market, and deepening centralized authoritarian leadership.

The revamping of the SAMI model from the A to B versions addresses a very different set of domestic and external opportunities and challenges that Xi and his leadership believe China faces compared to the past few decades. Three in particular stand out. First is the assessment that a global S&T revolution is taking place both in the civilian and defense domains, which represents a golden opportunity for China to take advantage of and leapfrog into first place. Second is an intensifying strategic technological competition with the United States and many other Western countries that is turning into a long-term Cold War that leaves China shut off from Western technology and markets. Third is China's growing prosperity and access to an increasingly diverse array of resources to support its technology development, especially from the marketplace.

Selectivity Shifts from Exclusive to Expansive

Selectivity as a guiding principle in the SAMI model has been most effective when clear overarching objectives exist and the purpose is compatible with existing national strategies. Moreover, selectivity has been most efficient when resources, whether plentiful or limited, are carefully managed. The Chinese techno-civilian system thrived between the 1980s and early 2010s because its goals of catching up and integrating with the global economic and technological order fitted very well with the objectives of the country's open-door and reform strategy.

By comparison, the techno-security base was initially in a quandary during the 1980s and early 1990s because it had no clear overarching security threat to focus its attention. This changed from the mid-1990s as Beijing's concerns over Taiwanese moves to seek independence and the threat from US strategic capabilities escalated. Even though these threats provided the techno-security base with a clear mission, it was at cross-purposes with the goals of the Chinese developmental state. Not surprisingly, the techno-security base has flourished with the rise of the techno-security state since the early 2010s.

Poor resource management is a chronic headache for the techno-civilian system and likely also for the techno-security apparatus, although a lack of transparency in this domain makes it difficult to assess the scale of the problem in the latter. The national S&T system enjoyed a strong and sustained increase in budgetary allocations from the early 2000s as innovation rose in national priorities. Annual national R&D expenditures increased by 23 percent on average between the early 2000s and early 2010s.[94] China invested 1.98 percent of its gross domestic product on R&D between 2006 and 2012, which amounted to RMB 2.42 trillion (US$383.5 billion based on 2012 exchange rates). Of the total amount spent on R&D, the Chinese government invested RMB 1.21 trillion (US$191.7 billion) or 12 percent of the central budget in S&T efforts.

On taking office, Xi made clear that he wanted to expand and accelerate this pace of investment with his calls for breakthroughs across a diverse array of technological fields. Although this would be extremely costly, it would help to spread the risk by not relying excessively on any one emerging technological domain that might not pan out. The nature of selectivity within the new SAMI model under Xi changed from being exclusive to being more expansive in breadth and scale.

Xi soon discovered that a far-reaching reform of the S&T management system was a prerequisite as the enormous investments being made did not actually translate into efficient technological advancement. The reality was that there was massive waste and inefficiency. In his first major speech on S&T policy in 2014, Xi offered a critical assessment of the state of the country's innovation prowess: "China's foundation for science and technology innovation is still not firm. China's capability for indigenous innovation, and especially original innovation, is still weak. Fundamentally, the fact that we are controlled by others in critical fields and key technologies has not changed."[95]

In a diagnosis of what Xi referred to as "the chronic malady of impotence, obstruction, and gridlock in converting science and technology achievements into actual productive forces," a key bottleneck was that "the link between innovation and conversion is insufficiently tight at every phase." Xi said that the only way to overcome this fundamental problem was that "reform of the science and technology system must be deepened. All ideological barriers and institutional obstructions that constrain scientific innovation must be broken down."

Xi gave a long list of structural and policy reform measures that were needed:

- Place science, technology, and innovation at the "core of overall national development and accelerate the formulation of top-level designs that promote the strategy of innovation-driven development."
- Remake the national S&T innovation strategy.
- Overhaul the structure and process for resource allocations to support S&T development.
- Strengthen unified planning and coordination of science, technology, and innovation efforts.
- Tackle fragmentation, especially of stovepiping and overlapping redundancies.
- Improve the basic research system.
- Implement key national science plans.

A fundamental problem was that there were far too many competing state agencies involved in managing the distribution of this funding. The allocation process resembled a sieve rather than a firehose. MOST minister Wan Gang (万钢) pointed out at a press conference in March 2015 that nearly forty government departments and one hundred planning channels were dealing with S&T project management, which has "caused duplication and closures, affecting efficiency. The problem of resource fragmentation is prominent."[96] MOST only had control of 20 percent of the total state S&T budget.

The State Council embarked on a far-reaching reform of the S&T funding system in 2015 to tackle many of the problems outlined by Xi with the issuance of the Management Reform Plan of Central Science and Technology Finance Plans (Special Items, Funds) (中央财政科技计划（专项、基金等）管理改革方案, *Zhongyang Caizheng Keji Jihua (Zhuanxiang, Jijin Deng) Guanli Gaige Fangan*).[97] One of the plan's most important reform measures was to consolidate several hundred existing special S&T plans and funds into five comprehensive programs and funds to reduce duplication, allow for economies of scale, and concentrate resources on select projects:

- National Natural Science Fund (国家自然科学基金, *Guojia Ziran Kexue Jijin*): This fund supports basic and cutting-edge research as well as the development of research personnel and teams to strengthen original innovation.
- National Major Science and Technology Projects (国家科技重大专项, *Guojia Keji Zhongda Zhuanxiang*): This program supports large-scale strategic projects and major industrialization projects that require coordination at the national level.
- National Key Research and Development Program (NKRDP; 国家重点研发计划, *Guojia Zhongdian Yanfa Jihua*): This program focuses on national-level major strategic tasks and subsumes all of the specialized civilian S&T programs that cover these responsibilities, such as the 863 Program, National Basic Research Program (known as the 973 Program), National Science and Technology Support Plan, and International Science and Technology Cooperation and Exchange Project. This program addresses basic and long-range scientific questions, critical technologies and products, and large-scale international cooperation. Another goal is to strengthen interdepartmental, interindustrial, and cross-regional R&D efforts through coordinated innovation.
- Special Fund for Technology Innovation Projects (技术创新引导专项, *Jishu Chuangxin Yindao Zhuanxiang*): This fund streamlines funding activities by consolidating various funding plans supervised by the NDRC, Ministry of Finance, MOST, MIIT, and Ministry of Commerce. It encourages the use of private capital to foster technology innovation

and is helping to create government-guided angel investing, venture capital, and risk compensation mechanisms. In addition, the government is using indirect measures to support innovation and improve tax incentives and government purchasing policies to promote innovation.
- R&D Base and Professional Special Projects (基地和人才专项, *Jidi He Rencai Zhuanxiang*): This plan improves the support of the development of research facilities and human resources, which includes MOST-managed state key laboratories, state engineering research and technology centers, S&T infrastructure platforms, and the Creative Talents Promotion Plan. The plan also covers NDRC-managed state engineering laboratories, state engineering research centers, and state-certified enterprise technology centers. It has sought to improve and better link talent development plans.[98]

With the National Major Science and Technology Projects and NKRDP dedicated to strategic technology development projects, this reform effort demonstrates that the selective prioritization of high-priority capabilities remains a core operational guidance for the Chinese leadership. The State Council reform plan detailing these changes pointed out that one of the basic principles of the initiative was to "focus on major national strategic tasks," which meant "optimizing resource allocations," directing efforts at "making breakthroughs," and "establishing new mechanisms to promote science and technology innovation around major tasks." This last point may be a reference to the setting up of new large-scale national laboratories. The reform plan highlighted the importance of the National Major Science and Technology Projects as the key vehicle for highly select projects, explaining in its description of this program that "it is necessary to insist on doing some things but not others . . . control the number of special projects, and concentrate on doing big things."

The possession of indigenous capability to produce core technology as a criterion for project selection has steadily risen in prominence and urgency during Xi's tenure. Xi has emphasized the critical importance of acquiring core technologies since coming to office, but this priority has become even more pressing as Western countries, led by the United States, have stepped up efforts to curb Chinese access to their technologies and innovation systems since the mid-2010s. This reached a turning point in May 2018 when the US government imposed a complete ban on the export of US technology goods to ZTE, one of China's star technology champions, for flouting international trade sanctions with North Korea and Iran.[99] Follow-up efforts to curb other Chinese entities such as Huawei further reinforced growing perceptions in Beijing that its cutoff from the Western-dominated advanced technology order was under way and that it would be far-reaching and permanent.

At a meeting of the Central Finance and Economic Affairs Commission a couple of months after the announcement of sanctions on ZTE, Xi talked at length about the importance of key and core technologies to China's economic and national security. "It is necessary to conscientiously enhance the innovation capability of China's key and core technologies," Xi stressed and referred to the Two Bombs, One Satellite spirit as the ideological context with which to embark on this technological development effort.[100]

Using the ZTE affair as an inflection point to significantly step up China's strategic technology drive, Xi said that it was necessary to "increase the sense of urgency and crisis" to achieve original breakthroughs. The SAMI model would be the organizational basis for this undertaking as Xi said that it was necessary to "focus on the needs of the state [authoritarianism], make overall planning to integrate all of our strengths, bring into play the advantage of internal and external markets [mobilization], strengthen planning and guidance, and form a more targeted science and technology innovation system [selectivity]."[101]

NATIONAL MAJOR SCIENCE AND TECHNOLOGY PROJECTS PROGRAM AND AFFILIATED PLANS

The principal role of the National Major Science and Technology Projects is to manage the portfolio of megaprojects contained in the 2006–2020 MLP and the STI 2030 program. The implementation of STI 2030 even before the completion of the MLP megaprojects is based on the principle of "as a project matures, another project begins" (成熟一项, 启动一项, *chengshu yixiang, qidong yixiang*), which is enshrined in the regulations guiding the management of these projects (see table 5.3).[102]

Each of these megaproject programs covers five domains:

- Electronics and information: The MLP has three projects on new-generation broadband wireless mobile communication networks—core electronic devices, high-end universal chips, and basic software products—and very-large-scale integrated circuit manufacturing equipment and turnkey techniques. STI 2030 has five projects: quantum communications and quantum computers, cyberspace security, big data, AI, and earth-space integrated information networks.
- Advanced manufacturing: The MLP has two projects on large passenger aircraft and high-grade numerical control machinery and basic manufacturing equipment. STI 2030 has three projects: aircraft engines and combustion turbines, smart manufacturing and robotics, and key new materials.
- Energy and environment: The MLP has three projects on large-scale oil and gas fields and coalbed methane, large-scale, advanced nuclear power

TABLE 5.3   The sixteen megaprojects of the Science, Technology, and Innovation 2030 major projects program

PROJECT	DESCRIPTION
Aircraft engines and combustion turbines	Research on general basic technologies such as materials, manufacturing techniques, experimentation and testing, and interdisciplinary studies to tackle design and other key technologies
Deep-sea stations	Research on deep-sea exploration and universal, specialized, mobile, and fixed deep-sea stations
Quantum communications and quantum computers	In-city, intercity, and open space quantum communication technologies; universal quantum computer prototype and functional quantum simulators will be developed and manufactured
Cerebrology and brain-inspired research	Brain cognition is main focus along with brain-inspired computing, brain-computer intelligence, and the diagnosis and treatment of major brain diseases
Cyberspace security	Cyberspace security technologies and systems encompassing information and networks will be developed
In-orbit services and maintenance systems for deep-space exploration and spacecraft	Improving China's efficiency in space resource utilization and ensuring in-orbit safety and reliable operations for spacecraft
Independent innovation in the seed industry	Agricultural plants, animals, forests, and microorganisms are key areas of focus to apply heterosis and molecular design breeding and provide support for national grain security strategies
Clean and efficient utilization of coal	R&D on green coal exploitation, high-efficiency coal power generation, clean coal conversion, coal pollution control, and coal capture, utilization, and sealing; demonstrate and popularize advanced applicable technologies, achieve leadership in coal-fired power generation and ultra-low-emission technology, and make breakthroughs on modern coal chemical engineering and poly-generation technology
Smart power grids	Regulation and control of large-scale renewable energy grids, flexible interconnection of large-scale power grids, interaction of supply and demand in power consumption by diversified users, and basic supporting technology for smart power grids, to achieve domestic production of technical equipment and systems for smart power grids and improve the share of electric power equipment in the global market
Earth-space integrated information networks	Comprehensive fusion of space-based information networks, the internet of the future, and mobile communication networks, forming earth-space integrated information networks with global coverage
Big data	Research common key technologies for big data, construct standard system and exchange platforms for open data sharing throughout China, form common knowledge application model and technical plan oriented toward typical application, and form big data industry clusters

(continued)

TABLE 5.3   (continued)

PROJECT	DESCRIPTION
Smart manufacturing and robotics	Construct a network of cooperative manufacturing platforms and research and develop smart robots, high-end turnkey equipment, and 3D printing and other equipment to solidify basic support capabilities for manufacturing
Key new materials	Research and production of carbon fiber and composite materials, high-temperature alloys, advanced semiconductor materials, new displays and their materials, high-end equipment using special alloys, rare earth new materials, and new materials for military use
Comprehensive environmental governance of Beijing, Tianjin, and Hebei	Building of core technologies, industrial equipment, standards and policy systems for coordinated governance of water/earth/air, coordinated resource cycling for labor/agriculture/city, and coordinated regional environment management and control; establishing a batch of comprehensive demonstration projects
Health care	Research of precision medicine, prevention and control of chronic noninfectious diseases and frequently occurring diseases, and research of reproductive health and birth defect prevention and control
Artificial intelligence	R&D of new-generation AI basic theory, core key technologies, and smart chips and systems

plants with pressurized water reactors and high-temperature gas-cooled reactors, and water pollution control and treatment. STI 2030 also has three projects: clean and efficient utilization of coal, smart power grids, and comprehensive environmental governance of Beijing, Tianjin, and Hebei.

- Biosciences and health: The MLP has three projects on new varieties of genetically modified organisms, formulation and manufacturing of major new medicines, and the prevention and treatment of AIDS, viral hepatitis, and other major contagious diseases. STI 2030 also has three projects: brain science research, health care, and innovation of the seed industry.

- Maritime and space: The MLP has two projects on a high-resolution earth observation system, and manned spaceflight and lunar exploration programs. STI 2030 also has two projects: deep-sea stations, and in-orbit services and maintenance systems for deep-space exploration and spacecraft.

The 13th Five-Year Science and Technology Innovation Plan stressed that STI 2030 was targeted for the next fifteen years to 2030 and that projects selected "embody China's strategic intentions to . . . strive to take the lead on breakthroughs on important directions." (see table 5.4)[103]

TABLE 5.4   Selection criteria for major strategic projects from the 1950s to the present day

PERIOD	KEY CRITERIA
1950s–1970s	Building strategic defense and deterrence forces, principally nuclear and missile capabilities
	Fostering basic and applied high-technology and advanced engineering capabilities to support defense and strategic needs, especially in electronics, automation, and manufacturing
1980s–early 2010s	Focusing on major national strategic tasks, such as enabling economic competitiveness (top priority) and national security
	Supporting technological catching-up
	Developing key basic and generic technologies
	Having long-term technological and economic impact
Early 2010s–present	Focusing on major national strategic tasks, such as enabling economic competitiveness and national security (top priority)
	Gaining international leadership
	Pursuing technological disruption and making breakthroughs, especially in new and emerging domains
	Establishing critical core technology essential to national and economic security
	Enhancing original domestic innovation and advancing technological self-sufficiency

STI 2030 does not make reference to any projects of a primarily defense or national security purpose, but ten of its sixteen projects have dual-use applications. They include all the projects in the electronics and information, advanced manufacturing, and maritime and space domains. To provide coordination on these dual-use projects on the defense side, one of the likely principal players is SASTIND's Major Special Projects Engineering Center (重大专项工程中心, *Zhongda Zhuanxiang Gongcheng Zhongxin*). This organization has been actively involved with MLP-related megaprojects.[104]

NATIONAL KEY RESEARCH AND DEVELOPMENT PROGRAM

The NKRDP is a mainstay of the Chinese government's research funding apparatus and supports an extensive array of disciplinary fields with particular emphasis during the 13th Five-Year Plan on strategic and key S&T topics as well as agriculture, energy and resources, environment, and health issues. Projects usually run from between three and five years and are intended to cover activities spanning from basic research through to commercialization. Around two-thirds of NKRDP-funded research projects are awarded to universities and research outfits, while 12 percent are given to state-owned enterprises and 10 percent to private firms.[105]

The NKRDP has funded scores of strategic and techno-security-related research projects. In 2020, for example, there were more than twenty of these projects listed (see table 5.5). Here are a few of the most significant:

- Strategic Advanced Electronic Materials Key Project: This project was started in 2016 and was funded throughout the 13th Five-Year Plan to conduct research on third-generation semiconductor materials and lighting, high-power laser materials, high-end optoelectronics, and microelectronics materials.[106]
- High-Performance Computing Key Project: This project was funded throughout the 13th Five-Year Plan period. Its focus was on the development of exascale high-performance computing hardware and application software. Key technological goals included making breakthroughs in exascale computer architecture, new processor architecture, high-speed interconnection networks, and software applications. There were plans to establish two to three high-performance computing application software centers to support these development efforts.[107]
- Additive Manufacturing and Laser Manufacturing Key Project: A central goal of this five-year project during the 13th Five-Year Plan was to make technological breakthroughs in additive manufacturing and laser manufacturing. This project was key in efforts being made in the Made in China 2025 and MLP programs.[108]
- Quantum Control and Quantum Information Key Project: More than RMB 1 billion (US$154 million based on 2021 exchange rates) has so far been allocated to this project, which started in 2016 with the initial goals of developing prototype devices, building a wide-area quantum communications network, and supporting the development of large-scale quantum computing projects.[109]

There is substantial continuity in the priorities of the NKRDP in the 14th Five-Year Plan, but there is also a sizable increase in new strategic projects. This includes funding for the development and utilization of strategic mineral resources, deep-sea and polar region technologies, biosafety technologies, and controllable industrial software platforms and digital ecosystems to help secure China's industrial supply chains.[110]

Mobilization

To credibly pursue the grand technological ambition of "doing big things," leapfrogging to the global frontier, and turning China from big to strong, especially in the techno-security realm, Xi and his administration have had to devise new

TABLE 5.5   Select list of funded research projects in the National Key Research and Development Program during the 13th Five-Year Science and Technology Innovation Plan, 2016–2020

Manufacturing Basic Technology and Key Components Key Project

Network Collaborative Manufacturing and Intelligent Factory Key Project

Intelligent Robotics Key Project

Key Basic Material Technology Promotion and Industrialization Key Project

Strategic Advanced Electronic Materials Key Project

Comprehensive Transportation and Intelligent Transportation Key Project

Smart Grid Technology and Equipment Key Project

Renewable Energy and Hydrogen Technology Key Project

Nuclear Safety and Advanced Nuclear Technology Key Project

Broadband Communication and New Network Key Project

Internet of Things and Smart City Key Technology and Demonstration Key Project

Earth Observation and Navigation Key Project

Research, Development, and Application Demonstration of Common Key Technologies in Modern Service Industry Key Project

Major Natural Disaster Monitoring, Early Warning, and Prevention Key Project

Public Security Risk Prevention and Control and Emergency Technical Equipment Key Project

Nanotechnology Key Project

Quantum Control and Quantum Information Key Project

Frontier Research of Large Scientific Devices Key Project

Global Change and Responses Key Project

High-Performance Computing Key Project

Additive Manufacturing and Laser Manufacturing Key Project

Key Scientific Issues of Transformative Technology Key Project

Synthetic Biology Key Project

---

and improved ways to mobilize, concentrate, and target the resources available from an increasingly developed economy and educated society. One important initiative is called the New Whole-of-Nation System (新型举国体制, *Xinxing Juguo Tizhi*), which is being actively promoted by the Chinese authorities as a more effective way of assembling the necessary state and market resources and leading talent into a winning combination of national champions able to achieve clearly defined strategic objectives.[111] The New Whole-of-Nation System concept has been applied widely—from the S&T domain to the sports world to offer the same message that China has found a winning formula of putting together world-beating teams. The success, for example, of the Chang'e 4 lunar exploration project and the 2019 world championship-winning Chinese women's national volleyball team are attributed to the New Whole-of-Nation System approach.[112]

The New Whole-of-Nation System framework became an authoritative operational concept at the Chinese Communist Party's (CCP) Central Committee

Fourth Plenum in October 2019. The plenum called for the building of a "new whole-of-nation system for key core technologies under a socialist market economy."[113] Chinese analysts point out that the New Whole-of-Nation System mobilizational approach is significantly different from the traditional top-down-led management model in two ways that are especially applicable for tackling core and emerging technologies.[114]

First is in the assembly and makeup of project teams. Analysts argue that contemporary core technologies are by their nature highly complex, cross-disciplinary, and involve cutting-edge capabilities that require putting together large-scale teams drawn from numerous sectors. This is especially true of next-generation core technologies like quantum and AI/machine learning. Past development of core technologies in the industrial era were more narrowly confined to single industries such as aeroengines, advanced electronics, and nuclear weapons technology. This meant that projects were usually given to a single research outfit to carry out. Under the New Whole-of-Nation System approach, project teams are drawn competitively from an extensive range of qualified entities across different industries. In the Chang'e 4 project, for example, research bids were accepted from institutions outside of the aerospace industry that had "a positive track record of breaking down barriers into the aerospace industry, accelerating space innovation, reducing engineering costs, and improving investment returns."[115]

A second important new feature of the New Whole-of-Nation System concept is the inclusion of the market economy as a key source for resources and other inputs into the development process. The goal is to reduce reliance on state funding and increase access to market-based resources. Considerable effort has been exerted since the early 2010s to develop linkages that would allow the insular techno-security state to access lucrative investment capital from the financial markets to supplement state funding for techno-security priorities. Two types of initiatives have been especially important: asset securitization and government guidance funds, which were examined in chapter 3.

MOBILIZATION, TECHNO-INDUSTRIAL POLICY, AND MADE IN CHINA 2025

Mobilizational activities in the industrial economy have centered on the pursuit of industrial policies, of which Made in China 2025 has been the most prominent and controversial during Xi's reign so far.[116] The origins of this top-down effort to turn China from a mid-level to an advanced manufacturing power was a joint research project by the Chinese Academies of Engineering (CAE) and MIIT in 2013 that examined how to raise the manufacturing quality of Chinese products.[117] An influential external source was Germany's Industry 4.0 strategy that highlighted the importance of intelligent or smart manufacturing and the onset of the fourth Industrial Revolution.[118]

Made in China 2025 was intended as a ten-year blueprint to empower China through advanced manufacturing.[119] The plan outlined a three-step strategy for China to comprehensively upgrade its industrial economy and become a world-leading manufacturer by mid-century. The first step, which Made in China 2025 was responsible for, is to make significant advances in innovation as well as manufacturing efficiency to realize basic industrialization by 2025. The second step, the focus of a successor plan, is to be able to compete with developed manufacturing powers by 2035. The last step is to be a leading world manufacturer by mid-century.

To achieve these goals, Made in China 2025 set up clear principles and tasks, and prioritized ten industrial sectors.[120] The plan's guiding principles were to establish innovation-driven manufacturing, emphasize quality over quantity, achieve green development, optimize the structure of Chinese industry, and nurture human talent. Policies were intended to deepen institutional reforms, strengthen financial and tax support, complete a multilevel talent training system, facilitate small and micro enterprises, and improve organizational and implementation mechanisms.

The ten industrial sectors prioritized by Made in China 2025 for policy and funding support were as follows:

1. New-generation information technology
2. Automated machine tools and robotics
3. Space and aviation equipment
4. Maritime equipment and high-tech shipping
5. Modern rail transportation equipment
6. New-energy vehicles and equipment
7. Power-generation equipment
8. Agricultural equipment
9. New materials
10. Biopharmaceutical and advanced medical products

There were extensive plans and detailed targets for each of these domains. In the new-generation information technology industry, for example, development priorities included microchips and associated equipment, information and communication equipment, and processor systems and industrial software. In the space and aviation equipment industry, priorities included accelerating the development of single-aisle commercial airliners, beginning work on wide-bodied two aisle aircraft, achieving self-reliance in manufacturing advanced jet engines, developing the capability to produce high bypass ratio turbofan engines, and building a next generation of space launch vehicles and heavy launch vehicles.

Nine tasks were identified as leading priorities, of which six stand out. They were (1) enhancing national innovation capabilities in manufacturing; (2) advancing the integration of information technologies and industrialization, strengthening industrial capability in core components, advanced basic technologies, key basic materials, and the industrial technology base; (3) enhancing quality and brand building; (4) promoting structural adjustment of the manufacturing sector; (5) actively developing service-oriented manufacturing and producer services; and (6) raising the level of the internationalization of manufacturing development.

To fulfill these tasks, Made in China 2025 had five subplans to facilitate government involvement because of inadequate market mechanisms:

- Manufacturing Innovation Center (Industrial Technology Research Base) Construction Plan: Establish fifteen manufacturing innovation centers by 2020 and forty by 2025 to conduct R&D on basic and common technologies for key industries.
- Intelligent Manufacturing Plan: Significantly improve the level of intelligent manufacturing in key areas by 2020 through the integration of new information technologies and equipment innovation.
- Core Industrial Capability Strengthening Plan: Support development in core components and industrial technology and raise the ratio of domestic core components and materials to 40 percent by 2020 and 70 percent by 2025 of overall supply, which is currently dominated by foreign products with more than 80 percent in certain areas.[121]
- Green Manufacturing Plan: Implement a special technological transformation project in traditional manufacturing sectors and cut emissions by 20 percent by 2020, compared to the 2012 level.[122]
- High-End Equipment Innovation Plan: Establish independent design and manufacture of advanced equipment capabilities in aviation, transportation, marine engineering, manufacturing, nuclear, and health care by 2020.

In addition to these subplans, the government drew up other specific industrial policies and guidelines for the development of specific industrial technologies and sectors. One of the most important was the "Guidelines on Developing and Promoting the National Integrated Circuit Industry," which saw the creation of a leading group named the State Integrated Circuit (IC) Industry Development Leading Group and the setting up of the National Integrated Circuit Industry Investment Fund.[123] An MIIT Special Action Implementation Program calls for creating military IC products and the promotion of civil-military IC production lines, and a 2016 MCF special action plan states that a Dual-Use Integrated Circuit Development Special Action Plan will be drafted along with a document outlining "high-level plans and programs" for the IC industry development in MCF areas.[124] As China deepens its MCF implementation, the desired end result of these efforts is a techno-security base more capable of sourcing basic and core technology domestically.

Development priorities for the information technology and space and aviation industries show extensive civil-military dual-use complementarity. Many of the other industrial sectors listed in Made in China 2025 also have dual-use overlap, which should not be surprising as Made in China 2025 was drawn up as leadership attention on MCF was ramping up in the mid-2010s. As pointed out in an earlier chapter, there is a parallel defense version of Made in China 2025 known as the Defense Science and Technology Industry Strong Basic Engineering Project 2025.

After Made in China 2025 became a lightning rod of criticism from the US government for being economically coercive and protectionist, the Chinese authorities stopped making public references to the plan in 2018, although it continues to be implemented.[125] Even though the Made in China 2025 moniker is no longer officially mentioned, its contents and norms remain core to Xi's goals of making China a global innovation and manufacturing champion, so they will feature prominently in any future plans and guidances. In the 14th Five-Year Plan, even though all references to Made in China 2025 have disappeared, the central importance of industrial and manufacturing policy continues to be emphasized. The 14th Five-Year Plan repeats the call from its predecessor plan that China should push to become a "Manufacturing Strong State" (制造强国, *Zhizao Qiangguo*).[126]

MOBILIZATION AND HUMAN TALENT

The mobilization of high-level human talent has been another area that the Xi regime has devoted extensive effort to nurture. Xi has made clear that "we must take the development of human talent resources as the highest priority in science and technology innovation."[127] Xi inherited a robust and proactive human talent development program from the Hu administration.[128] In 2002, the Party Organization Department established a Central Talent Coordination Leading Group that comprised representatives from numerous party and state agencies to help oversee efforts to build up the country's limited talent pool, especially in S&T. Party leaders declared that the "Communist Party controls talent" (党管才, *dang guan cai*)." Among the key mechanisms that were established was the Global Experts Recruitment Program, which is more commonly referred to as the Thousand

Talents Program (TTP; 千人计划, *Qianren Jihua*), in March 2008 that was masterminded by Li Yuanchao (李源潮), head of the Party Organization Department. The TTP had modest initial goals of permanently bringing back two thousand leading mainland-born scientists, business executives, and academics within five years. This reverse brain-drain approach did not generate much interest, however, and a brain circulation component was added to recruit participants on a part-time basis, allowing them to keep working in their host countries. This part-time option was far more appealing and attracted plenty of recruits but was also kept confidential because many recipients did not want their primary employers to know they were also working for Chinese entities. Consequently, recruitment rates for the TTP stopped being publicly released from 2011, although occasional Chinese media reports offered snippets of data that suggested that the TTP had signed up around eight thousand participants in its first eleven years from 2008 to 2018.[129] Another study of returning Chinese scientists from the United States and Europe offers a rough estimate that at least sixteen thousand scientists and high-tech entrepreneurs had been recruited back to China by the Chinese government by 2018, which would mean that TTP is responsible for 50 percent of the return rate.[130] Two-thirds came back from the United States and the remaining one-third from Europe. Variants of the TTP have been established in subsequent years such as the Thousand Young Talents Program.

In the five years that the TTP was under the Hu administration from 2008 to 2012, it is estimated to have hired around 3,320 talents. In the first six years under the Xi regime from 2013 to 2018, 4,700 participants were signed up, a 41 percent increase in the recruitment rate. This is one indicator of the stepped-up efforts for human talent by the Xi regime. In an assessment of the TTP and its use of state mobilization techniques, Hong Kong–based scholars David Zweig and Siqin Kang (康思勤) question whether this was an acceptable approach. They argue that the employment of traditional Communist Party tactics such as quotas, financial incentives, and implicit threats to party and state officials for noncompliance created trouble for policy implementation by allowing "institutions and local officials to cut corners."[131]

The TTP came under scrutiny from the US government in the mid-2010s as a vehicle for intellectual property theft and espionage, especially against the US academic and research communities. One of the first publicly disclosed US government assessments of the TTP and China's talent programs was a Federal Bureau of Investigation counterintelligence report in September 2015. Although the assessment began by pointing out that "associating with these talent programs is legal and breaks no laws," it eventually concludes that these programs "pose a serious threat to U.S. businesses and universities through economic espionage and theft of IP [intellectual property]."[132]

US concerns about the TTP and other Chinese talent programs gained growing prominence in the late 2010s and became increasingly caught up in the intensifying US-China great power competition. A US Senate investigation of the TTP issued in November 2019 concluded that "China's talent recruitment plans, including the Thousand Talents Plan, undermine the integrity of our research enterprise and harm our economic and national security interests."[133] In response, the Chinese authorities banned any public mention of the TTP and replaced or simply changed the name of the program to the Foreign High-End Expert Recruitment Plan (高端外国专家引进计划, *Gaoduan Waiguo Zhuanjia Yinjin Jihua*).[134] MOST was put in charge of this new recruitment plan so it would not be associated with the CCP apparatus.

The Foreign High-End Expert Recruitment Plan has objectives that are central to the purpose of the SAMI model. First is the recruitment of leading experts who are able to work on strategic S&T development, especially STI 2030 projects. The plan emphasizes "aggressively recruiting [大力引进, *dali yinjin*] those whose research interests are in international cutting-edge science and technology fields." Second is attracting foreign talent to tackle breakthrough areas such as AI, 5G, cloud computing, big data, the internet of things, and blockchain, as well as to address critical and core technologies such as rare earth materials, semiconductors, fuel cells, biotechnology, and marine S&T.

Another major human talent program aimed at high-level expertise that was established in the final months of the Hu administration and pursued by the Xi regime is the National High-Level Talent Special Support Program (国家高层次人才特殊支持计划, *Guojia Gaocengci Rencai Teshu Zhichi Jihua*), which is more commonly known as the Ten Thousand Talents Program (万人计划, *Wanren Jihua*).[135] This domestically focused program is directed primarily at S&T talent cultivation, although there is token inclusion of experts from the social sciences and humanities. Four batches of recipients had been announced as of 2019 totaling over four thousand experts.[136]

Although much of the focus of the achievements of the TTP and other Chinese talent programs have been directed on their nefarious access to foreign technology and know-how, of greater significance has been the professional impact and prominent roles played by returned experts within the Chinese S&T system. Official Chinese data show that 70 percent of the heads of key national research projects are overseas returnees while more than 80 percent of academicians from CAS and CAE have studied or worked overseas.[137] This recalls the pivotal roles played by returnees such as Qian Xuesen (钱学森) in the Two Bombs, One Satellite program in the Maoist era. Their contemporaries in today's Chinese techno-security state include the likes of quantum physicist Pan Jianwei (潘建伟), who earned a doctorate at the University of Vienna, and former

NUDT president and hypersonics expert Deng Xiaogang (邓小刚), who spent time as a postdoctoral researcher in Japan. Measured in research quality and impact, a 2020 bibliometric study of overseas and returned Chinese authors found that Chinese returnees published higher impact work in leading international journals compared to their domestic counterparts.[138]

A Revamped Authoritarian Leadership System

The leadership and management structure of the Chinese techno-security state underwent a major overhaul after Xi took office. Long-standing organizations and institutional arrangements made way for a very different approach under a hands-on leader who was far more interested and engaged in techno-security matters than his predecessors. Several characteristics of this revamped authoritarian leadership system stand out.

A first distinguishing feature is that the new institutional setup is highly personalized and revolves around Xi. He has personally taken charge of several of the most important top-level decision-making bodies within or closely affiliated with the techno-security state. This is despite his heavy political and state responsibilities as party general secretary and state president, not to mention his wide-ranging political and coercive efforts at consolidating power. These positions include being in charge of the CMC, CNSC, 995 Leading Group, CMCFDC, and Central Cyberspace Affairs Commission. This active personal involvement from Xi has helped to ensure that the SAMI model enjoys the powerful top-level political support that is critical to its success.

A second hallmark is that Xi has brought much of the locus of power and authority of the techno-security state back under the auspices of the Communist Party apparatus. This is a return to the Maoist Two Bombs, One Satellite model and a shift away from the 1979–2012 period when state agencies were given expanded roles in the leadership and management of key parts of the techno-security apparatus. The State Council is still an important player in the management and implementation of techno-security affairs, which is primarily carried out by MOST and SASTIND. However, the state's top-level influence in policymaking is considerably diminished compared to prior administrations. A key reason is that Xi has taken over the S&T portfolio that has traditionally belonged to the premier. Li Keqiang (李克强) still takes part in S&T matters and is the chair of a revamped National Science and Technology Leading Group, but he has adopted a lower profile and ceded the stage on S&T pronouncements and guidance to Xi.[139]

A third characteristic is that the revamped authoritarian leadership system appears, at least on paper, to be better integrated and coordinated. One of the biggest shortcomings of the techno-security state that Xi pointed to when he took charge was its entrenched bureaucratic fragmentation that caused waste, corruption, and chronic inefficiency. Coordination problems have been especially severe between the civilian, military, and defense industrial systems, and also between long-standing vertically integrated civilian systems.

In the case of the management of civilian S&T megaprojects, as part of the 2015 reform of S&T special projects and plans, an interagency committee was established to oversee the management of major S&T programs that was previously the responsibility of MOST. The Inter-Ministerial Joint Meeting of Science and Technology Program Management (国家科技计划管理部际联席会议, *Guojia Keji Jihua Guanli Buji Lianxi Huiyi*) is managed by MOST, the Ministry of Finance, and NDRC, which meet regularly to oversee funding activities and management issues and involves thirty other ministries and agencies.[140] Whereas the NDRC and Ministry of Finance wield enormous bureaucratic power, MOST is a relatively small and specialized ministry with limited political and administrative clout. MOST, though, has been given the lead role in the running of the interagency committee because of its expertise and experience. The MOST minister chairs these meetings, while NDRC and Ministry of Finance representatives are present at the deputy minister level.[141]

The interagency committee oversees a number of project management organizations, such as the National Natural Science Foundation of China, that are responsible for soliciting proposals, making grant awards, monitoring work, and evaluating results. These project management organizations are supposed to rely on outside groups of vetted expert reviewers to conduct peer review of applications.[142]

From Incremental to Breakthrough Innovation

Original innovation, and especially breakthrough S&T, is what Xi is demanding from the SAMI-B model. High-end innovation is the sole providence of a select elite of the world's most advanced, wealthy, and open societies, and Xi expects China to join this exclusive club by the mid-2030s and contest for outright leadership by mid-century.

The absorption-based SAMI-A model has been the engineering launchpad for the takeoff of both the Chinese techno-civilian and techno-security bases since the 1990s and will continue to play an influential role for many more years. However, important segments of the techno-security apparatus are now beginning to transition to domestically inspired and led innovation. To reach the level of a high-end breakthrough innovation country, though, China will need to go through several other stages of the innovation process. Although a few emerging sectors are hoping to bypass this step-by-step advance and leapfrog straight into the lead, the historical record for innovation demonstrates that the race is a marathon and not a long jump.

The Chinese authorities define progress to become an advanced innovation country as a three-step process. The initial stage is reinnovation, which China has accomplished, and is followed by integrated innovation. This refers to the synthesis of related technologies and processes that facilitates the development of competitive products and industries. These technologies and processes can be both foreign and domestic. As a concept, integrated innovation overlaps with the work on technology and systems integration from Western business academics such as Marco Iansiti and Michael Best who argue that the most effective way for technology advancement to occur in the business sector is through the tight integration of R&D with design, manufacturing, marketing, and other business-oriented functions aimed at conceptualizing new generations of technologies and products for customers.[143] Apple Inc. is the poster child of a company whose integrated approach to technology and business development has allowed it to have a revolutionary impact on the consumer technology market. At the sectoral and national levels, this means closer coordination and integration between universities and research institutes with industrial enterprises.

Although the United States is an effective role model for integrated innovation, there are significant socioeconomic, market, and regulatory differences that would make emulation by China enormously difficult. A more compatible role model would be the examples of its East Asian neighbors Japan and South Korea. Firms such as Toyota, Samsung, and Sony were pioneers in organizing their research, development, design, production, marketing, and sales channels into an integrated process, which has helped turn them into global innovation powerhouses. Many of these firms, however, have fallen behind in the global innovation competition in recent years, which calls into question their long-term competitiveness.

An alternative integration approach that has been adopted by Western defense establishments to improve their management of defense research, development, and acquisition processes is concurrent engineering. This was first popularized in the Japanese automobile industry in the 1980s and was subsequently adopted by US firms in the 1990s. This views the innovation process as made up of parallel but integrated activities across organizational functions. Activities such as idea generation, R&D, testing and evaluation, manufacturing, and marketing would occur in parallel but with close coordination through integrated product teams made up of representatives from all these disciplines working together. The Pentagon embraced this practice in the mid-1990s, although with mixed results.[144]

Original innovation is the final step and refers to scientific discovery and technological invention carried out by Chinese research institutions that are successfully developed and commercialized domestically. The meaning of original innovation appears to have expanded under Xi to include an emphasis on breakthrough innovation.[145]

To analyze the accelerating Chinese efforts to shift from reinnovation to indigenous innovation, a four-stage process will be employed that offers a more nuanced and analytically sophisticated framework compared to the official Chinese approach. Building from the imitation-to-innovation typology that was examined earlier in this chapter and that focused on the first four steps of the imitation cycle, the next stages are incremental innovation, architectural innovation, modular innovation, and finally breakthrough or radical innovation.

Incremental innovation is the limited and routinized updating and improvement of existing indigenously developed systems and processes. Incremental innovation can be the gradual upgrading of a system through the introduction of improved subsystems, but it is also often the result of organizational and management inputs aimed at producing different versions of products tailored to different markets and users, rather than significant technological improvements through original R&D. This is the most basic and standardized form of innovation that takes place and is widely practiced by defense establishments whose acquisition of highly expensive technologies means that they are in service for long periods of time and require periodic upgrading. The Chinese defense establishment has been a keen advocate of incremental innovation and updates its weapons and equipment on a regular basis. The SAMI model, though, is not designed or intended for incremental innovation, which can be carried out by the regular conventional parts of the techno-security base.

The next rung up on the innovation ladder is architectural innovation, which can be distinguished by its product and process variants. Architectural product innovation refers to "innovations that change the way in which the components of a product are linked together, while leaving the core design concepts (and thus the basic knowledge underlying the components) untouched."[146] Architectural process innovation refers to the redesign of production systems in an integrated approach (involving management, engineers, and workers as well as input from end users) that significantly improves processes but does not usually result in radical product innovation. The primary enablers are improvements in organizational, marketing, management, systems integration, and doctrinal processes and knowledge that are coupled with a deep understanding of market requirements and close-knit relationships between producers, suppliers, and users. As these are also the same factors responsible for driving incremental innovation, distinguishing between these different types of innovation poses a major analytical challenge.

Even though many of the soft capabilities enabling architectural innovation may appear modest and unremarkable, they have the potential to cause significant, even discontinuous, consequences through the reconfiguration of existing technologies in far more efficient and competitive ways that challenge or overturn the dominance of established leaders. Architectural innovation overlaps most closely with integrated innovation. The Chinese space and missile industry's development of the DF-21 family of anti-ship ballistic missiles, especially the DF-21D, is a prime example of architectural innovation.

Next on the innovation ladder is component or modular innovation, which involves the development of new component technology that can be installed into existing systems architecture. A fundamental requirement for modular innovation is the need for an advanced research, development, and engineering ecosystem consisting of research institutes, engineering facilities, and a cadre of experienced scientists and engineers that can produce advanced component hardware. The Chinese techno-security state has been investing heavily in component innovation over the last couple of decades, but the fruits of this labor often take many years to materialize. There have been growing signs since the mid- to late 2010s that this return on investment is beginning to be rewarded in areas such as military aircraft engines and advanced manufacturing capabilities such as CNC machine tools. Component innovation is a key area of focus for the SAMI model and the megaprojects contained in the STI 2030, Made in China 2025, and other long-term strategic S&T programs.

At the summit of the innovation mountain is radical or breakthrough innovation that requires both component and architectural innovation to be occurring at the same time to produce transformational changes in hardware, software, and processes—not only at the product or sector level but across many systems. The Chinese techno-security state is making big bets on key breakthrough innovations, including hypersonics, high-energy fusion, quantum technology, 5G, and AI.

Becoming a bona fide high-end breakthrough-capable techno-security power is a paramount goal for Xi by the first half of the 2030s. To make this possible, a prerequisite is to transform the reactive and balkanized reinnovation-oriented research, development, and engineering ecosystem into a proactive apparatus that has high-end research entities, a discovery-facing institutional culture, and tightly integrated linkages and networks able to conduct pathbreaking work. The 13th Five-Year Science and Technology Innovation Plan identifies the need for an "appropriate consolidation of existing national scientific research bases and platforms" and emphasizes the need for changes to two key categories of basic and applied research and engineering application.[147] The first category is strategic integration, which refers to national laboratories. The second category is technological innovation, which covers national technology innovation centers, national engineering and technology research centers, national engineering research centers, national engineering laboratories, and national key enterprise laboratories. The Xi regime considers the formation of a system of large-scale comprehensive national laboratories as essential platforms to accelerate fundamental and applied research, especially for big science, strategic, and national security–related endeavors.

The reform and repurposing of research and engineering centers in the technological innovation category underscores the shift from reinnovation to original innovation. This part of the national innovation system has played a vital role in the IDAR process by being responsible for turning the know-how and technologies acquired from abroad into reengineered domestic manufactured output. The 13th Five-Year Science and Technology Innovation Plan points out that the entities in this category are focused on serving strategic industrial needs and their missions will be directed "toward global competition . . . and industrial development."[148] The civilian defense industry also began to pivot from absorption to original innovation from the mid-2010s with the establishment of defense S&T industry technology innovation centers.

The Prospects for the SAMI Model

The SAMI model has been the secret sauce in explaining the stellar track record of achievements in China's development of large-scale strategic and defense-related programs between the 1950s and the present day. This was a collective and dogged brute-force approach to technological advancement that was heavily reliant on absorption and engineering. The fundamental challenge for Xi is whether this selective authoritarian mobilization framework is compatible with the new science, technology, and innovation–based approach that is being established.

The answer will only become evident as the exact nature of the Chinese techno-security state emerges and its performance becomes clearer over the coming years. The extensive efforts and enormous investment that have been made since the beginning of the 2010s to build a more capable SAMI-B original innovation model while still employing the SAMI-A approach in tandem suggest that the Chinese techno-security state has a fighting chance of meeting its goals and ambitions of challenging for global technological leadership by mid-century.

THE TECHNO-SECURITY STATE IN CONCEPTUAL AND COMPARATIVE PERSPECTIVE

China under Xi Jinping (习近平) is relentless in its pursuit of technological and security preeminence but is far from being alone in this quest. Many other states, past and present, have shown similar techno-security traits and impulses. This chapter examines the nature of the techno-security state from a conceptual and comparative perspective with the goal of developing an analytical framework to identify key common characteristics. Of particular interest is the development of the US techno-security state, which stands out as the world's most powerful and successful model.

Competing Schools of Thinking on the Role of the State

Scholarship on the nature, role, and purpose of the modern state is expansive and cuts across many disciplinary fields.[1] This chapter concentrates on the economic-centric and bello-centric schools of thinking.[2] Economic-centric states emphasize the central role of economic development in accounting for how states are organized and ruled, engage internally and externally, and pursue outcomes, of which wealth generation is the foremost goal. By contrast, bello-centric states are primarily concerned with the impact that the threat of or actual war has on their survival and development, so their main priority is to safeguard national security through internal mobilization and external posturing.[3]

Techno-security states fall under the bello-centric label, but they combine significant elements of economic-centric states. Economic development is a high priority for them, especially in areas critical for national security such as industrialization and technological innovation. Consequently, techno-security states often perform a delicate act of balancing between competing security and economic priorities and needs.

The Economic-centric School

Numerous types of economic-centric states have been identified and studied. Developmental states are underdeveloped but highly motivated interventionist regimes seeking to rapidly catch up through industrialization and export-led growth.[4] Trading states pursue international trade and investment and refrain as much as possible from building and maintaining costly military capabilities. Japan and Germany in the aftermath of World War II have been the role models of trading states; they vigorously promoted global economic interdependence while limiting their defense burdens by enjoying the benefits of US security protection.[5] Welfare states are another major type of economic-centric state in which the state plays a central role in providing for the socioeconomic well-being of its citizens through the establishment of comprehensive social welfare programs. Welfare states first emerged in Europe in the late nineteenth century and became increasingly entrenched with industrialization, democratization, and the aftermath of the two world wars.[6] More recently, there has been growing research on the role of the state in innovation and entrepreneurship, especially in the examination of state-market relations and the important influence that state actors have in the organization and running of complex ecosystems like national innovation systems that are responsible for ensuring the prosperity and power of modern societies.

These different types of economic-centric states share common attributes. First, they tend to see the world from a liberalist win-win perspective in which economic engagement is far more preferable to the use of military power. Second, military and national security issues are secondary to economic and social priorities. Third, policymaking is dominated by economic or social coalitions. The approaches of two types of economic-centric states are especially relevant in relationship to the techno-security state concept: the developmental state and innovation-entrepreneurial state.

THE DEVELOPMENTAL STATE SCHOOL

The developmental state approach has generated rich and varied insights into the role of the state in the development process. The framework was first put forward in the early 1980s by Chalmers Johnson to explain the success of Japan's development after the end of World War II and was subsequently applied to other catch-up states in East Asia and eventually to the politics and economics of growth itself.[7]

The developmental and techno-security state concepts have much in common. First, they are both fundamentally concerned about how to understand the relationship between the state and development. For the developmental state, this is primarily about the state's role in catch-up economic development while for the techno-security state it is about national security and technological development. Second, developmental states often have significant linkages to national security and technological interests, sometimes to the extent that some of them could be labeled as techno-security states at certain stages in their evolution. Japan is a classic example of a state that was originally heavily techno-security oriented in the interwar period but transitioned to become a developmental state after World War II. South Korea also had strong military roots in the formative stages of its economic development in the 1960s and 1970s but also followed the developmental state path in subsequent decades.

On the question of the nature and extent of the state's role in economic development, Johnson identified three ideal types of developmental states of which two were variants of contemporary capitalist economies and the third was the state socialist command economy. The first capitalist model is the plan rational state, which manages developmental functions by setting goals and policies through a market-based framework and actively intervenes to ensure implementation. Industrial and innovation policies are among the most important initiatives pursued. The plan rational state is what Johnson identifies as the developmental state. The second capitalist category is the market rational state, which plays an indirect regulatory role and is concerned primarily with process and form but not the substance of competition. The third type is the plan ideological state, which refers to socialist centrally planned economies in which ideological considerations overwhelmingly drive development goals.

Another way to distinguish between state control and market competition is through the prism of statism and anti-statism. In looking at how the United States grappled with nation building and national security during the Cold War with the Soviet Union during the 1950s to 1980s, Aaron Friedberg argues that the United States did not fall victim to a wholesale takeover by the national security establishment and its political allies like its Soviet archrival because of a strong anti-statist inclination.[8] This is also a characteristic that Linda Weiss points out in her study of the relationship between innovation and national security in the United States.[9]

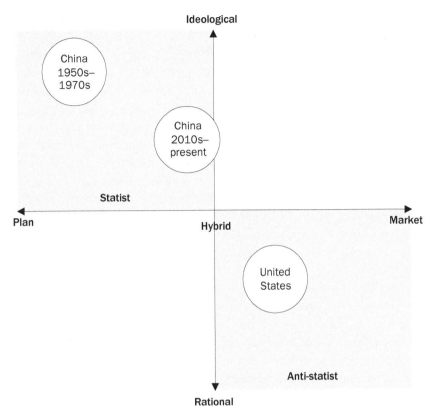

FIGURE 6.1. Techno-security state types

This statist versus anti-statist differentiation is a more meaningful analytical approach to examining the techno-security state than the classical political science tradition of distinguishing political regimes as authoritarian, totalitarian, or democratic (see figure 6.1). Although a large majority of national security and techno-security states are authoritarian in nature, there are also a small but not inconsequential number that are democratic. The most prominent democratic national/techno-security states are Israel and the United States during the Cold War or under the George W. Bush administration during its global war against terrorism.

Johnson's 1982 history of Japan's Ministry of International Trade and Industry (MITI) offers a close-up account of the evolution and workings of the plan rational model. He puts forward four essential features of the Japanese developmental state. Two are closely related and address how the state takes the lead in policy-making and implementation. The first general lesson from the Japanese experience is the importance of establishing a small but highly elite state bureaucracy to manage the state's top-down intervention. The second more specific insight is the necessity for a pilot organization like MITI that has a broad policy portfolio combining domestic and international responsibilities and also enjoys wide-ranging independence that even extends into the control of financial resources, allowing the ministry unfettered authority to pursue industrial policy as it sees fit. Although MITI was instrumental in guiding the development of the post–World War II Japanese civilian economy, it had its origins in the Ministry of Munitions, which was responsible for the rise of the interwar Japanese techno-security state.

The third feature of the Japanese developmental state is a political system that allows the government bureaucracy considerable scope to undertake initiatives of its own making rather than being beholden to its executive masters. In other words, administrative rather than political guidance is the central driver. This means that "top-down" strategies come not from the very apex of the political system but from one or two rungs down the hierarchy at the level of career civil servants. The last feature identified by Johnson focuses on the development of market-conforming methods of state intervention. In Japan, there is a prolifera-tion of special vehicles that include the setting-up of governmental financial in-stitutions, extensive use of tax incentives, the use of indicative plans, extensive reliance on public corporations, and the creation of special investment budgets that are separate from the government's general account. University of Califor-nia, San Diego professor Stephan Haggard pithily summarized Johnson's over-arching finding that "politicians 'reigned' but bureaucrats ultimately 'ruled.'"[10]

The study of the techno-security dimensions of the Japanese developmental state by Richard Samuels of the Massachusetts Institute of Technology is also rel-evant.[11] Samuels argues that the foundations of the Japanese techno-security state are based on a coherent set of beliefs revolving around three fundamental con-cepts. The first is the importance of "autonomy," which has been a constant theme throughout the course of Japan's industrialization, especially in the defense sec-tor.[12] The second notion is "diffusion" in which technology is regarded as a "quasi-public good to be developed and distributed through elaborate networks of producers and bureaucracies."[13] On this point, there is an important difference between Samuels and Johnson. The former sees the relationship between the state and private actors as defined by cooperation and constant negotiations, while Johnson views the state as dominant, imposing its policies unilaterally.[14] The third belief is "nurturing," which is the effort to support and sustain companies so that they can indigenize and diffuse technology.[15] Under state direction, companies are provided the necessary resources and work so they are able to become stable pil-lars of the industrial base. Competition is restrained and government contracts are carefully shared among a small group of hand-picked firms.

There are several important takeaways from the Japanese developmental state that are relevant when looking at the twenty-first century Chinese techno-security state. First is the pivotal role of administrative guidance, especially how this is delegated from the top and flows down into the implementation bureaucracy. Second is the importance of pilot organizations and how they are organized, led, and operated. Third is the identification of key tools of state intervention and the extent to which they are market conforming. Of particular significance are institutional creations.

The developmental state literature offers several additional insights that are helpful in framing the concept of the techno-security state. First is that actual policy coordination and implementation is far more complicated, multilayered, and contested. Although Johnson's thesis that MITI's powerful central role was a useful starting point in thinking about the development state model, subsequent work showed that a more nuanced understanding of other types of actors, including quasi–state institutions and intermediate level actors, was required, especially in weaker states and also between the state and the private sector.[16] This is especially relevant for the techno-security state concept because a key focus of this model is overcoming coordination problems between compartmentalized and competing actors, including between the state and the corporate sector and the civilian and defense domains.

A second contribution of the developmental state literature is its examination of the roles that technology, the pursuit of indigenous innovation capabilities, and learning have played in state development, especially for latecomer states such as South Korea that have been able to successfully catch up to the global innovation frontier in high-technology sectors such as semiconductors.[17] One pertinent insight is the importance that absorption and learning played in the initial stages of technological development as opposed to the pursuit of original innovation. Another lesson is the close collaboration between the state and corporate sectors in technological development, most notably in Japan and South Korea. A division of labor existed in which the state concentrated on research, development, and seeking technology transfers through market access controls while corporations concentrated on commercialization and production. These findings offer useful comparative insights into the technology development trajectories for techno-security states, especially those engaged in latecomer catching-up, which is the case for China.

A third takeaway is the crucial importance of the geostrategic environment and historical context in which states were situated, especially those in northeast Asia. Meredith Woo-Cummings points out that the rise of the developmental state in Japan, South Korea, and Taiwan was decisively shaped by war, colonialism, and the fear of war.[18] In addition, the security relationships that these countries had with their superpower benefactors, either the United States or Soviet Union, also had a profound impact. These experiences accounted for a distinctive overarching regional pattern of industrialization and technological development that was geared toward a "perpetual mobilization for war" during the Cold War.[19]

In the technological arena, these shared security concerns—although viewed from opposing sides—led northeast Asian states to become ardent proponents of the techno-nationalist school of grand strategic thinking in their initial stages of industrialization, especially in placing national security considerations at the very top of their development priorities. This accounted for the region-wide emphasis on the building of heavy, strategic, and technology-intensive industries.

Two distinct types of techno-nationalist grand strategies and models were adopted by northeast Asian states during this period: commercial and military techno-nationalism.[20] The commercial variant emphasizes the importance of technological autonomy for economic security, especially to allow homegrown vertically integrated firms to be competitive in the international marketplace. Military techno-nationalism stresses the overriding importance of military-security priorities in technological development. Which model states chose depended on the nature of their political and economic systems, whether those in power supported or opposed international engagement, and their strategic alignments within the Cold War system. Japan and South Korea chose the commercial-techno-nationalist variant as their catch-up development model, while Maoist China and the Democratic People's Republic of Korea picked military techno-nationalism.

THE INNOVATION-ENTREPRENEURIAL STATE SCHOOL

In contrast to the developmental state literature, innovation scholars regard the state as simply one actor in a crowded field that includes firms, universities, research centers, and financial institutions. In a discipline dominated by economists and management and business specialists, the private sector is viewed as the primary source for innovation activity and the state plays only a limited role, which is to address market failures and provide indirect regulatory guidance.[21]

There is one research cluster, the national innovation systems approach, that pays more attention to the state and is part of the broader systems of innovation camp, which examines the interaction between different actors and how this engagement is influenced by broader social, institutional, and political factors. There are different levels of systems of innovation analysis that range from the firm to the global level, but it is at the national level that the state plays a more prominent role. The national innovation systems model was the original starting point for the systems of innovation framework as scholars sought to understand the lessons of Japan's developmental success in the 1980s through an examination of its national characteristics for innovation.[22]

There have been efforts by scholars and governments in recent years to give more emphasis to the role of the state in enabling innovation, and the national innovation systems approach has been used and adapted as a platform from which to do this. One of the most prominent advocates of the innovation/entrepreneurial state argument is Mariana Mazzucato, who says that the state is a proactive, entrepreneurial, and risk-taking agent that plays a leading role in achieving high-end breakthroughs in innovation.[23] Mazzucato points out that the state is able to create strategies around new high-growth areas even before the business community is aware of or willing to invest in the growth potential, such as with the internet or nanotechnology. She argues that it is not enough for the state to deal with market or system failures, which is the mainstream view of innovation experts, but that "the state must also lead."

Among government agencies that Mazzucato spotlights as leading innovation from the front is the Department of Defense's (DoD's) Defense Advanced Research Projects Agency (DARPA). She points out that the DARPA model goes well beyond the funding of basic science, which is what most state science and technology (S&T) research agencies do. Instead, DARPA targets resources in specific areas and directions, opens new windows of opportunities, brokers the interactions between public and private agents involved in technological development, and facilitates commercialization.[24]

The Bello-centric School

Charles Tilly, a leading bello-centric scholar, put forward the classic argument that war made the state because "the building of an effective military machine imposed a heavy burden on the population involved: taxes, conscription, requisitions, and more." This in turn led to the promotion of "territorial consolidation, centralization, differentiation of the instruments of government and monopolization of the means of coercion, all the fundamental state-making processes."[25]

In the eyes of bello-centric scholars, the creation of military power led to the building of strong, modern states with the central objective of safeguarding national security. Bello-centrists can be equated with the international relations camp of neorealist thinking. Two bello-centric state schools are of particular relevance in the examination of the techno-security state: the national security state and the great power state.

THE NATIONAL SECURITY STATE SCHOOL

National security states (NSSs) come in many forms. Predatory security states are regimes in which elements of the national security bureaucracy manipulate their influence for political, economic, business, or other rewards for institutional and/or personal gains. The intelligence apparatus in Russia, for example, has been able to leverage its unrivaled authority in the post-Soviet era to occupy some of the most important power centers, including the presidency and key economic and business sectors. A garrison state is preoccupied with danger, especially war, and as a consequence, the military establishment emerges as the dominant institutional player. Harold Lasswell defined the garrison state as "under conditions of continual crisis and perpetual preparedness for total war, every aspect of life would eventually come under state control" so that "the specialists on violence" become "the most powerful group in society." NSSs are often associated with authoritarian political systems, and there is certainly a long list of states that fit this bill. They include the Soviet Union, Nazi Germany, and Japan in the interwar era to name just a few. However, there have also been a sizable number of democratic NSSs. The United States during World War II and into the Cold War had many of the features of an NSS, such as a sprawling and immensely influential national security establishment and a zero-sum competitive view of the world.[26]

THE GREAT POWER STATE SCHOOL

Techno-security states come in all sizes, but the most consequential of them are large and powerful and fit the description of great power states, a central concept in the study of international relations. The great power concept is relevant in the discussion of the techno-security state because the nature of these states is closely tied to the distribution of power within the international system and so an understanding of their techno-security capabilities offers geostrategic ramifications.

Great powers refer to a small elite of powerful states that exert far-reaching influence and authority on the workings of the international system. Each great power represents a pole, so the number of these states corresponds to the number of power centers in the global system. Despite the importance of the great power concept, there is no precise definition of what constitutes such a state. As Barry Buzan has noted, "even among neorealists who stage themselves as devoted to the development of rigour in IR [international relations] there is a willingness to duck the task of defining great power."[27]

Most of the criteria put forward to identify a great power have been material indicators because hard power capabilities are easier to measure and compare than ideational and soft power factors. Kenneth Waltz, for example, gives five key attributes of a great power: size of population and territory, resource endowment, economic capability, military strength, and political stability and competence. Waltz adds that a state needs to "score on all" of these areas to be ranked as a great power.[28] Another confusing issue is the label of great power itself, which has sometimes been used interchangeably with terms such as superpower or regional power.

William Wohlforth and Stephen Brooks employ the great power framework to assess the prospects of China attaining the same level of capabilities as the United States to become a superpower and transform the international system from a unipolar to a bipolar arrangement.[29] They focus on military, technological, and economic power and look at a variety of measurements in each of these areas to determine the distribution of capabilities between the two countries. Although Wohlforth and Brooks point to the potency of these elements interacting with each other, their analysis is mostly confined to assessing within rather than between these domains. In the examination of technological capacity, for instance, they look at patents, national research and development expenditures, technical skill levels, and high-technology exports, which provide general trends of civilian science and technology dynamics but are of limited value in assessing the impact on China's military capabilities.

Besides the academic debates on the constantly changing configuration of great powers and international polarity, there has also been a return to the primacy of great power competition for policymakers from Washington, DC to Beijing since the 2010s. The DoD in the early 2010s announced that it was refocusing its main attention from counterinsurgency, which had consumed much of its efforts and resources since the September 2001 terrorist attacks, to dealing with peer and near-peer state competitors because of mounting concerns about China and Russia. Tied with this shift in defense strategy was the implementation of new defense technology, innovation, and operational initiatives intended to allow the United States to find a competitive advantage without resorting to like-for-like arms races or even direct military confrontation. China has also been pursuing a defense technological strategic competition with the United States since the late 1990s. What the techno-security state concept offers to the analysis of great power dynamics is a more nuanced understanding of the complex interplay of security, technology, and political economy factors at the academic and policy levels.

Case Study of the US Techno-Security State

Can the United States compete and win the long-term techno-security competition against China? To answer this question, it is necessary to examine the nature of the US techno-security state and compare its strengths and weaknesses with its twenty-first-century archnemesis.

The Origins and Character of the US National Security State

World War II transformed the United States from a trading nation with a restrained international profile into a permanent NSS, an advanced techno-security state, and an assertive global military titan beginning from the Harry Truman administration in the second half of the 1940s. The character, size, and reach of the emergent NSS was subject to the nature of the US political system, especially to three sets of factors, according to Friedberg. They were (1) the basic structure of American governmental institutions, (2) the interests and relative strengths of competing groups within the government and society, and (3) the content of prevailing ideas and ideology. Friedberg argues that the core American ideals of anti-statism and anti-militarism were able to shape and contain the excessive tendencies of powerful state and military actors so that the United States did not become an all-consuming Frankenstein-like garrison state. The post–World War II US NSS can be generally defined as defensive in nature.

The grand struggle between competing coalitions and ideologies is also seen by Michael Hogan as the primary driving force behind the making of the US NSS.[30] He identifies two camps of which the first consisted of traditionalist "old world" conservative politicians who advocated for anti-statist, anti-militarist, and isolationist views that derived directly from the founding days of American independence. The opposing camp was made up of a "new world" breed of national security elites drawn from academia, government, industry, and Wall Street alongside the Truman administration, its congressional supporters, large portions of the media, industrialists, and the expansive military establishment who "celebrated American exceptionalism and American destiny" and fit well within the emerging national security ideology of American global leadership and anti-Soviet containment.

The intense rivalry between these dueling coalitions demonstrates two key structural features of the US political system. First is the open, robust, and pluralistic nature of the US democratic process, which not only permitted this no-holds-barred exchange of ideas but encouraged the debates beyond the Washington elites and across American society. Second is that the decision-making process leading to the creation of the NSS was not top down but a mixed approach of selective and limited high-level intervention, extensive bureaucratic and political delegation, and active bottom-up inputs from many different social groups. Although the White House played a leading role, especially on foundational decisions, there were extensive negotiations between the president and powerful actors of which the most influential were the military top brass. President Truman sometimes found himself having to compromise with his military chiefs and was occasionally outmaneuvered by them.

The personal role that President Truman played in the making of the NSS is contested by scholars. For a start, President Truman was not a strategic thinker and did not offer much of a grand vision to help guide the policy debate. Although Truman was aligned with the national security coalition, he also shared some of the anti-statist and anti-militarist reservations of the conservative camp. These conflicting views have led some scholars to conclude that Truman was a weak and hesitant leader who had difficulty making key decisions.[31] However, others take a contrary view and say that Truman was strong and decisive and owned the important decisions that he made. David Unger argues that Truman was deliberate in his actions and not beholden to the views of his advisers or generals.[32] Yet, other analysts point to the institutional limitations of the presidency that restricted the decision-making authority of the president without executive branch support. The final result—a restrained but durable NSS—was the desired outcome that President Truman and his successor Dwight Eisenhower had sought.

Another noteworthy feature of the birth of the US NSS was a sweeping makeover of its organizational structure at the outset. A big bang approach was taken through the 1947 National Security Act, which laid down a new set of powerful high-level bodies that provided expanded and comprehensive coverage of national security matters, which became increasingly broadly defined in an era of preparing for total war. They included the National Military Establishment (subsequently renamed the DoD), Joint Chiefs of Staff, National Security Council, and Central Intelligence Agency.

The external threat imperative is what Douglas Stuart sees as the overriding reason for the establishment of the US NSS. Whereas Friedberg identifies the Soviet Union as the raison d'être behind the rise of the US NSS, Stuart traces the catalyst further back to the Japanese attack on Pearl Harbor in 1941 that traumatized the American psyche. As Stuart writes, "Overnight, the powerful isolationist movement disappeared and *preparedness* was established as the new standard against which all future US foreign and defense policies would be judged."[33] Stuart believes that even if there was no Cold War between the United States and the Soviet Union following World War II, the post–Pearl Harbor NSS would have been established.

The end result was, according to Friedberg, a manageable and affordable strategic synthesis in which the United States was able to execute an external military strategy and geostrategic force posture to confront the Soviet Union that could be supported by a set of domestic power-creating mechanisms that generated the military capabilities needed "without doing grievous harm to American institutions or values."[34] This accommodative strategic synthesis sought to limit excessive fiscal, resource, and manpower extraction and keep in check the militarization of the economy and innovation system. The US NSS was essentially a threat-driven but affordable anti-statist defensive regime.

Comparing the Origins of the US and Chinese National Security States

There are some intriguing similarities, as well as fundamental differences, between the US historical experience and China's contemporary efforts in forging an NSS. The strands of commonality come mainly from the security sphere. The search for a strategic synthesis is one shared issue that stands out. This was a prolonged struggle in the US case, but Chinese leaders have also had to grapple with the challenge of balancing competing external and domestic concerns. Chinese leaders from Jiang Zemin (江泽民) to Xi have also regularly and prominently talked about the need to find their own strategic equilibrium between being a rich country and having a strong military (富国强兵, fuguo qiangbing). The phrasing that is commonly used is that a "strategic task of China's socialist modernization" is to "build a national defense and strong armed forces commensurate with China's international status and compatible with China's national security and development interests."[35] The US strategic synthesis took around fifteen years to come together, and although the authoritarian nature of the Chinese system may provide for a more efficient process, the prospects for finding a manageable and stable Chinese strategic synthesis may still be years away.

A second common thread is the catalytic role of threats. For the United States, Pearl Harbor was a profound wake-up call that then metamorphosed into the long-term Cold War threat from the Soviet Union. These events were instrumental in the making of the US NSS. Sixty years later, the terrorist attacks of September 11, 2001 led to a similar traumatic response and return to an NSS mentality, which subsequently transitioned to great power competition in the mid-2010s.

For China, there does not appear to be a single transformative shock comparable to Pearl Harbor but a series of external and internal threats and incidents extending over nearly twenty-five years that cumulatively led to the creation of the twenty-first-century NSS. The process can be traced back to the unwinding and collapse of the Soviet empire starting in 1989, followed quickly by the 1991 First Gulf War, which sent shock waves through the Chinese military establishment. Leadership attention then turned to prolonged crisis and tensions across the Taiwan Strait beginning in the early 1990s and continuing to the present day, the US bombing of the Chinese embassy in Belgrade in 1999, and finally intensifying but hidden US-China strategic competition throughout the 2000s that eventually emerged into the open in the early 2010s and became fully fledged by the mid-2010s. A persistent threat environment that is started or punctuated by major shocks appears to be an important ingredient in the recipe for making an NSS.

In dealing with a heightened threat environment, both the United States and China have emphasized the importance of military preparedness. Stuart highlights the central preoccupation with preparedness by the US NSS following Pearl Harbor. Preparedness is also a central organizing concept that Xi uses in explaining the building of a more capable NSS, especially the military dimensions. On taking office and becoming commander in chief, one of the first priorities that Xi assigned to the People's Liberation Army was to be fully prepared and ready to fight and win a military conflict, which has since become a core military operational requirement.

A third common strand that has contributed to the rise of both the US and Chinese NSSs is the role of strategic opportunities and especially the lure of becoming a world leader. For the United States, the biggest opportunity was the ability to become the new hegemonic leader of the Western world following the end of World War II. Many wartime allies welcomed the United States assuming the mantle of global leader, or what John Ikenberry has called the building of an empire by invitation.[36] Western European countries were especially keen for the United States to maintain a powerful presence in Europe to provide security protection against the looming Soviet threat and for postwar reconstruction aid. Some leading proponents of the national security camp such as George Kennan believed that adopting a strong Cold War posture was an exercise in national rejuvenation that allowed the United States to "recapture the moral discipline and the civic virtue" from earlier periods of American history.[37] Xi has emphasized that a strategic window of opportunity has opened up in the early twenty-first century with the country's economic development, which allows it to become a central player on the global stage. However, Xi cautions that there is strong international, especially Western, resistance to China's rise that requires strong national security safeguards to protect and ensure its rise is not blocked.

In the top-level design of the US and Chinese NSSs, there have also been some parallel elements of thinking. This has included the need to increase centralization of authority, especially to the country's top leader, improve coordination, in particular within the military establishment, and expand reach and coverage of the national security apparatus. The United States built a disciplined and effective command apparatus set out in the National Security Act. Chinese policymakers appear to have carefully studied the US model and applied some of the lessons that were relevant to their specific circumstances, which included the establishment of a national security commission and pushing for joint integration of the military high command.

The overall nature of the US and Chinese NSSs are, however, fundamentally different because of the political regimes they are nested within. The restrained US NSS was a hard-fought compromise between statist and national security advocates and anti-statist and anti-militarist forces. The intense struggle was a democratic safeguard to help mitigate the rise of an untamed garrison state. The Chinese authoritarian state does not have these political, institutional, or normative checks and balances. Until Xi came to power, there was only lukewarm interest in and support for an NSS, which were mostly confined to the military and internal security establishments. The overwhelming priority among the official establishment and society was the pursuit of economic development and maintaining a docile international profile. This healthy skepticism was reflected in failed efforts to establish a high-level national security council during the tenures of Jiang and Hu Jintao (胡锦涛). However, this long-standing economic-centric consensus proved to be an insufficient bulwark after Xi took office and began to put in place the critical pieces of his NSS.

Nonetheless, there are still some constraints on the rise of an overly expansive Chinese NSS. Most obviously, the growth in defense spending has not risen in relative terms since Xi has come to power and he has so far not advocated for significant increases. However, internal security spending has been expanding rapidly. The military also remains firmly under civilian control, so there is little threat of the emergence of a military-dominated garrison state. However, the Chinese NSS is still a work in progress and there is plenty of historical precedent from the Maoist era to show that these present restraints can be pushed aside.

Another glaring difference separating the US and Chinese cases is the orientation of their security regimes. The US NSS has been overwhelmingly directed externally beyond its borders, with some limited domestic ramifications. China under Xi is emphasizing both the external and internal dimensions, with heightened attention toward the domestic realm dealing with ideological, ethnic, and social stability matters that go well beyond traditional national security parameters.

The Origins and Character of the US Techno-Security State during the Cold War

Not surprisingly, the US NSS has had a profound influence in shaping its techno-security component, but the institutional identity and organizational culture of the techno-security state also owed much to the science state that emerged from the late 1940s onward. The relationship between the national security and science establishments was extremely close at its inception, organizationally as well as normatively. An important reason for this tight bond was that the chief architect of both the techno-security and science states was Vannevar Bush. He led the establishment of a centralized US defense research and development enterprise during World War II, overseeing a wide range of portfolios that included the Manhattan Project, and subsequently played an influential role in the founding of critical pillars of the postwar science state such as with the National Science Foundation.[38]

An underlying philosophical belief held by Bush and widely shared by the US scientific elite that cut to the very heart of the US-Soviet techno-security competition was that science and innovation would be far more successful and enduring under a democracy than a totalitarian system. This was because top-down totalitarian regimes were "rigid, arbitrary, hierarchical, and regimented," while the US system was "essentially adapted for the purpose" of pursuing pioneering science and technology.[39] The United States was the clear techno-security winner against the Soviet Union, and this issue of contesting scientific and political systems is once again at the forefront of the rivalry between the US and Chinese techno-security states.

What were the core features of the US techno-security state in its formative stages of development in the second half of the 1940s to the late 1950s that made it so effectively suited for the intense and prolonged technological struggle with the Soviet Union? The first was its pluralistic and decentralized nature.[40] The military services each had their own research and development outfits, such as the Office of Naval Research, that competed far more than they cooperated with each other. This was also the case for the federal science system where funding agencies and research institutions were established that pursued their own agendas with limited coordination with one another. They included the likes of the National Science Foundation, National Institutes of Health, and the Atomic Energy Commission. Initial efforts to establish centralized top-down coordination mechanisms were met with fierce resistance and were largely unsuccessful. The DoD made a couple of attempts during the late 1940s and early 1950s to create central coordination bodies and positions for science and technology oversight with the Research and Development Board and an assistant secretary of defense for research and development, but the individual armed services fatally undermined these initiatives.[41]

A second feature was the establishment of an expansive and robust system of large-scale federal laboratories engaged in cutting-edge defense and dual-use-related big science endeavors such as nuclear weapons and space research.[42] This included a nationwide system of nuclear weapons laboratories such as Los

Alamos, Lawrence Livermore, Sandia, and Oak Ridge, and the Jet Propulsion Laboratory that worked on ballistic missile and space propulsion technologies. A third feature was the federal government's permanent shift in becoming the principal and long-term source of funding for foundational scientific research, which initially occurred during World War II. The DoD and military services became the biggest funders of basic research during the Cold War, but the National Science Foundation and National Institutes of Health also emerged to become prominent players.

A fourth feature was the emergence of a strong public-private partnership between the government and private corporations in defense industrial production, which demonstrated the limits of the government in the affairs of the techno-security state. In the formulation of the 1947 National Security Act, which was the legal basis for the establishment of the NSS, the National Security Resources Board was authorized and its role was to "advise the president concerning the coordination of military, industrial, and civilian mobilization."[43] However, there was considerable debate about the authority and reach of the National Security Resources Board over the economy and especially on matters such as industrial policy. Some of the board's architects had hoped that it would be the economic counterpart to the National Security Council that was also created by the National Security Act. However, in the face of strong opposition and his own concerns, President Truman decided to keep the board a relatively powerless body that only engaged in low-key mobilization planning and accounting activities. The fate of the National Security Resources Board was a clear signpost that the realm of the US NSS would not reach deep into the economic sphere.

Following its initial establishment, the US techno-security state underwent subsequent rounds of adjustment to take into account major strategic, technological, and domestic changes. The first revamp occurred in the late 1950s in response to major Soviet technological and military industrial advancements of which the most prominent was the 1957 launch of the Sputnik manned spacecraft coupled with concerns over a growing bomber and missile gap. The fragmented and decentralized nature of the US techno-security state was identified as the prime reason for the United States falling behind the Soviet Union in vital defense and strategic sectors, and this led to the formation of centralized civilian-led agencies reporting to the defense secretary, which included DARPA, and the director of defense research and engineering, who was given the same rank as the secretaries of the armed services. Around the same time, in the science state, a group of talented young scientists and engineers known as the Fairchildren established a start-up semiconductor enterprise that laid the seeds for the creation of Silicon Valley and several powerhouses of the late-twentieth-century US innovation system, such as Intel and AMD.[44] These developments in the national S&T system, especially in the electronics and computing sectors, had profound consequences for the rise of the techno-security state. Another important turning point for the US techno-security state took place beginning in the mid-1970s and extended into the 1980s with what became known as the second offset strategy. This was again in response to the external threat posed by growing Soviet quantitative superiority in conventional and strategic military capabilities.[45] The United States could not compete on a like-for-like basis with the Soviet Union, so the DoD leadership headed by Harold Brown decided instead to seek technological superiority in advanced capabilities such as precision strike, intelligence, surveillance, and reconnaissance, as well as radar-evading stealth capabilities.[46] This eventually gave the United States a decisive technological edge by emphasizing US strengths over Soviet weaknesses, most notably in the air defense arena, and helped to contribute to the collapse of the Soviet Union at the end of the 1980s.

With the US techno-security state emerging triumphant at the end of the Cold War, it no longer faced any peer-to-peer rivals and turned instead to dealing with threats from regional states, nonstate actors, and technological challenges brought on by the shift from warfare in the industrial era to the information age. The next major turning point for the US techno-security state has been coping with the intensifying great power rivalry with China in the twenty-first century.

The Key Ingredients to the Success of the US Techno-Security State

In an examination of the contemporary US techno-security state, Weiss argues that there are three main reasons for the success of the United States as an advanced innovation power.[47] First, is the role of the NSS as a technological enterprise, which she defines as the role "played by a cluster of federal agencies that collaborate closely with private actors in pursuit of security-related objectives." Second, are geopolitical factors, and specifically threat perceptions, that have been "the original catalyst for the NSS formation and its evolution as an innovation engine." Third is anti-statism, which, as pointed out earlier, Weiss sees as pushing the public and private sectors toward hybrid ways of close cooperation.

More specifically, Weiss pointed to several distinctive features to explain why the US techno-security state has performed so well. The first factor is that the creative institutional design of the US NSS innovation enterprise has allowed it to fulfill two often competing purposes. The first is to meet the national security–focused public purpose and mission-oriented problem sets of the NSS, while the second is to satisfy the goals of the private sector, which are to absorb risk and ensure commercial viability. To foster collaboration, the NSS has established a set of mechanisms to align and bind its interests and goals with private actors such as cost sharing and various forms of support. However, the NSS also has to actively and directly monitor and manage the relationship to make sure that private actors are performing as required. This is done by providing incentives and rewards rather than through control and penalties. Weiss describes this as governed interdependence.

A second feature that Weiss says is an essential component of the US NSS innovation engine is hybridization, which refers to the merging of public and private institutions in novel ways to produce fused hybrid entities. There are many types of these hybrids in the US techno-security ecosystem. They include public interest corporations such as Science Applications International Corporation, federally funded research and development centers such as the Department of Energy's national laboratories, commercialization consortia between industry, academia, and national security entities, and public venture investment funds like the Central Intelligence Agency's In-Q-Tel located in Silicon Valley. Weiss argues that the hybridized NSS is a consequence of the US anti-statist tradition as these hybrid public-private partnerships are "a preferred American way of organizing state-society links."[48]

A third factor that Weiss believes is behind the success of the US NSS is its embrace of decentralized bottom-up coordination. The techno-security state divides responsibility among multiple mission-oriented agencies. Although this policy pluralism and fragmented authority has often been highlighted as a source of waste and inefficiency, Weiss argues that multiple models and sources of government support have played an essential role in driving the US innovation process. Key sectors such as computers and nanotechnology have benefited from this approach. The US experience shows that "a state need not have centralized powers, dispensing policies in a highly orchestrated effort from the top. A less centralized, bottom-up but agency-directed process could deliver better results."[49]

The notion of a broad-based science, technology, and innovation system that is engaged in national security–related activities has gradually entered into mainstream US official strategic thinking since the beginning of the 2010s. The Barack Obama administration sought to use the terminology and related narrative of the US national security science, technology, and innovation enterprise to upgrade and redefine the contours of the prevailing and deeply ingrained paradigm of the defense industrial base that dates back to the mid-twentieth century.[50] As one senior DoD official responsible for defense industrial affairs argued in 2015, "when the term 'Defense Industrial Base' is used, entrepreneurs, inventors, and other nontraditional suppliers do not immediately come to mind."[51]

The most explicit effort by the Obama administration to put forward the concept of the national security science, technology, and innovation enterprise occurred in 2016 when it issued a detailed long-term development strategy to "address the challenges and opportunities imposed by a new landscape of national security technology concerns in the 21st century."[52] The importance and relevance of this strategy, titled "A 21st Century Science, Technology, and Innovation Strategy for America's National Security," has to be questioned because it was only released in the final lame duck months of the Obama presidency, but the drafters from the White House's National Science and Technology Council Committee on Homeland and National Security and the Office of Science and Technology Policy had intended the document to be nonpartisan and to provide guidance for the next administration in thinking about the national security innovation challenge.

The starting premise of the Obama strategy is that "national security involves much more than military power and homeland defense" and consequently the "national security science, technology, and innovation enterprise includes not just the scientists and engineers working in federal and national laboratories, but also a much larger ecosystem of academic and industry stakeholders." The strategy document points out that although the national security innovation enterprise was created and organized to "respond to the military threats and economic opportunities of the last century"—and achieved many successes—in the twenty-first century, the "enterprise" must be able to not only retain military technological superiority but also "respond effectively to new challenges, such as asymmetric threats enabled by the globalization of science and technology; threats to stability, such as natural disasters and the effects of climate change; and other humanitarian and security crises, such as epidemic disease." These new challenges were "not anticipated in the design of the current US national security ST&I [science, technology, and innovation] enterprise," which primarily consists of a "closed network of national security laboratories and engineering centers and an inwardly-focused national security workforce." Today, "the best science and technology is often found outside the national security ST&I enterprise, in academic and commercial sectors in the United States or in other countries," and so "promoting technology development by the private sector at home and around the world and then harnessing that development in ingenious ways will be increasingly important for economic prosperity as well as for national security."

The Donald Trump administration embraced the concept of the inclusive national security innovation establishment, although it made some minor adjustments to distinguish it from the preceding administration, most notably by replacing "enterprise" with "base." The National Security Innovation Base featured prominently in the Trump administration's first national security strategy issued in December 2017. The national security strategy defined the National

Security Innovation Base as "the American network of knowledge, capabilities, and people—including academia, National Laboratories, and the private sector—that turns ideas into innovations, transforms discoveries into successful commercial products and companies, and protects and enhances the American way of life."[53]

A crucial difference between the Obama and Trump administrations in their thinking about the US techno-security state is that the former believed the national security science, technology, and innovation enterprise could benefit from international cooperation, while the latter emphasized a narrower techno-nationalist approach. The Trump national security strategy points out that the National Security Innovation Base reflects "the genius of creative Americans, and the free system that enables them, [which] is critical to American security and prosperity."

In conclusion, the US case offers a proven model of a successful relationship between the state and innovation, national security, and development. The key elements accounting for this outcome are governed interdependence, hybridization, decentralized coordination, and a looming threat environment. Whether the United States is able to maintain its preeminent technological leadership, especially in the national security and defense realms, is up for debate. Can a very different Chinese model that emphasizes a top-down, state-centric approach to innovation compete successfully?

An Analytical Framework of the Techno-Security State

This examination of the literature on economic-centric and bello-centric states and the US techno-security state offers a wealth of insights in the task of developing an analytical framework of the techno-security state that can robustly evaluate its performance, identify and assess long-term development trends, and allow for comparative analysis of different types of regimes. This framework is especially pertinent in considering the long-term competition between the US and Chinese techno-security states that is at the heart of their great power rivalry.

In constructing this framework, a number of key questions will be addressed. What are the principal factors contributing to the successful development and functioning of the techno-security state? What is the nature of the relationship and balance between the state and market? What is the nature of the relationship between the civilian and national security domains? How is the techno-security state organized, led, and managed? How does the techno-security establishment fit into the strategic, technological, and security calculations and needs of the governing regimes that they serve? How technologically advanced and self-reliant is the techno-security state? What are the key obstacles and weaknesses of the techno-security state?

A first step in building this framework is to draw up a taxonomy to distinguish between different types of techno-security states according to the relationship between the state and market. Borrowing from the developmental state school literature, three categories can be defined:

- Plan ideological states in which socialist central planning is dominant. These states were in the ascendancy during the twentieth-century Cold War with the Soviet Union and China under Mao Zedong (毛泽东) as archetypal representatives. In the twenty-first century, only North Korea remains active in this category.
- Plan rational states where governments set general policy directions and objectives and actively intervene in key strategic priorities while letting the market be responsible for implementation. Japan and France are strong examples of plan rational states.
- Hybrid rational states in which there is an interdependent and carefully balanced and orchestrated relationship between the state and market.[54] They come in two types: (1) statist-derived hybrid rational states where the state has traditionally been dominant but is moving to significantly reduce its authority and intervention and (2) anti-statist-derived hybrid rational states in which the state has historically maintained a limited but active leadership role and allowed the private sector to be in charge. The United States is the leading model of the anti-statist hybrid rational state while the United Kingdom is an example of a statist hybrid rational state.

The next step in this framework-building process is a more granular identification of factors that help to explain the nature of development and functioning of the techno-security state. The analyses done by Weiss and others in examining the successful development of the US techno-security state point to four factors that are especially pertinent. First is the nature of coordination of leadership and management entities within the techno-security ecosystem, which could be either decentralized bottom up, centralized top down, or a combination of the two. Second is the nature of the governance regime employed by the state to secure the participation of enterprises and other actors. Is it by incentives and rewards or through control and penalties? Third is the degree of hybridization taking place between public and private institutions as well as integration between the military and civilian spheres.

Fourth is the nature of threat perceptions and the threat environment. Techno-security states tend to view their national security as under severe

TABLE 6.1 The techno-security state analytical framework

Developmental model type

Plan ideological, plan rational, or hybrid rational

Key development and functional factors

External threat perceptions and the threat environment
Leadership and management coordination
Governance regime
Hybridization
Techno-nationalist ideology and strategies

---

danger and see these threats in zero-sum terms. Consequently, they are highly suspicious of the intentions of other states, pursue nationalistic, beggar-thy-neighbor postures that offer little room for accommodation, prefer to go it alone in their policy conduct, and are distrustful of international institutions. If war is the mother of invention, then the threat of war is the patron saint of innovation.

The developmental state scholarship offers an important fifth factor, which is the role of techno-nationalist ideology and strategies. Techno-nationalism is at the center of a techno-security state's identity and institutional culture. At one end of the techno-nationalist spectrum are statist-minded regimes that believe that only a state-controlled and closed-door approach to technological innovation can safeguard national security, economic competitiveness, and international status. Emphasis is placed on nurturing indigenous capabilities through the adoption of highly regulated protectionist regimes that sharply restrict foreign direct investment. However, many of these states are underindustrialized and struggling to catch up and find themselves dependent on the importation of advanced technology and knowledge. China between the 1950s and 2010s was a classic example of a techno-nationalist-dependent state. At the other end of the spectrum are anti-statist regimes that are market oriented, self-reliant, and technologically advanced but are willing to share their technological capabilities for profit and strategic advantage. The United States is the prime model of a state that pursues this strategy of techno-nationalist primacy.

Taken together, this list offers a broad mix of structural, process, and normative factors covering strategic, security, political, and economic topic areas (see table 6.1). This framework will be applied in the concluding chapter to compare the US and Chinese techno-security states and the prospects for their long-term competition for global technological dominance in security affairs.

CONCLUSIONS
The Prospects and Implications
of the Chinese Techno-Security State

China is making determined progress in its ascent to the pinnacle of the global techno-security order, but stern challenges await as the path to the very top narrows and becomes more arduous and treacherous. Externally, the United States is finally stirring to thwart China's techno-security rise while endeavoring to preserve its own long-cherished dominance. Domestically, the Chinese techno-security state along with the rest of the country is scrambling to turn from a dependent follower into an advanced and self-reliant science, technology, and innovation power. Nothing less than China's long-term power and prosperity and the continued rule of the Chinese Communist Party is at stake. What can the world expect as the Chinese techno-security state becomes more capable, confident, and confrontational?

Several major issues will be scrutinized in this concluding chapter that are especially salient in thinking about the prospects and implications of the Chinese techno-security state. First, how large and integrated is the Chinese techno-security state in both absolute terms and relative to the rest of the country; and compared with the United States? Second, how institutionalized or personalistic is the Chinese techno-security state and how dependent is its fortunes on Xi Jinping (习近平)? Third, what are the similarities and differences between the US-Soviet Cold War and US-Japan geo-economic competition in the late twentieth century and the US-China strategic rivalry today? Fourth, what are the prospects for the US and Chinese techno-security states in their long-term techno-security competition? Who is likely to emerge on top? Last, what is the future development path for the Chinese techno-security state over the course of the 2020s and into the 2030s and beyond, especially in the realm of economic securitization?

How Large and Sustainable Is the Chinese Techno-Security State?

The Chinese techno-security state is strategically important and wields considerable clout, but how big is it and why does it matter? To answer these questions, it is necessary to delineate the constituent parts of the techno-security state. The approach taken here is to define these components according to the extent to which they are engaged in national security–related activities (see table C.1).[1] Entities whose responsibilities are primarily devoted to national security activities are included in what will be referred to as the "core" base. The main components of this inner ring are (1) the national security–oriented research and development (R&D) apparatus, (2) armed forces, (3) domestically focused security agencies (law enforcement and paramilitary forces), (4) externally focused national security agencies (foreign affairs, intelligence, private security contractors), and (5) the defense industrial base that is engaged in defense activities.

Beyond this inner core is an outer ring or "expanded" techno-security and techno-strategic base that covers a diverse array of organizations that have broader and looser affiliations with national security affairs. The notion of the expanded techno-security base has its roots in the industrial mobilization systems that many states maintained during the Cold War in heightened preparation for war. Many of these legacy mobilization apparatuses are now outdated and do not incorporate components of the twenty-first-century high-technology economy. This outer band is divided into two parts. The first component is the

TABLE C.1 Components of the core and expanded techno-security state

Core techno-security base

National security-oriented research and development apparatus

Armed services

Domestic national security agencies: law enforcement, paramilitary forces

Externally oriented national security agencies: foreign affairs, private security contractors, and intelligence agencies

Defense industrial base

Expanded techno-security and techno-strategic bases

Dual-use civil-military base: commercial entities with actual or potential capabilities with national security applications

Techno-strategic base: sectors engaged in strategic but nondefense-related activities dual-use civil-military base that is composed of commercial entities that have actual or potential civilian capabilities with national security applications. The second component is the techno-strategic base that is composed of sectors engaged in strategically important but nondefense-related activities, such as economic competitiveness and resource resiliency.

Determining what should be included in the expanded techno-security/strategic base is far more contestable because of the lack of precision in the application of key terms and also because of larger political and policy considerations. What, for example, constitutes dual use? Should only realized capacity be counted or potential capacity as well? What should be deemed as of essential national strategic importance even if it is not of national security significance? What type and level of participation should qualify entities to be deemed part of the civil-military base? If a university, for example, receives military funding for research, should it be counted as a civil-military outfit? If this funding was significant and continuous, then a valid case could be made that the entity would be a civil-military affiliate, but what if the funding was small and ad hoc? These are complex and constantly evolving issues that governments are grappling with against the backdrop of intensifying political and national security pressures.

This study takes a narrower, formal approach in counting what should be included in this expanded outer layer. Those included are (1) entities that are formally approved as (actual or potential) contractors of national security products and services to the government and national security apparatus, (2) the rest of the defense industrial base that is not included in the core techno-security state, and (3) economic sectors specifically identified by their governments in official policies to be of critical geostrategic, geo-economic, or technological importance to the country's overall well-being.

Two key elements will be measured in quantifying the size of the core techno-security state. First is the financial component: how much financial resources are spent by the state on national security activities among the entities identified as belonging to the inner core? This would include the defense budget, internal security budget, nuclear weapons spending, and other expenditures included in state budgets related to national security. The second element is the industrial component, which primarily consists of the annual economic output of the defense industrial base.

Not surprisingly, the size of core techno-security states varies widely according to a broad array of factors such as the threat environment and regime type. Highly militarized plan ideological states are one group where the national security apparatuses wield extensive influence and consequently the cost of maintaining techno-security priorities accounts for a very large share of national resources. This is exemplified by the former Soviet Union, North Korea, and

China under Mao Zedong (毛泽东), where the defense burden alone (not including allocations to other parts of the techno-security enterprise) is estimated to have consumed anywhere between 10 percent and 20 percent of annual gross domestic product (GDP).[2]

Measuring the size of the contemporary core Chinese techno-security state is problematic and imprecise because of a chronic lack of transparency in the country's reporting of its defense and national security costs. Official external security expenditures in 2019 totaled US$180.9 billion (RMB 1.25 trillion based on 2019 exchange rates) or the equivalent of 1.3 percent of GDP, which consisted of defense spending of US$172.1 billion (RMB 1.189 trillion based on 2019 exchange rates) and foreign affairs expenditures of US$8.91 billion (RMB 61.6 billion based on 2019 exchange rates).[3] For a country building aircraft carriers, intercontinental ballistic missiles, several models of advanced combat aircraft, and numerous other advanced capabilities and with one of the world's largest standing armies, paying for these costly activities on such a meager slice of the GDP is highly questionable.

A number of major defense-related activities are not included in the official budget, including expenditures for the People's Armed Police (which falls into the domestic security budget), imports of major weapons systems, and the military portions of the space program.[4] One especially important category that is mostly absent from the official defense budget is R&D funding, which is accounted for elsewhere in the general state budget, such as science and technology (S&T) expenditures or the budget for the State Administration for Science, Technology, and Industry for National Defense (SASTIND). There are no official Chinese figures for defense R&D spending, but interviews and other research suggest that it could be equivalent to between 15 percent and 20 percent of the official defense budget, which would be between US$27.3 and US$36.4 billion annually at the end of the 2010s.[5] Adding this figure to the defense and foreign affairs budgets would bring total 2019 external security spending to around US$217–US$246 billion (RMB 1.5–1.7 trillion based on 2019 exchange rates).

Domestic security expenses are also substantial. Total Chinese government expenditures in this domain for 2019 are estimated to be around US$211 billion (RMB 1.46 trillion based on 2019 exchange rates), which is based on a 6.1 percent share of overall state funding for domestic security when it was last officially disclosed in 2017.[6] Only official central-level spending on domestic security in 2019 was revealed, which was US$26.6 billion (RMB 184 billion based on 2019 exchange rates) or around 12.5 percent of total domestic security spending. In total, the national security financial component for 2019 totals between US$434 billion and US$478 billion (RMB 3–3.3 trillion based on 2019 exchange rates), or between 3.1 percent and 3.3 percent of GDP.

For the industrial component, the only publicly available statistical data to measure the size of the defense industrial base are corporate revenue and profits. Value-added industrial output is not readily accessible. Corporate revenue, though, is significantly larger than value-added industrial output as it does not deduct the costs involved in production such as materials, labor, and services.[7] Total revenue reported by China's principal state-owned defense industrial conglomerates in 2019 was US$364.3 billion (RMB 2.517 trillion based on 2019 exchange rates),[8] which, if adjusted by a nominal 50 percent reduction into value-added industrial output, would be the equivalent of US$182.34 billion (RMB 1.26 trillion based on 2019 exchange rates) in value-added industrial output of 1.55 percent of GDP. A leading People's Liberation Army (PLA) center for military-civil fusion (MCF) analysis estimated in the mid-2010s that civilian production accounted for between 70 percent and 80 percent of total defense industry output value, a level that has been holding steady for the past couple of decades.[9] This would mean that for 2019, defense industry value-added industrial output value was between US$35.45 billion (RMB 245 billion based on 2019 exchange rates) and US$54.63 billion (RMB 377.5 billion) or the equivalent of between 0.3 percent and 0.5 percent of GDP. Added together with the financial component, the overall size of the core Chinese techno-security state would be between 3.4 percent and 3.6 percent of GDP.

For the outer layer of the Chinese techno-security state, the civil-military base covers several major components. The first is the remaining components of the defense industrial base not included in the core techno-security state as many of these activities would come under the definition of actual or potential dual-use activities. This would account for around 1.2 percent of GDP. The second component is the nonstate civilian MCF sector outside of the traditional defense industrial base. This sector has steadily expanded, and as of the late 2010s, there were more than three thousand civilian firms that had obtained state licenses allowing them to participate in the defense acquisition system. However, as the development of the civil-military base only began in earnest from the mid-2010s, the scale and range of activities is modest so far.

Key MCF-related activity can be divided into four buckets: R&D, financial investment, industrial production, and the provision of goods and services. Anecdotal information exists to show that there is considerable MCF-related R&D, but there has so far been no rigorous and comprehensive accounting of this effort. In the industrial domain, one proxy indicator of the scale of MCF-related activity is the number of civilian firms with little or no defense background that have been awarded official licenses to bid for participation in major military equipment projects, which is estimated to be around fifty as of the late 2010s.[10]

More significant MCF activity is taking place in logistics and support services such as maintenance, transportation, and the provision of food, clothing, and fuel supplies as the PLA has sought to increasingly outsource its requirements.

The sector that has witnessed the most intensive MCF growth is financial investment, where asset securitization (AS) and the proliferation of MCF-centered government guidance funds (GGFs) have brought in significant sums of new market-sourced funding streams for defense and dual-use projects. Nearly US$370 billion (RMB 2.55 trillion) of asset securitized funds were raised by China's major state-owned defense conglomerates between 2012 and 2020 or US$41 billion on average annually (see chapter 3 for more details). MCF-focused GGFs raised at least US$126 billion (RMB 872 billion) between 2012 and 2019, or an annual average of US$17.5 billion (RMB 121 billion), according to publicly available data, although a considerable number of MCF funds have not disclosed any information, so the actual figure is likely to be significantly higher. The combined annual average of investment funding raised through the AS and MCF GGF channels between 2012 and 2019 is at least US$54.4 billion (RMB 376 billion based on 2019 exchange rates) or the equivalent of 41 percent of the average official annual defense budget during this same period, which was US$143 billion (RMB 987 billion) or around 0.5 percent of GDP.

MCF-related R&D, industrial production, and supporting goods and services are likely to be much smaller in scale than this financial investment activity, so a reasonable estimate is that cumulative annual MCF-generated economic output at the beginning of the 2020s would not exceed 1 percent of GDP and could be substantially lower. The size of the MCF economic contribution to the techno-security state can be expected to steadily expand as the implementation of the MCF development strategy gathers momentum. Combined with the defense industrial MCF component, the estimated size of the expanded Chinese techno-security base is around 2.25 percent of GDP.

There are also industrial and technology efforts that could fall under the techno-strategic category. One of the most prominent is the strategic emerging industries (SEI) initiative that targets the development of next-generation information technology, high-end equipment manufacturing, new materials, biotechnology, new-energy vehicles, new energy, energy-efficient and environmental technologies, and digital innovation. The industrial sectors under the SEI cumulatively accounted for 10 percent of China's GDP in 2017.[11] Although a few of these sectors such as equipment manufacturing and new materials have potential dual-use applications, the overwhelming bulk of these activities have little or no national security utility and are intended to enhance the country's economic competitiveness. Consequently, although the SEI would fit under the techno-strategic label, it would not fall under the techno-security state rubric.

By comparison, the economic footprint of the US techno-security state appears to be considerably larger than its Chinese rival in absolute and relative terms. The core US techno-security state in 2019 was 5.9 percent of GDP while the size of the expanded techno-security variant was 1.2 percent of GDP. This is broken down as follows:

- The national security financial component in 2019 totaled US$1.13 trillion, or 5.27 percent of GDP, and was made up of three components: (1) external security (defense, intelligence, nuclear, international affairs) at US$863 billion, (2) homeland security (Department of Homeland Security, state-level law enforcement) at US$268.2 billion, and (3) miscellaneous supporting items (veteran affairs, national security portion of debt servicing) at US$372 billion. Whether this last supporting category should be included in the overall financial component is debatable because these items do not contribute directly to national security capabilities. If this supporting segment is excluded, then the overall figure falls to US$1.13 trillion, or 5.3 percent of GDP.[12]
- The industrial portion consisting of the aerospace and defense base totaled US$396 billion in 2019, which was equivalent to 1.8 percent of GDP.[13] However, a large majority of the industrial value-added output was for civilian products, such as commercial airliners. The Aerospace Industries Association said in the mid-2010s that defense sales accounted for 34 percent of total aerospace and defense sector sales.[14] Using this ratio, this would mean that the defense industrial base contributed US$132 billion, or 0.6 percent of GDP, to the size of the core techno-security state in 2019.
- For the expanded techno-security state, the civil-military portion would include the elements of the aerospace and defense industrial base not counted in the core techno-security state, which in 2019 would have been US$264 billion, or 1.2 percent of GDP. There are no sectors that are readily identifiable as currently belonging to the techno-strategic component, although there are long-term candidates such as artificial intelligence (AI), quantum computing, and 5G communications. The Department of Defense (DoD) identifies a number of sectors that are of vital importance to national security, such as the electronics sector, software engineering sector, machine tools and industrial controls sector, and the materials sector, especially specific items such as high-performance aluminum, titanium, beryllium, tungsten, rare earths, and synthetic carbon fibers, but the share of national security–related production in these sectors is small and makes it difficult to justify their inclusion into the expansive

techno-security state.[15] Only 6 percent of global electronics production, for example, is for the military market.[16]

One important finding from this financial analysis is that the Chinese and US techno-security states account for only a relatively modest stake of their national economies. In the case of the United States, the core techno-security state is around 5.9 percent of GDP, while the expanded variant is around 7.1 percent. The situation is similar for China, where the core techno-security state is likely no more than around 3.5 percent of GDP and the expanded version is estimated to be between 5.5 percent and 5.7 percent of GDP (see table C.2).

This lengthy discussion in quantifying the size of the Chinese techno-security state and providing a comparison with the United States is important for at least two major policy reasons. The first revolves around how the United States and its allies perceive the nature and reach of the Chinese techno-security state and how to calibrate efforts to control engagement with it. There is a growing perception by Western governments that the Chinese techno-security state, or key elements such as the PLA and MCF, are pervasive within the Chinese economy and society, and so only by fully decoupling and imposing sweeping export controls is it possible to prevent any assistance from ending up in the hands of techno-security-affiliated entities. But as the size of the Chinese techno-security state is relatively modest, this is akin to wielding a sledgehammer to fix an errant nail. Finding a more targeted and nuanced approach will help to mitigate collateral economic damage on all sides.

One approach could be to distinguish between the core techno-security base and the expanded outer system. The core base could be cordoned off and sub-

TABLE C.2 Quantifying the economic sizes of the Chinese and US techno-security states in the late 2010s

	CHINA	UNITED STATES
Core techno-security state (% of GDP)		
National security outlays: defense expenditures, defense research and development, foreign affairs, intelligence, domestic security	3%	5.3%
Defense industrial value-added output (for defense only–related activities)	0.3%–0.5%	0.6%
Expanded techno-security and techno-strategic state (% of GDP)		
Civilian and dual-use output of the defense industrial base	1.2%	1.2%
Military-civil fusion activities	1%	
Overall total	5.5%–5.7%	7.1%

ject to tight controls, while economic engagement would be allowed with the expanded system with careful due diligence and monitoring. But as linkages between the inner and outer parts of the Chinese techno-security state grow closer and become more integrated, such distinctions may become increasingly difficult to distinguish.

A principal tool that the US government has been using to curtail engagement with the Chinese techno-security state is to issue public lists of Chinese institutions and individuals that are subject to stringent export, investment, and other controls that lock them out of the US market and prevent any US entity from engaging in any type of business dealings with them. There has been a proliferation of these lists in the past few years of which the most important is the Department of Commerce's Entity List, which restricts the export of sensitive technologies and components that threaten US national security or foreign policy interests to foreign individuals and institutions placed on this list.

The number of mainland Chinese entities on the Entity List has significantly increased since its establishment in 1998.[17] There were fewer than twenty Chinese firms on the Entity List between 1998 and 2008, accounting for under 7 percent of total listed entities. The number of Chinese firms on the Entity List grew steadily but modestly throughout the 2010s in absolute but not relative terms and only significantly expanded from 2019 onward. Mainland Chinese firms made up nearly 10 percent of total firms on the Entity List in 2019, 17 percent in 2020, and 24 percent by the first quarter of 2021. Hong Kong–registered firms also feature prominently on the Entity List. There were more Hong Kong firms than mainland Chinese firms on the Entity List in the first half of the 2010s. In the second half of the 2010s, Hong Kong firms on average accounted for around 5 percent of total firms listed annually on the Entity List, numbering ninety-four firms by the first quarter of 2021. Counted together, mainland Chinese and Hong Kong firms made up close to 30 percent of the Entity List by 2021 (see table C.3).

The Department of Commerce's Bureau of Industry and Security (BIS), which is largely responsible for administering the US government's export control regime, created a new Military End User list in April 2020 that added further licensing requirements for exports going to China, Russia, and Venezuela. By the end of 2020, 102 companies had been put on this new list and the overwhelming number were Chinese companies already on the Entity List.[18]

The DoD also began to issue a list from June 2020 of "Communist Chinese military companies" that are operating directly or indirectly in the United States to support the PLA's modernization drive through MCF and other initiatives. This list is regularly updated and had more than forty entities by the beginning of 2021.[19] The US Congress has requested such a list since 1999, but this was a low priority for the DoD until China became a pressing bipartisan political issue two

TABLE C.3   Representation of Chinese and Hong Kong firms on the US Department of Commerce Entity List, 1998–2021

YEAR	TOTAL ENTITIES ON LIST	PRC ENTITIES	HONG KONG ENTITIES	PRC ENTITIES AS PERCENTAGE OF TOTAL LIST	HONG KONG ENTITIES AS PERCENTAGE OF TOTAL LIST
1998	13	1	0	7.69	0.00
1999	317	1	0	0.32	0.00
2000	326	7	0	2.15	0.00
2001	274	7	0	2.55	0.00
2002	286	19	0	6.64	0.00
2003	286	19	0	6.64	0.00
2004	286	19	0	6.64	0.00
2005	281	19	0	6.76	0.00
2006	285	19	0	6.67	0.00
2007	285	19	0	6.67	0.00
2008	292	19	0	6.51	0.00
2009	423	22	19	5.20	4.49
2010	427	22	23	5.15	5.39
2011	471	27	36	5.73	7.64
2012	544	33	46	6.07	8.46
2013	724	32	40	4.42	5.52
2014	783	38	49	4.85	6.26
2015	916	62	61	6.77	6.66
2016	1,001	76	67	7.59	6.69
2017	1,206	89	78	7.38	6.47
2018	1,228	87	77	7.08	6.27
2019	1,366	135	81	9.88	5.93
2020	1,554	271	86	17.44	5.53
2021	1,847	445	94	24.09	5.09
As of end of March 2021	1,872	454	92	24.25	4.91

decades later. The criteria applied to entities on the DoD list are not the same as those defined in the US government's Export Administration Regulations, and so these entities are not necessarily subject to export controls. To partially address this loophole, the Trump administration issued an executive order in November 2020 preventing US entities and individuals from making investments and purchasing securities in Chinese companies on the DoD list.[20] The Joseph Biden administration in June 2021 extended this executive order and added more Chinese companies to the investment ban.[21]

The proliferation of these lists offers a useful but reactive and limited defense against the vaunted Chinese absorption and acquisition apparatus. Chinese entities have shown themselves to be highly adept in this cat-and-mouse world by constantly adjusting how they gain access to foreign technology and knowledge transfers and obscuring their identities.[22]

The US government is cognizant of the limitations of these national control lists focused on entities and individuals and has sought to add other layers of protection to their export control regime. One of the most promising mechanisms is the development of multilateral export controls on categories of specific emerging and foundational technologies. BIS has been deliberating this approach since 2018, and there was initial concern that sweeping controls on broad technological categories such as for AI and semiconductors might be issued.[23] After extensive consultation, BIS finally began to issue highly targeted controls on an initial batch of six specific technologies in October 2020. Items included additive manufacturing machines, computational lithography software used in semiconductor production, technology for finishing five nanometer silicon wafers, software for surveillance and monitoring used by law enforcement authorities, and suborbital near-space vehicles.[24]

Building a stringent and tightly managed export control regime that safeguards the most crucial techno-security-related crown jewels while allowing technologies not included in this domain to be freely traded promises to be a more credible and proactive policy mechanism. However, the effectiveness of this new system will depend heavily on having an organization in charge that has the cutting-edge technical expertise, bureaucratic clout, high-level political access, and ability to balance competing national security and industry and commercial interests. BIS is presently in charge of this initiative but is chronically underfunded and understaffed, so it lacks many of these necessary institutional attributes required for success.[25]

A second policy implication stemming from this assessment of the size of the Chinese techno-security base is that it appears to be an affordable economic burden that can be sustained over the long term. Even when economic growth slows down significantly and permanently from its high rates of the post-1978 reform era, the Chinese economy will still be able to support the techno-security state as long as the burden does not appreciably escalate from current levels. China is a very long way from approaching the huge financial strains that crippled the Soviet Union or even the Maoist techno-security state. Like the United States during the Cold War, China appears to have found an accommodative strategic synthesis that allows for a sustainable security posture without overtaxing the country. This means that China may be able to sidestep the "guns versus butter" trade-off that it confronted at the beginning of the reform and opening-up era and its citizens can have both prosperity and power at the same time.

In summary, in terms of size, the Chinese techno-security state in the twenty-first century is not the overwhelming colossus it is sometimes imagined to be. This recognition is important in tempering exaggerated perceptions that the Chinese state and its economy is becoming militarized. It also belies the assumption that only comprehensive and sweeping decoupling between China and the West will prevent assistance from inadvertently supporting the continued development of the Chinese techno-security state.

Size, though, is just one factor in measuring the importance and impact of the techno-security state. Other considerations such as the strategic location and connections of the techno-security state within the overall national economy and society are also significant.

A Personalistic or Institutionalized Chinese Techno-Security State?

The making of the Chinese techno-security state has been deeply personalistic in nature, centering on the domineering influence of Xi. He has been the chief architect, builder, and enforcer of the techno-security state, which is integral in securing and maintaining his long-term hold on power. The leadership and organizational structure of the Chinese techno-security state are hyperconcentrated under Xi's authority; he wields absolute authority as the chairman of the Central National Security Commission, Central Military Commission, and Central Military-Civil Fusion Development Commission, which make up the triumvirate of the most important organizational components of the techno-security system.

Moreover, as Xi has been anointed as the core (核心意识, *hexin yishi*) of the party, he is regarded as its personification, and the ever-intensifying campaigns to enhance and safeguard the party's control over the country are primarily a proxy to fortify his grip on political power. The formulation that is put forward is the need to "safeguard the party's leadership, safeguard the socialist system with Chinese characteristics, and safeguard the authority of the party Central Committee with Comrade Xi Jinping as the core."[26] But as Susan Shirk points out, there is a paradox in Xi's efforts: "Despite his apparent grip on power, his insecurity is glaring."[27]

This overwhelmingly personalistic leadership arrangement will very likely continue as long as Xi remains in power and is active. The consequences for the Chinese political system and for its techno-security state are profound. No one is as well qualified to assess this impact as Deng Xiaoping (邓小平), who succeeded Mao and sought to prevent a repeat of the deep political strife and chronic mismanagement of the Maoist era. When Deng undertook reforms, he identified several of the most important root problems, which were the overconcentration of power, patriarchy, and life tenure.[28] Deng pointed out that "overconcentration of power is liable to give rise to arbitrary rule by individuals at the expense of collective leadership," while patriarchal ways "within the revolutionary ranks place individuals above the organization, which then becomes a tool in their hands." All this has "a very damaging influence on the party." On lifetime tenure, Deng attributed this in part to feudal practices and demanded that "no leading cadre should hold any office indefinitely."

In assessing the extent of Xi's influence within the techno-security state, it is useful to distinguish two ways that this has been carried out. First, there is Xi's direct personalistic involvement through the holding of formal positions and active participation in decision making, providing strategic guidance, and attending meetings and events. Second is the level of politicization in which the Communist Party has extended its political control, oversight, and intervention within the leadership and administrative apparatuses. Institutionalization, which is the ability of organizations to promote professional bureaucratic norms and practices and meritocratic procedures, can offset these politicized and personalistic trends.

In applying these three criteria to the Chinese techno-security state (see table C.4), the results show a mixed picture. Not surprisingly, the national security state is at the core of Xi's tight personalistic and politicized control with a low level of institutionalization. Xi also has highly personalistic engagement with the military strengthening and MCF domains, but the politicization of these two components is low. As for institutionalization, it is high for the military strengthening arena but in its infancy for MCF. Last, in the innovation realm, Xi's personal involvement has been moderate, politicization has been low, and institutionalization has been high.

Can the techno-security state remain intact if Xi is no longer in charge? His departure would certainly leave a huge power vacuum, especially if he did not have a clear succession plan beforehand. His current deputies lack the political

TABLE C.4 Personalization, politicization, and institutionalization within the Chinese techno-security state under Xi Jinping

TECHNO-SECURITY COMPONENTS	PERSONALIZATION	POLITICIZATION	INSTITUTIONALIZATION
National security	High	High	Low
Military strengthening	High	Low	High
Military-civil fusion	High	Low	Low
Innovation-driven development	Moderate	Low	High

qualifications to take over in anything more than a short-term acting capacity. Consequently, there would be serious doubts over the long-term sustainability of a post-Xi techno-security setup. This open-ended overconcentration of power and authority in Xi represents the gravest risk to the future prospects of the techno-security state as well as to China more generally.

Other Key Findings

Several additional findings are worth highlighting briefly in considering the prospects and implications of the Chinese techno-security state. First is that a top goal for the Chinese techno-security state is to achieve comprehensive and seamless fusion across the entire civilian-national security spectrum. Limited steps have so far been taken, especially in the military-civil domain, but the overarching problems of deep-rooted structural compartmentalization and overcoming powerful vested interests remain. Without meaningful integration, a fragmented techno-security state will be severely handicapped in its ability to compete with its external rivals.

A second finding is that the Chinese techno-security state is presently undergoing a far-reaching pivot from a tried-and-trusted absorption-based technology development model to emphasizing indigenous original innovation while maintaining this reinnovation approach. Becoming a full-fledged high-end and self-reliant innovation nation able to produce consistently disruptive and breakthrough S&T at the global innovation frontier is essential to China's goal of becoming a world-class innovation champion. This transformation will take place over the course of the 2020s and early 2030s in step with long-range plans such as the Science, Technology, and Innovation (STI) 2030 program and the 2021–2035 Medium- and Long-Term Science and Technology Development Plan (MLP). Although success is far from assured, the Chinese authorities are investing heavily to have a credible chance of accomplishing core goals.

A third finding is that the Chinese techno-security state is steadily shifting from a defensive realist posture emphasizing economic development and low-key international engagement, to embracing a more stridently offensive zero-sum security-maximizing approach in the Asia-Pacific region and in new technology domains such as cyber and outer space while still retaining a defensive approach at the global level. This strategic adjustment to a more forward-based assertive posture can be seen in China's military strengthening guidance and national security strategy as well as in its heavy investment in power projection capabilities. These findings paint a portrait of an ambitious techno-security state that is at a major crossroads in its development and orientation.

Comparing the US-China Rivalry with the US-Soviet Cold War and US-Japan Geo-economic Competition

The intensifying great power competition between the United States and China is sometimes referred to as a new Cold War because of the echoes to the all-consuming grand struggle between the United States and Soviet Union in the second half of the twentieth century. There are some similarities between these two episodes—the contest between authoritarian and democratic systems and geostrategic and military competition—but the differences are far more pronounced and consequential.[29]

Although national security is a core component of the contemporary US-China rivalry, there are other critical elements that make the current competition far more complicated and comprehensive than the US-Soviet standoff. First is the depth and scope of the geo-economic competition between the United States and China, which can be compared to the trade, investment, and technological rivalry between the United States and Japan in the 1980s and 1990s. Second, the civil-military technological arena is much more blurred and expansive and plays a far more influential role in shaping power dynamics today than in the past.

Two related but distinct points show the enormous challenge the United States faces in dealing with long-term competition with China in the technological-economic-security nexus. The first is that the lessons of the late-twentieth-century Cold War should not be drawn from simply examining the US-Soviet confrontation but rather from a broader and more holistic perspective of the US-Soviet-Japanese competition of the 1980s–1990s (see figure C.1). The second point is that the long-term challenge posed by China is taking place at the intersection between the military and civilian domains and is focused on strategic and emerging technologies and innovation (see figure C.2). Whether the top-down authoritarian statist approach offered by China or the bottom-up democratic anti-statist model championed by the United States will be the best suited to meeting this challenge will be one of the defining contests of this century.

Fortunately for the United States, the full brunt of the strategic and economic challenges posed by the Soviet Union and Japan during the second half of the twentieth century occurred at different periods. The Soviet military threat was primarily between the 1950s and 1970s. By the 1980s, the Soviet Union was in serious economic decline and its ability to compete militarily with the United States was lagging, especially technologically. For Japan, it only became a strong economic and technological competitor in the 1980s and subsequently faded in the 1990s.

Although the authoritarian Soviet Union and democratic Japan were very different political regimes, they did share some important characteristics. First,

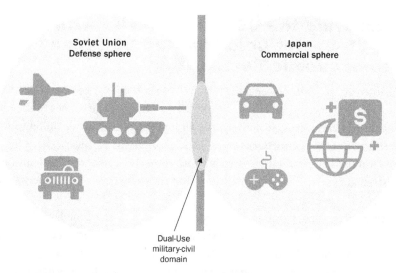

FIGURE C.1. The Cold War and geo-economic competition between the United States, Soviet Union, and Japan in the mid- to late twentieth century

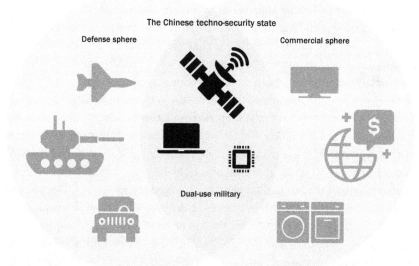

FIGURE C.2. The new US-China adversarial rivalry: The integrated commercial, defense, and dual-use challenge of China toward the United States in the twenty-first century

they were both techno-nationalist states whose technology development policies were predicated on closed technological borders and emphasized indigenous technological development. However, Japan pursued a commercial techno-nationalist approach while the Soviet Union emphasized military techno-nationalist development. Second, both were statist regimes in which the role of the state was central in guiding development; the Soviet plan ideological state had absolute hands-on control, while the Japanese plan rational state's relationship with the nonstate sector was more negotiable. Third, the foundations of technological and industrial development for both states (military-industrial for the Soviet Union, commercial-export for Japan) were based on absorption (relying on foreign sources) and engineering (incremental industrial development).

The United States had a fundamentally different development model. It had both a military techno-nationalist base and a commercial techno-globalist system, which were integrated to varying degrees but shared vital components of the innovation system, such as vibrant R&D, especially a strong university-based basic research apparatus. Having an integrated military and civilian technological and economic system provided enormous benefits and synergies that included strong corporations and powerful innovation systems, which the Soviet Union and Japan did not have and was critical for long-term sustainable competition.

When the geo-economic and geostrategic competition between the United States and the Soviet Union and Japan came to a head in the 1980s (Soviet Union) and early 1990s (Japan), profound technological changes were under way. There was a revolution in military affairs in the defense realm with the advent of precision strike and stealth, which occurred alongside a technological-economic paradigm shift with the arrival of the information age. This allowed the United States to excel because of the structural advantages created by its market-oriented and technologically innovative system.

Comparing the US and Chinese Techno-Security States and the Prospects for Long-Term Competition

With the US and Chinese techno-security states locked in a titanic struggle for global supremacy, the long-term outcome will hinge on whoever is most effective in harnessing their constituent core strengths while mitigating against critical weaknesses. Although the two countries draw on profoundly contrasting tenets, attributes, and approaches, they do share comparable strategic designs and desired outcomes for the configuration of their sprawling techno-security ecosystems. Moreover, unlike in the twentieth-century Cold War when the

United States far outmatched the Soviet Union economically and technologically, the gap between the United States and China in economic might, human resources, and technological capabilities is much narrower.

From an overarching ideological perspective, the US techno-security state is anchored on a deeply held anti-statist ethos that emphasizes limited government and an expansive leading role for the private sector. The Chinese techno-security state on the other hand is overwhelmingly statist with the party-state dominating ownership, control, and management. Although these distinctions are broadly true, the anti-statist versus statist divide between the two countries is less black and white than is generally assumed. Strong pro-statist forces in the United States have allowed the government to exert a powerful influence in making and shaping the techno-security state. In China, pro-market forces have steadily gained acceptance and prominence, although the techno-security state has lagged in opening up compared to other parts of the economy.

Nonetheless, the consequences of this statist versus anti-statist divergence is that the US and Chinese techno-security states are designed, configured, and operated very differently from each other. This makes for an intriguing matchup because of their dissimilar sources of strengths and weaknesses. The analytical framework put forward at the end of chapter 6 will now be applied to compare the US and Chinese techno-security states.

The Changing Strengths and Weaknesses of the Contemporary US Techno-Security State

For the US techno-security state, four key features have made major contributions to its overall success. The mutually rewarding partnership between the public and private sectors has been a particularly important driver of US performance. Nonetheless, the public-private relationship has become increasingly stale and less central and relevant in the twenty-first century. This threatens to turn this pillar of strength into a source of weakness. Two factors in particular have contributed to this state of affairs. First, the defense acquisition system has become increasingly rigid and risk averse, which has meant that business is mostly carried out with longtime trusted contractors. The result is that the techno-security state, and especially the defense establishment, is isolated from large portions of the most innovative and thriving commercial sectors of the economy. Second, the US techno-security state is struggling to have its voice heard in guiding innovation, as its once-dominant position as the biggest source of investment in R&D has eroded. The DoD at the beginning of the 2020s accounts for a mere 3.6 percent of global R&D outlays compared to 36 percent at its height in 1960.[30]

Moreover, the Pentagon has gone from being a first adopter of technologies to being increasingly an investor in technology research. This means that many technologies originate in the civilian sphere and are subsequently—and often belatedly—adapted for defense and dual-use applications.[31] Even though this is cost efficient and allows access to a more extensive pool of innovation, the US techno-security state risks becoming a follower rather than a leader unless it steps up to fill the gaps in defense-specific areas where the commercial sector is reluctant or unable to participate.

If these trends persist, the US techno-security state could find its influence and place in the US innovation system increasingly marginalized. This is already happening in the corporate sector. By the second half of the 2010s, the top five US technology companies such as Google, Amazon, and Apple spent ten times more annually on R&D than the top five US defense prime contractors including Lockheed Martin, Boeing, and Raytheon.[32] This growing imbalance in the public-private relationship could lead firms to decide that doing business with the techno-security state is not sufficiently lucrative and encourage them to focus instead on more profitable commercial markets domestically and internationally, including in China. Reinvigorating the public-private relationship will be critical in any effort by the United States to credibly compete against China over the long term.[33]

Calls have mounted since the late 2010s across the US political and policy establishments for a more robust and concerted government-driven response to technological, industrial, economic, and military competition with China.[34] This includes support for the return of industrial policy initiatives, which have fallen out of political favor since the 1970s. The Trump administration issued a national strategy for critical and emerging technologies in October 2020 that sought a "unity of effort across the United States government . . . from which deliberate action will affect multiple technology areas in a coordinated manner."[35] The strategy identified twenty technologies that would be targeted ranging from advanced computing to space technologies. One of the first areas to receive tangible government support has been the US semiconductor industry, which was allocated fifty-two billion dollars in financial incentives in the 2021 US Innovation and Competition Act.[36] The Biden administration has also advocated a comprehensive manufacturing and innovation strategy that it calls "build back better" that will "marshall the resources of the federal government in ways that we have not seen since World War II."[37]

US threat perceptions and responses to China's techno-security rise, typically a catalytic factor that exerts a powerful influence in spurring the techno-security state into action, only had a peripheral impact until the late 2010s. As China ramped up its efforts at innovation and military modernization from the beginning of the 2000s, US assessments of these efforts were that they posed little strategic threat as Chinese capabilities were far behind US levels.[38] The United States was also consumed by the global war on terror and threats emanating from the Middle East after the September 11, 2001 terrorist attacks. This meant that security worries over China, especially over escalating tensions across the Taiwan Strait, which had begun to gain heightened attention by US leaders at the turn of the twenty-first century, were relegated in priority.

The United States only elevated China to the top of its threat list with the unveiling of the Third Offset Strategy by then–secretary of defense Chuck Hagel in 2014, which was intended to address the erosion in US military technological superiority caused by initiatives such as China's so-called anti-access/area-denial capabilities.[39] China came to be referred to as the "pacing threat."[40] After Trump came to office, the Third Offset Strategy was replaced with the 2017 National Security Strategy and 2018 National Defense Strategy, which made great power competition the foremost priority, with China identified as the principal competitor.[41] Consequently, threat perceptions of China was a lagging factor for the US techno-security state until the late 2010s. This was fundamentally different from the US-Soviet Cold War when threat assessments were a driving factor behind the establishment and rapid buildup of the US techno-security state.

Techno-nationalist primacy has played a secondary role in the development of the US techno-security state, but the promotion of US technology and industrial relationships with advanced allied countries offers considerable potential going forward. Techno-nationalist primacy refers to the nature of US techno-security relations and engagement with foreign countries. As the world's most advanced techno-security power since World War II, the United States has been the dominant exporter of advanced technology, knowledge, and industrial products, both in the military and civilian spheres. This possession of a comprehensive world-class S&T base, especially in the defense technological arena, has meant the United States has traditionally had little appetite to acquire foreign technology or know-how, and this sense of industrial and technological superiority led to the building of a fierce and enduring techno-nationalist ideology and posture in which the US techno-security state viewed itself as head and shoulders above the rest of the world.

However, the global technological landscape has been undergoing rapid change in the twenty-first century with the advent of a diverse array of emerging technologies, many of which have defense and dual-use applications. This has created a window of opportunity for new leadership at the technological frontier in many new areas. With its shrinking overall share of global R&D investment, the United States has found that it is increasingly difficult and costly to keep abreast of technological advances in all the key domains, which has made collaboration with foreign partners increasingly attractive and necessary. This cooperation is taking place in areas such as 5G, quantum computing, and communications—areas where China has been especially active and is vying for global leadership. However, techno-nationalist primacy has been deeply entrenched for so long within the institutional culture of the US techno-security state that a fundamental shift toward a more collaborative techno-globalist approach is likely to encounter entrenched resistance and will take time to effectively implement.

There have been occasional attempts to establish the foundations of a more globalist-oriented techno-security approach, although with limited success so far. A prime example is the national technology and industrial base, which was initially established in the 1990s to facilitate US-Canadian national security and dual-use technological and industrial cooperation and was expanded in the late 2010s to include the United Kingdom and Australia.[42] The establishment of the Australia, United Kingdom, and United States (AUKUS) trilateral security partnership in 2021 represents a major step forward in these efforts to forge a US-centered global techno-security base. The White House pointed out that AUKUS is intended to "foster deeper integration of security and defense-related science, technology, industrial bases, and supply chains," which will begin with the building of nuclear submarines for the Royal Australian Navy.[43]

However, the national technology and industrial base has faced substantial political, legislative, and bureaucratic hurdles from within the US techno-security state that seek to limit such technology-sharing arrangements. These hurdles include the Buy America Act and International Traffic in Arms Regulations export controls, among others.

One area that the United States has been able to pursue a more collaborative partnership with foreign allies is in controlling the spread of sensitive technologies. In dealing with the technological challenges of the Soviet Union and Japan in the twentieth century, the United States established a number of institutional frameworks to control the flow of technologies and know-how to these countries. A robust multilateral export control regime, the Coordinating Committee for Multilateral Export Controls, was forged to deal with the Soviet Union and its allies, and investment control mechanisms, such as the Committee on Foreign Investment in the United States were created to manage the Japanese commercial challenge. These regimes worked effectively in their own spheres, but the integrated civil-military challenge coming from China requires the US government to develop a more robust and joint whole-of-government approach than the ad hoc and underdeveloped intra-agency process that currently exists.

The United States has been revamping these legacy regimes through incremental reforms such as the 2018 Foreign Investment Risk Review Modernization Act and a revamped export control regime. Even though these reforms will strengthen export and investment control regimes, there is still a gaping hole in the dual-use and strategic emerging high-technology domains that requires a new wholly dedicated institutional mechanism that is able to more effectively respond and deal with this highly fluid intersection between economics, trade, investment, technology, defense, and national security.

Revamping How the Chinese Techno-Security State Works

For China's techno-security state, heightened threat perceptions, centralized top-down coordination, and techno-nationalist dependence have been the principal drivers in its development. As detailed in earlier chapters, the Chinese authorities have used deepening concerns over the external security environment since the late 1990s, and especially the grand techno-security threat posed by the United States, as a catalyst to ramp up the development of its techno-security capabilities. This has especially been the case in areas such as strategic deterrence and anti-access/area-denial capabilities that led to the establishment of defense R&D initiatives such as the 995 Project. These perceptions of the US threat have only grown more dire, pressing, and expansive under Xi's tenure and are a hugely powerful existential motivating factor in driving the development of the Chinese techno-security state.

Centralized top-down coordination, or what this study has termed the selective authoritarian mobilization and innovation (SAMI) model, has been instrumental to many, if not most, of China's signature strategic technological achievements from nuclear weapons and ballistic missiles to the manned space program and high-performance computers. The SAMI approach is being revamped and reprioritized from foreign absorption to original innovation so that it continues to play a leading long-term role. However, a key and intentionally designed limitation of this model is that it can only manage a select number of the highest-priority strategic and defense-related projects.

Controlled interdependence has been the principal governance model used by the Chinese techno-security state since its inception. This refers to the adoption of a plan ideological or central planning system that relies on directly enforced administrative controls from state and party agencies and the use of penalties to ensure compliance by enterprises, research institutes, and other actors. Although there has been some relaxation and rollback of this pervasive state control in the post-1978 reform era, state planning, management, and intervention have remained extensive because the techno-security ecosystem continues to be overwhelmingly under state ownership.

Efforts to shift from direct to more indirect modes of governance or from a plan ideological to a plan rational approach gained traction starting in the twenty-first century with the state focusing its attention on setting broad high-level developmental directions instead of hands-on micromanagement. This is what Barry Naughton describes as "grand steerage" in which the Chinese authorities have issued numerous development "plans" that refer to "initiatives that involve real expenditure of resources to achieve concrete outcomes."[44] Naughton points to a slew of techno-industrial policies such as the 2006–2020 MLP, SEI, and Innovation-Driven Development Strategy (IDDS) as examples of this grand steerage, which would fall within the purview of the techno-security state. This less direct but still significant engagement of the state in economic management combined with more effective coordination with market mechanisms can be labeled as steered interdependence.

Another newly emerging example of this steered interdependence approach is the New Whole-of-Nation System concept, which is being applied especially to the development of key S&T projects. The New Whole-of-Nation System mechanism, which began to be rolled out only toward the end of the 2010s, seeks to acquire investment funds by tapping financial markets using AS and GGF as key vehicles. If the New Whole-of-Nation System approach becomes widely adopted, it would mark an important shift from the heavy hand of the state to a more balanced and coordinated state-market partnership.

Hybridization has yet to make a significant impact on the Chinese techno-security state, but the foundations for a robust and expansive MCF framework have been laid since the second half of the 2010s. The Chinese ambition is that its hybrid MCF model will become as extensively developed as in the United States within the next decade or so. Although the structural barriers to realizing this goal are high, the top-level political will to achieve this, as exemplified by Xi Jinping's active leadership of the MCF initiative, means the prospects for success are favorable. The challenge for the United States is whether it can stay ahead through revamping its civil-military integration setup and finding ways to undermine the Chinese effort.

The heightened priority of achieving original homegrown innovation and self-reliance may see techno-nationalist dependence become a less important force in supporting the Chinese techno-security state's race to the global innovation frontier. However, gaining access to and leveraging foreign technology and knowledge will continue to be an essential feature for the foreseeable future, especially for other parts of the techno-security ecosystem that are still catching up. Techno-nationalist dependence is a well-proven low-risk, high-reward development strategy and provides a safeguard, while the forging of an original innovation capacity is a long-term high-risk endeavor.

However, the long-term viability of the techno-nationalist dependence model will be put in grave doubt if the US-led efforts to significantly reduce and perhaps fully decouple technological relations with China is carried out. Before the US-China relationship turned acrimonious in the late 2010s, the two countries enjoyed broad and deep economic interdependence and societal engagement. Although the US and Chinese techno-security ecosystems have had far fewer interactions because of tight restrictions imposed by their governments, there has nonetheless been considerable cooperation and transactions taking place on matters deemed to not infringe on national security concerns. This more permissive climate became an early casualty of the intensifying great power rivalry, and policy debates have turned to how far the two countries should decouple from each other.

The implications of decoupling are markedly different in the techno-security realm compared to the economic or academic spheres. In the nonsecurity arenas, decoupling is costly and detrimental to both sides.[45] In the techno-security domain, however, the circumstances are more asymmetric. China is a clear beneficiary from being able to access the United States for advanced technology and knowledge, while the advantages for the United States are mixed. In the aggregate, though, the US techno-security state would be far less negatively impacted by decoupling than its Chinese counterpart.

The Chinese techno-security state is no stranger to decoupling. The current situation represents the third occasion where it has faced a far-reaching shutdown in access to critical technologies and know-how since the founding of the People's Republic. The first time was in the 1960s when the Soviet Union abruptly cut off industrial and technical assistance to China, especially to the techno-security establishment. This severely impacted the development of the nascent Chinese techno-security base but forced the country to urgently step up its efforts at technological self-reliance.[46] The second time was in the aftermath of the June 1989 Tiananmen Square crackdown when the United States and the European Economic Community (the forerunner to the European Union) imposed economic sanctions and halted all military cooperation with China. This cutoff in US-China military technological engagement has continued to the present day. Consequently, the Chinese authorities are well aware of what decoupling means and what steps to take to mitigate the fallout.

Decoupling would only be the opening gambit, however. The next phase would be a competition to gain dominance in the resultant bifurcated global technological order.[47] This would require the United States and China to find a stable of partners, build alliances, and establish their own techno-security orders. The United States has a powerful advantage because it played a central role in establishing the existing global techno-security order. However, the current revolution in global technology affairs offers a window of opportunity for China to stake a leadership claim on emerging domains such as 5G, AI, quantum technology, cybersecurity, clean energy, and biotechnology. Forging a winning multilateral coalition will not be easy for these techno-nationalist-minded countries.

In conclusion, the US techno-security state in the opening years of the 2020s remains much stronger and more innovative than its Chinese counterpart (see table C.5). This dominance is being steadily eroded, however, by US institutional sclerosis, far-reaching global technological changes, and China's intensive pace of techno-security development. Revitalizing key components of the US techno-security state, especially governed interdependence and techno-nationalist primacy, will allow the United States to retain its global leadership over the long term, although the gap with China will continue to shrink. The United States will need to undertake more transformative reforms to stay well ahead. Much will also depend on how serious the United States is about dealing with the long-term Chinese techno-security challenge to its national security and global leadership role given numerous competing domestic and international demands.

For China, the revamping of the techno-security state that has taken place in the past couple of decades, and especially under Xi's watch, has seen the gap steadily close with the United States and the global technology frontier. However, even more significant structural changes will be required to successfully transition from catching up to gaining parity or even leading. Moving more of the techno-security ecosystem from controlled interdependence to steered interdependence will be essential. Allowing hybridization to be fully implemented will also be a vital step. The enhancement of the centralized top-down coordination model will be especially important in the race for the development of emerging core technologies as active early state intervention can play a more effective and decisive role than bottom-up market support. The Chinese techno-security state will need to address these key deficiencies if it is to mount a realistic challenge against the United States for long-term global techno-security leadership.

The Chinese Techno-Security State's Continuing Evolution with Economic Securitization

The Chinese techno-security state that Xi Jinping built in his first decade in power rested on four core pillars: innovation-driven development, national security, military strengthening, and MCF. Toward the end of the 2010s, Xi and the Chinese leadership determined that a fifth component—the securitization

TABLE C.5 Key characteristics of the US and Chinese techno-security states

	CHINA	UNITED STATES
DEVELOPMENTAL MODEL TYPE	**PLAN RATIONAL**	**HYBRID RATIONAL**
KEY DEVELOPMENT AND FUNCTIONAL FACTORS		
External threat perceptions and threat environment	**Leading catalytic factor:** China assessed United States as a high-priority techno-security threat since end of the 1990s	**Lagging catalytic factor:** United States was distracted and slow to assess China as a serious techno-security concern until late 2010s
Leadership and management coordination	**Centralized top-down coordination:** Selective authoritarian mobilization and innovation model is a central source of success in the development of China's techno-security state	**Decentralized bottom-up coordination:** Responsibility is divided among multiple, mission-oriented government agencies that coordinate closely together
Governance regime	**Controlled interdependence:** This governance model originated from the Maoist central planning command system culture and relies on administrative controls and the use of penalties to ensure compliance	**Governed interdependence:** The state uses incentives and rewards like cost sharing to ensure that private firms meet requirements. This design allows national security–focused purpose and mission-oriented problem sets of the techno-security state to be met while also satisfying the goals of private sector, which are absorbing risk and ensuring profit
Hybridization	**Early-stage hybridization:** Military-civil fusion is at a preliminary stage of development, but the public sector will remain the dominant player with the private sector limited to a minor role	**Mature-stage hybridization:** The merging of public and private institutions in novel ways produces fused hybrid entities. Vehicles include public interest firms, federally funded R&D centers, and commercial consortia between industry, academia, and government entities
Techno-nationalist ideology and strategies	**Techno-nationalist dependence:** China seeks long-term technological self-reliance but is heavily dependent on foreign technology and know-how in the meantime	**Techno-nationalist primacy:** The United States is able to meet its own security needs through its domestic techno-security base but also supplies foreign countries through export and collaboration

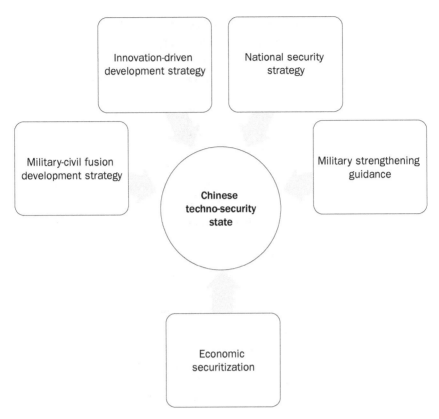

FIGURE C.3. The key components of the Chinese techno-security state in the 2020s

of the domestic foundations of the Chinese economy—was urgently needed in the wake of rising external economic threats (see figure C.3).

The Chinese authorities had identified economic security as an important element of the overall strengthening of national security priorities from the early 2010s. Economic security was listed among eleven categories in the 2015 National Security Law, but the concept was viewed largely from a microeconomic-level perspective in which the focus was on enhancing the protection of specific economic sectors, such as food security, energy security, and financial security.

The leadership's attention since the late 2010s has turned to the macrofoundations of economic securitization. This has meant the safeguarding of the Chinese economy by ensuring resilience, economic and technological selfreliance, and the ability to prevent external shocks from causing severe internal disruptions. Economic securitization was elevated to a first-order priority because of a profound reevaluation by the Chinese leadership of the international geostrategic and geo-economic environment surrounding China from the late 2010s.[48] When the foundations of the techno-security state were laid in the early to mid-2010s, the official strategic assessment was that China enjoyed a generally favorable external environment and that deepening interdependence into the global economic and technology systems was essential for long-term development.[49] The IDDS, for example, stressed the importance of expanding China's global development engagement through greater openness, cooperation, and ensuring that the country becomes a global leader.

The IDDS did not explicitly raise any serious concerns about strategic threats to China's security or the possible curtailment of the country's access to global supply chains or technology. However, it did identify a number of externally related matters that posed major challenges and risks for China's development prospects. These included the advent of commercial and military technological and industrial revolutions that were reshaping the global competitive landscape, along with the warning that critical core technologies, which China was overly reliant on, were under foreign control.

As strategic, economic, and technological tensions began to intensify between China and the United States and its allies from the mid-2010s, Chinese policymakers began to rethink its pro-globalist development posture. The first reported signs of this reassessment came at the Central Economic Work Conference in December 2017 when Xi put forward the idea that the country's advance from the existing model of high-paced quantitative growth to a more efficient and sustainable "high-quality development" (高质量发展, *gao zhiliang fazhan*) depended on having a smooth and unimpeded cycle (循环畅通, *xunhuan changtong*) of economic activity from production to distribution, circulation, and consumption.[50] What this referred to was how to ensure that China was able to mitigate the emergence of foreign efforts to impose obstacles intended to undermine its economic development. Chinese leaders and analysts called this drastically altered development landscape the New Development Stage (新发展阶段, *Xin Fazhan Jieduan*).

Concern that China's economic rise could be thwarted by external forces quickly gained currency from 2018 as the Trump administration undertook a concerted and expansive economic and technological campaign to impose costly sanctions, tariffs, and other restraints against China and its companies. The United States' imposition of crippling sanctions on ZTE Corporation, a Chinese technology national champion, in May 2018 was a major wake-up call for Beijing, which some Chinese analysts have likened to China's version of the Sputnik moment in which the Soviet Union's ability to launch the first person into space only galvanized the United States to engage in an all-out technology arms race.[51] (See chapter 5 for a more detailed discussion.)

The Chinese macroeconomic strategic response to this increasingly hostile international environment and the growing threat that its long-standing unfettered access to the global economic and technology order might be significantly curtailed or even cut off began to crystallize in 2020 under the rubric of the dual circulation (双循环, *shuang xunhuan*) economy. The dual circulation approach was first publicly raised in a speech by Xi at a meeting of the Central Financial and Economic Commission in April 2020. Xi pointed out the need to establish a complete system of domestic demand (完整的内需体系, *wanzhengde neixu tixi*) that would have a crucial bearing on China's long-term development and stability. Building up domestic economic resilience was essential, Xi explained, because the external environment was experiencing far-reaching changes, especially the accelerating trend of deglobalization.[52]

The Chinese leadership's push for a more domestically based economy and stepped-up securitization was driven by a mix of economic, geo-economic, and geostrategic factors. In a speech to a symposium of economic experts and social scientists in August 2020, Xi said that in recent years domestic markets had become the main engine of the country's overall economic growth while access to international markets and resources had significantly weakened. Xi said that the downturn in the global economy was caused by noneconomic factors and that the headwinds were likely to worsen in coming years, and so "we must be prepared to deal with a series of new risks and challenges."[53]

Vice-premier and economic czar Liu He(刘鹤) said in a *People's Daily* article in November 2020 that the principal macroeconomic reasons for this strategic shift included the fact that domestic demand was now adequate to sustain the country's long-term economic development and that there were deepening problems in China's access to the global supply of goods and services, especially the threat of having its neck choked (卡脖子, *qiabozi*). This refers to the potential cutoff in exports by the United States of critical high-technology components such as semiconductors.[54] The central goal of the dual circulation strategy, according to Liu, was to "increase the autonomy, sustainability, and resilience of economic development." This far-reaching adjustment in economic growth trajectory has been coined as the New Development Pattern (新发展格局, *Xin Fazhan Geju*).

Constituencies advocating for national security, protectionist, technonationalist, and mercantilist interests undoubtedly view the dual circulation strategy as a siren call to safeguard and promote the building-up of a securitized and self-reliant domestic economic base, especially sectors deemed to be of critical and strategic importance, against the escalating risks posed by deglobalization and decoupling with the West. The security of supply chains has received special prominence. Xi talked about the importance of supply chains at the April 2020 Central Economic and Financial Commission meeting, pointing out that "in order to safeguard China's industrial security and national security, we must focus on building production chains and supply chains that are independently controllable, secure and reliable, and strive for important products and supply channels to all have at least one alternative source, forming the necessary industrial backup system."[55]

The Chinese leadership stressed two prime considerations in the formulation of the 14th Five-Year Plan that took place in 2019–2020. First was how to "properly handle the relationship between development and national security," and second was how to "effectively prevent and respond to systemic risks that may affect the modernization process."[56] The Fifth Plenum of the 19th Party Congress Central Committee in the run-up to the finalization of the 14th Five-Year Plan in October 2020 made clear that there was increasing awareness that "national security is the prerequisite for development and development is the guarantee of security," and risk factors are "increasing significantly." Consequently, the Chinese authorities "must persist in coordinating development and security, enhance the awareness of opportunities and risks, establish a bottom-line thinking, estimate difficulties more fully, think more deeply about risks, pay attention to plugging loopholes, strengths and weaknesses, and play first and play well."[57] This meant adopting a more security-minded, risk-based, and preemptive mindset to "effectively prevent and resolve various risks and challenges."

The Chinese economy's rapid mobilized response to the COVID-19 pandemic is held up as a prime example of the importance of possessing a self-sufficient and comprehensive industrial supply chain for ensuring the country's national security. An article in *China National Defense News* argued that the battle against COVID-19 "fully demonstrates the significant advantages of the socialist system with Chinese characteristics and the national governance system as well as its strong social mobilizational and organizational power" that "provides a strong guarantee for fighting the pandemic and gaining control of the people's war."[58]

The Techno-Security Dimensions of the 14th Five-Year Plan and 2035 Vision

These pessimistic perspectives on China's global situation provided the strategic overview in the introduction of the 14th Five-Year Plan, which was officially released in March 2021 and became the authoritative road map of China's midterm development priorities. Befitting a document directly overseen by Xi himself, the 14th Five-Year Plan is long on political rhetoric and short on specifics.[59] Detailed guidance is contained in the proliferation of open and classified subordinate functional and sectoral five-year plans accompanying this master document.

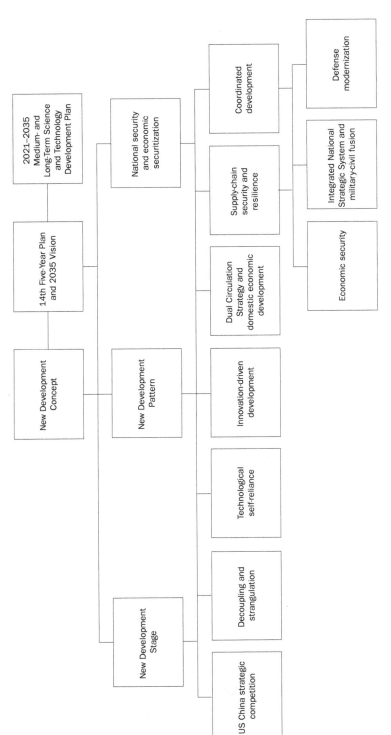

FIGURE C.4. The new development concept, economic securitization, and the Chinese techno-security state

The need for a far-reaching adjustment in China's approach to national development was put forward in the 14th Five-Year Plan under the nondescript label of the New Development Concept (新发展理念, *Xin Fazhan Linian*) (see figure C.4). The New Development Concept was required, according to the plan, because China was now in the "New Development Stage" and pursuing the "New Development Pattern."[60] The New Development Concept incorporates many of the existing development priorities that the Chinese authorities have already been pursuing such as innovation-driven development and green development but with an overarching emphasis on national security.[61]

This focus on national security, both explicitly and implicitly, has received central attention in the 14th Five-Year Plan compared to its cameo appearances in past five-year plans in the reform era. Nine out of the sixty-four chapters of the plan are devoted to national security–related topics covering domestic security, economic security, and defense modernization. National security and economic development are treated as of coequal importance and the plan emphasizes the need to closely integrate these two domains.

The plan highlights the "profound and complex changes" that China is facing in the international environment, which has not been witnessed in a century.[62] In other words, the external arena is more volatile and worrisome than at any time in the existence of the People's Republic of China, even during the Cold War days of bitter Sino-Soviet and Sino-US rivalry. Even though the plan does not explicitly identify the United States as the chief culprit responsible for China's worsening international security situation, speeches given by Xi around the time that the 14th Five-Year Plan was being finalized make clear that the United States is the main adversary.

At the World Economic Forum in January 2021, Xi accused the United States in all but name of being an existential threat to China's rise and igniting an all-out confrontation. Xi said that "to build small circles or start a new Cold War, to reject, threaten or intimidate others, to willfully impose decoupling, supply disruption or sanctions, and to create isolation or estrangement will only push the world into division and even confrontation."[63] In internal remarks circulated among Communist Party officials to explain the geostrategic reasoning behind the 14th Five-Year Plan, Xi spelled out that "the biggest source of chaos in the world today is the United States" and "the United States is the biggest threat (最大的威胁, *zuidade weixie*) to China's development and security."[64]

The 14th Five-Year Plan pointed to other major trends that would profoundly impact China's development and security over the next five years or more. The most noteworthy is an S&T revolution happening alongside a deep-seated industrial transformation and a far-reaching adjustment in the balance of international forces. Although not explicitly stated, this likely refers to the power transition under way with China's rise, which is challenging the long-standing global dominance of the United States. This has made the existing international order increasingly complex, unstable, and uncertain and brought in an era of "turbulent change, unilateralism, protectionism, and hegemonism that poses threats to world peace and development."[65]

The 14th Five-Year Plan contains a number of major themes that offer important clues as to what the next stage of the development of the Chinese techno-security state will entail. First, economic securitization at both the macro and micro levels is receiving prominent attention. Macrolevel economic securitization is set out in the "dual circulation" concept in which "China will form a formidably large domestic market and create a new development framework."[66] Using a combination of supply- and demand-side policies, the intention is to reconfigure and unblock domestic supply chains so they are protected from international disruptions.

At the micro level, the plan calls for "strengthening economic risk early warning, prevention, and control mechanisms and capabilities, achieving security and controllability of key industries, infrastructure, strategic resources, science and technology, and other key areas, and improving the secure development of food, energy, finance and other fields."[67] There is a detailed list of specific economic security measures to be carried out:

- Ensure food security and the security of energy and strategic mineral resources.
- Safeguard critical infrastructure facilities such as electric power, water supply, oil and gas, transportation, communications, internet, and the financial system.
- Protect ecological security, strengthen nuclear safety regulation, and maintain security in new and emerging domains.
- Expand oil, gas, and coal strategic reserves and diversify the sources of oil and gas imports.
- Build up early warning and risk prevention capabilities to protect overseas interests.
- Improve oversight of the financial system by enhancing risk prevention and early warning systems, strengthening supervision of systemically important financial institutions and holding companies, resolving hidden debts of local governments, and tightening cross-border currency flows.

This list covers much of the Chinese domestic economy and extends outward across the world. How far, deep, and rigorous this effort to securitize the Chinese economy will be and whether it will make the Chinese economy more self-reliant will depend on future Chinese leadership assessments of the international strategic environment and the trajectory of its great power rivalry with the United States and its allies. Although the prospects in the early 2020s of a full-scale retreat to the militarized autarkic Maoist development model of the 1950s–1970s are low, there are updated and refined elements of that era that are being embraced, especially in the strategic, defense, dual-use, and advanced technology domains.

The second major theme is an urgent need to achieve techno-nationalist independence and self-reliance. China's ease of access to foreign technology and knowledge over the past few decades has meant that self-reliance has been a fuzzy, aspirational long-term objective, but the rapid tightening of US-led export controls has forced the Chinese authorities into concerted action to prevent technological "strangulation." The developmental response has been to place science, technology, and innovation firmly at the commanding heights of the 14th Five-Year Plan policy agenda. The plan points to the critical importance of "adhering to the core position of innovation in China's modernization drive" and to "take science and technology independence and self-reliance as the strategic support for national development."[68] Several types of effort are highlighted:

- Resource allocations: The plan calls for a significant boost in basic research spending from around 6 percent at the end of the 13th Five-Year Plan to 8 percent by 2025. This is still around half of what advanced economies such as the United States (17 percent in 2017), France (21 percent in 2016), and Japan (13 percent in 2017) spend on basic research,[69] but in absolute terms, it could mean a doubling in the size of Chinese basic research outlays by the mid-2020s. Moreover, the plan calls for increasing annual R&D expenditures by 7 percent.
- Structural reforms: A long-awaited establishment of large-scale national laboratories is finally taking place with the plan calling for the setting-up of these institutions in the areas of quantum information, photonics and micro-nanoelectronics, network communications, AI, biomedicine, and modern energy systems.
- Prioritization of select technology domains: Seven areas are expressly identified in the plan, which are AI, quantum information, integrated circuits, genetics and biotechnology, neuroscience, advanced clinical medicine, and deep-space, deep-sea, and polar exploration. These areas have already been highlighted in other S&T development plans such as STI 2030.

Third is the continuing emphasis on the pursuit of industrial policy, especially in the advanced manufacturing and techno-industrial domains. The plan talks about the need for China to become a manufacturing superpower, although it avoids the use of terms that have sparked international backlash such as Made in China 2025 and MCF. These initiatives are continuing to move ahead but have been relabeled or are no longer transparent. SEI is one industrial policy platform that has not been affected by external notoriety and so has not been brushed out of the 14th Five-Year Plan. Although a new goal has been placed on SEI to generate 17 percent of GDP by 2025, there is no mention as to whether the SEI initiative met its 13th Five-Year Plan target of 15 percent. Core manufacturing sectors constitute the prime areas of SEI, which include precision machinery, robotics, materials, and electric vehicles.

Fourth, even though MCF as a phrase has disappeared from the 14th Five-Year Plan, the pursuit of the convergence between the civilian and defense economies remains a pressing priority.[70] The general objective outlined in the plan is to build an overarching integrated strategic system in which the civilian, defense, and national security sectors are closely aligned and coordinated. An extensive list of goals is put forward:

- Expand efforts to share resources, which means allowing the defense industrial sector to increase access to the financial markets.
- Encourage the coordinated civil-military development of key regions. A top priority of the 14th Five-Year Plan is regional and infrastructure development, especially the construction of high-speed transportation networks and the building of major urban clusters around the country. Military requirements will likely feature prominently in these projects.
- Deepen civil-military R&D collaboration. The civilian S&T R&D system will be increasingly leveraged for defense requirements.[71]
- Strengthen military-civil joint development (军民统筹发展, *junmin tongchou fazhan*) in maritime, space, cyber, biotechnology, new energy, AI, and quantum technology.
- Promote spin-on (civilian to military) and spin-off (military to civilian) applications in research, development, and production activities.
- Improve the development of the national defense mobilization system to ensure that the national economy can be rapidly and effectively repurposed for defense and national security uses in crisis and wartime conditions. The COVID-19 pandemic in 2020 is a prime example of activating the defense mobilization system to deal with a health crisis.
- Guarantee the national security (安全保障, *anquan baozhang*) of critical economic capabilities and beef up the early warning, risk prevention, and control mechanisms of the economy. Sectors explicitly identified in the plan include the grain, food, infrastructure, energy, and financial industries.[72]

MCF will become even more important under the new economic securitization paradigm with the emphasis on domestic economic and technological self-sufficiency and safeguarding against external economic threats. As the Chinese authorities no longer use the term *MCF*, it may also be time to replace this moniker with a new term, such as military-civil joint development, which the Chinese authorities are now using, or revert to the generally used label of *civil-military integration*.

A fifth important theme is the need to accelerate the pace and scale of defense modernization, especially with the goal of "improving the strategic ability to defend national sovereignty, national security, and development interests" by the hundredth anniversary of the founding of the PLA in 2027.[73] This centennial target was first disclosed at the Fifth Plenum in November 2020, which reviewed an earlier draft of the 14th Five-Year Plan and was the first time that such a target date had been publicly disclosed. Neither the 14th Five-Year Plan nor the Fifth Plenum communiqué provided specific details of what is meant by the 2027 target date, however. The *Global Times*, a nationalistic mainland Chinese newspaper affiliated with the party mouthpiece, *People's Daily*, reported that the 2027 centennial goal is to build a "fully modern" military force that will enable China to securely defend its sovereignty and national security interests in the Asia-Pacific region, especially concerning Taiwan, the South China Sea, and the western Pacific.[74] The *South China Morning Post* also reported that the 2027 centennial objective referred to a modernization plan that calls for the PLA to "become a real combat-ready force with counter strategic capabilities," with the PLA Air Force, Navy, and Rocket Force being accorded higher priority in order to enable China to defend core interests, especially Taiwan and the South China Sea.[75] The 14th Five-Year Plan emphasizes the need to "strengthen strategic and new combat forces in new domains as well as creating high-level strategic deterrence and joint combat systems."[76] At an all-army armament conference in October 2021 presided by Xi, the assembled heads of the PLA's armament apparatus were told to "go all out to accelerate weapons and equipment modernization" to meet the 2027 target.[77]

A number of other military modernization objectives are detailed in the plan. One is accelerating the integration of mechanization, informatization, and intelligenization. Mechanization refers to industrial age warfare that is predominantly fought by large-scale, low-tech, ground-based forces, which constitutes a large majority of PLA units. Informatization involves network-centric, highly mobile, and smaller-sized forces that are set up for information-intensive warfare. Intelligenization refers to future warfare in which emerging technologies such as AI, quantum information, big data, cloud computing, and the internet of things will play a central role, which means a growing emphasis on autonomous and unmanned military capabilities. The plan also calls for optimizing the layout of the defense industry. A top priority is promoting advanced high-end defense science, technology, and innovation along with high-quality defense production. Reforms are taking place to improve the structure and process of the defense innovation system and to reinvigorate the defense industrial base by allowing competition and addressing obstacles such as monopolies and corruption.

Last is the relationship between state planning and the market. In a demonstration of its inherently contradictory nature, the 14th Five-Year Plan calls for the continuation of market reforms and opening up to international engagement as well as expanded state intervention and control of the economy. In techno-security-related issues such as basic research, technological self-reliance, industrial policy, and MCF, the state's reach is expanding. Finding a solution to forging a viable market-conforming approach to state planning will be crucial to the long-term development prospects of the country. However, this goldilocks balance is absent in the 14th Five-Year Plan and the broader techno-security grand development strategy.

The 14th Five-Year Plan also provided a very brief outline of a longer term 2035 Vision (2035 年远景目标, 2035 Nian Yuanjing Mubiao) that declares that China will "basically realize socialist modernization" by 2035.[78] This means that the country's comprehensive national strength, of which economic, scientific, and technological capabilities are explicitly highlighted, will "rise sharply." Major breakthroughs in key core technologies will occur and China will reach the global innovation frontier. A modern economic system will be built from new modes of industrialization, informatization, urbanization, and agricultural development, which will allow China to reach the per capita income levels of a moderately developed country. China will also reach a higher level of security and stability of which a key contributing factor is the "basic realization" of defense modernization. This 2035 Vision was intended as a preview of a detailed 2021–2035 MLP that was drawn up to replace the 2006–2020 version, but its public release appears to have been a victim of increased secrecy by the Chinese authorities over its science, technology, and innovation activities.

The stage is set for the continuing rise of an even more capable and expansive but anxious and isolated Chinese techno-security state in the 2020s and 2030s. At the same time, the US techno-security state is assertively stepping up its efforts to meet this grand challenge from China. The world can only hope that this wide-ranging techno-security struggle remains peaceful and contained but should prepare for all-out competition that will be increasingly combustible and dangerous.

Notes

PREFACE AND ACKNOWLEDGMENTS

1. Cheung, *Fortifying China*.

INTRODUCTION

1. Xi Jinping, "Secure a Decisive Victory."
2. White House, *National Security Strategy*.
3. Relevant studies include Weiss, *America Inc.?*; Samuels, *Rich Nation, Strong Army*; Block and Keller, *State of Innovation*; and Brooks, *Producing Security*.
4. Economy, *The Third Revolution*.
5. Ringen, *The Perfect Dictatorship*. For a contrasting perspective, see Dickson, *The Dictator's Dilemma*.
6. Whiting, "China's Use of Force," 103–31.
7. See Liu Yanqiong, "Success of the Two Bombs and One Satellite Project"; and Dong Sheng, *The Eulogy of Heaven and Earth*.
8. See Gu Shulin, *China's Industrial Technology*; Lan Xue, "China's Innovation System Reform," 67–81; and Yuan Qingming, *Institutional Structure of Technological Innovation*, 219–26.
9. Xie Guang, *Contemporary Chinese Defense Science and Technology Sector*, 33.
10. Cheung, *Fortifying China*.
11. Yao Yunzhu, "Military Doctrine of the Chinese PLA."
12. Chinese Communist Party Central Committee Editorial Committee for Party Literature, *Selected Works of Deng Xiaoping 1975–1982*.
13. See Gao Liansheng and Guo Jingtan, *Construction of the Army in the New Period of Deng Xiaoping*, 167–218.
14. Zhang Wannian Writing Team, *Biography of Zhang Wannian*, 419.
15. Jiang Zemin National Defense Technology Industry Construction Thought Research Group, *Thinking of Jiang Zemin*, 363–88.
16. General Headquarters of Shenzhou VI Manned Space Flight Mission, "Spectacular Accomplishment out of a Strategic Decision."
17. Hu Jintao, "Hu Jintao's Speech."
18. See Posen, *The Sources of Military Doctrine*.
19. Fravel, *Active Defense*, 230–34.

1. INNOVATION-CENTERED DEVELOPMENT

1. Cheng Li identifies four networks that Xi draws from: (1) the "Yellow Earth Attachment" that hails from Shaanxi Province where Xu came from, (2) princelings and friends from Xi's formative years, (3) protégés who became associated with Xi during his time as a provincial leader, and (4) former assistants and secretaries (秘书, *mishu*) of top leaders who had themselves risen to leading official positions. See C. Li, "Xi Jinping's Inner Circle, Part 1"; C. Li, "Xi Jinping's Inner Circle, Part 2"; C. Li, "Xi Jinping's Inner Circle, Part 3"; C. Li, "Xi Jinping's Inner Circle, Part 4"; and C. Li, "Xi Jinping's Inner Circle, Part 5."

2. C. Li, "Xi Jinping's Inner Circle, Part 1."

3. C. Li, "Xi Jinping's Inner Circle, Part 1."

4. C. Li, "Xi Jinping's Inner Circle, Part 2."

5. C. Li, "Xi Jinping's Inner Circle, Part 1."

6. C. Li, "Xi Jinping's Inner Circle, Part 2."

7. Hu Jintao, "Report to the 18th National Congress."

8. "Xi Jinping Addresses Ninth Collective Study Session."

9. "Xi Jinping Addresses Ninth Collective Study Session."

10. Mu Rongping, "Innovation-Driven Development in China."

11. "Xi Jinping Addresses Ninth Collective Study Session."

12. "Xi Jinping Addresses Ninth Collective Study Session."

13. "Speech by Xi Jinping at the 17th Conference."

14. For a classic study of the general problem of bureaucratic fragmentation within the Chinese policy process, see Lieberthal and Oksenberg, *Policy Making in China.*

15. "Outline of the National Strategy of Innovation-Driven Development."

16. "Xi Jinping Chairs Seventh Meeting."

17. "Opinions of the CPC Central Committee."

18. "Xi Jinping Chairs Seventh Meeting."

19. See An Baijie, "Vice-Premier Highlights Innovation for Development."

20. "Outline of the National Strategy of Innovation-Driven Development."

21. Naughton, *The Rise of China's Industrial Policy.*

22. Elder and Fagerberg, "Innovation Policy," 5.

23. "Struggle to Build a Strong Country in Science and Technology."

24. "Communiqué of the Fifth Plenary Session."

25. Shirk, "China in Xi's 'New Era,'" 22–36.

26. "Xi Jinping Delivers a Speech at the Opening of the 19th Meeting."

27. "13th Five-Year National Science and Technology Innovation Plan."

28. "13th Five-Year National Science and Technology Innovation Plan."

29. Yuan Dongming, Ma Jun, and Wang Huaiyu, "It Is Necessary to Give Full Play."

30. "13th Five-Year National Science and Technology Innovation Plan."

31. "Xi Jinping Attends Plenary Meeting of PLA Delegation."

32. Xi Jinping, "Secure a Decisive Victory in Building a Moderately Prosperous Society."

33. "Xi Jinping Addresses Politburo 17th Collective Study Session."

34. "Xi Jinping Addresses Politburo 17th Collective Study Session."

35. Besides these five categories, Xi has also mentioned the management process as another area deserving to be shaken up with innovation. See "Xi Underlines Innovation."

36. "Xi Jinping Addresses Politburo 17th Collective Study Session."

37. "Xi Jinping Addresses Politburo 17th Collective Study Session."

38. Office of the US Secretary of Defense, *Annual Report to Congress*, 2018, 45.

39. State Council, *China's Military Strategy.*

40. Luo Derong, "Action Guidelines," 88–96. As the MSG is classified, its actual contents are unknown.

41. Luo Derong, "Action Guidelines."

42. Sun Sijing, "Strong Military Path Requires."

43. Xu Qiliang, "Do a Good Job in Studying the Military Strengthening Theory."

44. Xi Jinping, "Speech at Rally Celebrating 90th Anniversary."

45. See Saunders et al., *Chairman Xi Remakes the PLA.*

46. "Central Military Commission Issues 'Opinions concerning Deepening the Reform.'"

47. "Ministry of National Defense Holds News Conference."

48. "Former GAD Director Zhang Youxia Becomes New Director."

49. Zhao Lei, "PLA Says Chief of Its Arms Wing Replaced."

50. "2016 National Defense Science, Technology and Industry Working Conference."

51. "Nurture and Train a Large Number of Excellent Talents."

52. "Forge Talent Matrix That Wins Information Wars."

53. "Army Kicks Off Plan."

54. "Chinese Military Launches High-Level Scientific and Technological Innovation Talent Selection and Training Project"; "PLA Emphasizes High-Level Scientific and Technological Personnel Cultivation"; "China's National Defense in 2010."

55. "General Armaments Department Confirms First Batch of Project Experts."

56. "General Political Department Conducts Special Study."

57. "Cultivate Scientific and Technological Innovation."

58. "General Armament Department Talent Development 2020 Plan."

59. Interview with Chinese military acquisition expert, Changsha, September 2013.

60. Schwartz, *Defense Acquisition Reform*.

61. "Xi Jinping Addresses Ceremony."

62. "All-Army Political Work Conference Held"; "CPC Central Committee Retransmits the Decision."

63. "Strengthen Political Army Building."

64. "Chinese Military to Be Subject to Stricter Discipline."

65. Xi Jinping, "Secure a Decisive Victory in Building a Moderately Prosperous Society."

66. "Xi Jinping Attends Plenary Meeting of PLA." See also "Xi Jinping's Speech at Rally Celebrating 90th Anniversary."

67. "Give Full Play to the Role of Innovation in Driving Development."

68. "Establishment of Defense Industry Development Strategy Committee"; "Carrying the Reform Through to the End, Part 8"; and "Xi Jinping Gives Important Speech to PLA Delegation."

69. "Strategic Cooperation Relationship Officially Launched."

70. "Xi Jinping Attends Plenary Meeting of PLA."

71. "Xi Leads China's Military Reform."

72. "Zhang Youxia: Member of Political Bureau."

73. "Former GAD S&T Committee Director Liu Guozhi Appointed Director."

74. Mai, "Chinese Universities Should Produce Inquisitive Thinkers."

2. THE NATIONAL SECURITY STATE

1. Lasswell, *Essays on the Garrison State*.

2. Greenberg, *Reimagining the National Security State*.

3. Yuhua Wang and Carl Minzner call China a security state in their examination of the development of its "stability maintenance" regime centered on the political-legal apparatus of police, the courts, and procuratorates. Wang and Minzner, "The Rise of the Chinese Security State," 339–59. See also Guo, *China's Security State*, and Zenz and Leibold, "Securitizing Xinjiang," 324–48.

4. See Jervis, "Cooperation under the Security Dilemma," 167–214; Glaser and Kaufmann, "What Is the Offense-Defense Balance," 44–82; and Tang, "From Offensive to Defensive Realism."

5. Hu Jintao, "Unswervingly Advance Along the Path of Chinese Characteristics."

6. State Council Information Office, *The Diversified Employment*.

7. McGregor, "Party Man," 22.

8. See Osnos, "How Xi Jinping Took Control of China."

9. Beach, "Leaked Speech Shows Xi Jinping's Opposition to Reform."

10. "Hu Jintao, Xi Jinping Attend Enlarged Meeting."

11. "Xi Jinping Chairs Political Bureau Meeting."

12. "National Security Matter of Prime Importance."

13. Sun Jianguo, "Unwaveringly Take the National Security Path." See also Chen Xiangyang, "Seize the Opportunity to Plan."

14. Ramzy and Buckley, "'Absolutely No Mercy.'"

15. "Decision of the CPC Central Committee."

16. Guoping, "Increase Reform Confidence." Guoping is a pen name that the Chinese authorities use to comment on major issues in the official media.

17. Natalie Wong, "Hong Kong Protesters."

18. Huang, "Chinese President Accuses Fallen Top Officials."

19. The Commission for Discipline Inspection, *Excerpts from Xi Jinping's Discussion*, 28–29.

20. Wang Qishan, "Speech at the 18th Meeting."

21. Wendy Wu and Choi Chi-yuk, "Coup Plotters Foiled."

22. For example, see Anderlini, "Beijing on Edge amid Coup Rumours." A fascinating, plausible but thinly sourced account of this period focusing on Bo's attempts to gain power, the efforts of Zhou to build his power base within the national security apparatus, and the pivotal role of the Ministry of State Security is by Faligot, *Chinese Spies*, chap. 13.

23. Demick, "China Coup Rumors."

24. Baranovitch, "A Strong Leader for a Time of Crisis."

25. Greitens, *Dictators and Their Secret Police*.

26. "Communiqué on the Current State of the Ideological Sphere."

27. Sun Jianguo, "Unwaveringly Take the National Security Path."

28. "Sun Jianguo: China Is in Danger."

29. Wuthnow, "China's New 'Black Box.'"

30. L. Li, "Politics of Anticorruption in China," 47–63.

31. Xi Jinping, "Explanations of the CPC Central Committee's Resolution."

32. Xi Jinping, "Explanations of the CPC Central Committee's Resolution."

33. Hua Yiwen, "'Three in One System.'"

34. Hua Yiwen, "'Three in One System.'"

35. There has been plenty of scholarly attention on the role of the CNSC. See Wuthnow, "China's New 'Black Box'"; Lampton, "Xi Jinping and the National Security Commission," 749–77; Ji, "China's National Security Commission," 178–96; Sun, *Chinese National Security Decision-Making*; and Johnston, "The Evolution of Interstate Security Crisis."

36. "Xi Calls for Holistic National Security Outlook."

37. "Xi Calls for Efforts to Break New Ground."

38. Liu Yuejin, "Fully Implement the Holistic National Security Concept."

39. People's Daily Commentator, "Build a Firm System Dam."

40. Wong, "Chinese Security Laws."

41. "Xi Jinping Chairs Political Bureau Meeting."

42. Wang Xinjun, "Six Major Characteristics."

43. "Xi Jinping Presided over the First Meeting." For a broader context of this insecurity paradox, see Shirk, *Fragile Superpower*.

44. "National Security Matter of Prime Importance."

45. Yan Xuetong, *Analysis of China's National Interests*.

46. Deng, "The Chinese Conception of National Interests," 308–29.

47. "Xi Jinping Chairs First NSC Meeting."

48. "Xi Jinping's Speech at Opening."

49. Hu Angang, Yan Yilong, and Tang Xiao, *Xi Jinping's New Development Philosophy*.

50. "Xi Calls for Holistic National Security Outlook."

51. "Xi Jinping Chairs First NSC Meeting."

52. Li Yongsheng, "People's Security Is the Purpose."

53. Zhong Guoan, "Take General Secretary Xi Jinping's Overall National Security Concept."

54. Yang Dazhi, "Political Security Is Fundamental."

55. Li Daguang, *National Security*.

56. "Xi Jinping Presided over the First Meeting."

57. "Xi Jinping Presided over the First Meeting."

58. "Xi Jinping Presided over the First Meeting."

59. Guo, "Controlling Corruption in the Party," 597–624; L. Li, "The Rise of the Discipline and Inspection Commission," 447–82.

60. Li Li and Peng Wang, "From Institutional Interaction to Institutional Integration," 967–89.

61. Guo, "Controlling Corruption," 603.

62. Ji Renli, Wu Hairui, and Zong Haini, *Black Box of the Chinese Communist Party*, chap. 6.

63. Yuhua Wang quotes a figure of 1.6 million based on media reports dating to 2007 and believes this includes PAP personnel, which would mean police numbers would be closer to five hundred thousand. Y. Wang, "Empowering the Police," 627. Then–Public Security minister Guo Shengkun said in 2014 that the "public security contingent is a two-million-strong disciplinary force." Guo Shengkun, "Deeply Study and Comprehend."

64. Mattis and Brazil, *Chinese Communist Espionage*.

65. Liu Zhen, "Chinese Army Now."

66. Cheung, "Guarding China's Domestic Front Line," 525–47.

67. "Armed Police Command System."

68. Ma Haoliang, "Armed Police Reform."

69. Wuthnow, *China's Other Army*.

70. See Wang and Minzner, "The Rise of the Chinese Security State"; L. Li, "The Chinese Communist Party and People's Courts," 37–74; and Yang, "China's Troubled Quest for Order," 35–53.

71. "Xi Jinping Addresses Provincial, Ministerial-Level Cadres." References to "black swan" and "gray rhino" became popular in China from 2017. See "Facing 'Black Swan' and 'Grey Rhino.'"

72. Schwarck, "Intelligence and Informatization."

73. Zenz, "China's Domestic Security Spending"; Zenz, "Xinjiang's Re-education and Securitization Campaign."

74. This refers to how the public security apparatus "has adapted to the proliferation of IT by transforming the way it collects, analyzes, and disseminates information." Schwarck, "Intelligence and Informatization," 10–11.

75. Schwarck, "Intelligence and Informatization," 11.

76. Schwarck, "Intelligence and Informatization," 12–13.

77. Mattis and Brazil, "Chinese Communist Espionage," 21.

78. "Xi Jinping Addresses Provincial, Ministerial-Level Cadres Workshop."

79. "Xi Calls for Efforts to Break New Ground."

80. Sanger and Perlroth, "N.S.A. Breached Chinese Servers."

81. Greitens, *Dictators and Their Secret Police*.

82. Greitens, *Dictators and Their Secret Police*.

83. Greitens, *Dictators and Their Secret Police*.

84. Geddes, Wright, and Frantz, *How Dictatorships Work*.

85. For a detailed history, see Guo, "China's Security State."

86. Schwarck, "Intelligence and Informatization."

87. See Ghiselli, "Diplomatic Opportunities and Rising Threats," 611–25.

88. Liu Mingfu and Wang Zhongyuan, *The Thoughts of Xi Jinping*, 337–38.

89. "Chinese Police Must Guard against 'Color Revolutions.'" See also Lam, "Xi Jinping Warns against the 'Black Swans' and 'Gray Rhinos.'"

90. "Chen Li Talks."

91. See Huotari et al., *China's Emergence as a Global Security Actor.*

92. "Xi Calls for Holistic National Security Outlook."

93. Statement by senior Chinese diplomat Luo Zhaohui at a UN conference on December 24, 2019, http://www.chinesemission-vienna.at/eng/hyyfy/t1727584.htm.

94. Lu Lai, "Behind the Mysterious National Security Commission."

95. Yuan Peng, "China's International Strategic Thinking."

96. Chen Wenqing, "Vivid Practice and Rich Development."

3. THE PROMISE AND PERIL OF MILITARY-CIVIL FUSION

1. Pompeo, "Silicon Valley and National Security."

2. Mao Zedong, Deng, Jiang, Hu, and Xi all sought to put their personal stamps on CMI policy. MCC during the Deng era was primarily about how to leverage the dominant defense economy for civilian-oriented economic development. MCC was part of a longer sixteen-character strategic guidance that also included "combining peacetime and wartime preparations (平战结合, *pingzhan jiehe*), giving priority to military products (军品优先, *junpin youxian*), and letting the civilian sector support the military sector (以民养军, *yimin yangjun*)." These other parts of the guidance were largely ignored under Deng's tenure. For Jiang, the goal of his *Yujun Yumin* banner strategy was to find a more equitable two-way interaction between the civilian and military economies that would lead to the "mutual promotion and coordinated development" of these two spheres. This meant adjusting the locus of CMI from its lopsided focus on defense conversion under Deng to a relationship in which economic development would remain the top priority, but with more attention paid to military requirements. *Yujun Yumin* was also part of a sixteen-character guidance that included MCC to denote its overlap with Deng's slogan, along with "vigorously promote coordination and cooperation (大力协同, *dali xietong*) and conduct indigenous innovation (自主创新, *zizhu chuangxin*)." These last two concepts were also actively promoted and embraced. See Cheung, *Fortifying China.*

3. Liu Zhiwei, "Interpretation of the Deep-Seated Contradictions."

4. Bi Jingjing and Ren Tianzuo, *China Military-Civil Fusion Development Report 2014.*

5. Jiang Luming, Wang Weihai, and Liu Zuchen, *Discussion of a Military Civil Fusion Development Strategy*, 41–42.

6. Zhen Yujun, Ma De, and Yi Fei, "Military-Civil Fusion Makes Chinese Military Different."

7. Yin Jun and Tan Qingmei, "Degree of Military-Civil Fusion and Its Optimization Measures."

8. Jiang Luming, "Military-Civil Fusion Uses Security and Development."

9. "Hu Jintao's Report at the 17th Party Congress"; see also Du Zhongwu, "A Historical Investigation"; Li Chaomin, "A Major Composition That Must Be Written Well"; and Yu Chuanxin and Zhou Jianping, *Military-Civil Fusion-Style Development*, 93–98.

10. Hu Jintao, "Report to the 18th National Congress."

11. "Xi Jinping Talks about Military-Civil Fusion."

12. "Decision of the Chinese Communist Party Central Committee."

13. "Military-Civil Fusion Is the Strategic Decision."

14. The opinions have not been publicly released, but there has been detailed reporting of its contents. See "Opinions on the Integrated Development."

15. Other studies have put forward different translations of these terms. Alex Stone and Peter Wood define these concepts as full element, multidomain, and high return. Stone and Wood, *China's Military-Civil Fusion Strategy.*

16. Liu Zhiwei, "Interpretation of the Deep-Seated Contradictions."

17. Jiang Luming, "Military-Civil Fusion Uses Security and Development."

18. For a discussion of the Chinese context of total factor productivity, especially related to technology and innovation, see Zhang, "Productivity in China," 1–21.

19. Millett, Murray, and Watman, "The Effectiveness of Military Organizations," 37–71.

20. These four systems were the weapons and equipment research, development, and production system; talent cultivation system; military socialized support and logistics system; and defense mobilization system.

21. The official Chinese term is the Advanced Defense Science, Technology, and Industrial System with Chinese Characteristics (中国特色先进国防科技工业体系, *Zhongguo Tese Xianjin Guofang Keji Gongye Tixi*).

22. The official Chinese term is the Military-Civil Science and Technology Coordinated Innovation System (军民科技协同创新体系, *Junmin Keji Xietong Chuangxin Tixi*).

23. The official Chinese term is the Military Talent Training System (军事人才培养体系, *Junshi Rencai Peiyang Tixi*).

24. The official Chinese term is the Fundamental Domain and Resource Sharing System (基础领域资源共享体系, *Jichu Lingyu Ziyuan Gongxiang Tixi*). This is overseen by the Cybersecurity and Infrastructure Security Agency under the Department of Homeland Security, https://www.cisa.gov/critical-infrastructure-sectors.

25. The official Chinese term is the Military Support and Socialization System (军队保障社会化体系, *Jundui Baozhang Shehuihua Tixi*). Liao Xilong, "More Quickly Promote Military Support Socialization."

26. Luce and Richter, "Handling Logistics in a Reformed PLA," 257–92; McCauley, "Modernization of PLA Logistics."

27. "Xi Stresses Integrated Military, Civilian Development."

28. The official Chinese term is National Defense Mobilization System (国防动员体系, *Guofang Dongyuan Tixi*).

29. See Cheung, "Does the People's Republic of China?"

30. Wu Weichao, "A Brief Analysis," 68–69.

31. Liu Jinyu, "New Trends, New Policies, and New Ideas."

32. "The Strategic Move of the Rich Country and Strong Army"; Li Yizhong, "Exploring Practical Development Paths."

33. Jin Zhuanglong, "Opening Up a New Era." *Qiushi* is sometimes used to explain key national policies and strategies that have not been publicly disclosed. This was the case, for example, with the HNSC.

34. "Carry Out In-Depth Implementation." Xi's statement was subsequently incorporated into the 2016 opinions.

35. Jiang Luming, "China's Special Path in the Development of Military-Civil Fusion."

36. Defense Economics Research Center, National Defense University, "Overview of the Annual Development of China's Military-Civil Fusion."

37. Zhang Jiantian, "An Analysis of the Problems."

38. Minzner, "China's Turn against Law," 935–84.

39. National Defense Economics Research Center, "Overview of the Annual Development of China's Military-Civil Fusion."

40. See, for example, *The Contest for Innovation.*

41. Jackson, *The Four Aspects of Joint.*

42. Snider, "Jointness, Defense Transformation."

43. See Cheung, "A Conceptual Framework of Defense Innovation."

44. Ho, "Has China Gone into Stealth Mode."

45. Sichuan's provincial MCF Development Committee, for example, met in February 2019. See "How to Do a Good Job in MCF."

46. In 2020, the CMCFDC General Office director was Han Zheng (韩正), while his counterparts were Politburo member Ding Xuexiang (丁薛祥) in the CCP General Office, State Councillor Xiao Jie (肖捷) in the State Council General Office, and Lieutenant General Zhong Shaojun in the CMC General Office.

47. "Xi Jinping Chairs Second Plenum." The 13th Military-Civil Fusion Science and Technology Five-Year Plan has been published. See "13th Five-Year Special Plan for Science and Technology Military-Civil Fusion Development." The Center for Security and Emerging Technology at Georgetown University did an English translation of this plan.

48. Wu Hongxing and Wang Guizhi, "Vigorous Promotion of Military-Civilian Scientific and Technological Collaborative Innovation."

49. "In-Depth Study and Implementation."

50. "What New Changes Will Occur."

51. Hagt, *China's Civil-Military Integration.*

52. Hagt, *China's Civil-Military Integration,* 427.

53. Yin Weijun, "Seize the Key Systems."

54. "MIIT's 2018 Military-Civil Fusion."

55. Liu Jinyu, "New Trends, New Policies, and New Ideas." See also "To Implement the Military-Civil Development Strategy."

56. Yin, "Seize the Key Systems."

57. Before joining the CMCFDC, Jin headed the Commercial Aircraft Corporation of China, which is in charge of building advanced airliners able to compete with Airbus and Boeing beginning with the C919 passenger airliner, one of the megaprojects under the MLP. "The 'Head' of the Large Domestic Aircraft Project."

58. You Guangrong, Yan Hong, and Zhao Xu, "The Construction of the Military-Civil Fusion Policy System." You is a leading MCF and acquisition expert at the Academy of Military Sciences.

59. Cozad, "Toward a More Joint, Combat-Ready PLA."

60. "Xi Jinping Stresses Military-Civil Fusion."

61. "National Development and Reform Commission Makes Major Progress."

62. The GAD enjoyed a seventeen-year life span before it was reorganized into the CMC EDD in 2016. On the establishment of the Strategic Support Force, see Costello and McReynolds, "China's Strategic Support Force."

63. "Build Dragon Head and Quality Military-Civil Fusion Projects."

64. "13th Five-Year Special Plan for Science and Technology Military-Civil Fusion Development."

65. Li Yizhong, "Exploring Practical Development Paths"; "National Development and Reform Commission Makes Major Progress." No comprehensive list of these twenty-one projects has so far been published.

66. Miao Ye, "Research on the Current Situation." Miao is a researcher at the Defense Mobilization Research and Development Center affiliated with the NDRC. The commission is playing a leading role in the rolling-out of these zones. See also Zhang Jiaguo and Li Zhengfeng, "Analysis and Countermeasures of Problems."

67. "Many Provinces Are Striving to Establish Military-Civil Fusion Innovation Demonstration Zones."

68. Li Yizhong, "Exploring Practical Development Paths."

69. "National Military-Civil Fusion Innovation Demonstration Zones."

70. Miao Ye, "Research on the Current Situation."

71. "Ministry of Science and Technology and CMC Science and Technology Commission Jointly Issue 13th Five-Year Special Plan"; "13th Five-Year Special Plan for Science and Technology Military-Civil Fusion Development."

72. "Six Members of the Central Military Commission Gathered."

73. Four licenses were originally required, but this was streamlined to three in 2017. For details of these licenses, see "Introduction to 'The Three Military Industrial Certificates.'" In addition, the service arms also play a major role with their equipment development departments.

74. Tan Yungang, "See Opportunities, Challenges and Actions of China's Science and Technology Innovation Development."

75. "More than a Thousand Private Enterprises." One reason for the discrepancy in the number of firms reported to hold WERPLs is that a sizable number of these licenses have been canceled. See "SASTIND Cancels 200 Weapons and Equipment Research and Production Licenses."

76. Wu Boyi and Qi Zhongying, "Thoughts on the National Defense Science and Technology Industry."

77. See "Hot Weapons Licenses."

78. "The Achievements of Military-Civil Fusion; "About 3000 Private Enterprises in China Have Entered the Front Lines."

79. Tan Yungang, "Thoughts on Further Promoting 'Civilian Participation in Military.'"

80. "2018 Version of the Weapons and Equipment Research and Production License Catalog."

81. "2018 Version of the Weapons and Equipment Research and Production License Catalog."

82. Tan Yungang, "Opportunities and Challenges."

83. Tan Yungang, "Opportunities and Challenges."

84. Chinese Communist Party Central Party Literature Research Office, *Selection of Xi Jinping's Comments*, 50–51.

85. "Name List of 20 National Laboratories."

86. "13th Five-Year Science and Technology Innovation Plan," chap. 9, sec. 2.

87. There is considerable debate within the S&T community about how the national laboratory system should be built. One issue is whether these entities should copy the existing institutional culture of the research institute apparatus or forge new identities. See Wu Wei and Zhu Jiazan, "Push Out the Stereotypes."

88. "Promote Collaborative Innovation."

89. 14th Five-Year Plan, chap. 4, sec. 1.

90. "COSTIND Starts Construction of Defense S&T National Laboratories."

91. "SASTIND Holds 2016 Science and Technology Work Conference"; "SASTIND Take Measures to Accelerate National Defense."

92. "Name List of 60 Defense Science and Technology Key Laboratories."

93. "Defense Research Institute Reforms May Be Implemented Soon."

94. "Defense Research Institute Reforms Need to Deal with Six Issues."

95. "Defense Research Institute Reforms May Be Implemented Soon."

96. "Defense Conglomerates Will Start Classification Reform."

97. "How Will China's SOE Reform Fare."

98. "China Great Wall Plans to Implement Second Phase"; "How to Lay Out Plans for the Military Industrial Sector."

99. For example, in January 2007, CSSC subsidiary Hudong Heavy Machinery issued a private placement of US$1.5 billion (RMB 12 billion). The funds were used to buy

shipyards and invest in new technology. See "Hudong Heavy Eyes 12b Yuan in Placement."

100. "SASTIND Issues Notice on Rules for Defense."

101. "Li Keqiang Stresses Innovative Macroeconomic Measures."

102. "CSIC Releases Plan for 8.48 Billion Set."

103. "China Navy Plots Course to Stock Market."

104. "How Will China's SOE Reform Fare."

105. Yifei Gong, Peiyue Li, and Ziqiao Shen, "Research on Operating Efficiency."

106. "Four Things to Know about China's $670 Billion Government Guidance Funds."

107. Luong, Arnold, and Murphy, *Understanding Chinese Government Guidance Funds.*

108. One 2016 government audit of 235 funds found only 15 percent of them had actually raised money. Luong et al., *Understanding Chinese Government Guidance Funds*, 14.

109. A 2018 report on GGFs by the China Center for Financial Research at Tsinghua University found that only 6.4 percent of funding by GGFs went to initial seed-stage ventures, 18.7 percent were given to start-up stage outfits, 42.3 percent of funds went to entities in the expansion stage, and 31.2 percent of money went to mature stage firms. *Government Guidance Fund Report*, 18–19.

110. "Li Keqiang Hosts State Council Executive Meeting."

111. "13th Five-Year Science and Technology Innovation Plan."

112. ChinaVenture Institute, *2019 Chinese Government Guidance Fund Special Report.* Figures compiled by independent Chinese financial sources such as ChinaVenture and Zero21PO have to be taken with caution because they are often based on press releases and aspirational statements by start-up funds rather than actual funds raised. These firms also often have close ties to Chinese central and local government agencies dealing with venture capital and investment matters. The research arm of Zero21PO, for example, states on its website (https://www.pedata.cn/jsp/research.html) that it provides advisory services for many GGFs, including MOST and numerous provincial governments.

113. *Government Guidance Fund Trends.*

114. This information is based on the examination of the websites of Chinese defense corporations, Ministry of Finance, MIIT, State Intellectual Property Office, stock brokerages, fund shareholders, and media reports.

115. "State Council Promotes Military-Civil Fusion."

116. "Opinions of the General Office of the State Council on Promoting the Deep Development."

117. There have been occasional mentions of project areas that the fund is looking to make investments in. In 2018, for example, the Fujian Provincial Economic and Informatization Commission issued a province-wide notice soliciting investment projects for the fund. "Notice on Soliciting Investment Projects."

118. Fritz and Kennedy, "China's Military-Civil Fusion Funds."

119. ChinaVenture Institute, *2019 China Military Civil Fusion White Paper.*

120. CSRF's website is http://www.cctfund.cn.

121. "China's State-Owned Enterprise Structural Adjustment Fund."

122. Beijing Zhongwang Investment Development Corp. is a subsidiary of China Zhongwang Holdings Ltd., which is one of the world's largest manufacturers of industrial aluminum extrusion products and is owned by Liu Zhongtian (劉忠田). The National MCF Investment Fund appears to be one of Zhongwang's first investments in the MCF sector. "China Zhongwang Makes Strategic Investment."

123. Tus Holdings is the development, construction, and operational arm of Tsinghua Science and Technology Park.

124. "AVIC Capital Invests in the Establishment."
125. "National Military-Civil Fusion Industry Investment Fund Co., Ltd."
126. "Is China at the Forefront of Drone Technology?"
127. Tabrizi and Bronk, *Armed Drones in the Middle East Proliferation.*
128. Fangqi Xu and Hideki Muneyoshi, "A Case Study of DJI."
129. Newman, "The Army Grounds Its DJI Drones over Security Concerns."
130. A sizable number of commercial drone firms have been participating in defense and MCF exhibitions. See "UAVs at 2017 Military-Civil Fusion Expo"; and Hille, "China's Drone Makers Zero in on Armed Forces."
131. "Northwestern Polytechnical University a Leader."
132. "AEE Technology Co. Corporate Introduction."
133. "Military-Civil Fusion Makes Chinese Military Different."
134. "'One Belt One Road' Space Information Corridor Construction; see Chase, "The Space and Cyberspace Components."
135. Gu Yang, "'Digital Silk Road' Construction."
136. "Nuclear Power in China."
137. Crowe, "After Huawei, the Nuclear Question Looms Large"; Lee Jeong-ho, "China Scales Back Iran Nuclear Cooperation."
138. Necsutu, "Romania Cancels Deal with China."
139. Chen Yanxin, "Coordinate the Promotion of Military-Civil Fusion."
140. "13th Five-Year Special Plan for Science and Technology Military-Civil Fusion Development."
141. Joske, *The China Defence Universities Tracker.*
142. See also Tiffert, *Global Engagement.*
143. See Leslie, *The Cold War and American Science.*
144. Arkin and O'Brien, "The Most Militarized Universities in America."
145. In a speech in March 2020, Ford said that "over the past year, I have been sounding alarm bells to the United States' partners and allies, U.S. corporations, and to the American public about Beijing's strategy of 'Military-Civil Fusion.'" US State Department, "The PRC's 'Military-Civil Fusion' Strategy."
146. This point is incorrect as efforts to pass a comprehensive MCF law have so far been unsuccessful.
147. Vergun, "Addressing China Threats Requires Unity of U.S."
148. "President Donald J. Trump Is Protecting America."
149. O'Keeffe, "Bill Aims to Stop Theft of U.S. University Research."
150. "Has China Gone into Stealth Mode."
151. "The Fight against the Epidemic Demonstrates."
152. "Xi Jinping: Gradually Build a National Strategic System."
153. Huang Chaofeng and Ma Junyang, "Research on the Integrated National Strategic System."
154. Jiang Luming and Wang Weihai, "Building an Integrated National Strategic System."
155. "State Council Decision on Accelerating the Development of Strategic Emerging Industries."
156. "13th Five-Year Plan for the Development of Strategic Emerging Industries."

4. MILITARY STRENGTHENING

1. Chinese military strategic thinking can be categorized into four tiers. At the top is military thought (军事思想, *junshi sixiang*), which is the responsibility of the country's paramount leader and commander in chief. The second level is military strategy (军事战略, *junshi zhanlüe*), which is the responsibility of the PLA high command. The third

level is campaigns (战役, *zhanyi*), which addresses operational-level thinking, and the fourth tier is tactics (战术, *zhanshu*).

2. Xi Jinping, "Secure a Decisive Victory in Building a Moderately Prosperous Society."

3. See Cheung, *Fortifying China*.

4. "Hu Jintao, Xi Jinping Attend Enlarged Meeting."

5. Xi has participated in many more defense-related visits, meetings, and activities that are not disclosed. Information from all of these publicly reported visits, meetings, and conference participation comes from the monitoring of Chinese state media outlets and official party, state, and military websites.

6. "70th Anniversary Military Parade Is Here!" Xi's first military parade was in September 2015 in Beijing to commemorate the seventieth anniversary of China's victory against Japan. The second was an August 2017 parade in Zhurihe in Inner Mongolia to celebrate the ninetieth anniversary of the founding of the PLA. The third was an April 2018 naval parade held in the South China Sea. The fourth was another large-scale naval parade in April 2019 to commemorate the seventieth anniversary of the establishment of the PLA Navy.

7. This is what James Mulvenon has called conditional compliance, in which the PLA conditionally supports the top leader but in return expects autonomy over core corporatist issues such as military modernization and the making of military doctrine and strategy. Mulvenon, "China: Conditional Compliance," 317–35. See also Kiselycznyk and Saunders, *Civil-Military Relations in China*.

8. "Xi Jinping and His Era"; Wu Zhongshu, Wang Dengchao, and Ren Dalong, "Rule the Army by Law"; Choi and Chan, "President Xi Jinping Takes Aim at More Top Chinese Generals"; State Council Information Office, *China's National Defense in the New Era*, 5.

9. Chan, "China's Military Demotes over 70 Senior Officers."

10. "All-PLA Political Work Conference Concludes in Gutian."

11. Fravel, *Active Defense*, 28. See also Finkelstein, "China's National Military Strategy," 67–140.

12. For a fascinating case study of the process behind the making of the 1993 MSG, see Zhang Wannian Writing Team, *Biography of Zhang Wannian*, 59–72. Although a number of the key players in MSG policy formulation changed with the reorganization of the PLA high command in 2016, the policy-making process likely remains the same.

13. Wang Faan, *China's Strategy for Invigorating the Armed Forces*.

14. Wang Faan, *China's Strategy for Invigorating the Armed Forces*.

15. Wang Faan, *China's Strategy for Invigorating the Armed Forces*.

16. Hu Xin, "'Air-Sea Battle' Sword Pointed at East Asia."

17. "Central Military Commission Issues 13th Five-Year Plan."

18. Mei Xiangbin, "Evolution of Military Strategic Guidelines."

19. Fravel, *Active Defense*, 30.

20. Wen Bing, "Correctly Locate the Basic Point."

21. State Council Information Office, *China's Military Strategy*.

22. State Council Information Office, *The Diversified Employment of China's Armed Forces* and State Council Information Office, *China's National Defense in 2010*.

23. Luo Derong, "Action Guidelines for Armed Forces Building," 88–96.

24. Snow, "The Corps Is Axing All of Its Tank Battalions."

25. State Council Information Office, *China's National Defense in the New Era*.

26. "Xi Jinping's Speech at Rally Celebrating 90th Anniversary."

27. "For Seventeen Years, We Walked Together."

28. Yu Gaoda and Zhao Lusheng, *The Study of Military Equipment*, chap. 9.

29. Fu Guangming and Ji Hongtao, "Research on Hu Jintao's Strategic Thinking."

30. Liu Cheng, "Creating a New Situation in the Weapons and Equipment Modernization Effort."

31. "Administrative Measures of the State Administration."

32. Yan Xin, *Overview of the Development of China's Contemporary Defense Science and Technology, Part 1*, 168–70.

33. Liu Huaqing, *Memoirs of Liu Huaqing*, chap. 17.

34. Yu Gaoda and Zhao Lusheng, *The Study of Military Equipment*.

35. Yu Gaoda and Zhao Lusheng, *The Study of Military Equipment*, chap. 9.

36. Yu Gaoda and Zhao Lusheng, *The Study of Military Equipment*, chap. 9.

37. Li Andong, "Implement the Scientific Development Concept."

38. "Key Points of Zhang Youxia's Speech."

39. "Xi Jinping Attends PLA Armament Work Conference."

40. "Wu Shengli Speaks at the Eighth Plenary Meeting."

41. *China's National Defense in the New Era*, 5.

42. Informationized warfare refers to war-fighting in the information era involving highly networked military forces sharing enormous amounts of information together. Intelligentized warfare refers to the military application of AI/machine learning to fighting wars through algorithms and data.

43. Xiao Tianliang, *The Science of Strategy*.

44. Liberation Army Daily Commentator, "Give Full Play to the Role of Innovation."

45. For background, see Cheung, *Fortifying China*.

46. Mao Guohui, *Introduction to the Military Armament Legal System*, 46.

47. Mao Guohui, *Introduction to the Military Armament Legal System*, 45.

48. "Speech by Zhang Youxia at General Armament Department Party Committee."

49. "Decision of the Chinese Communist Party Central Committee."

50. "Xi Jinping Chaired the First Meeting of the CMC."

51. "Documentary of the Design Process of Deepening Defense."

52. Wu Ming, "Commentary on the Importance of the CMC Chairman Responsibility System."

53. Liberation Army Daily Commentator, "Give Full Play to the Role of Innovation in Driving Development."

54. "Central Military Commission Issues 'Opinions Concerning Deepening the Reform.'"

55. "Former GAD Director Zhang Youxia Becomes New Director."

56. "Casting a Shield, Honing a Sword, Never Removing Armor."

57. "Former GAD S&T Committee Director Liu Guozhi Appointed Director."

58. "Xi Jinping Gives Important Speech to PLA Delegation."

59. "Strategic Cooperation Officially Launched."

60. "The Country's First National Defense Science, Technology, and Innovation."

61. "Notice of Release of the Second Batch of Requirements"; "Notice on Holding the National Defense Science, Technology, and Innovation Rapid Response Small Group."

62. "Contributions of the Academy of Military Sciences."

63. Shao Longfei and Zhang Zhihua, "Academy of Military Science Retains Hundreds of Talents."

64. Shao Longfei and Zhang Zhihua, "National Innovation Institute of Defense Technology"; Wuthnow, "China's 'New' Academy of Military Sciences"; Kania, "Chinese Military Innovation in Artificial Intelligence."

65. "Academy of Military Science, China Aerospace Science and Technology Corp."

66. "Xi Demands High-Level Research Institutions for Strong Military."

67. "Xi Jinping Addresses Ceremony."

68. Xi paid a visit to AMS in May 2018 to signal his close ties and support for the institution. "When Inspecting the Academy of Military Science, Xi Jinping Stresses the Need to Work Hard."

69. Chan, "Chinese Military Sets Up Hi-Tech Weapons." This committee is also mentioned in the 2019 Chinese defense white paper in the same sentence that references AMS and other service research institutes. This suggests that the steering committee will coordinate and oversee research activities within the military academic system.

70. Interview with a senior AMS researcher, Hong Kong, June 2019.

71. "China Sets Up National Defense Science, Technology, and Industry Development."

72. "National Defense Technology Industry Development Strategy Committee."

73. The committee's secretary-general, Wu Zhijian, has been an especially prominent representative of the entity. See, for example, An An, "2016 Military-Civil Fusion Enterprise Summit" and "Interview with National Defense Technology Industry Development Strategy Committee Secretary-General Wu Zhijian."

74. For a detailed analysis of the history and role of the Science and Technology Committee under COSTTIND and SASTIND, see Hagt, "The Science and Technology Committee."

75. "National Defense Technology Industry Science and Technology Committee."

76. See Nan Tian and Fei Su, *Estimating the Arms Sales of Chinese Companies*.

77. See Cheung, *Fortifying China*.

78. "Two Major Chinese Aerospace Groups Sign an Agreement."

79. "President Xi Urges Independent R&D." See also Wood, Wahlstrom, and Cliff, *China's Aeroengine Industry*.

80. "Interim Measures for Administration of Defense"; "China Will Build a Number of Defense S&T Industry Innovation Centers."

81. Tang Taoyi, "Defense S&T Industrial Aviation Technology."

82. "Defense S&T Industry Efficient CNC Machining Technology."

83. Li Bin et al., "Thoughts on the Construction of National Defense Technology Industry." Li is the deputy director of the National Defense Technology Information and Management Research Center.

84. This section draws from the chapter on "Weaknesses in PLA Defense Industries," in Chase et al., *China's Incomplete Military Transformation*.

85. Lieberthal and Oksenberg, *Policy Making in China*, 35–42. See also Lieberthal and Lampton, *Bureaucracy, Politics, and Decision Making in Post-Mao China*; and Lampton, *Policy Implementation in Post-Mao China*.

86. See Liu Hanrong and Wang Baoshun, *National Defense Scientific Research Test Project Management*.

87. Pomfret, "Chinese Army Tests Jet"; Bumiller and Wines, "Test of Stealth Fighter."

88. Cheung, *Fortifying China*, 83–85.

89. Interview with PLA acquisition specialist, Beijing, November 2011.

90. Mao Guohui, *Introduction to the Military Armament Legal System*, 158–59.

91. Zong Zhaodun and Zhao Bo, "Major Reform Considered in Work."

92. Zhang Xiaoqi, "Armament Work."

93. Li Xuanliang, "CMC Vice Chairman Stresses Effective Anti-Corruption."

94. "Second Central Inspection Team Sent to SASTIND Party Committee."

95. Ng, "Former Boss of China Aircraft Carrier Programme."

96. Chan, "12 Years behind Bars."

97. Zheng, "China's Aircraft Carrier Troubles Continue."

98. For a comprehensive examination of the role of S&T-related programs and plans, see Cheung et al., *Planning for Innovation*.

99. Commission on Science, Technology, and Industry for National Defense, "Outline of Defense Medium- and Long-Term Science and Technology Development Plan." See also "China Unveils Plan."

100. "Outline of the National Defense Science, Technology, and Industry Medium- and Long-Term Science and Technology Development Plan."

101. "SASTIND Publishes Guide to Publicize Military Industrial Intelligent Manufacturing."

102. The Chinese embassy was hit by several precision-guided munitions launched from a US strategic bomber on May 7, 1999, as part of a NATO bombing campaign against the Slobodan Milošević regime. The United States said that the attack was accidental and caused by inaccurate targeting data, but there was a strong negative reaction from the Chinese government that disputed the US explanations. The 995 refers to the year (99) and month (fifth month, or May) in which the Belgrade bombing took place.

103. See, for example, Sun Hong and Li Lin, "On the Modes of Advancing Weapons"; and "Chinese Defense Science and Technology Industry's Tasks."

104. "For Seventeen Years, We Walked Together."

105. In the defense S&T domain, *Shashoujian* is used by Chinese leaders and analysts to refer to the development of armaments that target an enemy's vulnerabilities. Other less precise, but more colorful, definitions of this term are assassin's mace, trump card, and silver bullet.

106. Zhang Wannian Writing Team, *Biography of Zhang Wannian*, 416.

107. Zhang Wannian Writing Team, *Biography of Zhang Wannian*, 419. Possible candidates that fit into the *Shashoujian* category include anti-ship ballistic missiles such as the DF-21D, anti-satellite missiles, and stealth aircraft.

108. Zhang Wannian Writing Team, *Biography of Zhang Wannian*, 416.

109. Cao Guosheng, "Do Some Things, Do Not Do Other Things."

110. Zhang Wannian Writing Team, *Biography of Zhang Wannian*, 416.

111. Talk by Yao Youzhi at the Shenzhen Culture Forum, Shenzhen Citizen Culture Lecture Hall (深圳市民文化大讲堂), August 18, 2012, http://www.szccf.com.cn/wqhg_content_662.html.

112. Zhou Bisong, *Weapons and Equipment Development and National Defense Technology Innovation*, 22.

113. Mao Nongxi, "Shaanxi Defense Industry Trade Union Promotes Transformation."

114. Zhou Bisong, *Research on the Path for the Construction of Weapons*, 39.

115. "AVIC Studies and Implements Spirit of All-Army Armament Work Conference."

116. "Notice of the Heilongjiang Provincial People's Government."

117. Guan Fei, "Continuous Innovation of Heilongjiang's Defense Industry Interview."

118. "Notice of the Provincial Defense Industry Office on Supporting the Construction Work."

119. "Heilongjiang Engineering University Launches High-Tech Project No. 1."

120. "Central Military Commission Promulgates the Outline of the 13th Five-Year Program."

121. "2016 National Defense Science, Technology and Industry Work Conference."

122. Zhou, "China Almost Doubles Weapons Exports."

123. Cooper, "Classifying Warships by Generation."

124. Data obtained from annual editions of the *Military Balance* between 1989 and 2019 published by the International Institute for Strategic Studies, London. Research assistance provided by Patrick Hulme.

125. ONI defines a modern state-of-the-art submarine as being able to employ submarine-launched intercontinental ballistic missiles or anti-ship cruise missiles. See

Murray, Berglund, and Hsu, *China's Naval Modernization and Implications for the United States*, 6–7.

126. O'Rourke, *China Naval Modernization*, 32.

127. Office of the Secretary of Defense, *Annual Report to Congress, 2020*, 45.

128. "Intensive Commissioning of Warships."

5. CHINA'S EFFECTIVE MODEL OF TECHNOLOGICAL ADVANCEMENT

1. This approach fits very well with the classic thinking on innovation by Josef Schumpeter. See Schumpeter, *The Theory of Economic Development*.

2. Mack, *From Engineering Science to Big Science*; Hughes, *The Manhattan Project*.

3. See Cheung, "Economics, Security and Technology in Northeast Asia."

4. See Haggard and Cheung, "North Korea's Nuclear and Missile Programs."

5. Huai Guomo, "Entering the Initial Period of the Nuclear Industry, Part 1," 66–68.

6. See Cheung, *Fortifying China*, chap. 2.

7. Z. Wang, "The Chinese Developmental State during the Cold War."

8. Xie Guang, *The Contemporary Chinese Defense Science and Technology*, 33. See also "Nie Rongzhen."

9. Feigenbaum, *China's Techno-Warriors*, 52.

10. Wen Xisen and Kuang Xinghua, *The Theory of National Defense Science and Technology*, 62. They pointed out that more than four hundred government research institutes belonging to twenty ministries were involved in research in the nuclear weapons development program. More than another one thousand higher educational research organizations and enterprises also took part.

11. Xie Guang, *The Contemporary Chinese Defense Science and Technology Sector*, 39–40, 129.

12. Lewis and Xue, *China Builds the Bomb*, 35–36.

13. See Liao Feng, "History and Development of the Predecessors." The administrative support vehicle was the State Council No. 3 Office.

14. For an early history of the CSC in the 1960s and early 1970s, see Yang Mingwei, "Zhou Enlai and the Central Special Commission," 4–11.

15. Xie Guang, *The Contemporary Chinese Defense Science and Technology Sector*.

16. Liu Jifeng, Liu Yanqiong, and Xie Haiyan, *The Project of "Two Bombs, One Satellite,"* 73–74.

17. Cao Yingwang, *China's Chief Steward Zhou Enlai*.

18. In December 1977, the CMC decided that military modernization priorities would shift away from strategic weapons to less expensive and less risky conventional armaments programs. Xie Guang, *The Contemporary Chinese Defense Science and Technology Sector*, 130. Nevertheless, the CSC under Hua enlarged its membership to twenty-one members, although Hua did subsequently complain that this expanded lineup was too large. See Dong Fanghe, *General Zhang Aiping*, 656. According to Zheng Sheng, one of Zhang Aiping's sons, Hua delegated the running of the CSC to Zhang Aiping, who was the CSC office director in the late 1970s. See Han Gang, "The Controversy Regarding Hua Guofang."

19. Although Deng did attend a number of CSC meetings at the end of the 1970s, it is not clear if he took the formal title of CSC director. He was named, though, as a CSC deputy director in August 1977.

20. Shen and Xia, *Between Aid and Restriction*, 52.

21. Bai Pengju, "Zhang Aiping's Thinking on Defense Science and Technology," 55.

22. Zhi and Pearson, "China's Hybrid Adaptive Bureaucracy," 407–24.

23. Other mostly failed attempts at long-range S&T planning initiatives included (1) a ten-year plan issued in 1963 that replaced the earlier twelve-year S&T blueprint but that was aborted during the Cultural Revolution, (2) a medium-term development plan for

1978–1985, and (3) a 1990–2000 S&T development outline. There were also a proliferation of other shorter planning efforts and development programs such as the regular five-year plans.

24. Geng Jiandong, *Review of 15 Years of the National High Technology*, 22–24.

25. "The Guidelines for the Implementation of the National Medium- and Long-term Program for Science and Technology Development (2006–2020)."

26. Hao Xin and Gong Yidong, "China Bets Big on Big Science," 1548.

27. "Ministry of Science and Technology Holds Media Conference."

28. See "2010 Annual Report of the Major Special S&T Programs."

29. For a detailed discussion of the Chinese efforts to build up its military, industrial, and infrastructure mobilization apparatus, see Cheung, "Industrial, Technological, Economic and Infrastructure Capacity."

30. See Zhu Qinglin, *Study Course of National Economic Mobilization*.

31. "Central Military Commission Vice-Chair Urges Retention."

32. Liu Huaqing, *Memoirs of Liu Huaqing*, 571–72.

33. Liu Huaqing, *Memoirs of Liu Huaqing*, 573.

34. For the 2003 notice, see "Notice of the State Council on the Establishment of Deliberative Coordination Institutions."

35. "Notice of the State Council on the Establishment of Advisory and Coordinating Organs."

36. "State Council Notice on the Adjustment of the State Council Central Military Commission Central Special Commission," originally published on the website of Tuanfeng County People's Government, Hubei Province (湖北省团风县人民政府门户网站), http://www.tfzf.gov.cn/Article/tfk/200810/45.html. Webpage is no longer accessible.

37. The premier, a CMC vice-chairman, and a vice-premier were the three officials given responsibility for overseeing the running of the CSC. Chen Xiaodong, "Decision on the Shenzhou," 38–51. *Shenjian* is a monthly journal belonging to the EDD.

38. Li Mingsheng describes a CSC meeting reportedly held in October 2002 in which the participants were Premier Zhu Rongji, who chaired the event, Vice-Premier Wu Bangguo, CMC Vice-Chairman Zhang Wannian, State Councilor and State Council Secretary-General Wang Zhongyu, PLA Chief of General Staff General Fu Quanyou, General Logistics Department Director General Wang Ke, General Armament Department Director Cao Gangchuan, COSTIND Director Liu Jibin, and Vice Foreign Minister Wang Guangya. See Li Mingsheng, *An Eternal Dream*, 326. Li writes in the book that his knowledge of this event is based on the meeting records.

39. "Internal Structure, Staffing, and Primary Duties"; Yu Chen, "Secret History of China's Aerospace Industry."

40. Hu Baomin, Wang Ting, and Li Zibiao, "Research on the Special Characteristics," 84. The key US agencies are the National Aeronautics and Space Administration and the National Nuclear Security Administration under the Department of Energy.

41. "Success of Hard-Won Achievements."

42. See chapter 4 for a discussion of Document No. 37.

43. Tu Senlin, "Serve the Construction of an Advanced Defense Industry."

44. Liu Huaqing, *Memoirs of Liu Huaqing*, 477.

45. "Major Events in the Chinese Aviation Industry in 1990."

46. "China's Long March V Carrier Rocket."

47. "The Secret History of China's Laser Weapons."

48. "The Father of China's Manned Space Program."

49. Chen Xiaodong, "Jueci Shenzhou," 41–42.

50. The leadership selection was decided at a follow-up CSC meeting in November 1992.

51. Li Mingsheng, *An Eternal Dream*, chap. 23.

52. Chen Long, "Lunar Exploration Project Leading Group."

53. "From Technology Introduction to Indigenous Innovation."

54. Even when Xi came to power, he criticized the effectiveness of the absorption process. At a Politburo study session in September 2013, Xi said that "the problems of heavy importation and light digestion is still widespread, forming a vicious circle of 'introduction-backwardness-reintroduction.'" "Xi Jinping's Strategy of Technological Catching Up."

55. Zahra and George, "Absorptive Capacity," 186.

56. Hu Angang, "The Path of Indigenous Innovation."

57. For Chinese writings on the IDAR strategy, see Qiao Weiguo and Chen Fang, "Research on the Policy System"; and Li Nong, Qian Li, and Chong Xinong, "A Discussion of China's Technology Introduction," 67–70.

58. "Opinions to Encourage Technology Transfer."

59. This is the standard approach to civilian commercial technology transfers. For useful studies examining China and international technology transfer, see De Prato and Nepelski, *International Technology Transfer between China and the Rest of the World*; Van Reenen and Yueh, "Why Has China Grown So Fast?"; and Albert G. Z. Hu, Gary H. Jefferson, and Qian Jinchang, "R&D and Technology Transfer," 780–86. For a dated perspective on civilian and dual-commercial technology transfers in the 1990s, see Bureau of Export Administration, *US Commercial Technology Transfers to People's Republic of China*.

60. Stockholm International Peace Research Institute, *The Trend in International Transfers of Major Arms*; Wezeman et al., "Trends in International Arms Transfers, 2018."

61. See Barabanov, Kashin, and Makienko, *Shooting Star*.

62. "Maj. Gen. Li Wujun Serves as Director."

63. Interview with senior Russian Defense Ministry official, Moscow, April 1993, and reported in Cheung, "China's Buying Spree." See also Cheung, "Ties of Convenience."

64. "Russian Weapons Were Illegally Copied."

65. "Reshetin Sentenced to 11.5 Years."

66. "Russia Professors Found Guilty of Spying for China."

67. See Kania and Costello, "The Strategic Support Force," 111.

68. On the role of the GAD S&T Committee, see Hagt, "The Science and Technology Committee."

69. See Hannas, Mulvenon, and Puglisi, *Chinese Industrial Espionage*, chap. 2.

70. Hannas et al., *Chinese Industrial Espionage*, 20–21.

71. Xu Guanghua, "The Development of the S&T Information Industry."

72. Hannas et al., *Chinese Industrial Espionage*, 22.

73. One study suggests that 80 percent or more of S&T technical information requirements can be obtained from open-source publications, while the remainder needs to be collected from "special means." Huo Zhongwen and Wang Zongxiao, *Sources and Techniques of Obtaining National Defense Science and Technology Intelligence*, 84–85.

74. "Science and Technology Vanguard."

75. "Science and Technology Vanguard."

76. National Science Board, *Science and Engineering Indicators 2014*, 2–39.

77. Falkenheim and Trapani, National Center for Science and Engineering Statistics, *Trends in Graduate Education*, 17, and National Science Board, *Science and Engineering Indicators 2020*, 50.

78. National Science Board, *Science and Engineering Indicators 2014*, 2–41.

79. Falkenheim and Trapani, *Trends in Graduate Education*, 26.

80. Yang Xinggen, "Transformation from 'Mechanical Military Factory' into a 'Digital Military Factory,'" 39–40.

81. Jiang Yan and Bai Yunchuan, "Interview with Professor Wang Tianmiao."

82. "Administrative Measures on National Engineering Research Centers."

83. "Technological Progress Is Changing with Each Passing Day."

84. "Defense Science and Technology Industry Advanced Technology Research."

85. "Four Defense Science and Technology Industrial Technology Research."

86. Perry, "World's Top Ten Manufacturing Nations."

87. Yu Ping, "The J-11B Comes from Su-27."

88. "China's Imitation of Su-27SK and Its Impact."

89. "China 'Cloning' Russian Weapons despite Intellectual Property Agreement."

90. Gao Lu, "Chinese Jetliner Development."

91. "Xi Jinping: Struggle to Build a Strong Country."

92. "Xi Jinping: Struggle to Build a Strong Country."

93. "Xi Jinping's Speech at Rally Celebrating the 90th Anniversary."

94. Qiu, "China Goes Back to Basics."

95. "Speech by Xi Jinping at the 17th Conference."

96. "Wan Gang: Funding of Central Science and Technology Projects."

97. "State Council Notice on Deepening the Management Reform Plan."

98. "Policy Explanation on Deepening the Management Reform."

99. Zhong, "Chinese Tech Giant on Brink of Collapse."

100. "Xi Jinping Chairs Second Meeting." See also Zhang Zhanbin and Du Qinghao, "Regarding Core Technology Breakthroughs"; and Segal, "Seizing Core Technologies."

101. "Xi Jinping Chairs Second Meeting."

102. "Provisions on the Administration of Major National Science and Technology Projects."

103. "13th Five-Year Science and Technology Innovation Plan."

104. Liu Yuxian, "Gaofen Hunan Data and Application Center."

105. These were the published figures for the first two years of the NKRDP in 2016 and 2017. See National Key R&D Programs of China, *China Innovation Funding.*

106. "Application Guides for Key Project on Strategic Advanced Electronic Materials."

107. "Application Guides for Key Project on High-Performance Computing."

108. "Application Guides for Key Project on Additive Manufacturing and Laser Manufacturing."

109. "Application Guides for Key Project of Quantum Control and Quantum Information."

110. Jin Yezi, "Announcement of the 14th Five-Year National Key R&D Program."

111. "Xi Jinping Talks about the New Whole-of-Nation System."

112. "Xi Jinping Talks about the New Whole-of-Nation System."

113. "Decision of the Chinese Communist Party Central Committee on Several Major Issues."

114. Hu Yongshun, "What Is the New Whole-of-Nation System?"; Liu Yin, "What Is the 'New' Meaning of the New Whole-of-Nation System?"

115. Hu Yongshun, "What Is the New Whole-of-Nation System?"

116. See Holz, "Industrial Policies and the Changing Patterns of Investment."

117. "Li Keqiang's Flagship Plan."

118. Wubbeke et al., *Made in China 2025.*

119. State Council, *Made in China 2025.*

120. "Interpret 'Made in China 2025.'"

121. Zhu Minghao, "Need to Work on Core Components"; Huang Xin, "Lay a Solid Foundation."

122. Manufacturing Power Strategic Research Committee, *Research on the Manufacturing Power Strategy,* 263–77.

123. "Guidelines on Developing and Promoting the National IC Industry"; "A Decade of Unprecedented Growth."

124. "SASTIND Issues '2016 SASTIND Military-Civil Fusion Special Action Plan.'"

125. Wei, "Beijing Drops Contentious 'Made in China 2025' Slogan."

126. "14th Five-Year Plan for National Economic and Social Development of the People's Republic of China (2021–2025) and the Outline of Long-Term Goals for 2035," chap. 8.

127. "Speech by Xi Jinping at the 17th Conference."

128. Zweig and Kang, "The Rise and Fall."

129. Zweig and Kang, *America Challenges China's National Talents Programs*, 5.

130. Cao et al., "Returning Scientists."

131. Zweig and Kang, "The Rise and Fall," 20.

132. Federal Bureau of Investigation, *Chinese Talent Programs*.

133. US Senate Permanent Subcommittee on Investigations, *Threats to the U.S. Research Enterprise: China's Talent Recruitment Plans*, 5.

134. The plan was translated from a Nankai University website by the Center for Security and Emerging Technology at Georgetown University: Ministry of Science and Technology, *Notice on Applying for 2020 National Foreign Expert Projects*.

135. "The First Batch of 'Ten Thousand People Plan' Released."

136. The first batch in 2013 totaled 546 participants, the second batch in 2016 was 620 recipients, the third batch in 2017 numbered 1,635, and the fourth batch in 2019 was for 1,419 awardees.

137. "China's Brain Gain Spurs Innovation." Figures quoted by Cheng Li show similar levels of returnee representation in the mid-2000s. Li, "Bringing China's Best and Brightest Back Home."

138. This study examined data from Scopus, which is a major international citation database of nearly 25,000 academic publications. Cao et al., "Returning Scientists."

139. Han Wei, "China Revamps Top National Technology."

140. "Establishment of Inter-Ministerial Joint Meeting System."

141. Chen Ying, "Inter-Ministerial Joint Meeting of Science and Technology Program Management."

142. "State Council Notice on Deepening the Management Reform Plan of Central Financial Science and Technology Plans."

143. Iansiti, *Technology Integration*; Best, *The New Competitive Advantage*.

144. The Pentagon issued a directive in 1995 to promote the adoption of this parallel development process in the defense S&T system and published a handbook in 1998. See Department of Defense, *Integrated Product and Process Development Handbook*. A 2001 US Government Accounting Office study of DoD's use of the integrated parallel model through the use of integrated product teams found poor implementation. See US Government Accounting Office, *Best Practices*.

145. Bai Chunli, "Strive to Make Breakthroughs in Original Innovation."

146. Henderson and Clark, "Architectural Innovation," 10.

147. "13th Five-Year Science and Technology Innovation Plan," chap. 9.

148. "13th Five-Year Science and Technology Innovation Plan."

6. THE TECHNO-SECURITY STATE IN CONCEPTUAL AND COMPARATIVE PERSPECTIVE

1. See Jessop, *The State*.

2. Nexon, *The Struggle for Power*, chap. 3. Nexon has a third camp that he labels ideationalists.

3. See Kaspersen and Strandsbjerg, *Does War Make States?*

4. For an excellent overview, see Haggard, *Developmental States.*

5. Rosecrance, *The Rise of the Trading State.*

6. Castles et al., *The Oxford Handbook of the Welfare State.*

7. Johnson, *MITI and the Japanese Miracle.*

8. Friedberg, *In the Shadow of the Garrison State.*

9. Weiss, *America Inc.?*

10. Haggard, *Developmental States*, 45.

11. Samuels, *Rich Nation, Strong Army.*

12. See Green, *Arming Japan.*

13. Samuels, *Japan as a Technological Superpower*, 2.

14. Samuels, *The Business of the Japanese State*, 2.

15. Samuels, *Rich Nation, Strong Army*, 30–39.

16. Haggard, *Developmental States*, 48.

17. Amsden, *The Rise of the Rest*; Evans, *Embedded Autonomy.*

18. Woo-Cummings, "Back to Basics," 91–117.

19. Woo-Cummings, "Back to Basics," 98.

20. See Cheung, "Economics, Security and Technology."

21. Fagerberg and Verspagen, "Innovation Studies."

22. Nelson, *National Innovation Systems.*

23. Mazzucato, *The Entrepreneurial State.*

24. Mazzucato, *The Entrepreneurial State*, 80.

25. Tilly, *The Formation of National States.*

26. Lasswell, "The Garrison State," 455–68; Stuart, *Creating the National Security State.*

27. Buzan, *The United States and the Great Powers*, 58.

28. Waltz, *Theory of International Relations*, 131.

29. Brooks and Wohlforth, *America Abroad.*

30. Hogan, *A Cross of Iron.*

31. Herspring, "Truman and the American Military."

32. Unger, "The Politics and Political Legacy."

33. Stuart, "Preparing for the Next Pearl Harbor," 18.

34. These mechanisms consisted of defense outlays, human capital recruitment, the privatization of military production, a supporting civilian industrial infrastructure, and an advanced research and development system.

35. "Remarks Made by Xi Jinping at the Rally Celebrating the 40th Anniversary."

36. Ikenberry, "Rethinking the Origins of American Hegemony."

37. Hogan, *A Cross of Iron*, 465.

38. Zachary, *Endless Frontier.*

39. Friedberg, *In the Shadow of the Garrison State*, 304–5; Bush, *Modern Arms and Free Men.*

40. Friedberg, *In the Shadow of the Garrison State*, 306–7; Block, "Innovation and the Invisible Hand," 20–21.

41. Friedberg, *In the Shadow of the Garrison State*, 316–17.

42. Block, "Innovation and the Invisible Hand of Government," 7.

43. Friedberg, *In the Shadow of the Garrison State*, 208–10.

44. Block, "Innovation and the Invisible Hand of Government," 8–9.

45. Martinage, *Toward a New Offset Strategy.*

46. This asymmetric strategy was known as the competitive strategies concept and was developed by Andrew Marshall, the legendary head of the Office of Net Assessments in the Pentagon. See Marshall, *Long-Term Competition with the Soviets.*

47. Weiss, *America Inc.?* See also Taylor, "Toward an International Relations Theory"; Gholz and Sapolsky, "The Defense Innovation Machine."

48. Weiss, *America Inc.?* 201.

49. Weiss, *America Inc.?* 203.

50. Some leading defense analysts such as Michael O'Hanlon had started to talk about the national security industrial base at the beginning of the 2010s, but they used the term interchangeably with the defense industrial base. O'Hanlon, *The National Security Industrial Base.*

51. Gudger, "Modernizing Our Industrial Base," 15.

52. US National Science and Technology Council Committee, *A 21st Century Science, Technology, and Innovation Strategy,* ii.

53. White House, *National Security Strategy of the United States of America.* In terms of policy implementation, however, the Trump administration's priority and focus was on supporting the traditional defense industrial base. See White House, *Presidential Executive Order.*

54. The hybrid rational state category replaces the market rational state type that is in the original developmental state taxonomy. This modification spotlights the influence and involvement of the state in the techno-security sphere, which is more pronounced than in economic-centric counterparts. This is because national security is overwhelmingly the responsibility of governments. Moreover, the focus of technological innovation is more military and strategic in nature, which also means more state intervention and a reduced role for market forces. This means market rational techno-security states do not exist.

CONCLUSIONS

1. By contrast, the US government differentiates its defense and manufacturing industrial base according to ownership type. There is the "organic" defense industrial base that is composed of only government-owned facilities, such as manufacturing arsenals, depots, and ammunition plants. There is also the much larger private sector industrial base that is home to private sector companies and approved foreign entities, which are engaged in defense-specific, dual-use, and commercial-specific activities. This approach offers far less analytical precision. See Interagency Task Force in Fulfillment of Executive Order 13806, *Assessing and Strengthening the Manufacturing and Defense Industrial Base,* 15–17.

2. On estimates of the Soviet defense burden, see Firth and Noren, *Soviet Defense Spending.*

3. Ministry of Finance, "Report on the Implementation of the Central and Local Budgets in 2019." The average US dollar to RMB exchange rate in 2020 was US$1 to RMB 6.58.

4. See Liff and Erickson, "Demystifying China's Defence Spending." There are also no publicly available figures or estimates for Chinese intelligence spending.

5. Interview with high-ranking Chinese Ministry of Science and Technology official, 2011; Sun Yutao and Cong Cao, "Demystifying Central Government R&D Spending in China."

6. Total domestic expenditures in 2017 were US$196 billion (RMB 1.24 trillion). See Chin, "China Spends More on Domestic Security." See also Zenz, "China's Domestic Security Spending." Zenz points out that central level public security budgets are only a fifth of overall spending on domestic security.

7. In the case of the US aerospace and defense sector in 2017, sales revenue was US$865 billion compared to value-added industrial output of US$348 billion, a difference of 2.5 times. It is very likely, though, that Chinese input costs, especially for labor, would be considerably lower than for their US counterparts, although there are little data to determine this difference. For the purposes of our analysis, we would conserva-

tively estimate the value-added industrial output for the Chinese defense industry to be half of its total revenue value.

8. These are the figures reported by the country's ten leading defense conglomerates. Data come from defense company websites, government websites (National Audit Office), and media reports.

9. National Defense University Defense Economics Research Center, "Overview of the Annual Development," 10.

10. Zhong Wen and Hong Hong, "Hot Handed Weapons Licenses."

11. "Value-Added Output of Strategic Emerging Industries."

12. See *Making Sense of the $1.25 Trillion National Security State Budget*; 2019 police expenditures of US$190 billion are from the national income and product accounts database of the Department of Commerce's Bureau of Economic Analysis, https://apps .bea.gov/iTable/iTable.cfm?reqid=19&step=2#reqid=19&step=2&isuri=1&1921=survey, and intelligence budget information comes from DeVine, *Intelligence Community Spending*. National intelligence spending for 2019 was US$60.2 billion, which excluded military-related intelligence expenditures that fall under the defense budget.

13. *2020 State of the American Aerospace and Defense Industry.*

14. *2016 State of the American Aerospace and Defense Industry*, 4.

15. Interagency Task Force, *Assessing and Strengthening the Manufacturing and Defense Industrial Base*, 87–103.

16. Interagency Task Force, *Assessing and Strengthening the Manufacturing and Defense Industrial Base*, 90.

17. Faulk and Bialos, "Unpacking U.S.-China Sanctions and Export Control Regulations."

18. "US Commerce Department Issues 'Military End User' List." There are additional export control lists put out by the US government that include the Unverified List, the Denied Persons List, and the Specially Designated Nationals and Blocked Persons List.

19. Ramachandran and Heck, "Chinese Military Companies Trading Ban."

20. Swanson, "Trump Bars Investment in Chinese Firms."

21. Sanger and McCabe, "Biden Expands Trump-Era Ban on Investment in Chinese Firms Linked to Military."

22. Klein, "US Security Focus on Chinese State Ownership."

23. Metz, "Curbs on A.I. Exports?"; Tongele, "Emerging Technologies."

24. Feng and Barak, "China's Semiconductors."

25. Swanson, "The Agency at the Center of America's Tech Fight."

26. Zhong Guoan, "Take General Secretary Xi Jinping's Holistic National Security Concept."

27. Shirk, "The Return to Personalistic Rule."

28. Deng Xiaoping, "On the Reform of the System of Party and State Leadership."

29. See McFaul, "Cold War Lessons and Fallacies," 7–39.

30. Sargent, Gallo, and Schwartz, *The Global Research and Development Landscape.*

31. Remarks by Michael Brown, director of the US Department of Defense's Defense Innovation Unit at a forum on "Fresh Options to Reinvigorate Defense Innovation for the World as It Is Now," organized by the Strategic Multilayer Assessment and National Defense University, February 3, 2021.

32. See *Department of Defense Emerging Technology Strategy*, 36.

33. Leading US technology figures such as former Google CEO Eric Schmidt have urged for the remaking of the hybrid public-private relationship. "Google Ex-CEO Has a Plan for US."

34. Whalen, "To Counter China."

35. White House, *National Strategy for Critical and Emerging Technologies.*

36. Edmondson, "Senate Overwhelmingly Passes Bill."

37. This goal was set out in Biden's presidential campaign. See "The Biden Plan to Ensure the Future." Within several weeks of coming into power, the Biden White House issued an executive order related to this industrial plan. White House, "Executive Order on Ensuring the Future." Maintaining US manufacturing and innovation leadership was included in the Biden administration's interim national security guidance. See White House, *Interim U.S. National Security Strategic Guidance.*

38. China's efforts at defense technological and industrial development received limited attention and coverage in the congressional-mandated annual reviews of China's military power issued by the Pentagon during the 2000s and first half of the 2010s.

39. Cheung, "The Emergence of Direct US-China Defense Technological Competition." See also remarks by deputy US defense secretary Bob Work on the Third Offset Strategy at the Reagan Defense Forum.

40. Brimley, "Offset Strategies and Warfighting Regimes."

41. *Summary of the 2018 U.S. National Defense Strategy*; White House, *National Security Strategy of the United States.*

42. See McCormick et al., *National Technology and Industrial Base Integration*; and Greenwalt, *Leveraging the National Technology Industrial Base.*

43. White House, *Joint Leaders Statement on AUKUS.*

44. Naughton, "Grand Steerage," 54. Other analysts like Nicholas Lardy also point to the resurgent role of the state in economic development, especially in resource allocations and boosting the importance and reach of the state sector. See Lardy, *The State Strikes Back.*

45. See US Chamber of Commerce China Center and Rhodium Group, *Understanding U.S.-China Decoupling.*

46. Shen and Xia, *Between Aid and Restriction*, 52.

47. On the issue of bifurcation and the need of the United States to form strong multilateral technological alliances with close allies, see China Strategy Group, *Asymmetric Competition.* This group is made up of influential US technology leaders and policy researchers that includes Eric Schmidt, former CEO of Google.

48. The meaning of securitization here comes from the concept put forward by Buzan, Waever, and Wilde, *Security: A New Framework for Analysis.*

49. This positive assessment of China's international situation came from the country's national security community and is detailed in outlets such as the defense white papers issued by the Ministry of National Defense.

50. *Qiushi* commentator, "Compose a New Chapter." High-quality development refers to the pursuit of higher-end economic and technological activities of which original advanced innovation is a cornerstone.

51. Li Yuan, "ZTE's Near-Collapse."

52. Xi Jinping, "Several Major Issues."

53. "Xi Jinping: Correctly Understand and Grasp the Major Issues."

54. Liu He, "Accelerate the Construction of a New Development Pattern."

55. Xi Jinping, "Several Major Issues."

56. "Xi Jinping: Explanation of the 'Recommendations.'" A useful background assessment is Pei, "China's Fateful Inward Turn," 66.

57. "Recommendations of the Chinese Communist Party Central Committee."

58. Xue Zhiliang, "Fight the 'Pandemic.'"

59. A useful explanation of the intentions and goals of the 14th Five-Year Plan is provided by the National Development and Reform Commission, which is the primary state agency responsible for drafting the plan. National Development and Reform Commission, "The Grand Blueprint."

60. 14th Five-Year Plan, chap. 1, sec. 2.

61. Zhou Yuehui, "The Dialectical Relationship between the New Development Pattern and the New Development Concept."

62. National Development and Reform Commission, "The Grand Blueprint," sec. 1, chap. 1.

63. "Special Address by Chinese President Xi Jinping at the World Economic Forum."

64. He Bin, "Speech at Special Seminar for County-Level Leading Cadre."

65. 14th Five-Year Plan.

66. 14th Five-Year Plan, chap. 4.

67. 14th Five-Year Plan, chap. 53.

68. 14th Five-Year Plan, introduction to pt. 2.

69. National Science Board, *Research and Development*, 32.

70. 14th Five-Year Plan, chap. 57.

71. "Promote the Simultaneous Improvement of National Defense."

72. 14th Five-Year Plan, chap. 53. See also "The Correct Way to Open the 'Outline.'"

73. 14th Five-Year Plan, sec. 16, introduction.

74. Liu Caiyu, "China's Centennial Goal."

75. Chan and Zheng, "Why Taiwan May Be a Key Factor."

76. 14th Five-Year Plan, chap. 56.

77. "Xi Jinping Gives Important Instructions."

78. 14th Five-Year Plan, chap. 3, sec. 1.

Bibliography

ENGLISH-LANGUAGE MEDIA AND ONLINE SOURCES

"A Decade of Unprecedented Growth: China's Impact on the Semiconductor Industry 2014. Update." PricewaterhouseCoopers, January 2015. https://www.pwc.com/gx /en/technology/chinas-impact-on-semiconductor-industry/assets/china -semicon-2014.pdf.

An, Baijie. "Vice-Premier Highlights Innovation for Development." *China Daily*, November 11, 2015. https://www.chinadaily.com.cn/china/2015-11/11/content_224277 72.htm.

Anderlini, Jamil. "Beijing on Edge amid Coup Rumours." *Financial Times*, March 21, 2012. https://www.ft.com/content/650bb0f6-735f-11e1-aab3-00144feab49a.

Arkin, William, and Alexa O'Brien. "The Most Militarized Universities in America." *Vice News*, November 6, 2015. https://www.vice.com/en_us/article/j59g5b/the-most -militarized-universities-in-america-a-vice-news-investigation.

Beach, Sophie. "Leaked Speech Shows Xi Jinping's Opposition to Reform." *China Digital Times*, January 23, 2013. https://chinadigitaltimes.net/2013/01/leaked-speech -shows-xi-jinpings-opposition-to-reform/

Brimley, Shawn. "Offset Strategies and Warfighting Regimes." *War on the Rocks*, October 15, 2014. https://warontherocks.com/2014/10/offset-strategies-warfighting -regimes/.

Bumiller, Elisabeth, and Michael Wines. "Test of Stealth Fighter Clouds Gates Visit to China." *New York Times*, January 12, 2011. https://www.nytimes.com/2011/01/12 /world/asia/12fighter.html.

Chan, Minnie. "12 Years behind Bars for Corrupt Former Boss of Chinese Warship Builder CSIC." *South China Morning Post*, July 4, 2019. https://www.scmp.com /news/china/politics/article/3017326/12-years-behind-bars-corrupt-former-boss -chinese-warship.

——. "China's Military Demotes over 70 Senior Officers 'For Bribing Fang Fenghui.'" *South China Morning Post*, June 25, 2019. https://www.scmp.com/news/china /military/article/3016059/chinas-military-demotes-over-70-senior-officers -bribing-fang.

——. "Chinese Military Sets Up Hi-Tech Weapons Research Agency Modelled on US Body." *South China Morning Post*, July 25, 2017. https://www.scmp.com/news /china/diplomacy-defence/article/2104070/chinese-military-sets-hi-tech -weapons-research-agency.

Chan, Minnie, and William Zheng. "Why Taiwan May Be a Key Factor in China's Military Modernisation Plan." *South China Morning Post*, October 30, 2020. https:// www.scmp.com/news/china/military/article/3107867/why-taiwan-may-be-key -factor-chinas-military-modernisation-plan.

Chin, Josh. "China Spends More on Domestic Security as Xi's Powers Grow." *Wall Street Journal*, March 6, 2018. https://www.wsj.com/articles/china-spends-more-on -domestic-security-as-xis-powers-grow-1520358522.

"China 'Cloning' Russian Weapons despite Intellectual Property Agreement." *Nezavisimoye Voyennoye Obozreniye*, December 3, 2010.

"China's Imitation of Su-27SK and Its Impact." *Kanwa Asian Defense Review*, May 2008.

"Chinese Police Must Guard against 'Color Revolutions,' Says Top Official." *Reuters News Agency*, January 18, 2019. https://www.reuters.com/article/us-china-politics-police /chinese-police-must-guard-against-color-revolutions-says-top-official-idUSK CN1PC0BS.

Choi, Chi-yuk. "'Political Mistakes,' More than Graft, Led to Downfall of Chinese Military Chiefs Guo Boxiong and Xu Caihou." *South China Morning Post*, May 26, 2016. https://www.scmp.com/news/china/policies-politics/article/1954587/politi cal-mistakes-more-graft-led-downfall-chinese.

Choi, Chi-yuk, and Minnie Chan. "President Xi Jinping Takes Aim at More Top Chinese Generals as Anticorruption Drive Rolls On." *South China Morning Post*, August 24, 2018. https://www.scmp.com/news/china/diplomacy-defence/article/2161 289/president-xi-jinping-takes-aim-more-top-chinese.

Cooper, Alastair. "Classifying Warships by Generation." *US Naval Institute, Naval History Blog*, July 8, 2016. https://www.navalhistory.org/2016/07/08/classifying-war ships-by-generation.

"Criminal Justice Expenditures: Police, Corrections, and Courts." Urban Institute. Accessed March 15, 2021. https://www.urban.org/policy-centers/cross-center -initiatives/state-and-local-finance-initiative/state-and-local-backgrounders /police-and-corrections-expenditures.

Crowe, Philip. "After Huawei, the Nuclear Question Looms Large for China-UK Relations." *The Diplomat*, July 20, 2020. https://thediplomat.com/2020/07/after-huawei -the-nuclear-question-looms-large-for-china-uk-relations/.

Demick, Barbara. "China Coup Rumors May Be Wild, but Tension is Real." *Los Angeles Times*, March 22, 2012. https://www.latimes.com/archives/la-xpm-2012-mar-22-la -fg-china-coup-rumors-20120323-story.html.

Edmonson, Catie. "Senate Overwhelmingly Passes Bill to Bolster Competitiveness With China." *New York Times,* June 8, 2021. https://www.nytimes.com/2021/06/08/us /politics/china-bill-passes.html.

Feng, Coco, and Masha Barak. "China's Semiconductors: Latest US Export Controls May Hinder Ambitions to Catch Up." *South China Morning Post*, November 6, 2020. https://www.scmp.com/tech/policy/article/3108706/chinas-semiconductors -latest-us-export-controls-may-hinder-ambitions.

"Google Ex-CEO Has a Plan for US to Stay Ahead of China's Government-Backed Tech." *C4ISR.Net*, March 25, 2021. https://www.c4isrnet.com/artificial-intelligence/2021 /03/26/google-ex-ceo-has-a-plan-for-us-to-stay-ahead-of-chinas-government -backed-tech/.

Hille, Kathrin. "China's Drone Makers Zero in on Armed Forces." *Financial Times*, November 8, 2018. https://www.ft.com/content/4f427fa2-e284-11e8-a6e5-792428 919cee.

Ho, Matt. "Has China Gone into Stealth Mode with Its Military-Civil Fusion Plans?" *South China Morning Post*, June 5, 2020. https://www.scmp.com/news/china /military/article/3087785/has-china-gone-stealth-mode-its-military-civil-fusion -plans.

Huang, Cary. "Chinese President Accuses Fallen Top Officials of 'Political Conspiracies.'" *South China Morning Post*, January 2, 2017. https://www.scmp.com/news/china /policies-politics/article/2058767/chinese-president-accuses-fallen-top-officials.

Klein, Jodi Xu. "US Security Focus on Chinese State Ownership Is Not Productive, Advisory Panel Is Told." *South China Morning Post*, March 20, 2021. https://www .scmp.com/print/news/china/article/3126246/us-security-focus-chinese-state -ownership-not-productive-advisory-panel.

Lee, Jeong-ho. "China Scales Back Iran Nuclear Cooperation 'due to Fears of US Sanctions.'" *South China Morning Post*, January 31, 2019. https://www.scmp.com/news/china/diplomacy/article/2184512/china-scales-back-iran-nuclear-cooperation-due-fears-us.

Li, Yuan. "ZTE's Near-Collapse May Be China's Sputnik Moment." *New York Times*, June 10, 2018. https://www.nytimes.com/2018/06/10/technology/china-technology-zte-sputnik-moment.html.

Liu, Caiyu. "China's Centennial Goal of Building a Modern Military by 2027 in Alignment with National Strength: Experts." *Global Times*, October 31, 2020. https://www.globaltimes.cn/content/1205238.shtml.

Liu, Zhen. "Chinese Army Now Makes Up Less than Half of PLA's Strength as Military Aims to Transform Itself into Modern Fighting Force." *South China Morning Post*, January 21, 2019. https://www.scmp.com/news/china/military/article/2183050/chinese-army-now-makes-less-half-plas-strength-military-aims.

Mai, Jun. "Chinese Universities Should Produce Inquisitive Thinkers Who Are Totally Loyal to the Communist Party, Xi Jinping Says." *South China Morning Post*, April 19, 2021. https://scmp.com/news/china/politics/article/3130187/chinese-universitiesshould-produce-inquisitive-thinkers-who.

Metz, Cade. "Curbs on A.I. Exports? Silicon Valley Fears Losing Its Edge." *New York Times*, January 1, 2019. https://www.nytimes.com/2019/01/01/technology/artificial-intelligence-export-restrictions.html.

Necsutu, Madalin. "Romania Cancels Deal with China to Build Nuclear Reactors." *Balkan Insight*, May 27, 2020. https://balkaninsight.com/2020/05/27/romania-cancels-deal-with-china-to-build-nuclear-reactors/.

Newman, Lily Hay. "The Army Grounds Its DJI Drones over Security Concerns." *Wired*, August 7, 2017. https://www.wired.com/story/army-dji-drone-ban/.

Ng, Teddy. "Former Boss of China Aircraft Carrier Programme in Corruption Probe." *South China Morning Post*, May 13, 2020. https://www.scmp.com/news/china/military/article/3084131/former-boss-china-aircraft-carrier-programme-corruption-probe.

O'Keeffe, Kate. "Bill Aims to Stop Theft of U.S. University Research by China, Others." *Wall Street Journal*, June 3, 2020. https://www.wsj.com/articles/bill-aims-to-stop-theft-of-u-s-university-research-by-china-others-11591174800.

Osnos, Evan. "How Xi Jinping Took Control of China." *New Yorker*, April 6, 2015. https://www.newyorker.com/magazine/2015/04/06/born-red.

Perry, Mark. "World's Top Ten Manufacturing Nations, 1970 to 2018." *American Enterprise Institute Blog*, January 28, 2020. https://www.aei.org/carpe-diem/animated-chart-of-the-day-worlds-top-ten-manufacturing-nation.

Pomfret, John. "China Tests Stealth Aircraft before Gates, Hu Meet." *Washington Post*, February 26, 2011. https://www.washingtonpost.com/national-security/china-tests-stealth-aircraft-before-gates-hu-meet/2011/01/11/ABssHkD_story.html.

——. "Chinese Army Tests Jet during Gates Visit." *Washington Post*, January 12, 2011.

Qiu, Jane. "China Goes Back to Basics on Research Funding." *Nature*, March 11, 2014. https://www.nature.com/news/china-goes-back-to-basics-on-research-funding-1.14853.

Rabinovitch, Simon. "China Navy Plots Course to Stock Market." *Financial Times*, September 11, 2013. https://next.ft.com/content/4f27d80a-1abb-11e3-a605-00144feab7de.

Ramzy, Austin, and Chris Buckley. "'Absolutely No Mercy': Leaked Files Expose How China Organized Mass Detentions of Muslims." *New York Times*, November 16, 2019. https://www.nytimes.com/interactive/2019/11/16/world/asia/china-xinjiang-documents.html.

"Reshetin Sentenced to 11.5 Years for Passing Technology to China." *RIA-Novosti News Agency,* December 3, 2007.

"Russia Professors Found Guilty of Spying for China." *Associated Press,* June 20, 2012.

"Russian Weapons Were Illegally Copied 500 Times Abroad over 17 Years, Says Rostec." *Tass Russian News Agency,* December 13, 2019. https://tass.com/defense/1099283.

Sanger, David, and David McCabe. "Biden Expands Trump-Era Ban on Investment in Chinese Firms Linked to Military," *New York Times,* June 3, 2021. https://www.nytimes.com/2021/06/03/us/politics/biden-ban-chinese-firms-trump.html.

Sanger, David, and Nicole Perloth. "N.S.A. Breached Chinese Servers Seen as Security Threat." *New York Times,* March 22, 2014. https://www.nytimes.com/2014/03/23/world/asia/nsa-breached-chinese-servers-seen-as-spy-peril.html.

Smithberger, Mandy. "America's $1.1 Trillion National Security Budget." *Center for Defense Information, Project for Government Oversight,* May 24, 2017. https://www.pogo.org/investigation/2017/05/americas-11-trillion-national-security-budget/.

Snow, Shawn. "The Corps Is Axing All of Its Tank Battalions and Cutting Grunt Units." *Marine Corps Times,* March 23, 2020. https://www.marinecorpstimes.com/news/your-marine-corps/2020/03/23/the-corps-is-axing-all-of-its-tank-battalions-and-cutting-grunt-units/.

So, Charlotte. "Hudong Heavy Eyes 12b Yuan in Placement." *South China Morning Post,* January 30, 2007. https://www.scmp.com/article/580095/hudong-heavy-eyes-12b-yuan-placement.

Swanson, Ana. "The Agency at the Center of America's Tech Fight with China." *New York Times,* March 26, 2021. https://www.nytimes.com/2021/03/26/business/economy/commerce-department-technology-china.html?action=click&module=Well&pgtype=Homepage&section=Technology.

——. "Trump Bars Investment in Chinese Firms with Military Ties." *New York Times,* November 12, 2020. https://www.nytimes.com/2020/11/12/business/economy/trump-china-investment-ban.html.

Vergun, David. "Addressing China Threats Requires Unity of U.S., World Effort, Esper Says." *DOD News,* January 24, 2020. https://www.defense.gov/Explore/News/Article/Article/2065332/addressing-china-threats-requires-unity-of-us-world-effort-esper-says/.

Wei, Lingling. "Beijing Drops Contentious 'Made in China 2025' Slogan, but Policy Remains." *Wall Street Journal,* March 5, 2019. https://www.wsj.com/articles/china-drops-a-policy-the-u-s-dislikes-at-least-in-name-11551795370.

Whalen, Jeanne. "To Counter China, Some Republicans Are Abandoning Free-Market Orthodoxy." *Washington Post,* August 26, 2020. https://www.washingtonpost.com/business/2020/08/26/republicans-favor-industrial-policy.

Wong, Edward. "Chinese Security Laws Elevate the Party and Stifle Dissent. Mao Would Approve." *New York Times,* May 29, 2015. https://www.nytimes.com/2015/05/30/world/asia/chinese-national-security-law-aims-to-defend-party-grip-on-power.html.

Wong, Natalie, Sum Lok-kei, and Ng Kang-chung. "Hong Kong Protesters Have Been Receiving Training From Foreign Forces, City's Security Chief Says." *South China Morning Post,* January 8, 2020. https://www.scmp.com/news/hong-kong/politics/article/3045255/hong-kong-protesters-have-been-receiving-training-foreign.

Wu, Wendy, and Choi Chi-yuk. "Coup Plotters Foiled: Xi Jinping Fended Off Threat to 'Save Communist Party.'" *South China Morning Post,* October 19, 2017. https://www.scmp.com/news/china/policies-politics/article/2116176/coup-plotters-foiled-xi-jinping-fended-threat-save.

Zhao, Lei. "PLA Says Chief of Its Arms Wing Replaced." *China Daily*, September 19, 2017. https://www.chinadaily.com.cn/china/2017-09/19/content_32187194.htm.

Zheng, William. "China's Aircraft Carrier Troubles Continue with More Researchers Charged with Corruption." *South China Morning Post*, December 28, 2018. https://www.scmp.com/news/china/military/article/2179855/chinas-aircraft-carrier-troubles-continue-more-researchers.

Zhong, Raymond. "Chinese Tech Giant on Brink of Collapse in New U.S. Cold War." *New York Times*, May 9, 2018. https://www.nytimes.com/2018/05/09/technology/zte-china-us-trade-war.html?action=click&module=RelatedCoverage&pgtype=Article&region=Footer.

Zhou, Laura. "China Almost Doubles Weapons Exports over Past Five Years, with Pakistan Biggest Buyer: Think Tank." *South China Morning Post*, February 22, 2016. http://www.scmp.com/news/china/diplomacy-defence/article/1915140/china-almost-doubles-weapons-exports-over-past-five.

ENGLISH-LANGUAGE JOURNAL ARTICLES AND BOOKS

2016 State of the American Aerospace and Defense Industry. Washington, DC: Aerospace Industries Association, December 2016. https://www.aia-aerospace.org/report/the-strength-to-lift-america-the-state-of-the-u-s-aerospace-defense-industry-2016/.

2018 State of the American Aerospace and Defense Industry. Washington, DC: Aerospace Industries Association, July 2018. https://www.aia-aerospace.org/report/2018-facts-figures/.

2020 State of the American Aerospace and Defense Industry. Washington, DC: Aerospace Industries Association, September 2020. https://www.aia-aerospace.org/wp-content/uploads/2020/09/2020-Facts-and-Figures-U.S.-Aerospace-and-Defense.pdf.

Amsden, Alice. *The Rise of the Rest: Challenges to the West from Late-Industrializing Economies*. Oxford: Oxford University Press, 2003.

Barabanov, Mikhail, Vasiliy Kashin, and Konstantin Makienko. *Shooting Star: China's Military Machine in the 21st Century*. Minneapolis: East View Press, 2012.

Baranovitch, Nimrod. "A Strong Leader for a Time of Crisis: Xi Jinping's Strongman Politics as a Collective Response to Regime Weakness." *Journal of Contemporary China* 30, no. 128 (2021): 249–65.

Best, Michael. *The New Competitive Advantage*. New York: Oxford University Press, 2001.

Black, Jeremy. *War and Technology*. Bloomington: Indiana University Press, 2013.

Block, Fred. "Innovation and the Invisible Hand of Government." In *State of Innovation: The U.S. Government's Role in Technology Development*, edited by Fred Block and Matthew Keller, 1–26. New York: Paradigm, 2011.

Block, Fred, and Matthew Keller, eds. *State of Innovation: The U.S. Government's Role in Technology Development*. New York: Paradigm, 2011.

Brooks, Stephen. *Producing Security: Multinational Corporations, Globalization, and the Changing Calculus of Conflict*. Princeton, NJ: Princeton University Press, 2011.

Brooks, Stephen G., and William C. Wohlforth. *America Abroad: Why the Sole Superpower Should Not Pull Back from the World*. Oxford: Oxford University Press, 2018.

——. "The Rise and Fall of the Great Powers in the Twenty-First Century: China's Rise and the Fate of America's Global Position." *International Security* 40, no. 3 (2015/16): 7–53.

Bush, Vannevar. *Modern Arms and Free Men: A Discussion of the Role of Science in Preserving Democracy*. New York: Simon & Schuster, 1949.

Buzan, Barry. *The United States and the Great Powers*. Cambridge, UK: Polity Press, 2004.

Buzan, Barry, Ole Waever, and Jaap de Wilde. *Security: A New Framework for Analysis.* Boulder, CO: Lynne Rienner, 1998.

Cao, Cong, Jeroen Baas, Caroline S Wagner, and Koen Jonkers. "Returning Scientists and the Emergence of China's Science System." *Science and Public Policy* 47, no. 2 (2020): 172–83.

Castles, Francis, Stephan Leibfried, Jane Lewis, Herbert Obinger, and Christopher Pierson, eds. *The Oxford Handbook of the Welfare State.* Oxford: Oxford University Press, 2010.

Chase, Michael, Jeffrey Engstrom, Tai Ming Cheung, Kristen Gunness, Scott W. Harold, Susan Puska, and Samuel K. Berkowitz. *China's Incomplete Military Transformation.* Washington, DC: RAND, October 2014.

Chase, Michael S. "The Space and Cyberspace Components of the Belt and Road Initiative." In *Securing the Belt and Road Initiative: China's Evolving Military Engagement along the Silk Roads,* edited by Nadège Rolland. Seattle: National Bureau of Asian Research Special Report no. 80, September 2019. https://www.nbr.org/wp-content/uploads/pdfs/publications/sr80_securing_the_belt_and_road_sep2019.pdf.

Cheung, Tai Ming. "A Conceptual Framework of Defense Innovation." *Journal of Strategic Studies* 44, no. 6 (2021): 775–801.

——. "China's Buying Spree." *Far Eastern Economic Review,* July 8, 1993.

——. "Does the People's Republic of China Have the Industrial, Technological, Economic and Infrastructure Capacity to Wage and Sustain a Successful Military Campaign to Subdue Taiwan?" In *If China Attacks Taiwan,* edited by Steve Tsang, 159–76. London: Routledge, 2006.

——. "Economics, Security and Technology in Northeast Asia: Maneuvering between Nationalist and Globalist Forces." In *The Economy-Security Nexus in Northeast Asia,* edited by T. J. Pempel, 65–88. Abingdon, UK: Routledge, 2013.

——. *Fortifying China.* Ithaca, NY: Cornell University Press, 2013.

——. "Guarding China's Domestic Front Line: The People's Armed Police and China's Stability." *China Quarterly,* no. 146 (1996): 525–47.

——. "The Emergence of Direct US-China Defense Technological Competition." In *The Gathering Pacific Storm,* edited by Tai Ming Cheung and Thomas G. Mahnken, 1–13. Amherst, NY: Cambria, 2018.

——. "Ties of Convenience: Sino-Russian Military Relations in the 1990s." In *China's Military: The PLA in 1992/1993,* edited by Richard H. Yang and Chinese Council of Advanced Policy Studies, Taipei. Boulder, CO: Westview, 1993.

Cheung, Tai Ming, Thomas Mahnken, Deborah Seligsohn, Kevin Pollpeter, Eric Anderson, and Fan Yang. *Planning for Innovation: Understanding China's Plans for Technological, Energy, Industrial, and Defense Development.* Washington, DC: US-China Economic and Security Review Commission, 2016.

China Strategy Group. *Asymmetric Competition: A Strategy for China and Technology.* 2020. https://assets.documentcloud.org/documents/20463382/final-memo-china-strategy-group-axios-1.pdf.

Costello, John, and Joe McReynolds, "China's Strategic Support Force: A Force for a New Era." In *Chairman Xi Remakes the PLA: Assessing Chinese Military Reforms,* edited by Philip C. Saunders, Arthur S. Ding, Andrew Scobell, Andrew N. D. Yang, and Joel Wuthnow, 437–515. Washington, DC: National Defense University Press, 2019.

Cozad, Mark. "Toward a More Joint, Combat-Ready PLA." In *Chairman Xi Remakes the PLA: Assessing Chinese Military Reforms,* edited by Philip C. Saunders, Arthur S. Ding, Andrew Scobell, Andrew N. D. Yang, and Joel Wuthnow, 203–26. Washington, DC: National Defense University Press, 2019.

Delury, John, and Orville Schell. *Wealth and Power: China's Long March to the Twenty-First Century*. New York: Random House, 2013.

Deng, Yong. "The Chinese Conception of National Interests in International Relations." *China Quarterly* 154 (1998): 308–29.

Department of Defense Emerging Technology Strategy: A Venture Capital Perspective. Silicon Valley: Silicon Valley Defense Working Group, April 2019. https://static1 .squarespace.com/static/5f82250a85dd3125aeba053d/t/5fb279560e8bbf646f9357e8 /1605532000435/DOD+Emerging+Tech+Strategy+from+a+VC+Perspective+SVD WG.pdf.

De Prato, Giuditta, and Daniel Nepelski. *International Technology Transfer between China and the Rest of the World*. Seville: European Commission Joint Research Centre Institute for Prospective Technological Studies, 2013.

DeVine, Michael. *Intelligence Community Spending: Trends and Issues*. Washington, DC: Congressional Research Service, 2019. https://fas.org/sgp/crs/intel/R44381.pdf.

Dickson, Bruce J. *The Dictator's Dilemma: The Chinese Communist Party's Strategy for Survival*. New York: Oxford University Press, 2016.

Economy, Elizabeth C. *The Third Revolution: Xi Jinping and the New Chinese State*. New York: Oxford University Press, 2018.

Elder, Jakob, and Jan Fagerberg. "Innovation Policy: What, Why, and How." *Oxford Review of Economic Policy* 33, no. 1 (2017): 2–23.

Evans, Peter. *Embedded Autonomy: States and Industrial Transformation*. Princeton, NJ: Princeton University Press, 1995.

Fagerberg, Jan, and Bart Verspagen. "Innovation Studies: The Emerging Structure of a New Scientific Field." *Research Policy* 38, no. 2 (2009): 218–33.

Faligot, Roger. *Chinese Spies: From Chairman Mao to Xi Jinping*. London: Hurst, 2019.

Falkenheim, Jaqui, and Josh Trapani. *Trends in Graduate Education*. Presentation to the Council of Graduate Schools, February 26, 2020. https://cgsnet.org/ckfinder /userfiles/files/2_26_2020%20Trends%20in%20Graduate%20Education%20We-binar_Final.pdf.

Faulk, Ginger, and Jeffrey Bialos. "Unpacking U.S.-China Sanctions and Export Control Regulations: The U.S. 'Entity List.'" *Global Trade Magazine*, November 24, 2020. https://www.globaltrademag.com/unpacking-us-china-sanctions-and-export -control-regulations-the-us-entity-list/.

Feigenbaum, Evan. *China's Techno-Warriors: National Security and Strategic Competition from the Nuclear to the Information Age*. Stanford, CA: Stanford University Press, 2003.

Finkelstein, David M. "China's National Military Strategy: An Overview of the 'Military Strategic Guidelines.'" In *Right Sizing the People's Liberation Army: Exploring the Contours of China's Military*, edited by Roy Kamphausen and Andrew Scobell, 69–141. Carlisle, PA: Army War College, 2007.

Firth, Noel, and James Noren. *Soviet Defense Spending: A History of CIA Estimates, 1950–1990*. College Station: Texas A&M University Press, 1998.

Fravel, Taylor M. *Active Defense: China's Military Strategy Since 1949*. Princeton, NJ: Princeton University Press, 2019.

Friedberg, Aaron L. *In the Shadow of the Garrison State: America's Anti-statism and Its Cold War Grand Strategy*. Princeton, NJ: Princeton University Press, 2000.

Fritz, Audrey, and Scott Kennedy. "China's Military-Civil Fusion Funds: Big but Not Necessarily Effective." *Center for Strategic and International Studies*, October 4, 2019. https://www.csis.org/blogs/trustee-china-hand/chinas-military-civil-fusion -funds-big-not-necessarily-effective.

Geddes, Barbara, Joseph Wright, and Erica Frantz. *How Dictatorships Work: Power, Personalization, and Collapse.* Cambridge: Cambridge University Press, 2018.

Ghiselli, Andrea. "Diplomatic Opportunities and Rising Threats: The Expanding Role of Non-traditional Security in Chinese Foreign and Security Policy." *Journal of Contemporary China* 27, no. 112 (2018): 611–25.

Gholz, Eugene, and Harvey M. Sapolsky. "The Defense Innovation Machine: Why the US Will Remain on the Cutting Edge." *Journal of Strategic Studies* 44, no. 6 (2021): 854–72.

Glaser, Charles, and Chaim Kaufmann. "What Is the Offense-Defense Balance and Can We Measure It?" *International Security* 22, no. 4 (1998): 44–82.

Gong, Yifei, Peiyue Li, and Ziqiao Shen. "Research on Operating Efficiency of Government Industry Guidance Funds." *Theoretical Economics Letters* 10, no. 1 (2020): 90–101.

Green, Michael J. *Arming Japan.* New York: Columbia University Press, 1995.

Greenberg, Karen, ed. *Reimagining the National Security State: Liberalism on the Brink.* Cambridge: Cambridge University Press, 2019.

Greenwalt, William. *Leveraging the National Technology Industrial Base to Address Great-Power Competition: The Imperative to Integrate Industrial Capabilities of Close Allies.* Washington, DC: Atlantic Council Scowcroft Center for Strategy and Security, April 2019. https://www.atlanticcouncil.org/wp-content/uploads/2019/04/Leveraging_the_National_Technology_Industrial_Base_to_Address_Great-Power_Competition.pdf.

Greitens, Sheena Chestnut. *Dictators and Their Secret Police: Coercive Institutions and State Violence.* Cambridge: Cambridge University Press, 2016.

——. "Rethinking China's Coercive Capacity: An Examination of PRC Domestic Security Spending, 1992–2012." *China Quarterly* 232 (2017): 1002–25.

Gu, Shulin. *China's Industrial Technology: Market Reform and Organisational Change.* London: Routledge, 1999.

Gudger, Andre. "Modernizing Our Industrial Base: The National Security Challenge of Our Time." *Defense AT&L*, July–August 2015. https://www.dau.edu/library/defense-atl/DATLFiles/Jul-Aug2015/Gudger.pdf.

Guo, Xuezhi. *China's Security State: Philosophy, Evolution, and Politics.* Cambridge: Cambridge University Press, 2012.

——. "Controlling Corruption in the Party: China's Central Discipline Inspection Commission." *China Quarterly* 219 (2014): 597–624.

Haggard, Stephan. *Developmental States.* Cambridge: Cambridge University Press, 2018.

Haggard, Stephan, and Tai Ming Cheung. "North Korea's Nuclear and Missile Programs: Foreign Absorption and Domestic Innovation." *Journal of Strategic Studies* 44, no. 6 (2021): 802–29.

Hagt, Eric. "China's Civil-Military Integration: National Strategy, Local Politics." PhD diss., Johns Hopkins School of Advanced International Studies, 2019.

——. "The Science and Technology Committee: PLA-Industry Relations and Implications for Defense Innovation." In *Forging China's Military Might: A New Framework for Assessing Innovation*, edited by Tai Ming Cheung, 66–86. Baltimore: Johns Hopkins University Press, 2014.

Hannas, William C., James Mulvenon, and Anna B. Puglisi. *Chinese Industrial Espionage: Technology Acquisition and Military Modernization.* London: Routledge, 2013.

Hao, Xin, and Gong Yidong. "China Bets Big on Big Science." *Science* 311, no. 5767 (2006): 1548–49.

Henderson, Rebecca, and Kim Clark. "Architectural Innovation: The Reconfiguration of Existing Product Technologies and the Failure of Established Firms." *Administrative Science Quarterly* 35, no.1 (1990): 9–30.

Herspring, Dale R. "Harry S. Truman and the American Military." In *Origins of the National Security State and the Legacy of Harry S. Truman*, edited by Mary Ann Heiss and Michael J. Hogan, 39–67. Kirksville, MO: Truman State University Press, 2014.

Hogan, Michael J. *A Cross of Iron: Harry S. Truman and the Origins of the National Security State, 1945–1954*. Cambridge: Cambridge University Press, 1998.

Holz, Carsten. "Industrial Policies and the Changing Patterns of Investment in the Chinese Economy." *China Journal* 81 (2019): 23–57.

Hu, Albert G. Z., Gary H. Jefferson, and Qian Jinchang. "R&D and Technology Transfer: Firm-Level Evidence from Chinese Industry." *The Review of Economics and Statistics* 87, no. 4 (2005): 780–86.

Hu, Angang, Yan Yilong, and Tang Xiao. *Xi Jinping's New Development Philosophy*. Singapore: Springer, 2018.

Hughes, Jeff. *The Manhattan Project: Big Science and the Atom Bomb*. New York: Columbia University Press, 2002.

Huotari, Mikko, Jan Gaspers, Thomas Eder, Helena Legarda, and Sabine Mokry. *China's Emergence as a Global Security Actor: Strategies for Europe*. Berlin: Mercator Institute for China Studies, July 2017.

Iansiti, Marco. *Technology Integration: Making Critical Choices in a Dynamic World*. Cambridge, MA: Harvard Business School Press, 1998.

Ikenberry, G. John. "Rethinking the Origins of American Hegemony." *Political Science Quarterly* 104, no. 3 (1989): 375–400.

"Is China at the Forefront of Drone Technology?" *CSIS ChinaPower Project*, March 20, 2020. https://chinapower.csis.org/china-drones-unmanned-technology/#easy-footnote-bottom-2-3704.

Jackson, Aaron P. *The Four Aspects of Joint: A Model for Comparatively Evaluating the Extent of Jointness within Armed Forces*, Joint Studies Paper Series no. 2. Canberra: Defence Publishing Service, 2018. https://www.defence.gov.au/ADC/publications/documents/joint_studies/JSPS_2_The_Four_Aspects_Of_Joint.pdf.

Jervis, Robert. "Cooperation under the Security Dilemma." *World Politics* 30, no. 2 (1978): 167–214.

Jessop, Bob. *The State: Past, Present, and Future*. Cambridge, UK: Polity, 2016.

Ji, You. "China's National Security Commission: Theory, Evolution and Operations." *Journal of Contemporary China* 25, no. 98 (2016): 178–96.

Johnson, Chalmers. *MITI and the Japanese Miracle: The Growth of Industrial Policy, 1925–1975*. Stanford, CA: Stanford University Press, 1982.

Johnston, Alastair Iain. "The Evolution of Interstate Security Crisis: Management Theory and Practice in China." *Naval War College Review* 69, no. 1 (2016): 29–71.

Joske, Alex. *The China Defence Universities Tracker: Exploring the Military and Security Links of China's Universities*. Canberra: Australian Strategic Policy Institute, 2019.

Kania, Elsa. "Chinese Military Innovation in Artificial Intelligence." Testimony to US-China Economic and Security Review Commission, June 7, 2019. https://www.uscc.gov/sites/default/files/June%207%20Hearing_Panel%201_Elsa%20Kania_Chinese%20Military%20Innovation%20in%20Artificial%20Intelligence.pdf.

Kania, Elsa B., and John K. Costello. "The Strategic Support Force and the Future of Chinese Information Operations." *The Cyber Defense Review* 3, no. 1 (2018): 105–21.

Kaspersen, Lars Bo, and Jeppe Strandsbjerg, eds. *Does War Make States? Investigations of Charles Tilly's Historical Sociology*. Cambridge: Cambridge University Press, 2017.

Kiselycznyk, Michael, and Phillip C. Saunders. *Civil-Military Relations in China: Assessing the PLA's Role in Elite Politics*. Washington, DC: National Defense University Press, 2010.

Lam, Willy Wo-Lap. "Xi Jinping Warns against the 'Black Swans' and 'Gray Rhinos' of a Possible Color Revolution." *China Brief*, February 20, 2019. https://jamestown.org/program/china-brief-early-warning-xi-jinping-warns-against-the-black-swans-and-gray-rhinos-of-a-possible-color-revolution/.

Lampton, David, ed. *Policy Implementation in Post-Mao China*. Berkeley: University of California Press, 1987.

Lampton, David M. "Xi Jinping and the National Security Commission: Policy Coordination and Political Power." *Journal of Contemporary China* 24, no. 95 (2015): 759–77.

Lardy, Nicholas R. *The State Strikes Back: The End of Economic Reform in China*. Washington, DC: Peterson Institute for International Economics, January 2019.

Lasswell, Harold D. "The Garrison State." *American Journal of Sociology* 46, no. 4 (1941): 455–68.

——, ed. *Essays on the Garrison State*. New York: Routledge, 2018.

Leslie, Stuart. *The Cold War and American Science: The Military-Industrial-Academic Complex at MIT and Stanford*. New York: Columbia University Press, 1993.

Lewis, John Wilson, and Xue Litai. *China Builds the Bomb*. Stanford, CA: Stanford University Press, 1988.

Li, Cheng. "Bringing China's Best and Brightest Back Home: Regional Disparities and Political Tensions." *China Leadership Monitor* 11 (2004). https://www.hoover.org/sites/default/files/uploads/documents/clm11_lc.pdf.

——. "Xi Jinping's Inner Circle, Part 1: The Shaanxi Gang." *China Leadership Monitor* 43 (2014).

——. "Xi Jinping's Inner Circle, Part 2: Friends from Xi's Formative Years." *China Leadership Monitor* 44 (2014).

——. "Xi Jinping's Inner Circle, Part 3: Political Protégés from the Provinces." *China Leadership Monitor* 45 (2014).

——. "Xi Jinping's Inner Circle, Part 4: The Mishu Cluster, Part I." *China Leadership Monitor* 46 (2015).

——. "Xi Jinping's Inner Circle, Part 5: The Mishu Cluster, Part II." *China Leadership Monitor* 47 (2015).

Li, Li, and Peng Wang. "From Institutional Interaction to Institutional Integration: The National Supervisory Commission and China's New Anti-Corruption Model." *China Quarterly* 240 (2019): 967–89.

Li, Ling. "Politics of Anticorruption in China: Paradigm Change of the Party's Disciplinary Regime, 2012–2017." *Journal of Contemporary China* 28, no. 115 (2019): 47–63.

——. "The Chinese Communist Party and People's Courts: Judicial Dependence in China." *American Journal of Comparative Law* 64, no. 1 (2016): 37–74.

——. "The Rise of the Discipline and Inspection Commission, 1927–2012: Anticorruption Investigation and Decision-Making in the Chinese Communist Party." *Modern China* 42, no. 5 (2016): 447–82.

Li, Xiaoting. "Cronyism and Military Corruption in the Post-Deng Xiaoping Era: Rethinking the Party-Commands-the-Gun Model." *Journal of Contemporary China* 26, no. 107 (2017): 696–710.

Lieberthal, Kenneth, and David Lampton, eds. *Bureaucracy, Politics, and Decision Making in Post-Mao China*. Berkeley: University of California Press, 1992.

Lieberthal, Kenneth, and Michel Oksenberg. *Policy Making in China: Leaders, Structures, and Processes*. Princeton, NJ: Princeton University Press, 1988.

Liff, Adam P., and Andrew S. Erickson. "Demystifying China's Defence Spending: Less Mysterious in the Aggregate." *China Quarterly* 216 (2013): 805–30.

Liu, Mingfu, and Wang Zhongyuan. *The Thoughts of Xi Jinping*. Salt Lake City, UT: American Academic Press, 2017.

Luce, LeighAnn, and Erin Richter. "Handling Logistics in a Reformed PLA." In *Chairman Xi Remakes the PLA: Assessing Chinese Military Reforms*, edited by Phillip C. Saunders, Arthur S. Ding, Andrew Scobell, Andrew N. D. Yang, and Joel Wuthnow, 257–292. Washington, DC: National Defense University, 2019.

Luong, Ngor, Zachary Arnold, and Ben Murphy. *Understanding Chinese Government Guidance Funds*. Washington, DC: Center for Security and Emerging Technology, 2021. https://cset.georgetown.edu/publication/understanding-chinese-government-guidance-funds/.

Mack, Pamela Etter. *From Engineering Science to Big Science: The NACA and NASA Collier Trophy Research Project Winners*. Washington, DC: National Aeronautics and Space Administration, NASA Office of Policy and Plans, NASA History Office, 1998.

Making Sense of the $1.25 Trillion National Security State Budget. Center for Defense Information, Project for Government Oversight, May 7, 2019. https://www.pogo.org/analysis/2019/05/making-sense-of-the-1-25-trillion-national-security-state-budget/.

Marshall, A. W. *Long-Term Competition with the Soviets: A Framework for Strategic Analysis*. Washington, DC: RAND, 1972. https://www.rand.org/pubs/reports/R862.html.

Martinage, Robert. *Toward a New Offset Strategy: Exploiting U.S. Long-Term Advantages to Restore U.S. Global Power Projection Capability*. Washington, DC: Center for Strategic and Budgetary Assessments, 2014. https://csbaonline.org/uploads/documents/Offset-Strategy-Web.pdf.

Mattis, Peter, and Matthew Brazil. *Chinese Communist Espionage: An Intelligence Primer*. Annapolis, MD: Naval Institute Press, 2019.

Mazzucato, Mariana. *The Entrepreneurial State*. New York: Public Affairs, 2015.

McCauley, Kevin. "Modernization of PLA Logistics: Joint Logistic Support Force." *US-China Economic and Security Review Commission Testimony*, February 15, 2018.

McCormick, Rhys, Samantha Cohen, Andrew Hunter, and Gregory Sanders. *National Technology and Industrial Base Integration: How to Overcome Barriers and Capitalize on Cooperation*. Washington, DC: Center for Strategic and International Studies, 2018. https://csis-website-prod.s3.amazonaws.com/s3fs-public/publication/180307_McCormick_NationalTechnologyAndIndustrialBaseIntegration_Web.pdf.

McFaul, Michael. "Cold War Lessons and Fallacies for U.S.-China Relations Today." *Washington Quarterly* 43, no. 4 (2021): 7–39.

McGregor, Richard. "Party Man: Xi Jinping's Quest to Dominate China." *Foreign Affairs* 98, no. 5 (2019): 18–25. https://www.foreignaffairs.com/articles/china/2019-08-14/party-man.

Millett, Allan R., Williamson Murray, and Kenneth H. Watman. "The Effectiveness of Military Organizations." *International Security* 11, no. 1 (1986): 37–71.

Minzner, Carl F. "China's Turn against Law." *American Journal of Comparative Law* 59, no. 4 (2011): 935–84.

Mu, Rongping. "Innovation-Driven Development in China: Strategy, Policy, and Practices." *Research Institute of Economy, Trade, and Industry*, April 12, 2013. https://www.rieti.go.jp/en/events/bbl/13041201.html.

Mulvenon, James. "China: Conditional Compliance." In *Coercion and Governance: The Declining Political Role of the Military in Asia*, edited by Muthiah Alagappa, 317–335. Palo Alto, CA: Stanford University Press, 2001.

Murray, Craig, Andrew Berglund, and Kimberly Hsu. *China's Naval Modernization and Implications for the United States*. Washington, DC: US-China Economic and Security Review Commission, 2013.

National Science Board. *Research and Development: U.S. Trends and International Comparisons (Science and Engineering Indicators 2020)*. Arlington, VA: National Science Foundation, January 2020. https://ncses.nsf.gov/pubs/nsb20203/.

——. *Science and Engineering Indicators 2014*. Arlington, VA: National Science Foundation, February 2014. https://www.nsf.gov/statistics/seind14/.

——. *Science and Engineering Indicators 2020: Higher Education in Science and Engineering*. Arlington, VA: National Science Foundation, September 4, 2019. https://ncses.nsf.gov/pubs/nsb20197/.

Naughton, Barry. "Grand Steerage." In *Fateful Decisions: Choices That Will Shape China's Future*, edited by Thomas Fingar and Jean C. Oi, 51–81. Stanford, CA: Stanford University Press, 2020.

——. *The Rise of China's Industrial Policy, 1978–2020*. Mexico City: Universidad Nacional Autónoma de México, 2021.

Nelson, Richard, ed. *National Innovation Systems: A Comparative Perspective*. Oxford: Oxford University Press, 1993.

Nexon, Daniel. *The Struggle for Power in Early Modern Europe*. Princeton, NJ: Princeton University Press, 2009.

"Nuclear Power in China." *World Nuclear Association*, July 2020. https://www.world-nuclear.org/information-library/country-profiles/countries-a-f/china-nuclear-power.aspx.

O'Hanlon, Michael. *The National Security Industrial Base: A Crucial Asset of the United States, Whose Future May Be in Jeopardy*. Washington, DC: Brookings Institution, February 2011. https://www.brookings.edu/research/the-national-security-industrial-base-a-crucial-asset-of-the-united-states-whose-future-may-be-in-jeopardy/.

O'Rourke, Ronald. *China Naval Modernization: Implications for U.S. Navy Capabilities—Background and Issues for Congress*. Washington, DC: Congressional Research Service, March 2021.

Pei, Minxin. "China's Fateful Inward Turn: Beijing's New Economic Strategy as Spelled Out by the Resolution of the CCP Central Committee's 5th Plenum." *China Leadership Monitor* 66 (2020). https://www.prcleader.org/pei-3.

Posen, Barry. *The Sources of Military Doctrine*. Ithaca, NY: Cornell University Press, 1984.

Ramachandran, Seetha, and David Heck. "Chinese Military Companies Trading Ban: Overview of OFAC's Ongoing Guidance." *National Law Review* 11, no. 108 (2021). https://www.natlawreview.com/article/chinese-military-companies-trading-ban-overview-ofac-s-ongoing-guidance.

Report of the Task Force on 21st-Century National Security Technology and Workforce. *The Contest for Innovation: Strengthening America's National Security Innovation Base in an Era of Strategic Competition*. Simi Valley, CA: Ronald Reagan Institute, December 2019. https://www.reaganfoundation.org/media/355297/the_contest_for_innovation_report.pdf.

Ringen, Stein. *The Perfect Dictatorship: China in the 21st Century*. Hong Kong: Hong Kong University Press, 2016.

Rosecrance, Richard N. *The Rise of the Trading State: Commerce and Conquest in the Modern World*. New York: Basic Books, 1986.

Samuels, Richard. *Japan as a Technological Superpower*. JPRI Working Paper no. 15. Oakland, CA: Japan Policy Research Institute, January 1996. http://www.jpri.org/publications/workingpapers/wp15.html.

——. *Rich Nation, Strong Army*. Ithaca, NY: Cornell University Press, 1994.

——. *The Business of the Japanese State*. Ithaca, NY: Cornell University Press, 1987.

Sargent, John F. Jr., Marcy E. Gallo, and Moshe Schwartz. *The Global Research and Development Landscape and Implications for the Department of Defense*. Washington, DC: Congressional Research Service, November 2018. https://fas.org/sgp/crs/natsec/R45403.pdf.

Saunders, Phillip C., Arthur S. Ding, Andrew Scobell, Andrew N. D. Yang, and Joel Wuthnow, eds. *Chairman Xi Remakes the PLA: Assessing Chinese Military Reforms*. Washington, DC: National Defense University, 2019.

Schumpeter, Josef. *The Theory of Economic Development*. Cambridge, MA: Harvard University Press, 1934.

Schwarck, Edward. "Intelligence and Informatization: The Rise of the Ministry of Public Security in Intelligence Work in China." *China Journal* 80 (2018): 1–23.

Schwartz, Moshe. *Defense Acquisition Reform: Background, Analysis, and Issues for Congress*. Washington, DC: Congressional Research Service, May 23, 2014. https://fas.org/sgp/crs/natsec/R43566.pdf.

Segal, Adam. "Seizing Core Technologies: China Responds to U.S. Technology Competition." *China Leadership Monitor* 60 (2019). https://www.prcleader.org/segal-clm-60.

Shen, Zhihua, and Yafeng Xia. *Between Aid and Restriction: Changing Soviet Policies toward China's Nuclear Weapons Program, 1954–1960*. Washington, DC: Woodrow Wilson Center, May 2012.

Shirk, Susan L. "China in Xi's 'New Era': The Return to Personalistic Rule." *Journal of Democracy* 29, no. 2 (2018): 22–36.

——. *Fragile Superpower*. Oxford: Oxford University Press, 2008.

Snider, Don M. "Jointness, Defense Transformation, and the Need for a New Joint Warfare Profession." *Parameters* 33, no. 3 (Autumn 2003): 17–30.

Stone, Alex, and Peter Wood. *China's Military-Civil Fusion Strategy*. Washington, DC: US Air Force China Aerospace Studies Institute, June 2020.

Stuart, Douglas. "Preparing for the Next Pearl Harbor: Harry S. Truman's Role in the Creation of the U.S. National Security Establishment." In *Origins of the National Security State and the Legacy of Harry S. Truman*, edited by Mary Ann Heiss and Michael J. Hogan, 17–38. Kirksville, MO: Truman State University Press, 2015.

Stuart, Douglas T. *Creating the National Security State: A History of the Law That Transformed America*. Princeton, NJ: Princeton University Press, 2012.

Sun, Yun. *Chinese National Security Decision-Making: Processes and Challenges*. Washington, DC: Brookings Institution, May 2013.

Sun, Yutao, and Cong Cao. "Demystifying Central Government R&D Spending in China." *Science* 345, no. 6200 (2014): 1006–8.

Tabrizi, Aniseh Bassiri, and Justin Bronk. *Armed Drones in the Middle East Proliferation and Norms in the Region*. London: Royal United Services Institute, December 2018. https://rusi.org/sites/default/files/20181207_armed_drones_middle_east_web.pdf.

Tang, Shiping. "From Offensive to Defensive Realism: A Social Evolutionary Interpretation of China's Security Strategy." In *China's Ascent: Power, Security, and the Future of International Politics*, edited by Robert Ross and Zhu Feng, 141–162. Ithaca, NY: Cornell University Press, 2015.

Taylor, Mark Z. "Toward an International Relations Theory of National Innovation Rates." *Security Studies* 21, no. 1 (2012): 113–52.

"The Trend in International Transfers of Major Arms, 1980–2019." Stockholm International Peace Research Institute, March 2020. http://www.sipri.org/research/armaments/transfers/measuring/recent-trends-in-arms-transfers.

Tian, Nan, and Fei Su. *Estimating the Arms Sales of Chinese Companies*. SIPRI Insights on Peace and Security, no. 2020/2. Stockholm: SIPRI, January 2020. https://www.sipri.org/sites/default/files/2020-01/sipriinsight2002_1.pdf.

Tiffert, Glenn, ed. *Global Engagement: Rethinking Risk in the Research Enterprise*. Palo Alto, CA: Hoover Institution Press, July 2020.

Tilly, Charles. *The Formation of National States in Western Europe*. Princeton, NJ: Princeton University Press, 1975.

Unger, David C. "The Politics and Political Legacy of Harry S. Truman's National Security Policies." In *Origins of the National Security State and the Legacy of Harry S. Truman*, edited by Mary Ann Heiss and Michael J. Hogan, 165–88. Kirksville, MO: Truman State University Press, 2014.

"US Commerce Department Issues 'Military End User' List." White & Case, January 7, 2021. https://www.whitecase.com/publications/alert/us-commerce-department-issues-military-end-user-list.

Van Reenen, John, and Linda Yueh. "Why Has China Grown So Fast? The Role of International Technology Transfer." Oxford: Oxford University Discussion Paper Series, 2012.

Waltz, Kenneth. *Theory of International Relations*. Reading, MA: Addison-Wesley, 1979.

Wang, Yuhua. "Empowering the Police: How the Chinese Communist Party Manages Its Coercive Leaders." *China Quarterly* 219 (2014): 625–48.

Wang, Yuhua, and Carl Minzner. "The Rise of the Chinese Security State." *China Quarterly* 222 (2015): 339–59.

Wang, Zuoyue. "The Chinese Developmental State during the Cold War: The Making of the 1956 Twelve-Year Science and Technology Plan." *History and Technology* 31, no. 3 (2015): 180–205.

Weiss, Linda. *America Inc.? Innovation and Enterprise in the National Security State*. Ithaca, NY: Cornell University Press, 2014.

Wezeman, Pieter, Aude Fleurant, Alexandra Kuimova, Nan Tian, and Siemon T. Wezeman. "Trends in International Arms Transfers, 2018." Stockholm International Peace Research Institute, March 2018. https://www.sipri.org/sites/default/files/2019-03/fs_1903_at_2018.pdf.

Whiting, Allen S. "China's Use of Force, 1950–56, and Taiwan." *International Security* 26, no. 2 (2001): 103–31.

Woo-Cummings, Meredith. "Back to Basics: Ideology, Nationalism, and Asian Values in East Asia." In *Economic Nationalism in a Globalizing World*, edited by Eric Helleiner and Andreas Pickel, 91–117. Ithaca, NY: Cornell University Press, 2005.

Wood, Peter, Alden Wahlstrom, and Roger Cliff. *China's Aeroengine Industry*. Beijing: China Aerospace Studies Institute, March 2020.

Work, Bob. "Deputy U.S. Defense Secretary Bob Work on the Third Offset Strategy at the Reagan Defense Forum." Speech delivered at Reagan Presidential Library, Simi Valley, CA, November 7, 2015. http://www.defense.gov/News/Speeches/Speech-View/Article/628246/reagan-defense-forum-the-third-offset-strategy.

Wubbeke, Jost, Mirjam Meissner, Max J. Zenglein, Jaqueline Ives, and Björn Conrad. *Made in China 2025: The Making of a High-Tech Superpower and Consequences for Industrial Countries*. Berlin: Mercator Institute for China Studies, December 2016.

Wuthnow, Joel. "China's 'New' Academy of Military Science: A Revolution in Theoretical Affairs?" *China Brief* 19, no. 2 (January 18, 2019). https://jamestown.org/program/chinas-new-academy-of-military-science-a-revolution-in-theoretical-affairs/.

——. "China's New 'Black Box': Problems and Prospects for the Central National Security Commission." *China Quarterly* 232 (2017): 886–903.

——. *China's Other Army: The People's Armed Police in an Era of Reform*. Washington, DC: Center for the Study of Chinese Military Affairs Institute for National Strategic Studies National Defense University, April 2019.

Xu, Fangqi, and Hideki Muneyoshi. "A Case Study of DJI, the Top Drone Maker in the World." *Kindai Management Review* 5 (2017): 97–104.

Xue, Lan. "A Historical Perspective of China's Innovation System Reform: A Case Study." *Journal of Engineering and Technology Management* 14, no. 1 (1997): 67–81.

Yang, Dali. "China's Troubled Quest for Order: Leadership, Organization and the Contradictions of the Stability Maintenance Regime." *Journal of Contemporary China* 26, no. 103 (2017): 35–53.

Yao, Yunzhu. "The Evolution of Military Doctrine of the Chinese PLA from 1985 to 1995." *Korean Journal of Defense Analysis* 7, no. 2 (1995): 57–80.

Yue, Xie. "Rising Central Spending on Public Security and the Dilemma Facing Grassroots Officials in China," *Journal of Current Chinese Affairs* 42, no. 2 (2013): 79–109.

Zachary, G. Pascal. *Endless Frontier: Vannevar Bush, Engineer of the American Century.* Cambridge, MA: MIT Press, 1999.

Zahra, Shaker, and Gerard George. "Absorptive Capacity: A Review, Reconceptualization, and Extension." *Academy of Management Review* 27, no. 2 (2002): 185–203.

Zenz, Adrian. "China's Domestic Security Spending: An Analysis of Available Data." *China Brief* 18, no. 4 (March 12, 2018).

——. "Xinjiang's Re-education and Securitization Campaign: Evidence from Domestic Security Budgets." *China Brief* 18, no. 17 (November 5, 2018).

Zenz, Adrian, and James Leibold. "Securitizing Xinjiang: Police Recruitment, Informal Policing and Ethnic Minority Co-optation." *China Quarterly* 242 (2019): 324–48.

Zhang, Yanqun. "Productivity in China: Past Success and Future Challenges." *Asia-Pacific Development Journal* 24, no. 1 (2017): 1–21.

Zhi, Qiang, and Margaret Pearson. "China's Hybrid Adaptive Bureaucracy: The Case of the 863 Program for Science and Technology." *Governance, International Journal of Policy, Administration, and Institutions* 30, no. 3 (2017): 407–24.

Zweig, David, and Siqin Kang. *America Challenges China's National Talents Programs.* Washington, DC: Center for Strategic and International Studies, May 2020. https://www.csis.org/analysis/america-challenges-chinas-national-talent -programs.

——. "The Rise and Fall of the Thousand Talents Program, 2008–2019." Paper presented at the 2019 Duke International Forum on "A New Age of Sino-US Higher Education Cooperation," Durham, NC, December 2019.

ENGLISH-LANGUAGE OFFICIAL GOVERNMENT SOURCES

Brown, Michael. "Fresh Options to Reinvigorate Defense Innovation for the World as It Is Now." Forum organized by the Strategic Multilayer Assessment and National Defense University, February 3, 2021.

Bureau of Export Administration. *US Commercial Technology Transfers to People's Republic of China.* Washington, DC: US Department of Commerce, 1999.

Chinese Communist Party Central Committee Editorial Committee for Party Literature. *Selected Works of Deng Xiaoping, 1975–1982.* Beijing: Foreign Languages Press, 1994.

Department of Defense. *Integrated Product and Process Development Handbook.* Washington, DC: Office of the Under Secretary of Defense, Acquisition and Technology, 1998.

Federal Bureau of Investigation. *Chinese Talent Programs.* September 2015. https://info .publicintelligence.net/FBI-ChineseTalentPrograms.pdf.

Interagency Task Force in Fulfillment of Executive Order 13806. *Assessing and Strengthening the Manufacturing and Defense Industrial Base and Supply Chain Resiliency of the United States.* Washington, DC: Office of the Under Secretary of Defense for Acquisition and Sustainment, and Office of the Deputy Assistant Secretary of Defense for Industrial Policy, September 2018.

Office of the Secretary of Defense. *Annual Report to Congress: Military and Security Developments Involving the People's Republic of China 2020.* Washington, DC: Office of the Secretary of Defense, August 2020. https://media.defense.gov/2020/Sep/01/2002488689/-1/-1/1/2020-DOD-CHINA-MILITARY-POWER-REPORT-FINAL.PDF.

Office of the US Secretary of Defense. *Annual Report to Congress: Military and Security Developments Involving the People's Republic of China 2018.* Washington, DC: Office of the US Secretary of Defense, August 2018.

Pompeo, Michael. "Silicon Valley and National Security." Speech to the Commonwealth Club, San Francisco, January 13, 2020. https://www.state.gov/silicon-valley-and-national-security/.

State Council. *Made in China 2025: Realizing the Manufacturing Power Strategy.* Beijing: State Council, May 8, 2015.

State Council Information Office. *China's Military Strategy.* Beijing: State Council Information Office, May 2015.

——. *China's National Defense in 2010.* Beijing: State Council Information Office, March 2011.

——. *China's National Defense in the New Era.* Beijing: State Council Information Office, July 2019.

——. *The Diversified Employment of China's Armed Forces.* Beijing: State Council Information Office, April 2013.

Summary of the 2018 U.S. National Defense Strategy. Washington, DC: US Department of Defense, January 2018. https://dod.defense.gov/Portals/1/Documents/pubs/2018-National-Defense-Strategy-Summary.pdf.

"The Biden Plan to Ensure the Future Is 'Made in All of America' by All of America's Workers." Biden Harris Democrats, July 10, 2020. https://joebiden.com/made-in-america/.

Tongele, Tongele N. "Emerging Technologies." Paper presented at the Bureau of Industry and Security Conference, September 2, 2020. https://www.bis.doc.gov/index.php/documents/2020-virtual-conference/2603-ea-plenary-emerging-technologies/file.

US Chamber of Commerce China Center and Rhodium Group. *Understanding U.S.-China Decoupling: Macro Trends and Industry Impacts.* Washington, DC: US Chamber of Commerce, 2021. https://www.uschamber.com/sites/default/files/024001_us_china_decoupling_report_fin.pdf.

US Department of Commerce, Bureau of Economic Analysis. *National Income and Product Accounts Database.* https://apps.bea.gov/iTable/iTable.cfm?reqid=19&step=2#reqid=19&step=2&isuri=1&1921=survey.

US Government Accounting Office. *Best Practices: DOD Teaming Practices Not Achieving Potential Results.* Washington, DC: GAO, April 2001.

US National Science and Technology Council Committee on Homeland and National Security. *A 21st Century Science, Technology, and Innovation Strategy for America's National Security.* Washington, DC: Executive Office of the President, May 2016. https://obamawhitehouse.archives.gov/sites/default/files/microsites/ostp/NSTC/national_security_s_and_t_strategy.pdf.

US Senate Permanent Subcommittee on Investigations. *Threats to the U.S. Research Enterprise: China's Talent Recruitment Plans.* Washington, DC: US Senate Committee on Homeland Security and Governmental Affairs, November 2019. https://www.hsgac.senate.gov/imo/media/doc/2019-11-18%20PSI%20Staff%20Report%20-%20China%27s%20Talent%20Recruitment%20Plans.pdf.

US State Department. *The PRC's "Military-Civil Fusion" Strategy Is a Global Security Threat.* Washington, DC: US State Department, March 16, 2020. https://2017-2021

.state.gov/the-prcs-military-civil-fusion-strategy-is-a-global-security-threat /index.html.

White House. *Executive Order on Ensuring the Future Is Made in All of America by All of America's Workers.* January 25, 2021. https://www.whitehouse.gov/briefing -room/presidential-actions/2021/01/25/executive-order-on-ensuring-the-future -is-made-in-all-of-america-by-all-of-americas-workers/.

——. *Interim U.S. National Security Strategic Guidance.* March 3, 2021. https://www .whitehouse.gov/wp-content/uploads/2021/03/NSC-1v2.pdf.

——. *Joint Leaders Statement on AUKUS.* September 15, 2021. https://www.whitehouse .gov/briefing-room/statements-releases/2021/09/15/joint-leaders-statement-on -aukus/.

——. *National Security Strategy of the United States of America.* December 2017. https:// trumpwhitehouse.archives.gov/wp-content/uploads/2017/12/NSS-Final-12-18 -2017-0905.pdf.

——. *National Strategy for Critical and Emerging Technologies.* October 2020. https:// www.hsdl.org/?view&did=845571.

——. *President Donald J. Trump Is Protecting America from China's Efforts to Steal Technology and Intellectual Property.* May 29, 2020. https://www.whitehouse.gov /briefings-statements/president-donald-j-trump-protecting-america-chinas -efforts-steal-technology-intellectual-property/.

——. *Presidential Executive Order on Assessing and Strengthening the Manufacturing and Defense Industrial Base and Supply Chain Resiliency of the United States.* July 21, 2017. https://www.govinfo.gov/content/pkg/FR-2017-07-26/pdf/2017-15860.pdf.

CHINESE-LANGUAGE MEDIA ARTICLES

"70th Anniversary Military Parade Is Here! Comparing Previous Military Parades in New China" (70 周年大阅兵来了! 对比新中国历次阅兵). *Sohu.com*, September 30, 2019. https://www.sohu.com/a/344477455_505583.

"2016 National Defense Science, Technology and Industry Work Conference Was Held in Beijing" (2016 年国防科技工业工作会议在京召开). *SASTIND* (国防科工局), January 9, 2016. http://www.gov.cn/xinwen/2016-01/09/content_5031770.htm.

"2018 Version of the Weapons and Equipment Research and Production License Catalog Was Overhauled and Military Market Access Threshold Was Significantly Lowered" ("民参军" 大幅降低门槛, 2018 年版武器装备科研生产许可目录大修). *New Beijing Daily* (新京报), December 27, 2018. http://www.81it.com/2018/1227/9240.html.

"About 3000 Private Enterprises in China Have Entered the Front Lines of Military Procurement" (我国大约 3000 家民企已进入军工采购一线). *Science and Technology Daily* (科技日报), March 14, 2018. http://m.xinhuanet.com/mil/2018-03/14/c _129829001.htm.

"Academy of Military Science Brings in Over 120 Top-Quality Personnel" (军事科学院 引进 120 多名高端人才). *Tencent* (腾讯网), April 13, 2018. https://xw.qq.com /cmsid/20180413A1IXI600.

"Academy of Military Science, China Aerospace Science and Technology Corp. Establish Qian Xuesen Military Systems Engineering Research Institute" (钱学森军事 系统工程研究院揭牌成立). *Weixin* (微信), April 20, 2018. https://www.sohu.com/a /229040069_162220.

"AEE Technology Co. Corporate Introduction" (一电科技公司简介). Accessed August 5, 2020. http://www.aee.com/index.php?case=archive&act=list&catid=256.

"All-Army Political Work Conference Held in Gutian; Xi Jinping Attends Meeting, Delivers Important Speech, Emphasizes Need to Develop Role of Political Work as Lifeline for Strengthening the Army and Invigorating the Military, and to Struggle for

Realization of the Party's Goal of Strengthening the Army under the New Situation" (全军政治工作会议在古田召开习近平出席会议并发表重要讲话). *Xinhua News Agency* (新华社), November 1, 2014. http://www.xinhuanet.com//politics/2014-11/01/c_1113074055.htm.

"All-PLA Political Work Conference Concludes in Gutian" (全军政治工作会议在福建古田闭幕). *Liberation Army Daily* (解放军报), November 3, 2014. http://china.cnr.cn/news/201411/t20141102_516711046.shtml.

An, An (安安). "2016 Military-Civil Fusion Enterprise Summit Successfully Held in 2016" (2016 军民融合企业峰会成功举办). *China Space News* (中国航天报), December 26, 2016. http://www.js7tv.cn/news/201612_73514.html.

"Armed Police Command System Adjustment a Major Political Decision: Xi" (确保党对武警部队绝对领导的重大政治决定). *Xinhua News Agency* (新华社), January 10, 2018. http://www.xinhuanet.com/mil/2017-12/27/c_129776912.htm.

"Army Kicks Off Plan to Give Priority Support for Science, Technology Innovation Talents" (陆军启动科技创新人才优先扶持计划). *Liberation Army Daily* (解放军报), April 9, 2018. http://www.81.cn/jfjbmap/content/2018-04/09/content_203359.htm.

"AVIC Capital Invests in the Establishment of Huihua Fund, Holding 51.28% as Controlling Shareholder" (中航资本出资设立惠华基金 持股 51.28% 为控股股东). *Securities Daily* (证券日报), September 21, 2018. http://finance.sina.com.cn/stock/s/2018-09-21/doc-ihkhfqnt3540512.shtml.

"AVIC Studies and Implements Spirit of All Army Armaments Work Conference" (中航工业学习贯彻全军装备工作会议精神). *China Aviation News* (中国航空报), December 13, 2014.

Bai, Chunli (白春礼). "Strive to Make Breakthroughs in Original Innovation" (着力突破性原始创新). *Economic Daily* (经济日报), January 15, 2013. http://views.ce.cn/view/ent/201301/15/t20130115_24027641.shtml.

"Build Dragon Head and Quality Military-Civil Fusion Projects Xi Jinping Emphasized When Visiting the 2nd Military-Civil Fusion Development High-Tech Achievements Exhibition" (习近平在参观第二届军民融合发展高技术成果展时强调打造军民融合龙头工程精品工程). *China Science News* (中国科学报), October 20, 2016. http://news.sciencenet.cn/sbhtmlnews/2016/10/316988.shtm?id=316988.

"Carry Out In-depth Implementation of the Military-Civil Fusion Development Strategy and Strive to Create a New Situation to Strengthen the Army" (深入实施军民融合发展战略开创新局面). *People's Daily* (人民日报), March 13, 2015. https://www.chinacourt.org/article/detail/2015/03/id/1566449.shtml.

"Carrying the Reform Through to the End, Part 8" ("将改革进行到底" 第八集: 强军之路 (下)). *China Central Television Channel 1* (中央电视台一频道), July 24, 2017. http://www.xinhuanet.com//politics/2017-07/24/c_1121372697.htm.

"Casting a Shield, Honing a Sword, Never Removing Armor: Roundup of CMC Equipment Development Department's Planning and Promotion of the Building of a Weapons and Equipment System" (铸盾砺剑不卸甲—军委装备发展部谋划推动武器装备体系建设综述). *Liberation Army Daily* (解放军报), September 20, 2017. http://cpc.people.com.cn/n1/2017/0920/c412690-29547030.html.

"Central Military Commission Issues 13th Five-Year Plan for Army Construction and Development" (中央军委颁发 《军队建设发展"十三五"规划纲要》). *Xinhua News Agency* (新华社), May 12, 2016. http://www.xinhuanet.com/mil/2016-05/12/c_1118855988.htm.

"Central Military Commission Issues 'Opinions Concerning Deepening the Reform of National Defense and the Armed Forces'" (中央军委印发 "关于深化国防和军队改革的意见). *Xinhua News Agency* (新华社), January 1, 2016. http://www.xinhuanet.com/mil/2016-01/01/c_1117646692.htm.

"Central Military Commission Promulgates the Outline of the 13th Five-Year Program for the Building and Development of the Armed Forces" (中央军委颁发"军队建设发展"十三五"规划纲要). *Xinhua News Agency* (新华社), May 12, 2016. http://www.xinhuanet.com/mil/2016-05/12/c_128978367.htm.

"Central Military Commission Vice-Chair Urges Retention of Essential Military Enterprises" (军委副主席敦促保留重要的军工企业). *Xinhua News Agency* (新华社), March 18, 1994. http://www.gov.cn/test/2009-04/22/content_1292428.htm.

"Chen Li Talks about 'Excerpts from Xi Jinping's Exposition on General National Security'" (陈理谈" 习近平关于总体国家安全观论述摘编). *People's Daily Online Theory Channel* (人民网-理论频道), August 14, 2018. http://theory.people.com.cn/n1/2018/0814/c40531-30227214.html.

Chen, Long (陈龙). "Lunar Exploration Project Leading Group Held Mobilization Meeting for Launch of Chang'e 3" (探月工程重大专项领导小组就嫦娥三号发射召开动员会). *China Space News* (中国航天报), November 29, 2013. https://www.chinanews.com/mil/2013/11-29/5563412.shtml.

Chen, Yanxin (沈雁昕). "Coordinate the Promotion of Military-Civil Fusion and the Belt and Road Initiative" (统筹推进军民融合与"一带一路"). *Red Flag Journal* (红旗文稿), April 2017. http://www.qstheory.cn/dukan/hqwg/2017-04/25/c_1120868189.htm.

Chen, Ying (陈莹). "Inter-Ministerial Joint Meeting of Science and Technology Program Management Was Held" (国家科技计划管理部际联席会议召开). *Science and Technology Daily* (科技日报), December 22, 2016. http://digitalpaper.stdaily.com/http_www.kjrb.com/kjrb/html/2016-12/23/content_358194.htm?div=-1.

"China Great Wall Plans to Implement Second Phase of Equity Incentives Program, and Mixed Reform of Military Industrial Central Enterprises Continues" (中国长城拟实施第二期股权激 励, 军工央企混改持续推进). *China Securities Research Development Department* (中信建投证券研究发展部), November 24, 2019. http://pdf.dfcfw.com/pdf/H3_AP201911251371064635_1.pdf.

"China Sets Up National Defense Science, Technology, and Industry Development Strategy Committee to Position a Strategic Consulting Platform" (中国设立国防科技工业发展战略委员会, 定位战略咨询平台). *The Paper* (澎湃新闻), April 4, 2015. http://m.thepaper.cn/kuaibao_detail.jsp?contid=1338404&from=kuaibao.

"China Unveils Plan for Developing Defense Technologies" (中国公布国防科技规划). *Xinhua News Agency* (新华社), May 25, 2006. http://www.cctv.com/news/china/20060525/100424.shtml.

"China Will Build a Number of Defense S&T Industry Innovation Centers" (中国将打造一批国防创新中心 建立若干国家实验室). *Science and Technology Daily* (科技日报), June 30, 2016. https://www.guancha.cn/Science/2016_07_01_366022.shtml.

"China Zhongwang Makes Strategic Investment into 3 Funds Including the National Military-Civil Integration Industry Fund" (中国忠旺获国家军民融合产业基金等三只基金战略投资). *China Economic Network* (中国经济网), October 31, 2019. https://finance.sina.cn/2019-10-31/detail-iicezuev6178216.d.html.

"China's Brain Gain Spurs Innovation." *Xinhua News Agency* (新华社), March 7, 2017. http://www.xinhuanet.com//english/2017-03/07/c_136109739.htm.

"China's Long March V Carrier Rocket Is Set to Have First Flight in 2014" (中国长征五号为全新运载火箭 将于 2014 年首飞). *Xinhua News Agency* (新华社), March 12, 2008. http://news.xinhuanet.com/mil/2008-03/12/content_7773226.htm.

"China's State-Owned Enterprise Structural Adjustment Fund Signed over RMB 70 Billion in Two Years" (中国国有企业结构调整基金两年签约超 700 亿元). *Xinhua News Agency* (新华社), August 30, 2018. http://www.xinhuanet.com/fortune/2018-08/30/c_1123355344.htm.

"Chinese Defense Science and Technology Industry's Tasks for the New High-Technology Program for This and Next Year Are Extremely Heavy" (中国国防科技工业今明两年高新工程任务繁重). *China News Service* (中国新闻网), April 20, 2004. https://www.chinanews.com/n/2004-04-20/26/427498.html.

"Chinese Military Launches High-Level Scientific and Technological Innovation Talent Selection and Training Project" (中国军队启动高层次科技创新人才选拔培养工程). *Liberation Army Daily* (解放军报), July 31, 2009. http://mil.news.sina.com.cn/2009-07-31/0812561134.html.

"Chinese Military to Be Subject to Stricter Discipline: Senior Official" (高级官员: 中国军队将受到更严格的纪律管理). *Xinhua News Agency* (新华社), January 17, 2018. http://www.xinhuanet.com/english/2018-01/17/c_136902781.htm.

"Contributions of the Academy of Military Science in the Last 50 Years" (军事科学院50年辉煌历程). *Liberation Army Daily* (解放军报), March 13, 2008. http://www.chinadaily.com.cn/hqzg/2008-03/22/content_6557735.htm.

"CSIC Releases Plan for 8.48 Billion Set, Creates Precedent for Defense Asset Injection" (中国重工 84.8 亿定增预案出炉 开创重大军工资产注入先河). *Shanghai Securities News* (上海证券报), September 11, 2013. http://finance.sina.com.cn/stock/s/20130911/023716724295.shtml.

Dai, Shaoli, and Shan Shigang (戴绍利和单世刚). "Cultivate Scientific and Technological Innovation Talent for a Strong Army" (为强军兴军培养造就科技创新人才). *Liberation Army Daily* (解放军报), September 1, 2015. http://81rc.81.cn/news/2015-09/01/content_6659464.htm.

"Defense Conglomerates Will Start Classification Reform, 87 Enterprises Are Listed" (军工集团将启动分类改革 已有87家企业上市). Cnstock.com (中国证券网), September 6, 2015. http://news.cnstock.com/industry/sid_zxk/201509/3553950.htm.

"Defense Research Institute Reforms May Be Implemented Soon" (军工科研院所分类改革文件或近期落地). *Xinhua News Agency* (新华社), January 15, 2016. http://news.xinhuanet.com/finance/2016-01/15/c_128631763.htm.

"Defense S&T Industry Efficient CNC Machining Technology Innovation Center/CNC Machine S&T and Equipment Engineering Laboratory" (国防科技工业高效数控加工技术创新中心/数控加工工艺技术与装备工程实验室). Efficient CNC Machining Technology Innovation Center website (高效数控加工技术创新中心). Accessed June 6, 2020. http://www.me.buaa.edu.cn/info/1179/1524.htm.

"Defense Science and Technology Industry Advanced Technology Research and Application Experience Exchange Conference Held" (国防科技工业先进技术研究应用经验交流会召开). COSTIND website (国防科工委网站), October 18, 2007. http://www.gov.cn/govweb/gzdt/2007-10/18/content_778869.htm.

"Documentary of the Design Process of Deepening Defense and Military Reform by Xi Jinping and the CMC" (习主席和中央军委运筹设计深化国防和军队改革纪实). *Sina News Center* (新浪新闻中心), December 30, 2015. http://news.sina.com.cn/o/2015-12-30/doc-ifxncyar6047368.shtml.

"Establishment of Inter-Ministerial Joint Meeting System for National Science and Technology Plan Management" (国家科技计划管理部际联席会议制度建立). *Science and Technology Daily* (科技日报), May 15, 2015. http://www.xinhuanet.com/politics/2015-05/15/c_127802657.htm.

"Facing 'Black Swan' and 'Gray Rhino' Events Have Been on Fire Recently!" (和"黑天鹅"对着干"灰犀牛"最近火了!). *Xinhua News Agency* (新华社), July 19, 2017. http://www.xinhuanet.com//world/2017-07/19/c_129659332.htm.

"For Seventeen Years, We Walked Together" (十七年, 我们一起走来). *China Military Industry News* (中国军工报), December 31, 2015. http://news.hit.edu.cn/zgjgb/list.htm.

"Forge Talent Matrix That Wins Information Wars: Roundup of National Defense and Army Building Achievements" (培养人才矩阵赢得信息战—国防和军队建设成就综述). *China Military Industry News* (中国军工报), October 27, 2012. https://china.huanqiu.com/article/9CaKrnJvNAu.

"Former GAD Director Zhang Youxia Becomes New Director of CMC Equipment Development Department" (原总装备部部长张又侠上将任新组建的军委装备发展部部长). *The Paper* (澎湃新闻), January 14, 2016. https://www.thepaper.cn/newsDetail_forward_1420521.

"Former GAD S&T Committee Director Liu Guozhi Appointed Director of New CMC S&T Commission" (原总装备部科技委主任刘国治中将任新组建军委科技委主任). *The Paper* (澎湃新闻), January 11, 2016. https://www.thepaper.cn/newsDetail_forward_1419368.

"Four Defense Science and Technology Industrial Technology Research and Application Centers Established" (我国四大国防科技工业技术研究应用中心成立). *China Broadcasting Network* (中国广播网), April 8, 2008. http://news.sohu.com/20080408/n256164022.shtml.

"From Technology Introduction to Indigenous Innovation, Era Shift Urgently Demands New Development Model: What Foundations Must Be Laid for Independent Innovation against Backdrop of Globalization: Interview with State Council Development Research Center Foreign Economic Relations Department Deputy Director Long Guoqiang" (从技术引进到本土创新, 时代转移迫切要求新的发展模式: 应对全球化背景下的自主创新必须打下哪些基础: 国务院发展研究中心对外经济关系部副主任隆国强专访). *China Economic Weekly* (中国经济周刊), June 19, 2018. http://finance.sina.com.cn/roll/2018-06-19/doc-iheauxvz5946697.shtml.

Gao, Lu (高路). "Chinese Jetliner Development Is on Track" (中国客机发展步入正轨). *International Herald Leader* (国际先驱导报), June 9, 2009. http://herald.xinhuanet.com/.

"General Armaments Department Confirms First Batch of Project Experts" (总装备部确认第一批项目专家). *China Military Industry News* (中国军工报), July 14, 2011. http://news.hit.edu.cn/zgjgb/list.htm.

"General Political Department Conducts Special Study and Planning on Topic of Strengthening Building of Talented Personnel for Armed Forces Science and Technology Innovation Teams" (总政专题研究部署加强军队科技创新团队人才建设). *Liberation Army Daily* (解放军报), July 27, 2012. http://mil.news.sina.com.cn/2012-07-27/0532696737.html.

Gu, Yang (顾阳). "'Digital Silk Road' Construction Will Become a New Engine for Global Development" ("数字丝路" 建设将成全球发展新引擎). *Economic Daily* (经济日报), September 9, 2019. http://www.gov.cn/xinwen/2019-09/09/content_5428411.htm.

Guo, Qiangli, and Wang Shibin (郭强利和王士彬). "PLA Emphasizes High-Level Scientific and Technological Personnel Cultivation" (高层次科技创新人才工程动员部署会召开). *Liberation Army Daily* (解放军报), December 18, 2009. http://news.mod.gov.cn/forces/2009-12/18/content_4112275.htm.

Guo, Shengkun (郭声琨). "Deeply Study and Comprehend Comrade Xi Jinping's Series of Important Speeches on Safeguarding National Security and Social Stability" (郭声琨: 把维护政治安全, 政权安全放在首要位置来抓). *People's Daily* (人民日报), January 3, 2014. http://www.chinanews.com/gn/2014/01-10/5719460.shtml.

Guoping (国平). "Increase Reform Confidence, Maintain Stable Force and Tenacity" (坚定改革信心 保持定力和韧劲). *CCTV Network Economy* (央视网经济), August 19, 2015. http://www.xinhuanet.com/politics/2015-08/19/c_128145875.htm.

Han, Wei. "China Revamps Top National Technology Strategy Body." *Caixin Global*, August 8, 2018. https://www.caixinglobal.com/2018-08-10/china-revamps-top-national-technology-strategy-body-101313443.html.

"Harbin Engineering University Launches High-Tech Project no. 1" (哈尔滨工程大学位列中国高科技项目第一). September 7, 2006. http://bbs.tianya.cn/post-university-39826-2.shtml.

He, Bin (何斌). "Speech at Special Seminar for County-Level Leading Cadre to Study and Implement the 5th Plenum of 19th Central Committee" (在县级领导干部学习贯彻党的十九届五中全会专题研讨班上的发言). *Qilian News* (祁连新闻), February 25, 2021. http://www.qiliannews.com/system/2021/02/25/013341147.shtml.

"How to Do a Good Job in MCF in Sichuan in 2019? Peng Qinghua Attends the Meeting" (如何抓好四川 2019 年军民融合发展工作? 彭清华在这个会上作了部署). Sichuan Online (四川在线), February 27, 2019. https://sichuan.scol.com.cn/gcdt/201902/56824444.html.

"How to Lay Out Plans for the Military Industrial Sector in the 14th Five-Year Plan?" (军工"十四五"如何布局谋篇?). China Galaxy Securities (中国银河证券股份公司), September 23, 2020. http://pdf.dfcfw.com/pdf/H3_AP202009241416879860_1.pdf.

"How Will China's SOE Reform Fare with Three Year Action?" *Xinhua News Agency* (新华社), January 29, 2021. http://www.xinhuanet.com/english/2021-01/29/c_139707120.htm.

Hu, Angang (胡鞍钢). "The Path of Indigenous Innovation with Chinese Characteristics" (中国特色自主创新道路). *Science Daily* (科学时报), April 6, 2014. http://news.sciencenet.cn/htmlnews/2014/4/291483.shtm.

"Hu Jintao, Xi Jinping Attend Enlarged Meeting of Central Military Commission, Deliver Important Speeches" (胡锦涛, 习近平出席中央军委扩大会议并发表重要讲话). *Xinhua News Agency* (新华社), November 17, 2012. http://www.xinhuanet.com/politics/2012-11/17/c_123965664_3.htm.

Hu, Yongshun (扈永顺). "What Is the New Whole-of-Nation System?" (新型举国体制什么样?). *Liaowang* (瞭望), January 7, 2020. http://paper.news.cn/2020-01/06/c_1210426434.htm.

Hua, Yiwen (华益文). "'Three in One System' Opens New Stage in National Security" (三位一体" 开启国家安全新阶段). *People's Daily Overseas Edition* (人民日报海外版), July 2, 2015. http://opinion.china.com.cn/opinion_90_132790.html.

Huang, Xin (黄鑫). "Lay a Solid Foundation to Grow Stronger" (夯实基础, 由大变强). *Economic Daily* (经济日报), February 26, 2014. http://paper.ce.cn/jjrb/html/2014-02/26/content_189990.htm.

"In-depth Study and Implementation, Strengthen Reform and Innovation, Accelerate the Formation of a New Pattern of In-depth Military-Civil Fusion Development" (深入学习贯彻 强化改革创新 加快形成军民融合深度发展新格局). *People's Daily* (人民日报), October 2, 2017. http://www.hnjgdj.gov.cn/2017/1002/33946.html.

"Intensive Commissioning of Warships Aims to Safeguard China's Maritime Rights, Interests" (中国海军一年来新型战舰密集入列). *Liberation Army Daily* (解放军报), January 9, 2014. http://www.81.cn/jmywyl/2014-01/09/content_5727593_2.htm.

"Interview with National Defense Technology Industry Development Strategy Committee Secretary-General Wu Zhijian" (科技是军民融合的核心要素—访国防科技工业发展战略委员会吴志坚秘书长). Guoding Capital (国鼎资本), April 1, 2017. http://www.guoding-capital.com/node/119.

Jiang, Luming (姜鲁鸣). "Military-Civil Fusion Uses Security and Development to Fight for National Interests as 'Single Piece of Steel'" (统筹国家安全和发展的总方略).

China National Defense News (中国国防报), June 2, 2016. http://www.81.cn /gfbmap/content/21/2016-06/02/03/2016060203_pdf.pdf.

Jiang, Luming, and Wang Weihai (姜鲁鸣和王伟海). "Building an Integrated National Strategic System and Capabilities" (构建一体化的国家战略体系和能力). *Guangming Daily* (光明日报), November 10, 2017. http://epaper.gmw.cn/gmrb/html/2017 -11/10/nw.D110000gmrb_20171110_1-06.htm?div=-1.

Jiantian, Zhang (张建田). "An Analysis of the Problems Restricting the Legislation of Military-Civil Fusion" (制约军民融合立法之问题分析). *Legal Daily* (法制日报), February 27, 2019. http://www.legaldaily.com.cn/army/content/2019-02/27 /content_7782179.htm.

Jin, Yezi (金叶子). "Announcement of the 14th Five-Year National Key R&D Program" ('十四五' 国家重点研发计划公布 透露哪些信号). *First Business News* (第一财经), February 5, 2021. https://finance.sina.com.cn/roll/2021-02-05/doc-ikftpnny476 4907.shtml.

"Key Points of Zhang Youxia's Speech at the General Armament Department Party Committee Enlarged Meeting" (张又侠在总装备部党委扩大会议上的讲话要点). *China Military Industry News* (中国军工报), January 9, 2014. http://news.hit.edu.cn /zgjgb/list.htm.

Li, Andong (李安东). "Implement the Scientific Development Concept, Strengthen the Strategic Direction of Armament Building" (贯彻科学发展观加强军备建设战略方向). *China Military Industry News* (中国军工报), December 5, 2012. http://news .hit.edu.cn/zgjgb/list.htm.

Li, Xuanliang (李宣良). "CMC Vice Chairman Stresses Effective Anti-Corruption" (许其亮: 把军队党风廉政建设和反腐败工作提高到新水平). *Xinhua News Agency* (新华社), January 17, 2014. http://www.gov.cn/jrzg/2014-01/16/content_2568885 .htm.

Li, Yizhong (李毅中). "Exploring Practical Development Paths in Carrying Out the Military-Civil Fusion Strategy" (贯彻军民融合战略探索实践发展路径). *China Enterprise Network* (中国企业网), October 13, 2017. http://www.zqcn.com.cn /huodong/201710/13/c501681.html.

"Li Keqiang Hosts State Council Executive Meeting" (李克强主持召开国务院常务会议). Chinese Central Government website (中央政府门户网站), January 14, 2015. http:// www.gov.cn/guowuyuan/2015-01/14/content_2804136.htm.

"Li Keqiang Stresses Innovative Macroeconomic Measures at CAS, CES Meeting" (李克强在两院院士大会作报告时强调创新宏观调控). *Xinhua News Agency* (新华社), June 10, 2014. http://www.gov.cn/guowuyuan/2014-06/10/content_2698215.htm.

"Li Keqiang's Flagship Plan: Made in China 2025" (李克强的王牌计划: 中国制造2025). *West China Metropolis Daily* (华西都市报), March 11, 2015. http://finance.ifeng .com/a/20150311/13545234_0.shtml.

Liberation Army Daily Commentator (解放军报评论员). "Give Full Play to the Role of Innovation in Driving Development: Eighth Commentary on Seriously Studying and Implementing Chairman Xi's Important Speech at the CMC Work Conference on Military Structural Reforms" (充分发挥创新驱动发展作用: 八论认真学习贯彻习主席在中央军委改革工作会议上的重要讲话). *Liberation Army Daily* (解放军报), December 5, 2015. http://www.xinhuanet.com/mil/2015-12/05/c_128501327.htm.

Liberation Army Daily Commentator (解放军报评论员). "Strengthen Political Army Building, Guarantee That the Armed Forces Will Advance along the Correct Political Line" (加强政治建军, 确保军队沿着正确政治方向前进). *Liberation Army Daily* (解放军报), February 27, 2016. http://www.81.cn/2017jj90/2016-12/21 /content_7668941.htm.

Liu, Cheng. "Creating a New Situation in the Weapons and Equipment Modernization Effort" (中国开创武器装备现代化建设的新局面). *Liberation Army Daily* (解放军报), October 14, 2002. http://news.sohu.com/19/73/news203667319.shtml.

Liu, Yin (刘垠). "What Is the 'New' Meaning of the New Whole-of-Nation System? Experts Explain in Detail the Spirit of General Secretary Xi Jinping's Important Instructions" (新型举国体制"新"意何在: 专家详解习近平总书记有关重要指示精神). *Science and Technology Daily* (科技日报), May 18, 2020. http://stdaily.com/index/kejixinwen/2020-05/18/content_941987.shtml.

Liu, Yuejin (刘跃进). "Fully Implement the Holistic National Security Concept" (全面贯彻落实总体国家安全观). *Banyuetan* (半月谈) no. 9 (May 15, 2018). http://m.banyuetan.org/szjj/detail/20180514/1000200033135991526261678827373975_1.html.

Liu, Yuxian (刘玉先). "Gaofen Hunan Data and Application Center Established to Help the Development of the Spatial Information Industry" (高分湖南数据与应用中心成立 助力空间信息产业发展). *Red Net* (红网), December 4, 2017. https://hn.rednet.cn/c/2017/12/04/886585.htm.

Liu, Zhiwei (刘志伟). "Interpretation of the Deep-Seated Contradictions in Military-Civil Fusion" (解读军民合合深层次矛盾: 军队非战斗机构人员偏多). *China National Defense News* (中国国防报), March 26, 2015. http://www.xinhuanet.com//mil/2015-03/26/c_127624181_2.htm.

Lu, Lai (路来). "Behind the Mysterious National Security Commission" (神秘国安委走上前台的背后). *Duowei News* (多维新闻), February 21, 2017. http://news.dwnews.com/china/news/2017-02-21/59801187.html.

Lu, Yongzhen (卢永真). "Defense Research Institute Reforms Need to Deal with Six Issues" (军工科研院所改制需直面六大问题). *Xinhua News Agency* (新华社), July 23, 2014. http://finance.ifeng.com/a/20140723/12778652_0.shtml.

Ma, Haoliang (马浩亮). "Armed Police Reform Establishes Mobile Contingent" (武警改革组建机动总队). *Ta Kung Pao* (大公报), February 14, 2018. http://news.takungpao.com/mainland/focus/2018-02/3544027.html.

"Maj. Gen. Li Wujun Serves as Director of the Equipment Technology Cooperation Bureau of the Central Military Commission Equipment Development Department" (李武军少将任中央军委装备发展部装备技术合作局局长). *The Paper* (澎湃新闻), April 27, 2016. https://www.sohu.com/a/71948589_260616.

"Major Events in the Chinese Aviation Industry in 1990" (1990 年中国航空业的重大事件). *Chinese News Net* (中国新闻社). No Date. http://60.13.141.177/cgi-bin/Ginfo.dll?DispInfo&w=westpower&nid=141230.

"Many Provinces Are Striving to Establish Military-Civil Fusion Innovation Demonstration Zones, and Many NPC Representatives Suggest Breaking the Ice and Removing the Threshold" (多省争设军民融合创新示范区, 多位代表委员建议破坚冰去门槛). *The Paper* (澎湃新闻), March 9, 2018. https://www.sohu.com/a/225166111_260616.

Mao, Nongxi (毛浓曦). "Shaanxi Defense Industry Trade Union Promotes Transformation and Upgrading of Labor Competition" (陕西国防工会推动劳动竞赛转型升级). *Workers' Daily* (工人日报), June 5, 2015. http://acftu.people.cn/n/2015/0605/c121801-27109170.html.

"Military-Civil Fusion Is the Strategic Decision for Enriching the Nation and Strengthening the Military" (军民融合是富国强军的战略抉择). *Liberation Army Daily* (解放军报), March 17, 2015. https://81-cn.newsproxy.info/jmywyl/2015-03/17/content_6399609.htm.

"Military-Civil Fusion Makes Chinese Military Different" (军民融合, 让中国军队不一样). *Southern Weekend* (南方周末), March 5, 2018. http://www.infzm.com/content/133809.

"Ministry of National Defense Holds News Conference on CMC Administrative Reform and Reorganization" (国防部召开军委机关调整组建专题新闻发布会). *China Military Online* (中国军网), January 11, 2016. http://www.81.cn/xwfyr/2016-01/11/content_6852766.htm.

"Ministry of Science and Technology Holds Media Conference" (科技部举行司局长媒体集中访谈会). *Ministry of Science and Technology* (科技部), February 22, 2017. http://www.scio.gov.cn/xwfbh/gbwxwfbh/xwfbh/kjb/Document/1543185/1543185.htm.

"More than a Thousand Private Enterprises Have Obtained Weapons and Equipment Research and Production Licenses" (千余家民营企业获武器装备科研生产许可证). *People's Net* (人民网), March 11, 2016. http://scitech.people.com.cn/n1/2016/0311/c1007-28192181.html.

"Name List of 20 National Laboratories" (20 家国家实验室名单). *Sciping.com* (科塔学术), October 17, 2018. https://www.sciping.com/21519.html.

"Name List of 60 Defense Science and Technology Key Laboratories" (60 家国防科技重点实验室). *Sciping.com* (科塔学术), November 21, 2019. https://www.sciping.com/33068.html.

"National Defense Technology Industry Development Strategy Committee Held Second Plenary Meeting" (国防科技工业发展战略委员会召开第二次全体会议). *SASTIND* (国防科工局), July 10, 2016. http://www.gov.cn/xinwen/2016-07/10/content_5090029.htm.

"National Development and Reform Commission Makes Major Progress in Military-Civil Fusion in 2017 and Key Preparations for 2018" (干货! 国家发改委军民融合工作 17 年主要进展和 18 年重点部署). *Cyber-Information Military-Civil Fusion* (网信军民融合), March 23, 2018. http://zgsc.china.com.cn/2018-03/23/content_40263308.html?f=pad&a=false.

"National Engineering Research Centers (国家工程研究中心)." *Sciping.com* (科塔学术), July 27, 2018. https://www.sciping.com/13626.html.

"National Key R&D Programs of China." *China Innovation Funding.* Accessed March 10, 2021. http://chinainnovationfunding.eu/national-key-rd-programmes/.

"National Military-Civil Fusion Industry Investment Fund Co., Ltd." (国家军民融合产业投资基金有限责任公司). *PEDaily* (投资界). https://zdb.pedaily.cn/enterprise/show79777/#business.

"National Security Matter of Prime Importance: President Xi" (习近平说国家安全是头等大事). *Xinhua News Agency* (新华社), April 15, 2014. http://www.xinhuanet.com//politics/2014-04/15/c_1110253910.htm.

"Nie Rongzhen: Creating an Unforgettable Chinese Technology 'Golden Age'" (开国元帅聂荣臻: 建国后开创新中国科技 "黄金时代"). *Science and Technology Daily* (科技日报), May 13, 2014. http://dangshi.people.com.cn/n/2014/0513/c85037-25012201-6.html.

Niu, Mingming (牛明明). "The 'Three Unprecedenteds' Indicate China's Current Position" ("三个前所未有"指明当前中国的方位). *Liberation Army Daily* (解放军报), April 10, 2014. http://www.81.cn/jmywyl/2014-04/10/content_5850141.htm?appinstall=0.

"Northwestern Polytechnical University a Leader in China's Unmanned Aerial Vehicle National Team" (西北工业大学"领飞"我国中高端民用无人机产业发展). *Ta Kung Pao* (大公报), February 10, 2018. https://rcussd.nwpu.edu.cn/info/1076/1494.htm.

"'One Belt One Road' Space Information Corridor Construction and Application Implementation Promotion Meeting Held" ("一带一路" 空间信息走廊建设与应用实施推进会召开). *State Administration of Science, Technology, and Industry for National Defense* (国防科技工业局), November 30, 2017. http://news.sina.com.cn/o/2017-11-30/doc-ifyphtze2791969.shtml.

People's Daily Commentator (人民日报评论员). "Build a Firm Systems Dam for National Security" (人民日报评论员: 筑牢国家安全的制度堤坝). *People's Daily* (人民日报), July 2, 2015. http://opinion.people.com.cn/n/2015/0702/c1003-27240271.html.

People's Daily Commentator (人民日报评论员). "Nurture and Train a Large Number of Excellent Talents in Science and Technology: On Studying and Implementing the Important Speech of General Secretary Xi Jinping at the Two Meetings of the Academicians of the Chinese Academy of Sciences and of the Chinese Academy of Engineering" (培养造就大批优秀科技人才: 五论学习贯彻习近平总书记两院院士大会重要讲话). *People's Daily* (人民日报), June 2, 2018. http://opinion.people.com.cn/n1/2018/0602/c1003-30029994.html.

"Promote Collaborative Innovation in Marine Science and Technology and Help Build a Community of Shared Oceanic Destiny" (推动海洋科技协同创新 助力构建海洋命运共同体). *People's Daily* (人民日报), December 27, 2019. http://www.xinhuanet.com/2019-12/27/c_1125393468.htm.

"Promote the Simultaneous Improvement of National Defense Strength and Economic Strength" (促进国防实力和经济实力同步提升). *Guangming Daily* (光明日报), March 14, 2021. https://news.gmw.cn/2021-03/14/content_34683946.htm.

Qiushi Commentator (求是评论员). "Compose a New Chapter in China's Economic Miracle by Accelerating the Construction of a New Development Pattern" (在加快构建新发展格局中谱写中国经济奇迹新篇章). *Qiushi* (求是), December 15, 2020. http://www.qstheory.cn/dukan/qs/2020-12/15/c_1126857440.htm.

——. "The Fight against the Epidemic Demonstrates the Significant Political Advantages of Military-Political and Military-Civilian Unity" (疫情防控斗争彰显军政军民团结的显著政治优势). *Qiushi Wang* (求是网), May 29, 2020. http://www.qstheory.cn/wp/2020-05/29/c_1126048519.htm.

"Reform of Defense Research Institutes Made Breakthroughs, Space Sector May Take the Lead" (军工院所分类改革迎突破 航天系望成"领头羊). *Shanghai Securities News* (上海证券报), February 4, 2016. http://www.cnstock.com/v_industry/sid_rdjj/201602/3703256.htm.

"Remarks Made by Xi Jinping at the Rally Celebrating the 40th Anniversary of Reform and Opening Up" (习近平在庆祝改革开放 40 周年大会上的讲话). *Xinhua News Agency* (新华社), December 18, 2018. https://baijiahao.baidu.com/s?id=1620162720919526107&wfr=spider&for=pc.

"Research Institutes Restructuring Starts, Greatest Potential in Electronics and Space" (军工行业: 院所改制发令枪响, 电科航天弹性最大). *Tencent Finance* (腾讯财经), May 12, 2016. http://finance.qq.com/a/20160512/026066.htm.

"SASTIND Holds 2016 Science and Technology Work Conference" (2016 年全国科技工作会议在京召开). *State Administration for Science, Technology and Industry for National Defense* (国防科工委), January 11, 2016. http://www.most.gov.cn/ztzl/qgkjgzhy/2016/2016ttxw/201601/t20160111_123671.htm.

"SASTIND Take Measures to Accelerate National Defense Science, Technology and Industry Coordinated Innovation" (国防科工局多措并举加快推进国防科技工业协同创新). *State Administration for Science, Technology and Industry for National Defense* (国防科技工业局), June 29, 2016. http://www.sastind.gov.cn/n112/n117/c6603042/content.html.

"Science and Technology Vanguard, Think Tank for Decision Making" (科技先锋, 决策智囊团). *China Military Industry News* (中国军工报), November 17, 2012. http://news.hit.edu.cn/zgjgb/list.htm.

Shao, Longfei, and Zhang Zhihua (邵龙飞和张志华). "Academy of Military Science Retains Hundreds of Talents for National Defense Frontier Technology Innovation"

(军事科学院保留数百名国防前沿技术创新人才). *Liberation Army Daily* (解放军报), February 4, 2018. http://www.81.cn/jwgz/2018-02/04/content_7931564.htm.

——. "National Innovation Institute of Defense Technology of the Academy of Military Science: Exploring a 'Matrix Style' Model of Scientific Research to Boost Innovation Capabilities" (军事科学院探索"矩阵式"科研模式提升创新能力). *Liberation Army Daily* (解放军报), April 2, 2018. http://military.people.com.cn/n1/2018/0402/c1011-29902586.html.

"Six Members of the Central Military Commission Gathered at the Military Museum. What Happened? Visit to the Military-Civil Fusion 4th Exhibition of High-Tech Equipment" (6 名中央军委成员齐聚军博, 所为何事? 原来是第四届军民融合发展高技术装备成果展览). *Jiefang Daily* (解放日报), October 12, 2018. https://www.jfdaily.com/wx/detail.do?id=110148.

"Special Address by Chinese President Xi Jinping at the World Economic Forum Virtual Event of the Davos Agenda." *Xinhua News Agency* (新华社), January 25, 2021. http://www.xinhuanet.com/english/2021-01/25/c_139696610.htm.

"Speech by Zhang Youxia at General Armament Department Party Committee Enlarged Meeting." *China Defense Industry News* (中国军工报), January 9, 2014.

"Success of Hard-Won Achievements Belong to the Party and the People" (成功来之不易, 成就属于党和人民). *Xinhua News Agency* (新华社), December 16, 2011. http://roll.sohu.com/20111216/n329253633.shtml.

"Sun Jianguo: China Is in Danger of Being Invaded; Using Struggle to Seek a Win-Win for China and the United States" (孙建国上将: 中国有被侵略危险用斗争谋中美共赢). *Huanqiu Wang* (环球网), March 2, 2015. http://mil.news.sina.com.cn/2015-03-02/1123822832.html.

Tan, Yungang (谭云刚). "Opportunities and Challenges for the Development of China's Technological Innovation in the New Era" (新时代中国科技创新发展机遇挑战与行动). *China Defense Conversion Journal* (中国军转民), March 2020. http://www.ecorr.org/news/industry/2020-05-27/177150.html.

——. "See Opportunities, Challenges and Actions of China's Science and Technology Innovation Development in the New Era" (新时代中国科技创新发展机遇挑战与行动). *Strategic Frontier Technology* (战略前沿技术), June 5, 2020. http://www.impcia.net/news/details_617.html.

——. "Thoughts on Further Promoting 'Civilian Participation in Military' in Weapons and Equipment Research and Production" (深入推进武器装备科研生产领域"民参军"的几点思考). *Cyber-Information Military-Civil Fusion* (网信军民融合), September 2018. https://www.sohu.com/a/275579733_465915.

Tang, Taoyi (唐焘逸). "Defense S&T Industrial Aviation Technology Innovation Center Established" (国防科技工业航空技术创新中心成立). *China Aviation News* (中国航空新闻网), January 17, 2017. http://www.cannews.com.cn/2017/0117/162034.shtml.

Tang, Ziyi, and Xue Xiaoli. "Four Things to Know about China's $670 Billion Government Guidance Funds." *Caixin Global*, February 25, 2020. https://www.caixinglobal.com/2020-02-25/four-things-to-know-about-chinas-670-billion-government-guidance-funds-101520348.html.

"The Achievements of Military-Civil Fusion Development in the Defense Industry" (国防科技工业军民融合发展取得阶段成果). *Liberation Army Daily* (解放军报), December 7, 2017. http://www.81.cn/jfjbmap/content/2017-12/07/content_193721.htm.

"The Correct Way to Open the 'Outline' of the 14th Five-Year Plan" ("十四五"规划"纲要"的正确打开方式). *Diyi Caijing* (第一财经), March 15, 2021. https://www.yicai.com/news/100986328.html.

"The Country's First National Defense Science, Technology, and Innovation Rapid Response Small Group Launched in Shenzhen" (全国首个国防科技创新快速响应小组在深圳启动). *Shenzhen Special Economic Zone News* (深圳特区报), March 18, 2018. https://www.thepaper.cn/newsDetail_forward_2032644.

"The Father of China's Manned Space Program" (中国载人航天之父: 我国离航天强国还有距离). *China Newsweek* (中国新闻周刊), June 21, 2012. http://news.sina.com.cn/c/sd/2012-06-21/163024635232.shtml.

"The First Batch of 'Ten Thousand People Plan' Released" ("万人计划" 首批入选名单发布). *People's Daily* (人民日报), October 30, 2013.

"The General Armament Department Talent Development 2020 Plan to Be Issued and Implemented" (总装部 2020 年人才发展计划将发布和实施). *China Military Industry News* (中国军工报), February 18, 2012. http://news.hit.edu.cn/zgjgb/list.htm.

"The 'Head' of the Large Domestic Aircraft Project: Jin Zhuanglong, Executive Deputy Director of the New Central Military-Civil Fusion Development Commission Office" (国产大飞机 "掌门人" 金壮龙履新中央军民融合办常务副主任). *The Paper* (澎湃新闻), September 1, 2017. http://m.thepaper.cn/wifiKey_detail.jsp?contid=1781224&from=wifiKey#.

"The Secret History of China's Laser Weapons" (中国激光武器秘史). *Study Times* (学习时报), September 17, 2010. https://news.qq.com/a/20100917/001726.htm?qqcom_pgv_from=aio.

"The Strategic Move of the Rich Country and Strong Army" (富国强军的战略之举). *People's Daily* (人民日报), September 25, 2017. http://www.msweekly.com/show.html?id=93455.

"To Implement the Military-Civil Fusion Development Strategy, We Must Give Full Play to the Role of Local Development and Reform Departments and Enterprises" (国家发改委: 实施军民融合发展战略, 要发挥好地方发改部门和企业的作用). *Finance and Economics Magazine* (财经界杂志), March 2018. https://www.secrss.com/articles/1592.

"Two Major Chinese Aerospace Groups Sign an Agreement to Deepen Strategic Cooperation" (中国航天两大集团签署深化战略合作协议). *China Aerospace News* (中国航天报), August 31, 2020. http://www.spacechina.com/n25/n2014789/n2414549/c2998607/content.html.

"UAVs at 2017 Military-Civil Fusion Expo: Innovative and Eye-Catching; Anti-UAV Devices on the Rise" (2017 军民融合装备展上的无人机: 创新亮眼 反无人机装备兴起). *Global Times Net* (环球网), April 13, 2017. https://uav.huanqiu.com/article/9CaKrnK1Vqa.

"Value-Added Output of Strategic Emerging Industries Will Account for about 10% of GDP by End of 2017" (2017 年底战略性新兴产业增加值占 GDP 比重将达 10% 左右). *Xinhua News Agency* (新华社), July 5, 2017. http://www.xinhuanet.com//politics/2017-07/05/c_1121270049.htm.

"Wan Gang: Funding of Central Science and Technology Projects Is Managed by Nearly 40 Departments, Affecting Efficiency" (万钢: 中央财政科技项目由近 40 个部门管理 影响效率). *China News Network* (中国新闻网), March 11, 2015. http://www.chinanews.com/gn/2015/03-11/7119802.shtml.

Wang, Fanhua, and Peng Liang (王凡华和彭亮). "Two National Engineering Research Centers Including UAV System Will Be Set Up at Northwestern Polytechnical University" (西工大获批立项建设 2 个国家工程研究中心). *China Aviation News* (中国航空新闻网讯), April 8, 2013. https://news.nwpu.edu.cn/info/1002/22605.htm?ixlgklnrzfkuotdx.

Wang, Xinjun (王新俊). "Six Major Characteristics of the Road of National Security with Chinese Characteristics" (中国特色国家安全道路六大特点). *People's Daily (Over-*

seas Edition) (人民日报海外版), January 26, 2015. http://opinion.people.com.cn/n /2015/0126/c1003-26449275.html.

Wen, Bing (温冰). "Correctly Locate the Basic Point for Preparation for Military Struggle" (定准军事斗争准备基点). *Study Times* (学习时报), June 4, 2015. http://www .cssn.cn/dzyx/dzyx_llsj/201506/t20150604_2021650.shtml.

"What New Changes Will Occur in the In-depth Development of China's Military-Civil Fusion in 2018?" (2018, 我国军民融合深度发展将会呈现哪些新变化). *Liberation Army Daily* (解放军报), January 27, 2018. http://www.mod.gov.cn/mobilization /2018-01/27/content_4803480.htm.

"When Inspecting the Academy of Military Science, Xi Jinping Stresses the Need to Work Hard to Build High-Level Military Scientific Research Institutions to Provide Strong Support for Realizing the Party's Goal of Strengthening the Armed Forces in the New Era" (习近平在视察军事科学院时强调 努力建设高水平军事科研机构 为 实现党在新时代的强军目标提供有力支撑). *Xinhua News Agency* (新华社), May 16, 2018. http://www.xinhuanet.com/video/2018-05/16/c_129874089.htm.

Wu, Hongxing, and Wang Guizhi (吴红星和王桂芝). "Vigorous Promotion of Military-Civilian Scientific and Technological Collaborative Innovation in Key Areas" (积极 推进重点领域 军民科技协同创新). *Liberation Army Daily* (解放军报), April 20, 2018. http://www.81.cn/jfjbmap/content/2018-04/20/content_204267.htm.

Wu, Ming (吴铭). "Commentary on the Importance of the CMC Chairman Responsibility System" (关于中央军委主席负责制重要性的评论). *Liberation Army Daily* (解 放军报), November 30, 2015. http://www.xinhuanet.com/mil/2015-11/30/c_1284 82461_2.htm.

Wu, Wei, and Zhu Jiazan (吴伟和朱嘉赞). "Push Out the Stereotypes of the Scientific Research System and Speed Up the Construction of National Laboratories" (跳出 科研体制陈规窠臼 加快建设国家实验室). *Science and Technology Daily* (科技日报), April 10, 2019. http://digitalpaper.stdaily.com/http_www.kjrb.com/kjrb/html /2019-04/10/content_418974.htm?div=-1.

Wu, Zhongshu, Wang Dengchao, and Ren Dalong (吴中书, 王登超和任大龙). "Rule the Army by Law: Writing a New Chapter in Formalization" (书写正规化建设新篇 章). *Liberation Army Daily* (解放军报), October 13, 2017. http://www.81.cn/jfjbmap /content/2017-10/13/content_189658.htm.

"Xi Calls for Efforts to Break New Ground In National Security" (习近平: 开创新时代国 家安全工作新局面). *Xinhua News Agency* (新华社), April 17, 2018. http://www .xinhuanet.com/politics/leaders/2018-04/17/c_1122697734.htm.

"Xi Calls for Holistic National Security Outlook" (习近平的总体国家安全观). *Xinhua News Agency* (新华社), February 17, 2017. http://www.xinhuanet.com//politics /2017-02/17/c_1120486809.htm.

"Xi Demands High-Level Research Institutions for Strong Military" (习近平: 努力建设高 水平军事科研机构). *Xinhua News Agency* (新华社), May 16, 2018. https://baijia-hao.baidu.com/s?id=1600618873076024972&wfr=spider&for=pc.

"Xi Jinping Addresses Ceremony, Symposium Marking Newly Reshuffled Military Academic Institutions" (习近平在新改组的军事学术机构座谈会上致辞). *Xinhua News Agency* (新华社), July 19, 2017. http://www.xinhuanet.com/politics/2017-07/19/c_112 1347127.htm.

"Xi Jinping Addresses Ninth Collective Study Session of the Chinese Communist Party Political Bureau" (习近平主持中共中央政治局举行第九次集体学习). *Xinhua News Agency* (新华社), October 1, 2013. http://www.gov.cn/ldhd/2013-10/01/content_249 9370.htm.

"Xi Jinping Addresses Politburo 17th Collective Study Session, Emphasizes Need to Accurately Grasp New Trends in the World's Military Development, Advance with the

Times to Vigorously Promote Military Innovation" (习近平: 准确把握世界军事发展新趋势 与时俱进大力推进军事创新). *Xinhua News Agency* (新华社), August 30, 2014. http://www.xinhuanet.com//politics/2014-08/30/c_1112294869.htm.

"Xi Jinping Addresses Provincial, Ministerial-Level Cadres Workshop on Developing Risk Solving Skills" (习近平在省部级主要领导干部坚持底线思维着力防范化解重大风险专题研讨班开班式上发表重要讲话). *Xinhua News Agency* (新华社), January 21, 2019. http://www.xinhuanet.com/politics/leaders/2019-01/21/c_1124022412.htm.

"Xi Jinping and His Era." *Xinhua News Agency* (新华社), November 17, 2017. http://www.xinhuanet.com//english/2017-11/17/c_136758372_6.htm.

"Xi Jinping Attends PLA Armament Work Conference, Emphasizes Quickening the Building of an Armament System Commensurate with the Requirements of Performing Missions, Providing Strong Material and Technological Support for the Fulfillment of the Strong Army Dream" (习近平在出席全军装备工作会议时强调: 加快构建适应履行使命要求的装备体系). *China Military Industry News* (中国军工报), December 6, 2014. http://cpc.people.com.cn/n/2014/1205/c64094-26151796.html.

"Xi Jinping Attends Plenary Meeting of PLA Delegation, Stresses Comprehensive Implementation of Innovation-Driven Development Strategy and Promote Realization of New Strides in National Defense and Army Building" (习近平: 全面实施创新驱动发展战略 推动国防和军队建设实现新跨越). *Xinhua News Agency* (新华网), March 13, 2016. http://www.xinhuanet.com//politics/2016-03/13/c_1118316426.htm.

"Xi Jinping Chaired the First Meeting of the CMC National Defense and Military Small Leading Group" (习近平主持中央军委深化国防和军队改革领导小组第一次全体会). *Xinhua News Agency* (新华社), March 15, 2014. http://www.gov.cn/xinwen/2014-03/15/content_2639427.htm.

"Xi Jinping Chairs First NSC Meeting, Stresses National Security with Chinese Characteristics" (习近平: 坚持总体国家安全观 走中国特色国家安全道路). *Xinhua News Agency* (新华社), April 15, 2014. http://www.xinhuanet.com//politics/2014-04/15/c_1110253910.htm.

"Xi Jinping Chairs Political Bureau Meeting on Outline for National Security Strategy" (习近平主持中共中央政治局召开会议 审议通过 国家安全战略纲要). *Xinhua News Agency* (新华社), January 23, 2015. http://www.xinhuanet.com//politics/2015-01/23/c_1114112093.htm.

"Xi Jinping Chairs Second Meeting of Central Financial and Economic Affairs Commission" (习近平主持召开中央财经委员会第二次会议). *Xinhua News Agency* (新华社), July 13, 2018. http://www.gov.cn/xinwen/2018-07/13/content_5306291.htm.

"Xi Jinping Chairs Second Plenum of Central Military-Civil Fusion Development Commission" (习近平主持召开中央军民融合发展委员会第二次全体会议). *Xinhua News Agency* (新华社), September 22, 2017. http://www.gov.cn/xinwen/2017-09/22/content_5226942.htm.

"Xi Jinping Chairs Seventh Meeting of Central Financial and Economic Leading Group, Stresses Need to Accelerate Pace of Implementing Innovation-Driven Development Strategy, Accelerate the Pace of Promoting Transformation of Economic Development Model" (习近平: 加快实施创新驱动发展战略 加快推动经济发展方式转变). *Xinhua News Agency* (新华网), August 18, 2014. http://www.xinhuanet.com/politics/2014-08/18/c_1112126938.htm.

"Xi Jinping: Fully Implement the Innovation-Driven Development Strategy to Promote the Construction of National Defense and the Army to Achieve a New Leap" (习近平: 全面实施创新驱动发展战略 推动国防和军队建设实现新跨越). *Xinhua News*

Agency (新华社), March 13, 2016. http://www.xinhuanet.com//politics/2016-03/13/c_1118316426.htm.

"Xi Jinping Gives Important Instructions to the All-Army Equipment Work Conference, Emphasizing the Comprehensive Creation of a New Situation in Weapons and Equipment Construction, and Making Positive Contributions to the Realization of the Goal of the Military's Centennial Struggle (习近平对全军装备工作会议作出重要指示强调 全面开创武器装备建设新局面 为实现建军一百年奋斗目标作出积极贡献). *Xinhua News Agency* (新华社), October 26, 2021. http://www.news.cn/politics/leaders/2021-10/26/c_1127998203.htm.

"Xi Jinping Gives Important Speech to PLA Delegation at 2016 NPC Meeting" (习近平出席解放军代表团全体会议并讲话). *Xinhua News Agency* (新华社), March 14, 2016. http://www.xinhuanet.com//politics/2016lh/2016-03/14/c_128796772.htm.

"Xi Jinping: Gradually Build a National Strategic System and Capability for Military-Civil Fusion" (习近平: 逐步构建军民一体化的国家战略体系和能力). *Xinhua News Agency* (新华社), June 20, 2017. http://www.xinhuanet.com/mil/2017-06/20/c_129637093.htm.

"Xi Jinping Presided over the First Meeting of the 19th Central National Security Commission and Delivered an Important Speech" (习近平主持召开十九届中央国家安全委员会第一次会议并发表重要讲话). *Xinhua News Agency* (新华社), April 17, 2018. http://www.gov.cn/xinwen/2018-04/17/content_5283445.htm.

"Xi Jinping Stresses Military-Civil Fusion at the Plenum of the PLA Delegation at NPC Session" (习近平在人大会议解放军代表团强调军民融合). *Xinhua News Agency* (新华网), March 2, 2017. http://cpc.people.com.cn/n1/2018/0313/c64094-29863762.html.

"Xi Jinping Talks about the New Whole-of-Nation System" (习近平谈新型举国体制). *Communist Party Construction Network Micro Platform* (党建网微平台), June 5, 2020. http://www.enping.gov.cn/jmepssjj/gkmlpt/content/2/2068/post_2068838.html#3923.

"Xi Jinping's Speech at Rally Celebrating the 90th Anniversary of the Founding of the People's Liberation Army" (习近平: 在庆祝中国人民解放军建军90周年大会上的讲话). *Xinhua News Agency* (新华社), August 1, 2017. http://www.xinhuanet.com/politics/2017-08/01/c_1121416045.htm.

"Xi Jinping's Strategy of Technological Catching Up: There Should be Asymmetric Assassin's Mace" (习近平论科技赶超战略: 应该有非对称性 "杀手锏"). *People's Daily Network* (人民网), March 22, 2016. http://theory.people.com.cn/n1/2016/0322/c40555-28216844.html.

"Xi Leads China's Military Reform, Stressing Building of Strong Army" (习近平领导军事改革, 强调强军目标). *Xinhua News Agency* (新华社), March 15, 2014. http://www.xinhuanet.com//politics/2014-03/15/c_119785243.htm.

"Xi Stresses Integrated Military, Civilian Development" (习近平强调军民融合发展). *Xinhua News Agency* (新华社), September 22, 2017. http://www.gov.cn/xinwen/2017-09/22/content_5226942.htm.

Xu, Guanghua (徐冠华). "The Development of the S&T Information Industry in the Building of an Innovation Country" (创新型国家建设中科技信息产业的发展). *Ministry of Science and Technology* (科技部), October 19, 2006. http://www.gov.cn/gzdt/2006-10/19/content_417635.htm.

Xue, Zhiliang (薛志亮). "Fight the 'Pandemic' and Refresh Thinking on National Defense Mobilization" (战 "疫", 刷新国防动员思路). *China National Defense News* (中国国防报), April 2, 2020. http://www.gfdy.gov.cn/topnews/2020-04/02/content_9783197.htm.

Yang, Dazhi (杨大志). "Political Security Is Fundamental to National Security" (政治安全是国家安全的根本). *Liberation Army Daily* (解放军报), April 20, 2018. http://www.81.cn/jfjbmap/content/2018-04/20/content_204248.htm.

Yao, Youzhi. Talk at the Shenzhen Culture Forum (姚有志在深圳文化论坛上的讲话). Shenzhen Citizen Culture Lecture Hall (深圳市民文化大讲堂), August 18, 2012. http://www.szccf.com.cn/wqhg_content_662.html.

Yin, Weijun (尹卫军). "Seize the Key Systems to Promote and Accelerate the Implementation of Military-Civil Fusion Reform Tasks" (军民结合推进司: 抓住重点系统推进, 加快军民融合改革任务落实), *Ministry of Industry and Information Technology* (工信部), December 31, 2016. http://zjiii.org/html/xinwendongtai/1348.html.

Yu, Chen (喻尘). "Secret History of China's Aerospace Industry" (中国航天历程揭秘). *Southern Metropolis Daily* (南方都市报), October 25, 2007. https://news.163.com/07/1025/10/3RL2N4PF00012EP4.html.

Yu, Ping (余萍). "The J-11B Comes from Su-27 and Becomes a Better Fighter Plane" (中国歼 11B 可同时探测 20 个目标并攻击 6 个目标). *Military Digest* (军事文摘) 12 (2007). http://mil.news.sina.com.cn/p/2008-01-15/0746481266.html.

Yuan, Dongming, Ma Jun, and Wang Huaiyu (袁东明, 马骏和王怀宇). "It Is Necessary to Give Full Play to the Role of the Market in Science and Technology Incubation" (充分发挥市场在科技孵化中的作用). *China Economic Times* (中国经济时报), June 16, 2014. http://www.chinareform.net/index.php?m=content&c=index&a=show&catid=28&id=13610.

Zhang, Xiaoqi (张晓祺). "Armament Work: It Is the Right Time for Reform and Innovation" (装备工作: 改革创新正当其时). *Liberation Army Daily* (解放军报), February 13, 2014. http://cpc.people.com.cn/n/2014/0213/c83083-24345683.html.

Zhang, Zhanbin, and Du Qinghao (张占斌和杜庆昊). "Regarding Core Technology Breakthroughs, How General Secretary Xi Lays It Out" (关于核心技术突破, 习总书记如何布局). *People's Tribune* (人民论坛), May 2018. http://opinion.haiwainet.cn/n/2018/0515/c456318-31316226.html.

"Zhang Youxia: Member of Political Bureau of CPC Central Committee" (张又侠: 中共中央政治局委员). *China Daily* (中国日报), October 26, 2017. https://www.chinadaily.com.cn/china/2017-10/26/content_33723562.htm.

Zhao, Lei. "PLA Says Chief of Its Arms Wing Replaced." *China Daily* (中国日报), September 19, 2017. https://www.chinadaily.com.cn/china/2017-09/19/content_32187194.htm.

Zhen, Yujun, Ma De, and Yi Fei (郑宇钧, 马德和易非). "Military-Civil Fusion Makes Chinese Military Different" (军民融合让中国军队不一样). *Nanfang Zhoumo* (南方周末), March 1, 2018. http://www.infzm.com/content/133719.

Zhong, Guoan (钟国安). "Take General Secretary Xi Jinping's Holistic National Security Concept as Guidance and Write a New Chapter of National Security" (以习近平总书记总体国家安全观为指引 谱写国家安全新篇章). *Qiushi* (求是), April 15, 2017. http://www.qstheory.cn/dukan/qs/2017-04/15/c_1120788993.htm.

Zhong, Wen, and Hong Hong (钟文和洪鸿). "Hot Handed Weapon Licenses" (炙手可热的武器许可证). *China Enterprise News* (中国企业报), August 9, 2016. http://epaper.zqcn.com.cn/content/2016-08/09/content_33087.htm.

Zhou, Yuehui (周跃辉). "The Dialectical Relationship between the New Development Pattern and the New Development Concept" (新发展格局与新发展理念的辩证关系). *Chengdu Daily* (成都日报), September 2, 2020. https://theory.gmw.cn/2020-09/02/content_34145932.htm.

Zong, Zhaodun, and Zhao Bo (宗兆盾和赵波). "Major Reform Considered in Work on the Prices of Our Army's Armaments" (我军装备价格工作酝酿重大改革). *Liberation*

Army Daily (解放军报), November 13, 2009. http://www.china.com.cn/military/txt /2009-11/12/content_18870203.htm.

CHINESE-LANGUAGE OFFICIAL GOVERNMENT PUBLICATIONS AND LEADERSHIP SPEECHES

"13th Five-Year National Science and Technology Innovation Plan" ("十三五" 国家科技 创新规划). *State Council* (国务院), July 28, 2016. http://www.gov.cn/zhengce /content/2016-08/08/content_5098072.htm.

"13th Five-Year Plan for the Development of Strategic Emerging Industries" (国务院关于印 发 "十三五" 国家战略性新兴产业发展规划的通知). *State Council* (国务院), November 29, 2016. http://www.gov.cn/zhengce/content/2016-12/19/content_5150090.htm.

"14th Five-Year Plan for National Economic and Social Development of the People's Republic of China (2021–2025) and the Outline of Long-Term Goals for 2035" (中华 人民共和国国民经济和社会发展第十四个五年规划和 2035 年远景目标纲要). *Xinhua News Agency* (新华社), March 12, 2021. http://www.gov.cn/xinwen/2021-03 /13/content_5592681.htm.

"2010 Annual Report of the Major Special S&T Programs" (国家科技年度报告2010(国家 科技重大专项)). *Ministry of Science & Technology* (科技部), 2010. http://www .most.gov.cn/ndbg/2011ndbg/201203/p020120330342474680592.pdf.

"Administrative Measures of the State Administration for Science, Technology, and Industry for National Defense for Basic Scientific Research" (国防科工局基础科研 管理办法). *State Administration for Science, Technology, and Industry for National Defense* (国防科工局), Document no. 136, publicly released April 28, 2018. http:// www.sastind.gov.cn/n4235/c6801289/content.html.

"Additive Manufacturing and Laser Manufacturing" Key Special Project 2018 Annual Project Application Guidelines" ("增材制造与激光制造" 重点专项 2018 年度项目 申报指南). *Ministry of Science and Technology* (科技部). http://zct.ideatob.com /mp/?at=5&lb=0&bno=8338&aid=

"Administrative Measures on National Engineering Research Centers" (国家工程研究中 心管理办法). *National Development and Reform Commission* (国家发展和改革委员 会), March 5, 2007. http://www.gov.cn/ziliao/flfg/2007-03/12/content_548451.htm.

"Central Committee of the Communist Party of China and the State Council issued the 'National Innovation-driven Development Strategy Outline'" (中共中央 国务院印 发《国家创新驱动发展战略纲要》). *Xinhua News Agency* (新华社), May 19, 2016. http://www.xinhuanet.com/politics/2016-05/19/c_1118898033.htm.

"Central Military Commission Issues 'Opinions Concerning Deepening the Reform of National Defense and the Armed Forces'" (中央军委印发《关于深化国防和军队改 革的意见》). *Xinhua News Agency* (新华社), January 1, 2016. http://www .xinhuanet.com/mil/2016-01/01/c_1117646692.htm.

China Statistical Yearbook (中国统计年鉴) China Statistics Bureau (中国统计出版社), Annual Editions. http://www.stats.gov.cn/tjsj/ndsj/.

"China's Military Strategy" (中国的军事战略). *State Council* (国务院), May 2015. http:// www.scio.gov.cn/zfbps/ndhf/2015/Document/1435161/1435161.htm.

"China's National Defense in 2010" (2010 年中国的国防). *State Council Information Office* (国务院新闻办公室), March 31, 2011. http://www.gov.cn/zhengce/2011-03/31 /content_2618567.htm.

Commission on Science, Technology, and Industry for National Defense (国防科学技术工 业委员会). "Outline of Defense Medium- and Long-Term Science and Technology Development Plan" (国防科技工业中长期科学和技术发展规划纲要颁布). May 29, 2006.

"Communiqué of the Fifth Plenary Session of the 18th Central Committee of the Communist Party of China" (中国共产党第十八届中央委员会第五次全体会议公报). *Xinhua News Agency* (新华网), October 29, 2015. http://www.xinhuanet.com//politics/2015-10/29/c_1116983078.htm.

"Communiqué on the Current State of the Ideological Sphere" (关于当前意识形态领域情况的通报). *Central Committee of the Communist Party of China General Office* (中共中央办公厅), April 23, 2013.

"COSTIND Starts Construction of Defense S&T National Laboratories: Interview with Sun Laiyan, COSTIND Deputy Director" (国防科工局开始建设国防科技实验室: 采访国防科工委副主任孙来燕). *Central Government* website (中央政府门户网站), September 16, 2007. http://www.gov.cn/zxft/ft59/wz.htm.

"CPC Central Committee Retransmits the Decision on Several Issues Concerning Military Political Work under the New Situation and Stresses Giving Even Better Play to the Role of Political Work as the Lifeline in the Course of Building a Strong Army and Rejuvenating the Army" (中共中央转发《关于新形势下军队政治工作若干问题的决定》强调在强军兴军征程中更好发挥政治工作生命线作用). *Xinhua News Agency* (新华社), January 30, 2015. http://www.xinhuanet.com//politics/2015-01/30/c_1114199584.htm.

"Decision of the Chinese Communist Party Central Committee on Several Major Issues Concerning the Comprehensive Deepening of Reforms" (Adopted by the Third Plenary Session of the 18th CPC Central Committee on November 12, 2013) (关于 《中共中央关于全面深化改革若干重大问题的决定》 的说明). *Xinhua News Agency* (新华社), November 15, 2015. http://cpc.people.com.cn/xuexi/n/2015/0720/c397563-27331312.html.

"Decision of the CPC Central Committee on Several Major Issues Concerning Comprehensive Deepening of Reforms" (中共中央关于全面深化改革若干重大问题的决定). *Xinhua News Agency* (新华社), November 12, 2013. http://www.gov.cn/jrzg/2013-11/15/content_2528179.htm.

"Establishment of Defense Industry Development Strategy Committee" (国防科技工业科学技术委员会在京成立). *State Administration for Science, Technology and Industry for National Defense* (国家国防科技工业局), June 5, 2015. http://www.miit.gov.cn/n11293472/n11293832/n11293907/n11368223/16625375.html.

Fourth Plenum of the 19th Chinese Communist Party Central Committee. "Decision of the Chinese Communist Party Central Committee on Several Major Issues Concerning Upholding and Improving the Socialist System with Chinese Characteristics and Promoting the Modernization of the National Governance System and Governance Ability" (中共中央关于坚持和完善中国特色社会主义制度推进国家治理体系和治理能力现代化若干重大问题的决定). *Xinhua News Agency* (新华社), November 5, 2019. http://www.xinhuanet.com/2019-11/05/c_1125195786.htm.

"Guidelines for the Implementation of the 'National Medium- and Long-term Program for Science and Technology Development (2006–2020)'" (国务院关于印发实施" 国家中长期科学和技术发展规划纲要 (2006–2020 年)" 若干配套政策的通知). *State Council* (国务院), February 2006. http://www.gov.cn/zwgk/2006-02/26/content_211553.htm.

"Guidelines on Developing and Promoting the National IC Industry" (国家集成电路产业发展推进纲要). *Ministry of Industry and Information Technology* (工信部), June 24, 2014. http://www.miit.gov.cn/n11293472/n11293832/n11293907/n1136822 3/16044261.html.

"High-Performance Computing" Key Special Project 2021 Annual Project Application Guidelines" (高性能计算" 重点专项 2021 年度项目申报指南). *Ministry of Science and Technology* (科技部). https://www.sdxz2050.com/5926.html.

Hu, Jintao (胡锦涛). "Hu Jintao's Speech at the Meeting Celebrating the Great Success of China's First Lunar Probe Project" (胡锦涛在庆祝我国首次探月工程成功大会上的讲话). *Xinhua News Agency* (新华社), December 12, 2007. http://www.gov.cn/ldhd/2007-12/12/content_832298.htm.

——. "Report to the 18th National Congress of the Communist Party of China" (胡锦涛在中国共产党第十八次全国代表大会上的报告). *Xinhua News Agency* (新华社), November 8, 2012. http://www.xinhuanet.com//18cpcnc/2012-11/17/c_113711665.htm.

——. "Unswervingly Advance along the Path of Chinese Characteristics, Struggle to Complete the Building of a Well-Off Society in an All-Round Way." Report to the 18th Chinese Communist Party National Congress (坚定不移沿着中国特色社会主义道路前进　为全面建成小康社会而奋斗), November 8, 2012. *Xinhua News Agency* (新华社), November 17, 2012. http://www.xinhuanet.com//18cpcnc/2012-11/17/c_113711665.htm.

"Hu Jintao's Report at the 17th Party Congress" (胡锦涛在党的十七大上的报告). *Xinhua News Agency* (新华社), October 24, 2007. http://politics.people.com.cn/GB/8198/6429196.html.

"Interim Measures for Administration of Defense Science and Technology Industrial Innovation Centers" (国防科工局关于印发《国防科技工业创新中心管理暂行办法》《国防科技工业创新中心设立评规则》的通知). *State Administration for Science, Technology and Industry for National Defense* (国防科工局), January 27, 2016. http://www.zj.gov.cn/art/2016/1/27/art_14072_265594.html.

"Internal Structure, Staffing, and Primary Duties of the Ministry of Industry and Information Technology" (工业和信息化部主要职责内设机构和人员编制规定). *State Council General Office* (国务院办公厅), July 17, 2008. http://www.gov.cn/gzdt/2008-07/17/content_1048292.htm.

"Interpret 'Made in China 2025': 'Three-Step' Strategy to Become a Manufacturing Power" ("中国制造 2025" 解读之六: 制造强国 '三步走' 战略"). *Ministry of Industry and Information Technology* (工信部), May 19, 2015. http://www.miit.gov.cn/n11293472/n11293832/n11294042/n11481465/16595227.html.

"Introduction to 'The Three Military Industrial Certificates': Confidential and Qualification Certification of Weapons and Equipment Research and Production Units" ("军工三证" 介绍: 武器装备科研生产单位保密资格认证). *Zhejiang Provincial Defense Science, Technology, and Industry Association* (浙江省国防科技工业协会), November 1, 2017. http://www.zjgfxh.com/szzx/show/id/122.html.

Liu, He (刘鹤). "Accelerate the Construction of a New Development Pattern with the Domestic Cycle as the Main Body and the Domestic and International Cycles Mutually Promoting Each Other" (加快构建以国内大循环为主体、国内国际双循环相互促进的新发展格局). *People's Daily* (人民日报), November 25, 2020. http://paper.people.com.cn/rmrb/html/2020-11/25/nw.D110000renmrb_20201125_1-06.htm.

"Made in China 2025: Realizing the Manufacturing Power Strategy" (中国制造 2025 文件印发: 实现制造业强国战略). *State Council* (国务院), May 8, 2015. http://www.gov.cn/zhengce/content/2015-05/19/content_9784.htm.

"MIIT's 2018 Military-Civil Fusion Work Ideas and Work Arrangements" (工信部 2018 年军民融合工作思路和工作安排). January 17, 2018. https://www.secrss.com/articles/338.

Ministry of Finance (财政部). "Report on the Implementation of the Central and Local Budgets in 2019 and Draft Central and Local Budgets for 2020" (关于 2019 年中央和地方预算执行情况与 2020 年中央和地方预算草案的报告), May 30, 2020. http://www.mof.gov.cn/gkml/caizhengshuju/202005/t20200530_3523307.htm.

"Ministry of National Defense Holds News Conference on CMC Administrative Reforms and Reorganization" (国防部召开军委机关调整组建专题新闻发布会). *China*

Military Online (中国军网), January 11, 2016. http://www.mod.gov.cn/info/2016 -01/11/content_4637928.htm.

Ministry of Science and Technology (科技部). *Notice on Applying for 2020 National Foreign Expert Projects* (关于申报 2020 年度国家外国专家项目的通知). Translated by Ben Murphy. Washington, DC: Center for Security and Emerging Technology, 2020. https://cset.georgetown.edu/wp-content/uploads/t0100_belt_road_young _experts_EN-1.pdf.

"Ministry of Science and Technology and CMC Science and Technology Commission Jointly Issue 13th Five-Year Special Plan for Science and Technology Military-Civil Fusion Development Assigning 16 Key Tasks in 7 Areas" (科技部和中央军委科学技术委员会联合印发《"十三五"科技军民融合发展专项规划》布局七大领域十六个关键任务). *Ministry of Science and Technology* (科技部), April 12, 2017. https:// cailiao.just.edu.cn/2017/1002/c4134a21999/page.htm.

"National Defense Technology Industry Science and Technology Committee Was Established in Beijing" (国防科技工业科学技术委员会在京成立). *State Administration for Science, Technology and Industry for National Defense* (国防科工局), November 14, 2018. http://www.sastind.gov.cn/n112/n117/c6803961/content.html.

National Development and Reform Commission (国家发展和改革委员会). "The Grand Blueprint for Starting a New Journey of Building a Modern Socialist Country in an All-Round Way" (开启全面建设社会主义现代化国家新征程的宏伟蓝图). *Qiushi* (求是), March 16, 2021. http://www.qstheory.cn/dukan/qs/2021-03/16/c_1127 209214.htm.

"National Military-Civil Fusion Innovation Demonstration Zones" (国家军民融合创新示范区). *Ministry of Industry and Information Technology* (工信部), July 2, 2018. http://www.ecorr.org/news/industry/2018-07-02/169431.html.

"Notice of Release of the Second Batch of Requirements of the National Defense Technology Innovation Rapid Response Small Group (Dalian)" (关于国防科技创新快速响应小组 (大连) 2020 年第 2 批需求发布的通知). *National Defense Technology Innovation Rapid Response Team (Dalian)* (国防科技创新快速响应小组(大连), March 12, 2020. http://www.dl.gov.cn/gov/detail/detail.vm?diid=100C010002003 11211020031217&lid=3_3.

"Notice of the Heilongjiang Provincial People's Government on Adjustment of Members of the Heilongjiang Provincial High-Technology Project Leading Group" (黑龙江省人民政府关于调整黑龙江省高新工程领导小组成员的通知). Heilongjiang Government Document no. 56 (黑龙江省政府no. 56 号文件), August 23, 2005. http:// www.law-lib.com/law/law_view.asp?id=104433.

"Notice of the Provincial Defense Industry Office on Supporting the Construction Work of the High-Technology Project" (黑龙江省人民政府办公厅转发省国防工办关于支持高新工程建设意见的通知). Heilongjiang Government Issued Document no. 78 (2001) (黑政办发 [2001]78 号), December 4, 2001. http://pkulaw.cn/fulltext _form.aspx?Gid=16858126&Db=lar.

"Notice of the State Council on the Establishment of Advisory and Coordinating Organs" (国务院议事协调机构设置). *Central People's Government of the People's Republic of China* (中华人民共和国中央政府), State Document no. 13, March 21, 2008. http://www.gov.cn/zwgk/2008-04/24/content_953488.htm.

"Notice on Holding the National Defense Science, Technology, and Innovation Rapid Response Small Group 'Chongqing Region' Proposal Day" (关于举办国防科技创新快速响应小组 "重庆地区" 提案日活动的通知). *Chongqing Science and Technology Bureau and National Defense Science, Technology, and Innovation Rapid Response Team* (重庆快响小组和重庆市科学技术局), May 26, 2020. http://kjj.cq.gov .cn/zwxx_176/tzgg/202005/t20200526_7480933.html.

"Notice on Soliciting Investment Projects from the National Defense Science, Technology, and Industry MCF Industrial Investment Fund" (关于征集国家国防科技工业军民融合产业投资基金投资项目的通知). *Quanzhou Economic and Informatization Commission* (泉州市经济和信息化委员会), July 16, 2018. https://www.sohu.com/a/241711225_100006481.

"Opinions of the CPC Central Committee and State Council on Deepening Reform of Institutional Mechanisms and Accelerating the Implementation of Innovation-Driven Development Strategy" (中共中央 国务院关于深化体制机制改革加快实施创新驱动发展战略的若干意见). *Xinhua News Agency* (新华社), March 23, 2015. http://www.xinhuanet.com//politics/2015-03/23/c_1114735805_5.htm.

"Opinions of the General Office of the State Council on Promoting the Deep Development of Military-Civil Fusion of Defense Science, Technology, and Industry" (国务院办公厅关于推动国防科技工业军民融合深度发展的意见). State Council General Office Document no. 91 (国办发 91 号), November 23, 2017. http://www.chinanews.com/cj/2017/12-04/8392248.shtml.

"Opinions on the Establishment and Perfection of an Armaments Development and Production System in Accordance with the Principles of Military-Civil Fusion and Embedding the Defense Sector within the Civilian Sector" (国务院中央军委关于建立和完善军民结合寓军于民武器装备科研生产体系的若干意见). *State Council* (国务院), October 24, 2010. http://www.jxzb.gov.cn/2011-1/20111111433114.htm.

"Opinions on the Integrated Development of Economic Construction and Defense Construction" (关于经济建设和国防建设融合发展的意见). *Xinhua News Agency* (新华社), July 21, 2016. http://www.xinhuanet.com//politics/2016-07/21/c_1119259282.htm.

"Opinions to Encourage Technology Transfer and Innovation and Promote the Transformation of the Growth Mode in Foreign Trade" (关于鼓励技术引进和创新, 促进转变外贸增长方式的若干意见). Ministry of Commerce, National Development and Reform Commission, Ministry of Science and Technology, Ministry of Finance, General Customs Administration, General Tax Administration, State Intellectual Property Office, and State Foreign Exchange Office (商务部、发展改革委、科技部、财政部、海关总署、税务总局、知识产权局、外汇局), July 14, 2006. http://www.most.gov.cn/ztzl/gjzctx/ptzcyjxh/200802/t20080225_59303.htm.

"Outline of the National Defense Science, Technology, and Industry Medium- and Long-Term Science and Technology Development Plan Promulgated" (国防科技工业中长期科技发展规划纲要颁布). *Xinhua News Agency* (新华社), May 25, 2006. http://www.edu.cn/rd/gai_kuang/xin_wen_gong_gao/200605/t20060525_180366.shtml.

"Outline of the National Strategy of Innovation-Driven Development" (国家创新驱动发展战略纲要). Background Briefing by the Minister of Science and Technology, May 23, 2016. http://www.china.com.cn/zhibo/zhuanti/ch-xinwen/2016-05/23/content_38515829.htm.

"Policy Explanation on Deepening the Management Reform Central Funding of S&T Plans (Items and Funds)" (关于深化中央财政科技计划 (专项、基金等) 管理改革的方案 政策解读). *Ministry of Science and Technology* (科技部), January 1, 2015. http://www.most.cn/kjzc/zdkjzcjd/201501/t20150106_117286.htm.

"President Xi Urges Independent R&D for Aviation Engines, Gas Turbines." *Xinhua News Agency* (新华社), August 28, 2016. https://www.globaltimes.cn/content/1003351.shtml.

"Provisions on the Administration of Major National Science and Technology Projects (Civilian Projects)" (国家科技重大专项 (民口) 管理规定). *Ministry of Science and Technology, National Development and Reform Commission, and Ministry of*

Finance (科技部, 发改委和财政部). Document no. 145, January 6, 2019. http://www
.most.gov.cn/mostinfo/xinxifenlei/fgzc/gfxwj/gfxwj2017/201706/t20170627
_133757.htm.

"Quantum Control and Quantum Information" Key Special Project 2020 Annual Project Application Guidelines" ("量子调控与量子信息" 重点专项 2020 年度项目申报
指南). *Ministry of Science and Technology* (科技部), September 2019. https://service
.most.gov.cn/u/cms/static/201909/24150950111y.pdf.

"Recommendations of the Chinese Communist Party Central Committee on Formulating
the 14th Five-Year Plan for National Economic and Social Development and Long-
Term Goals for 2035" (中共中央关于制定国民经济和社会发展第十四个五年规划和二
〇三五年远景目标的建议). *Xinhua News Agency* (新华社), November 3, 2020. http://
www.xinhuanet.com/politics/zywj/2020-11/03/c_1126693293.htm.

"SASTIND Cancels 200 Weapons and Equipment Research and Production Licenses"
(国防科工局注销 200 家单位武器装备科研生产许可证). SASTIND (国防科技工业
局), May 31, 2019. http://clep.org.cn/n112/n117/c6806419/content.html.

"SASTIND Issues '2016 SASTIND Military-Civil Fusion Special Action Plan'" (国防科
工局关于印发 "2016 年国防科工局军民融合专项行动计划" 的通知). *State Admin-
istration for Science, Technology and Industry for National Defense* (国防科工局),
March 13, 2016. http://www.acfic.org.cn/zzjg_327/nsjg/bgt/bgttzgg/201603
/t20160316_3356.html.

"SASTIND Issues Notice on Rules for Defense S&T and Industry Fixed Assets Investment Program Management" (国防科技工业固定资产投资项目管理规定). *State
Administration for Science, Technology and Industry for National Defense* (国防科
工委), August 27, 2013. http://www.opt.ac.cn/jg/glbm/kjyglb/xagjsjgglwj/201309
/W020140328373812704712.pdf.

"SASTIND Publishes Guide to Publicize Military Industrial Intelligent Manufacturing
Special Action Plan for Defense S&T Industry Strong Basic Project" (国防科工局公
开发布国防科技工业强基工程军工智能制造专项行动计划项目指南). *State Adminis-
tration for Science, Technology and Industry for National Defense* (国防科工局),
April 28, 2018. http://www.gov.cn/xinwen/2018-04/28/content_5286691.htm.

"SASTIND Take Measures to Accelerate National Defense Science, Technology and Industry Coordinated Innovation" (国防科工局多措并举加快推进国防科技工业协同
创新). *State Administration for Science, Technology and Industry for National Defense* (国防科工局), June 29, 2016. http://www.sastind.gov.cn/n112/n117/c6603
042/content.html.

"Second Central Inspection Team Sent to SASTIND Party Committee to Inspect the Situation" (中央第二巡视组向国防科工局党组反馈专项巡视情况). *Central Commission
for Discipline Inspection Supervision* website (中央纪委监察部网站), June 8, 2016.
http://www.ccdi.gov.cn/special/zyxszt/djlxs_zyxs/fkqk_18jzydjl_zyxs/201606
/t20160613_80395.html.

"Speech by Xi Jinping at the 17th Conference of the Chinese Academy of Sciences and
12th Conference of the Chinese Academy of Engineering" (习近平在中国科学院
第十七次院士大会、中国工程院第十二次院士大会上的讲话). *Xinhua News Agency*
(新华社), June 9, 2014. http://cpc.people.com.cn/n/2014/0610/c64094-25125594
.html.

"State Council Decision on Accelerating the Development of Strategic Emerging Industries" (国务院关于加快培育和发展战略性新兴产业的决定). *State Council* (国务院),
October 2010. http://www.gov.cn/zwgk/2010-10/18/content_1724848.htm.

"State Council Notice on Deepening the Management Reform Plan of Central Financial
Science and Technology Plans (Special Items, Funds, etc.)" (国务院印发关于深化
中央财政科技计划 (专项、基金等) 管理改革方案的通知). *Ministry of Science and*

Technology (科技部), January 7, 2015. http://www.most.gov.cn/ztzl/shzyczkjjhglgg /wjfb/201501/t20150107_117294.htm.

"State Council Notice on the Adjustment of the State Council Central Military Commission Central Special Commission" (国务院发 "关于调整国务院中央军委专门委员会的通知"). *State Council* (国务院), September 22, 2008. http://www.gansu.gov .cn/art/2008/9/22/art_420_187905.html.

"State Council Notice on the Establishment of Deliberative Coordination Institutions and Temporary Institutions" (国务院关于议事协调机构和临时机构设置的通知). State Council Document no. 10 (国务院 no.10 号文件), March 21, 2003. http:// www.gov.cn/gongbao/content/2003/content_62047.htm.

"State Council Promotes Military-Civil Fusion: Actively Introduce Social Capital to Participate in the Shareholding Reform of Military Industrial Enterprises" (国务院促军民融合: 积极引入社会资本参与军工企业股份制改造). *Xinhua News Agency* (新华社), December 4, 2017. https://m.huanqiu.com/article/9CaKrnK5VdK.

"Strategic Advanced Electronic Materials Key Special Project 2020 Annual Project Application Guidelines" (战略性先进电子材料重点专项 2020 年度项目申报指南), *Ministry of Science and Technology* (科技部). http://www.chinabx.org.cn/upload /202004/23/202004231051348806.pdf

"Strategic Cooperation Officially Launched between National Natural Science Foundation and CMC S&T Commission" (国家自然科学基金委员会与中央军委科学技术委员会战略合作正式启动). *National Natural Science Foundation* (国家自然科学基金会), August 15, 2016. http://www.nsfc.gov.cn/publish/portal0/tab440/info55759.htm.

"Struggle to Build a Strong Country in Science and Technology: Speech by Xi Jinping Delivered at the National Science and Technology Innovation Conference, the Conference of Academicians of the Chinese Academy of Sciences and the Chinese Academy of Engineering, and the 9th National Congress of the Chinese Association for Science and Technology" (抢占先机迎难而上建设世界科技强国: 习近平出席中国科学院第十九次院士大会、中国工程院第十四次院士大会开幕会并发表重要讲话). *Xinhua News Agency* (新华网), May 31, 2016. http://www.xinhuanet .com//politics/2016-05/30/c_1118956522.htm.

"Technological Progress Is Changing with Each Passing Day and the Innovation Drive is Outstanding: 15th Report on Economic and Social Development Achievements in the 40 Years of Reform and Opening" (科技进步日新月异 创新驱动成效突出—改革开放 40 年经济社会发展成就系列报告之十五). *State Statistics Bureau* (国家统计局), September 12, 2018. http://www.stats.gov.cn/ztjc/ztfx/ggkf40n/201809/t20180912 _1622413.html.

"The 13th Five-Year Special Plan for S&T Military-Civil Fusion Development" ("十三五"科技军民融合发展专项规划). *Ministry of Science and Technology* (科技部), August 24, 2017. https://web.archive.org/web/20200531235848/; http://www.most.gov .cn/mostinfo/xinxifenlei/fgzc/gfxwj/gfxwj2017/201708/W020170824580027341808 .doc.

"The Diversified Employment of China's Armed Forces" (中国武装力量的多样化运用). *State Council Information Office* (国务院新闻办公室), April 16, 2013. http://www .gov.cn/zhengce/2013-04/16/content_2618550.htm.

Wang, Qishan (王岐山). "Speech at the 18th Meeting of the 12th Standing Committee of the Chinese People's Political Consultative Conference National Committee" (在政协第十二届全国委员会常务委员会第十八次会议上的讲话). *Xinhua News Agency* (新华网), December 2, 2016. http://www.cppcc.gov.cn/zxww/2016/11/01/ARTI147795 9667104989.shtml.

"Xi Jinping: Correctly Understand and Grasp the Major Issues of Medium- and Long-Term Economic and Social Development" (习近平: 正确认识和把握中长期经济社

会发展重大问题). *Qiushi* (求是), January 15, 2021. http://www.xinhuanet.com
/politics/leaders/2021-01/15/c_1126987023.htm.

"Xi Jinping Delivers a Speech at the Opening of the 19th Meeting of the Academicians of
the Chinese Academy of Sciences and the 14th Meeting of the Academicians of the
Chinese Academy of Engineering" (习近平在中国科学院第十九次院士大会, 中国工
程院第十四次院士大会上的讲话). *Xinhua News Agency (新华网)*, May 28, 2018.

Xi, Jinping (习近平). "Explanations of the CPC Central Committee's Resolution Concerning Several Major Issues in Comprehensively Deepening Reform" (中共中央
关于全面深化改革若干重大问题的决定). *Xinhua News Agency* (新华社), Novem-
ber 15, 2013. http://www.gov.cn/jrzg/2013-11/15/content_2528179.htm.

——. "Secure a Decisive Victory in Building a Moderately Prosperous Society in All Re-
spects and Strive for the Great Success of Socialism with Chinese Characteristics
for a New Era" (决胜全面建成小康社会 夺取新时代中国特色社会主义伟大胜利).
Report to the 19th Chinese Communist Party National Congress, *Xinhua News
Agency* (新华社), October 18, 2017. http://www.xinhuanet.com//politics
/19cpcnc/2017-10/27/c_1121867529.htm.

——. "Several Major Issues in the National Medium- and Long-Term Economic and Social Development Strategy" (国家中长期经济社会发展战略若干重大问题). *Qiushi*
(求是), October 31, 2020. http://www.qstheory.cn/dukan/qs/2020-10/31/c_11266
80390.htm

"Xi Jinping: Struggle to Build a Strong Country in Science and Technology of the World."
National Science and Technology Innovation Conference, Academicians Conference of the Chinese Academy of Sciences and Chinese Academy of Engineering,
and Ninth National Congress of the Chinese Association for Science and Technology (习近平: 为建设世界科技强国而奋斗, 在全国科技创新大会、两院院士大会、
中国科协第九次全国代表大会上的讲话). *Xinhua News Agency* (新华社), May 31,
2016. http://www.xinhuanet.com/politics/2016-05/31/c_1118965169.htm.

Xi, Jinping (习近平). "Xi Jinping: Decisive Victory to Build a Moderately Prosperous Society in an All-Round Way and Win the Great Victory of Socialism with Chinese
Characteristics in the New Era. Report at the 19th National Congress of the Communist Party of China" (习近平: 决胜全面建成小康社会 夺取新时代中国特色社会主
义伟大胜利—在中国共产党第十九次全国代表大会上的报告). *Xinhua News Agency*
(新华社), October 18, 2017. http://www.xinhuanet.com/politics/19cpcnc/2017-10
/27/c_1121867529.htm.

——. "Xi Jinping: Explanation of the 'Recommendations of the Chinese Communist Party
Central Committee on Formulating the 14th Five-Year Plan for National Economic
and Social Development and Long-Term Goals for 2035'" (习近平: 关于《中共中央关
于制定国民经济和社会发展第十四个五年规划和二○三五年远景目标的建议》的说明).
Xinhua News Agency (新华社), November 3, 2020. http://www.xinhuanet.com
/politics/leaders/2020-11/03/c_1126693341.htm; http://www.xinhuanet.com/politics
/2018-05/28/c_1122901308.htm.

"Xi Jinping's Speech at Opening of Second World Internet Conference" (习近平在第二届
世界互联网大会开幕式上的讲话). *Xinhua News Agency (新华社)*, December 16,
2015. http://www.xinhuanet.com//politics/2015-12/16/c_1117481089.htm.

"Xi Jinping's Speech at Rally Celebrating 90th Anniversary of the Founding of the People's
Liberation Army" (习近平在庆祝中国人民解放军建军 90 周年大会上的讲话). *Xin-
hua News Agency* (新华社), August 1, 2017. http://www.xinhuanet.com/politics
/2017-08/01/c_1121416045.htm.

"Xi Jinping Talks about Military-Civil Fusion: It is About National Security and Overall Development" (习近平谈军民融合: 是国家战略 关乎国家安全和发展全局). *Qi-*

ushi (求是), October 16, 2018. http://cpc.people.com.cn/xuexi/n1/2017/0123 /c385474-29043923.html.

Ziwen, Jiang (蒋子文). "Former GAD Director Zhang Youxia Becomes New Director of CMC Equipment Development Department" (原总装备部部长张又侠上将任新组建的军委装备发展部部长). *The Paper* (澎湃新闻), January 14, 2016. https://www .thepaper.cn/newsDetail_forward_1420521.

CHINESE-LANGUAGE JOURNAL ARTICLES AND BOOKS

Bai, Pengju (白朋举). "Zhang Aiping's Thinking on Defense Science and Technology" (张爱萍国防科技思想探析). *Military History Research* (军事历史研究) 3 (2007): 51–58.

Bi, Jingjing, and Ren Tianzuo (毕京京和任天佑), chief eds. *China Military-Civil Fusion Development Report 2014* (中国军民融合发展报告2014). Beijing: National Defense University Press (北京; 国防大学出版社), 2014.

Cao, Guosheng (操国胜). "Do Some Things, Do Not Do Other Things: The Strategic Approach to Socialist Reform and Innovation" (有所为有所不为-社会主义改革创新的战略方针). *Journal of Chizhou Teachers College* (池州学院学报) 6 (2005): 1–6.

Cao, Yingwang (曹应旺). *China's Chief Steward Zhou Enlai* (中国的总管家周恩来). Shanghai: Shanghai People's Publishing House (上海; 上海人民出版社), 2006.

Chen, Wenqing (陈文清). "Vivid Practice and Rich Development of the Holistic National Security Concept" (总体国家安全观的生动实践和丰富发展). *Qiushi* (求是), April 15, 2020. http://www.qstheory.cn/dukan/qs/2020-04/15/c_1125856695.htm.

Chen, Xiangyang (陈向阳). "Seize the Opportunity to Plan China's National Security Strategy in a New Era" (抓紧运筹新时期中国国家安全战略). *Liaowang* (瞭望), December 2, 2013. http://theory.people.com.cn/n/2013/1202/c40531-23718303.html.

Chen, Xiaodong (陈晓东). "Decision on the Shenzhou" (决此神舟). *Shenjian* (神剑), June 2003, 38–51.

China's National Defense in the New Era (新时代的中国国防). Beijing: People's Republic of China State Council Information Office (北京; 国务院新闻办公室), 2019.

ChinaVenture Institute (投中研究院). *2019 China Military Civil Fusion White Paper* (2019 年中国军民融合白皮书), March 2019. https://www.dx2025.com/archives /7543.html.

ChinaVenture Research Institute (投中研究院). *2019 Chinese Government Guidance Fund Special Report* (2019 中国政府引导基金专题报告), October 2019. https:// chinaventure-static.obs.cn-north-1.myhuaweicloud.com/reportFiles /6591979882283008.pdf.

Chinese Communist Party Central Party Literature Research Office, ed. (中共中央文献研究室). *Selection of Xi Jinping's Comments on Science, Technology and Innovation* (习近平关于科技创新论述摘编). Beijing: Central Party Literature Press (北京; 中共文献出版社), 2016.

Commission for Discipline Inspection of the CPC Central Committee and the Literature Research Office of the CPC Central Committee (中共中央纪律检查委员会和中共中央文献研究室). *Excerpts from Xi Jinping's Discussion on the Party's Records and Rules* (习近平关于严明党的记录和规矩论述摘编). Beijing: Central Literature Press and China Founder Press (北京; 中央文献出版社, 中国方正出版社), 2015.

Deng, Xiaoping (邓小平). "On the Reform of the System of Party and State Leadership." In *Selected Works of Deng Xiaoping: Volume 2 (1975–1982)* (邓小平文选: 第二卷 (1975–1982)), 302–325. Beijing: Foreign Languages Press (北京; 外文出版社), 1995.

Dong, Fanghe (东方鹤). *General Zhang Aiping (Lower Volume)* (上将张爱萍 (下)). Beijing: People's Press (北京; 人民出版社), 2007.

Dong, Sheng (东生). *The Eulogy of Heaven and Earth: The Inside Story of "Two Bombs, One Satellite"* (天地颂: "两弹一星" 内幕). Beijing: Xinhua Press (北京: 新华出版社), 2000.

Du, Zhongwu (杜中武). "A Historical Investigation of the Formation of the Military-Civil Fusion Development Path with Chinese Characteristics: The Development of Military-Civil Fusion Thinking of Mao Zedong, Deng Xiaoping, Jiang Zemin, and Hu Jintao" (中国特色军民融合式发展之路形成的历史考察: 兼论毛泽东、邓小平、江泽民、胡锦涛军民融合式发展思想). *Military Historical Research* (军事历史研究) 4 (2012): 1–6.

Fu, Guangming, and Ji Hongtao (傅光明和吉洪涛). "Research on Hu Jintao's Strategic Thinking of Strengthening the Army through Science and Technology" (胡锦涛科技强军战略思想研探). *China Military Science* (中国军事科学) 5 (2011): 18–24.

Gao, Liansheng, and Guo Jingtan (高连升和郭竞炎). *The History of the Development and Construction of the Army in the New Period of Deng Xiaoping* (邓小平新时期军队建设思想发展史). Beijing: Liberation Army Press (北京: 解放军出版社), 1997.

General Headquarters of Shenzhou VI Manned Space Flight Mission (神舟六号载人航天飞行任务总指挥部). "Spectacular Accomplishment Out of a Strategic Decision, Successful Cause through Independent Innovation: Enlightenment from the Success of Shenzhou VI Manned Space Flight Mission" (战略决策绘宏图 自主创新成伟业). *Qiushi* (求是), December 1, 2005. http://www.cmse.gov.cn/zhuanti/news/show.php@itemid=220.

Geng, Jiandong (耿建东). *Review of 15 Years of the National High Technology and Research Development Program* (中国高技术研究发展计划十五年). Beijing: Science Press (北京: 科学出版社), 2001.

Government Guidance Fund Report (政府引导基金报告). Tsinghua University China Financial Research Center (清华大学中国金融研究中心), November 2018. http://ccfr.sem.tsinghua.edu.cn/view/page/1, 18–19.

Government Guidance Fund Trends (政府引导基金动态). Zero2IPO Research Center (清科研究中心), 2020. https://www.pedata.cn/special_do/govFund/web.

Guan, Fei (关非). "Continuous Innovation of Heilongjiang's Defense Industry: Interview with Heilongjiang Defense Science, Technology, and Industry Office Party Secretary Ben Qili and Director Sun Sheng" (锐意进取 不断创新的黑龙江军工—访黑龙江国防科技工业办公室党组书记贲起利、主任孙珅). *Military Industrial Culture* (军工文化), July 2011, 52–55.

Han, Gang (韩钢). "The Controversy Regarding Hua Guofang" (还原华国锋—关于华国锋的若干史实). *History Reference* (文史参考), August 2011. http://history.people.com.cn/GB/205396/15505844.html.

Hu, Angang, Yan Yilong, and Tang Xiao (胡鞍钢, 鄢一龙和唐啸). *Xi Jinping's New Development Philosophy* (中国新发展理念). Singapore: Springer, 2018.

Hu, Baomin, Wang Ting, and Li Zibiao (胡宝民, 王婷, 李子彪). "Research on the Special Characteristics of Major Science and Technology Programs" (重大科技专项的特征研究). *China Science and Technology Forum* (中国科技论坛) (September 2007): 81–85.

Hu, Xin (胡欣). "'Air-Sea Battle' Sword Pointed at East Asia" (空海一体战" 剑指东亚). *Contemporary Military Affairs* (现代军事) 10 (2011): 20–23.

Huai, Guomo (怀国模). "Entering the Initial Period of the Nuclear Industry, Part 1" (投身原子能工业的初创时期(上). *China Defense Conversion Journal* (中国军转民) 2 (2014): 66–68.

Huang, Chaofeng, and Ma Junyang (黄朝峰和黄浚洋). "Research on the Integrated National Strategic System and Capacity Composition and Construction" (一体化的国家战略体系和能力构成与构建研究). *Journal of Northwestern Polytechnical University (Social Science Edition)* (西北工业大学学报)(社会科学版) 4 (2019): 110–15.

Huo, Zhongwen, and Wang Zongxiao (霍忠文和王宗孝). *Sources and Techniques of Obtaining National Defense Science and Technology Intelligence* (国防科技情报源及获取技术). Beijing: Science and Technology Literature Press (北京; 科学技术文献出版社), 1991.

Ji, Renli, Wu Hairui, and Zong Haini (季仁禮, 吳青綸, 宗海妮). *Black Box of the Chinese Communist Party* (中共"黑匣子"). Hong Kong: Haya Press (哈耶出版社), 2009.

Jiang, Luming (姜鲁鸣). "China's Special Path in the Development of Military-Civil Fusion and the Fundamental Task of System Construction" (我国军民融合发展的特殊路径与制度建设的根本任务). *China Defense Conversion Journal* (中国军转民), October 2017. http://www.qlkzsh.com/index.php?s=/Home/Index/ql_front _detail_pc/gid/75/id/1359/orgid/81024347/umid/3300236.html.

Jiang, Luming, Wang Weihai, and Liu Zuchen (姜鲁鸣, 王海伟和刘祖辰). *Discussion of Military-Civil Fusion Development Strategy* (军民融合发展战略探论). Beijing: People's Press (北京; 人民出版社), 2017.

Jiang, Yan, and Bai Yunchuan (江彦和白云川). "Interview with Professor Wang Tianmiao, Group Leader of Advanced Manufacturing Technology in National 863 Program" (工业化与信息化融合促进先进制造技术发展—访国家 863 计划先进制造技术领域专家组组长王田苗教授). *China Manufacturing Industry and Informatization* (中国制造业信息化) (2008): 6–7.

Jiang Zemin National Defense Technology Industry Construction Thought Research Group (江泽民国防科技工业建设思想研究课题组). *Research into the Thinking of Jiang Zemin on the Building of the Defense Science and Technology Industry* (江泽民国防科技工业建设思想研究). Beijing: Electronics Industry Press (北京; 电子工业出版社), 2005.

Jin, Zhuanglong (金壮龙). "Opening Up a New Era for a New Situation for In-depth Military-Civil Fusion Development" (开创新时代军民融合深度发展新局面). *Qiushi* (求是), July 16, 2018. http://www.xinhuanet.com/politics/2018-07/16/c_1123133 733.htm.

Li, Bin, Lei Hegong, Cao Qi, and He Yijia (李斌, 雷贺功, 曹琪, 何艺佳). "Thoughts on the Construction of National Defense Technology Industry Think Tanks in the New Era" (关于新时代国防科技工业智库建设的思考). *Think Tank Theory and Practice* (智库理论与实践) 5, no. 3 (2020): 16–20.

Li, Chaomin (李超民). "A Major Composition That Must Be Written Well to Implement the Scientific Development Concept: An Exploration of Hu Jintao's View on Military-Civil Fusion Development with Chinese Characteristics" (贯彻科学发展观必须做好的—篇大文章—胡锦涛关于中国特色军民融合式发展体系探讨). *China Military Science* (中国军事科学) 5 (2011): 43–53.

Li, Daguang (李大光). *National Security* (国家安全). Beijing: Yanshi Publishing House (北京; 言实出版社), 2016.

Li, Mingsheng (李鸣生). *An Eternal Dream: The Story of the Chinese Person Who Left Earth for the First Time* (千古一梦: 中国人第一次离开地球的故事). Beijing: Baihuazhou Literature and Art Publishing House (北京; 百花洲文艺出版社), 2009.

Li, Nong, Qian Li, and Chong Xinong (李宏, 钱利和崇曦农). "A Discussion of China's Technology Introduction and Indigenous Innovation Policy" (试论技术引进与我国自主创新发展战略现代财经). *Modern Finance and Economics* (现代财经) 27, no. 12 (2007): 67–70.

Li, Yongsheng (李永胜). "People's Security Is the Purpose and Soul of National Security" (人民安全是国家安全的宗旨与灵魂). *Qiushi* (求是), April 27, 2018. http:// www.qstheory.cn/wp/2018-04/27/c_1122749045.htm.

Liao, Feng (廖锋). "History and Development of the Predecessors to the General Armament Department" (总装备部及其 "前身" 发展沿革辨). *Military Historical Facts* (军事史林) 12 (2005): 38–45.

Liao, Xilong (廖锡龙). "More Quickly Promote Military Support Socialization, Blaze a Trail of Military-Civil Fusion Development" (加快推进军队保障社会化 走出一条军民融合式发展路子). *Qiushi* (求是), May 16, 2012. https://www.cnki.com.cn/Article/CJFDTotal-QUSI201210020.htm.

Liu, Hanrong, and Wang Baoshun (刘汉荣和王保顺), eds. *National Defense Scientific Research Test Project Management* (国防科研试验项目管理). Beijing: National Defense Industry Press (北京; 国防工业出版社), 2009.

Liu Huaqing (刘华清). *Memoirs of Liu Huaqing* (刘华清回忆录). Beijing: Liberation Army Press (北京; 中国人民解放军出版社), 2004.

Liu, Jifeng, Liu Yanqiong, and Xie Haiyan (刘戟锋, 刘艳琼和谢海燕). *The Project of "Two Bombs, One Satellite": A Model for Big Science* (两弹一星工程与大科学). Jinan: Shandong Education Press (济南; 山东教育出版社), 2004.

Liu, Jinyu (刘晋豫). "New Trends, New Policies, and New Ideas in the Current Development of China's Military-Civil Fusion" (当前我国军民融合发展新态势、新政策与新思路). *Military and Civilian Technology and Products* (军民两用技术与产品) 9 (2018): 44–47.

Liu, Mingfu, and Wang Zhongyuan ((刘明福和王忠远). *The Thoughts of Xi Jinping* (习近平思想). Cambridge, MA: American Academic Press, 2017.

Liu, Yanqiong (刘艳琼). "The Experience and Enlightenment from the Success of the Two Bombs and One Satellite Project" (中国科学院与 "两弹一星" 工程). *Bulletin of the Chinese Academy of Sciences* (中国科学院院刊) 9 (2019): 1003–13.

Luo, Derong (骆德荣). "Action Guidelines for Armed Forces Building and Military Struggle Preparations—Several Points in Understanding the Military Strategic Guidelines in the New Era" (军队建设与军事斗争准备的行动纲领 -对新形势下军事战略方针的几点认识). *China Military Science* (中国军事科学) 1 (2017): 88–96.

Manufacturing Power Strategic Research Committee (制造强国战略研究项目组). *Research on the Manufacturing Power Strategy* (制造强国战略研究). Beijing: Electronics Industry Press (北京; 电子工业出版社), 2015.

Mao, Guohui (毛国辉等), ed. *Introduction to the Military Armament Legal System* (军事装备法律制度概论). Beijing: National Defense Industry Press (北京; 国防工业出版社), 2012.

Mei, Xiangbin (梅宪宾). "Evolution of Military Strategic Guidelines Since the Founding of New China" (新中国军事战略方针的历史演变及规律). *Military History* (军事历史) 4 (2010): 65–68.

Miao, Ye (苗野). "Research on the Current Situation and Countermeasures of the Construction of National Military-Civil Fusion Innovation Demonstration Zones" (我国军民融合创新示范区建设现状及对策研究). *Military Civil Fusion Observer* (军民融合观察), January 31, 2018. https://www.sohu.com/a/220111524_466840.

National Defense University Defense Economic Research Center (国防经济研究中心). "Overview of the Annual Development of China's Military-Civil Fusion" (中国军民融合年度发展概况). *China Defense Conversion Journal* (中国军转民) 3 (2016): 9–14.

Qiao, Weiguo, and Chen Fang (乔为国和陈芳). "Research on the Policy System and Implementation of Technology Importation, Absorption, and Reinnovation" (引进消化吸收再创新的政策体系与实施问题研究). *Science and Technology for Development* (科技促进发展) (May 2010): 37–40.

State Council Information Office (国务院新闻办公室). *The Diversified Employment of China's Armed Forces* (中国武装力量的多样化运用). Beijing: People's Press (北京; 人民出版社), 2013.

Sun, Hong, and Li Lin (孙宏和李霖). "On the Modes of Advancing Weapons and Equipment Development with Chinese Characteristics" (论中国特色装备建设的推进模式). *China Military Science* (中国军事科学) 6 (2005): 55–60.

Sun, Jianguo (孙建国). "Unwaveringly Take the National Security Path with Chinese Characteristics: Study General Secretary Xi Jinping's Major Strategic Thinking on the Holistic National Security Concept" (坚定不移走中国特色国家安全道路—学习习近平主席总体国家安全观重大战略思想). *Qiushi* (求是), March 1, 2015. http://news.12371.cn/2015/03/01/ARTI1425196310318229.shtml.

Sun, Sijing (孙思敬). "The Strong Military Path Requires That Military Theory with Chinese Characteristics Be Taken as a Guide" (强军之路要以中国特色军事理论为先导). *Qiushi* (求是) 15 (2013): 24–26.

Tu, Senlin (屠森林). "Serve the Construction of an Advanced Defense Industry and Vigorously Promote Military-Civil Fusion" (坚持先进军工建设推进军民融合发展). *Defence Industry Conversion in China* (中国军转民) 2 (2012): 26–33.

Wang Faan (王法安), ed. *China's Strategy for Invigorating the Armed Forces Amid Peaceful Development* (中国和平发展中的强军战略). Beijing: Military Science Press (北京; 军事科学出版社), 2011.

Wen, Xisen, and Kuang Xinghua (温熙森和匡兴华). *The Theory of National Defense Science and Technology* (国防科学技术论). Beijing: National University of Defense Technology Press (北京; 国防科技大学出版社), 1997.

Wu, Boyi, and Qi Zhongying (武博禕和齐中英). "Thoughts on the National Defense Science and Technology Industry Advancing in the Direction of Military-Civil Fusion Development with Chinese Characteristics" (关于国防科技工业走中国特色军民融合式发展之路的思考). *Military Economic Research* (军事经济研究) 4 (2010): 26–28.

"Wu Shengli Speaks at the Eighth Plenum of the 11th Navy Party Committee" (吴胜利在海军十一届八次全会上讲话). *People's Navy* (人民海军), January 7, 2015.

Wu, Weichao (吴卫超). "A Brief Analysis of the Main Content and Institutional Mechanisms behind the Military-Civil Fusion Style Development of National Defense Mobilization" (浅谈国防动员军民融合式发展的主要内容和体制机制). *National Defense Journal* (国防) 1 (2013): 68–69.

Xiao, Tianliang (肖天亮), ed. *The Science of Strategy* (战略学). Beijing: National Defense University Press (北京; 国防大学出版社), 2017.

Xie, Guang (谢光, 主编), chief ed. *The Contemporary Chinese Defense Science and Technology Sector* (当代中国的国防科技事业). Beijing: Contemporary China Press (北京; 当代中国出版社), 1992.

Xu, Qiliang (许其亮). "Do a Good Job in Studying the Military Strengthening Theory and Making Contributions to the Cause of Military Strengthening" (学好强军理论干好强军事业). *Qiushi* (求是) 15 (2014): 3–6.

Yan, Xin (闫新), ed. *Overview of the Development of China's Contemporary Defense Science and Technology, Part 1* (中国当代国防科技发展概况 (一)). Beijing (北京): Academic Video Publishing House (学苑音像出版社), 2004.

Yang, Xinggen (杨兴根). "Transformation from 'Mechanical Military Factory' into a 'Digital Military Factory'" (由"机械军工"向"数字军工"转变). *Aviation Science and Technology* (航空科学技术), (January 2004): 39–40.

Yan, Xuetong (阎学通). *Analysis of China's National Interests* (中国国家利益分析). Tianjin: Tianjin People's Press (天津; 天津人民出版社), 1997.

Yang, Mingwei (杨明伟). "Zhou Enlai and the Central Special Committee" (周恩来与中央专门委员会). *Zongheng* (纵横) (December 1997): 4–11.

Yin, Jun, and Tan Qingmei (尹君和谭清美). "Research on the Evaluation of the Degree of Military-Civil Fusion and Its Optimization Measures" (军民融合程度评价及其优化对策研究). *Science Research Management* (科研管理) 41, no. 1 (2020): 90–97.

You, Guangrong, Yan Hong, and Zhao Xu (游光荣, 闫宏和赵旭). "The Construction of the Military-Civil Fusion Policy System: Status, Problems and Countermeasures" (军民融合发展政策制度体系建设: 现状、问题及对策). *China Science and Technology Forum* (中国科技论坛) 1 (2017): 150–56.

Yu, Chuanxin, and Zhou Jianping (于川信和周建平), eds. *Military-Civil Fusion-Style Development: Theory and Practice* (军民融合式发展: 理论与实践). Beijing: Academy of Military Sciences Publishing House (北京; 军事科学出版社), 2010.

Yu, Gaoda, and Zhao Lusheng (余高达, 和赵潞生). *The Study of Military Equipment* (军事装备学). Beijing (北京): National Defense University Press (国防大学出版社), 2000.

Yuan, Peng (袁鹏). "China's International Strategic Thinking and Strategic Arrangements for a New Era" (新时代中国国际战略思想与战略布局). *Contemporary International Relations* (现代国际关系) 11 (2017): 1–8.

Yuan, Qingming (袁庆明). *The Analysis and Research of the Institutional Structure of Technological Innovation* (技术创新的制度结构分析). Beijing (北京): Economic Management Press (经济管理出版社), 2003.

Zhang, Jiaguo, and Li Zhengfeng (张嘉国和李正锋). "Analysis and Countermeasures of Problems in the Construction of Military-Civil Fusion Innovation Demonstration Zones" (军民融合创新示范区建设的问题分析与对策). *Journal of Northwestern Polytechnical University (Social Science Edition)* (西北工业大学学报(社会科学版)) 4 (2018): 84–88.

Zhang Wannian Writing Team (张万年传写作组). *Biography of Zhang Wannian* (张万年传). Beijing: Liberation Army Press (北京; 解放军出版社), 2011.

Zhang, Yuzhe, and Zhou Zhen (张于喆和周振). "Xi Jinping's Strategic Thoughts on the Integration of Military and Civil Development" (习近平关于军民融合发展的战略思想研究). *Comparative Economic and Social Systems* (经济社会体制比较) 204, no. 4 (2019): 9–16.

Zhou, Bisong (周碧松). *Research on the Path for the Construction of Weapons with Chinese Characteristics* (中国特色武器装备建设道路研究). Beijing (北京): National Defense University Press (国防大学出版社), 2012.

——. *Weapons and Equipment Development and National Defense Technology Innovation* (国防科技创新和武器装备发展). Beijing (北京): Economic Science Press (经济科学出版社), 2017.

Zhu, Minghao (朱明皓). "Need to Work on Core Components to Become a Manufacturing Power" (实现制造强国须先弥补基础短板). *China Industry Review* (中国工业评论), August 3, 2015. http://www.chinaeinet.com/article/detail.aspx?id=10690.

Zhu, Qinglin (朱庆林主编), chief ed. *Study Course of National Economic Mobilization* (国民经济动员学教程). Beijing (北京): Military Science Press (军事科学出版社), 2002.

Index

Photos are indicated by an italicized page number; tables are indicated by t; figures are indicated by f.

strengths and weaknesses of contemporary, 290–94
Trump and, 269–70
US compared to Chinese NSS origins and, 262–64
US NSS origins and character and, 260–62

Waltz, Kenneth, 258–59
Wang, Yuhua, 71, 313n3, 315n63
Wan Gang, 25, 230
Wang Qishan, 18, 58, 61
Wang Weihai, 140–41
Weapons and Equipment Acquisition Information Network (WEAIN), 116
Weapons and Equipment Construction Plans (WECPs), 151, 155, 156f
Weapons and Equipment Development Strategy (WEDS)
  on asymmetric development, 157–58
  classification of, 151
  composition elements of, 153–54
  contemporary state of, 158–59
  MCF and, 158
  MSG relationship with, 146–60
  national-level, 152
  on offensive capabilities, 157
  regional security periphery analysis by, 153–54
  revision of, 159–60
  selective development of, 158
  service-level, 152
  on strategic deterrence capabilities, 157
  on S&T trends, 154
  tasks of, 151–52
  unified central leadership for, 157
  WECPs compared to, 155
Weapons and Equipment Research, Development, and Production License Catalog, 115–16
weapons and equipment research and production licenses (WERPLs), 114–15
weapons systems, generational development of Chinese, 187–91, 188f–90f
WECPs (Weapons and Equipment Construction Plans), 151, 155, 156f
WEDS. See Weapons and Equipment Development Strategy
Weiss, Linda, 252, 267–68
welfare states, 251
Wen Jiabao, 31, 211
  MLP and, 205
Wen Xisen, 326n10

WERPLs (weapons and equipment research and production licenses), 114–15
Wohlforth, William, 259
Woo-Cummings, Meredith, 255
Work Conference on Military Structural Reforms, CMC, 2015, 162–63, 165
Wu Shengli, 159–60

Xi Jinping, 1
  on absorption process, 328n54
  advisers and inner circle to, 18–19, 78t, 311n1
  on AMS, 43–44
  authoritarian leadership system of, 244–45
  background of, 17–18
  on Belt and Road Initiative, 31
  on bureaucratic fragmentation, 23
  CAS and CAE speech of, 2014, 22–23
  Chinese techno-security state of, 2, 12–14, 13t
  Chinese techno-security state sustainability without, 285–86
  civil-military innovation and, 44–45
  as CMC chairman, 45–48, 55, 108, 144
  CMCFDC involvement of, 105–6
  on CNSC, 63
  creativity-driven innovation and, 41–44
  "cult of gold-plated innovation" and, 49
  on development-security relationship, 12–14, 65–66
  discipline enforcement initiative of, 61–62, 68
  FELG and, 24
  on 14th Five-Year Plan, 304
  on HNSC, 55
  IDDS development and, 18–25
  IDDS unveiled by, 2016, 29
  inauguration of, 19–20
  on INSS, 140–41
  MCF ambitions of, 83–84, 88–90, 94, 140–41
  on MCF obstacles, 95
  military and defense S&T engagements of, 2012–2020, 144, 144f
  military-driven innovation and, approach of, 37–47
  military-driven innovation and, assessment of, 47–50
  military leadership team under, 48–49
  military parades and, 144–45, 227, 322n6
  on Military Strengthening in the New Era, 142
  military strengthening strategic thinking of, 143–46, 144f

CPSIA information can be obtained
at www.ICGtesting.com
Printed in the USA
LVHW101641270722
724551LV00015B/390/J